Biotechnology and Agricultural Development

This book addresses the continuing controversy over the potential impact of genetically modified (GM) crops in developing countries. Supporters of the technology claim it offers one of the best hopes for increasing agricultural production and reducing rural poverty, while opponents see it as an untested intervention that will bring corporate control of peasant farming. The book examines the issues by reviewing the experience of GM, insect-resistant cotton, the most widely grown GM crop in developing countries.

The book begins with an introduction to agricultural biotechnology, a brief examination of the history of cotton production technology (and the institutions required to support that technology), and a thorough review of the literature on the agronomic performance of GM cotton. It then provides a review of the economic and institutional outcomes of GM cotton during the first decade of its use. The core of the book is four country case studies based on original fieldwork in the principal developing countries growing GM cotton (China, India, South Africa and Colombia). The book concludes with a summary of the experience to date and implications for the future of GM crops in developing countries.

This review challenges those who have predicted technological failure by describing instances in which GM cotton has proven useful and has been enthusiastically taken up by smallholders. But it also challenges those who claim that biotechnology can take the lead in agricultural development by examining the precarious institutional basis on which these hopes rest in most countries. The analysis shows how biotechnology's potential contribution to agricultural development must be seen as a part of (and often secondary to) more fundamental policy change. The book should be of interest to a wide audience concerned with agricultural development. This would include academics in the social and agricultural sciences, donor agencies and NGOs.

Robert Tripp has a doctorate in social anthropology and has spent his career working on issues related to agricultural technology development and dissemination. He spent 15 years with the Economics Program of the International Maize and Wheat Improvement Center (CIMMYT) and 12 years as a research fellow with the Overseas Development Institute (ODF).

Routledge Explorations in Environmental Economics
Edited by Nick Hanley
University of Stirling, UK

1. **Greenhouse Economics**
   Value and ethics
   Clive L. Spash

2. **Oil Wealth and the Fate of Tropical Rainforests**
   Sven Wunder

3. **The Economics of Climate Change**
   Edited by Anthony D. Owen and Nick Hanley

4. **Alternatives for Environmental Valuation**
   Edited by Michael Getzner, Clive Spash and Sigrid Stagl

5. **Environmental Sustainability**
   A consumption approach
   Raghbendra Jha and K.V. Bhanu Murthy

6. **Cost-Effective Control of Urban Smog**
   The significance of the Chicago cap-and-trade approach
   Richard F. Kosobud, Houston H. Stokes, Carol D. Tallarico and Brian L. Scott

7. **Ecological Economics and Industrial Ecology**
   Jakub Kronenberg

8. **Environmental Economics, Experimental Methods**
   Edited by Todd L. Cherry, Stephan Kroll and Jason F. Shogren

9. **Game Theory and Policy Making in Natural Resources and the Environment**
   Edited by Ariel Dinar, José Albiac and Joaquín Sánchez-Soriano

10. **Arctic Oil and Gas**
    Sustainability at risk?
    Edited by Aslaug Mikkelsen and Oluf Langhelle

11. **Agrobiodiversity, Conservation and Economic Development**
    Edited by Andreas Kontoleon, Unai Pascual and Melinda Smale

12. **Renewable Energy from Forest Resources in the United States**
    Edited by Barry D. Solomon and Valeria A. Luzadis

13. **Modeling Environment-Improving Technological Innovations under Uncertainty**
    Alexander A. Golub and Anil Markandya

14. **Economic Analysis of Land Use in Global Climate Change Policy**
Thomas Hertel, Steven Rose and Richard Tol

15. **Waste and Environmental Policy**
Massimiliano Mazzanti and Anna Montini

16. **Avoided Deforestation**
Prospects for Mitigating Climate Change
Edited by Stefanie Engel and Charles Palmer

17. **The Use of Economic Valuation in Environmental Policy**
Phoebe Koundouri

18. **Benefits of Environmental Policy**
Klaus Dieter John and Dirk T.G. Rübbelke

19. **Biotechnology and Agricultural Development**
Robert Tripp

Biotechnology and Agricultural Development

Transgenic cotton, rural institutions and resource-poor farmers

Edited by
Robert Tripp

Routledge
Taylor & Francis Group

LONDON AND NEW YORK

First published 2009
by Routledge
2 Park Square, Milton Park, Abingdon, Oxon, OX14 4RN

Simultaneously published in the USA and Canada
by Routledge
270 Madison Avenue, New York, NY 10016

Routledge is an imprint of the Taylor & Francis Group, an informa business

Typeset in Times New Roman by
Book Now Limited, London
Printed and bound in Great Britain by
CPI Antony Rowe, Chippenham, Wiltshire

British Library Cataloguing in Publication Data
A catalogue record for this book is available from the British Library

Library of Congress Cataloging in Publication Data
Biotechnology and agricultural development: transgenic cotton, rural
institutions and resource-poor farmers / edited by Robert Tripp.
    p. cm.—(Routledge explorations in environmental economics; 19)
1. Cotton—Biotechnology—Economic aspects—Developing
countries—Case studies. 2. Agricultural biotechnology—Economic
aspects—Developing countries. 3. Agriculture and state—Developing
countries—Case studies. I. Tripp, Robert Burnet. II. Series.

HD9088.D44B56 2009
338.1'763351091724—dc22   2008052124

ISBN10: 0–415–49963–1 (hbk)
ISBN10: 0–415–54384–3 (pbk)
ISBN10: 0–203–87646–6 (ebk)

ISBN13: 978–0–415–49963–7 (hbk)
ISBN13: 978–0–415–54384–2 (pbk)
ISBN13: 978–0–203–87646–6 (ebk)

Contents

List of illustrations   ix
List of contributors   xv
Acknowledgements   xvii
List of abbreviations   xix
Foreword   xxi
RAY OFFENHEISER AND KIMBERLY PFEIFER

1   Biotechnology and agricultural development   1
ROBERT TRIPP

2   Cotton production and technology   23
ROBERT TRIPP

3   Development, agronomic performance and sustainability
of transgenic cotton for insect control   49
ANN M. SHOWALTER, SHANNON HEUBERGER,
BRUCE E. TABASHNIK AND YVES CARRIÈRE

4   Transgenic cotton: Assessing economic performance
in the field   72
ROBERT TRIPP

5   Transgenic cotton and institutional performance   88
ROBERT TRIPP

6   Farmers' seed and pest control management for Bt cotton
in China   105
JIKUN HUANG, RUIJIAN CHEN, JIANWEI MI, RUIFA HU AND
ELLIE OSIR

7 India's experience with Bt cotton: Case studies from Gujarat
   and Maharashtra   135
   N. LALITHA, BHARAT RAMASWAMI AND P.K. VISWANATHAN

8 The socio-economic impact of transgenic cotton in Colombia   168
   PATRICIA ZAMBRANO, LUZ AMPARO FONSECA, IVÁN CARDONA
   AND EDUARDO MAGALHAES

9 Ten years of Bt cotton in South Africa: Putting the smallholder
   experience into context   200
   MARNUS GOUSE

10 Summary and conclusions   225
   ROBERT TRIPP

   References   246
   Index   268

Illustrations

Figures

6.1 Principal cotton-growing provinces of China   106
6.2 Cotton varieties sold in county capital and township
     shops in 2007   112
6.3 Variation of Bt cotton seed prices (yuan/kg) for nine
     major varieties in Hebei, Shandong and Henan in 2007   119
6.4 Chemical pesticides used in China, thousand tons,
     1991–2006   125
6.5 Insecticide application in sample villages, Henan,
     Shandong and Hebei, 2007   132
6.6 Insecticide application for bollworm in sample villages,
     Henan, Shandong and Hebei, 2007   132
7.1 Location of survey areas in India   136
7.2 Seed cotton yields (kg/ha) Gujarat, Maharashtra and
     all India   146
8.1 Colombia and cotton-growing regions   169
8.2 Cotton area (ha) and adoption of transgenic cotton
     (%), 2004–2008   170
8.3 The activities of cotton producer associations   175
8.4 The commercialization channels for transgenic cotton
     seeds, 2007   179
9.1 Cotton production area in South Africa   201
9.2 Main cotton production regions in South Africa   204
9.3 Market share of seed companies according to cotton
     delivered to gins per market season   210
9.4 Total October to March rainfall for Makhathini according
     to production season   215
9.5 Number of smallholder cotton producers on Makhathini Flats
     and the correlation with pre-season rainfall   222

Tables

2.1   Cotton insect-resistance transgenes available
      commercially, 2007   45
2.2   Area of cotton planted, in hectares, by type (and
      per cent of total cotton area), 2007   46
2.3   Area in hectares (and per cent of total cotton area) planted
      with transgenic, insect-resistant cotton, (single trait or
      stacked), by year   47
3.1   Characteristics of transgenic cotton cultivars for insect
      control commercialized or in development   54
3.2   Efficacy of transgenic cotton cultivars against key cotton
      pests based on corrected per cent mortality   56
3.3   Efficacy of transgenic cotton cultivars against key cotton
      pests based on the corrected per cent reduction of field
      pest density   57
4.1   Changes in yield and insecticide use with Bt cotton   74
4.2   Cost of conventional and Bt cotton seed (2007)   79
4.3   Resistance management for Bt cotton   85
5.1   Cotton technology for insect resistance, seed companies
      and varieties (2007)   91
5.2   Intellectual property rights and transgenic cotton   94
5.3   Seed regulations in countries growing transgenic cotton   98
6.1   Number of seed companies and seed dealers selling
      Bt cotton seeds in 6 county capitals, 8 townships and
      12 villages by the level of registration capital in 2007   111
6.2   Number of Bt cotton varieties sold in the shops located in
      county capitals in 2007   113
6.3   Number of Bt cotton varieties sold in the shops located in
      townships in 2007   113
6.4   Yield performance and insecticide use for Bt cotton varieties
      included and not included on China's Biosafety Committee
      approved list in 2006 and 2007   116
6.5   The level of Bt toxin expression, ng/g, by variety type and
      by location   117
6.6   Farmers' knowledge about seed companies   120
6.7   Number of varieties planted per household in Hebei,
      Shandong, Henan and Anhui in 2006   120
6.8   The percentage of seed saved and purchased from shops
      located in different places in Hebei, Shandong and
      Henan, 2006   121
6.9   Insecticide use on cotton varieties from different
      seed markets   121
6.10 Adoption of popular Bt cotton varieties,
      by village, 2006   122

6.11 Number of years that farmers have planted cotton varieties
used in 2007   122
6.12 Yields and Bt toxin expression for saved and purchased
seed of the same varieties   123
6.13 Relationship between seed saving and (a) number of shops,
(b) number of varieties in Hebei, Henan and Shandong
in 2006 and 2007   123
6.14 The number of pesticide shops and types of insecticides used
in cotton in Hebei, Shandong and Henan, 2007   126
6.15 Number of insecticide company names recalled by farmers
in Hebei, Shandong and Henan, 2007   126
6.16 The percentage of insecticide purchased from shops located
in different locations in Hebei, Shandong
and Henan, 2007   127
6.17 Types of insecticide applied by farmers in Hebei, Shandong
and Henan, 2007   127
6.18 The most important source of farmers' information for
selection of type of insecticide   128
6.19 Insecticide use (kg/ha) for all insects and for bollworm
in Hebei, Shandong, Henan and Anhui, 1999–2007   129
6.20 Insecticide use (kg/ha) for all other pests and mirids in
Hebei, Shandong, Henan and Anhui, 1999–2007   130
6.21 Relationship between insecticide application (kg/ha) and
(a) technology knowledge and (b) risk preference   133
7.1 The study sample   137
7.2 Sample farmer characteristics   138
7.3 Bt cotton adoption trends for sample farmers   141
7.4 Adoption trends by number of growers   142
7.5 The diffusion of illegal seeds in Gujarat (sample area)   142
7.6 Adoption of Bt in Maharashtra   143
7.7 Differences between growers who use unapproved seed
and others, Gujarat   143
7.8 Median seed cotton yields for sample farmers   145
7.9 Yields of approved and unapproved varieties in Gujarat,
2005–07 (kg seed cotton per hectare)   146
7.10 Yields of approved and unapproved varieties in Gujarat,
2003–04 (kg seed cotton per hectare)   146
7.11 Number of distinct varieties sown by sample
farmers, 2003–07   148
7.12 Number of varieties grown by sample farmers   149
7.13 Cumulative distribution of novice plantings,
sample farmers   151
7.14 Varietal history and area allocation: Maharashtra   152
7.15 Varietal history and area allocation: Gujarat   152

7.16   Types of planting (novice, experimental and imitation)
       for sample farmers, 2007   153
7.17   Sources of information about Bt cotton seeds
       (percentage responses)   154
7.18   Labour use for insecticide application and farm size   155
7.19   Number of insecticide sprays applied to fields (Gujarat)   156
7.20   Number of insecticide sprays applied to fields (Maharashtra) 156
7.21   Number of insecticides used in each spraying   157
7.22   Insecticide sprays per plot, by pest and by
       time period: Maharashtra   158
7.23   Insecticide applications per plot: Maharashtra   159
7.24   Insecticide use per ha against target pests in Maharashtra   159
7.25   Insecticide sprays per plot, by pest and by time period, Gujarat 160
7.26   Insecticide applications per plot, Gujarat   162
7.27   Insecticide use per ha against target pests in Gujarat   163
7.28   Number of insecticide sprays per plot in Gujarat:
       2003–04 versus 2007–08   164
7.29   Farmers' opinions about Bt cotton   165
7.30   Characteristics of 'Bollgard II' growers in Gujarat   165
7.31   Refuge management   166
8.1   Distribution of cotton area by size of holding   171
8.2   Number of farmers and variety use, by department   172
8.3   Cotton associations by area and number of farmers, 2008   174
8.4   Cotton associations in Córdoba by variety use, number
       of farmers and area   180
8.5   Characteristics of the survey sample, by department   182
8.6   Landholding and land quality for sample farmers   183
8.7   Characteristics of cotton farmers in the sample – percentages 184
8.8   Household characteristics of sample farmers   185
8.9   Costs of production and yields of sample cotton farmers,
       by variety and department   187
8.10   Costs of production and yield, by variety and
       farm size, Tolima   190
8.11   Costs of production and yields for 15 Tolima farmers
       growing both conventional and Bt varieties   191
8.12   Tolima: first stage – OLS estimation for Bt adoption   192
8.13   Tolima: second-stage – yield estimation   192
8.14   Coast: first stage – OLS estimation for Bt adoption   193
8.15   Coast: second-stage – yield estimation   194
8.16   Seeding rate, by type of variety and farm size, Tolima   195
8.17   Cost of insect control, by type of insect, cotton variety
       and department   196
9.1   Cotton production area by province   205
9.2   Percentage and estimated areas (hectares) planted to
       transgenic crops in South Africa   206

9.3   Cultivars received at cotton gins the past 22 years according
      to marketing seasons   208
9.4   Cotton seed prices and technology fees (Rands per 25 kg
      bag of seed)   211
9.5   Summary of the findings of the major studies   216
9.6   Smallholder production according to province   218
9.7   Variability in smallholders' and Makhathini's contribution
      to the total cotton crop   221

Boxes

1.1   Conflicting visions of genetic engineering   2
1.2   Socio-economic impact and the Cartagena Protocol
      on Biosafety   17
2.1   The distribution and development of cotton   24
2.2   Cotton and intellectual property   34
2.3   Cotton insects   39
2.4   Plant breeding for insect resistance   43
4.1   Seed price of transgenic cotton in the USA   77
5.1   Transgenic crop varieties and intellectual property rights 92

Contributors

Iván Cardona, Consultant, Colombian Cotton Confederation (CONALGODÓN)

Yves Carrière, Professor, Department of Entomology, University of Arizona

Ruijian Chen, PhD candidate, Center for Chinese Agricultural Policy (CCAP)

Luz Amparo Fonseca, Executive President, Colombian Cotton Confederation (CONALGODÓN)

Marnus Gouse, Research Fellow, Department of Agricultural Economics, Extension and Rural Development, University of Pretoria

Shannon Heuberger, PhD candidate, Department of Entomology, University of Arizona

Ruifa Hu, Professor, Center for Chinese Agricultural Policy (CCAP)

Jikun Huang, Professor and Director, Center for Chinese Agricultural Policy (CCAP)

N. Lalitha, Associate Professor, Gujarat Institute of Development Research (GIDR)

Eduardo Magalhaes, Consultant, International Food Policy Research Institute (IFPRI)

Jianwei Mi, PhD candidate, Center for Chinese Agricultural Policy (CCAP)

Ellie Osir, Senior Program Specialist, International Development Research Centre (IDRC)

Bharat Ramaswami, Professor, Indian Statistical Institute (ISI)

Ann M. Showalter, Research Specialist, Department of Entomology, University of Arizona

Bruce E. Tabashnik, Professor, Department of Entomology, University of Arizona

Robert Tripp, independent researcher and consultant.

P.K. Viswanathan, Associate Professor, Gujarat Institute of Development Research (GIDR)

Patricia Zambrano, Research Analyst, International Food Policy Research Institute (IFPRI)

Acknowledgements

This book is an attempt to examine a very complex and controversial subject as carefully as possible. It required considerable support in order to interpret diverse sources of information and to steer a reasonable course through a very heated debate. The endeavour was fortunate to have an exceptionally strong administrative and intellectual foundation.

The work reported here is the outcome of the Oxfam-America project, 'Learning from the Experience of Small-Scale Farmers. The Case of Transgenic Cotton', carried out with funding from the Rockefeller Foundation. The project was managed by Kimberly Pfeifer, the Head of Research for Oxfam-America. Her innovative approach to research management and her skillful administrative support were absolutely crucial to the success of the project.

The early history of the project linked it to a similar endeavour by the International Food Policy Research Institute (IFPRI) to examine the experience of transgenic food crops in developing countries, 'Best Practices for Assessing the Social and Economic Impacts of Transgenic Crop Varieties on Small-Scale Farmers', funded by the International Development Research Center (IDRC). One of the key people in making the link between the two projects was Tony La Viña (originally with the World Resources Institute). Despite his subsequent move to become the Dean of the Ateneo School of Government in the Philippines, he maintained a key coordinating role throughout the life of both projects and helped manage three joint meetings during the course of the research. The opportunity to be directly linked to IFPRI's project provided access to ground-breaking research led by Melinda Smale and her colleagues, particularly José Falck-Zepeda and Patricia Zambrano. Further contributions to the Oxfam project came from Xaq Frolich, Raquel Gomes and Lamissa Diatite.

The two projects were served by a joint advisory committee that met with project staff to advise and reflect on the research, and thanks go to Rafiq Chaudhry, Michelle Chauvet Sanchez, Suman Sahai, Assetou Samaké and Bert Visser for their investment in the project. Particular thanks go to committee member Glenn Davis Stone who contributed a wealth of experience from his own research on transgenic cotton in India. Dramane Diasso, Wu Konming and Ellie Osir also contributed to review meetings. The joint project meetings also allowed those working on cotton to learn from the experience of the researchers affiliated with IFPRI's project examining transgenic maize and soybeans, including Jessica Bercilla, Rodrigo Paz Ybarnegaray, Arie Sanders, Rogelio Carlos Trabanino and Jose Yorobe Jr.

The core of this book is four country case studies on transgenic cotton, and the project relied on an outstanding group of researchers. They carried out original research and explored novel hypotheses in an exceptionally wide range of environments, yet were always willing to compare notes and take an interest in what their colleagues in other countries were finding. The work in China was conducted under the leadership of Jikun Huang, the Director of the Center for Chinese Agricultural Policy Analysis (CCAP) and it relied on the long experience of Ruifa Hu and the additional work of Ruijian Chen and Jianwei Mi. In India, the work was managed from the Gujarat Institute of Development Research (GIDR) and led by N. Lalitha with P. K. Viswanathan; they collaborated on research design and analysis with Bharat Ramaswami of the Indian Statistical Institute. The research in Colombia was managed through the Colombian Cotton Federation (CONALGODÓN) with the support of its executive president Luz Amparo Fonseca and her staff; and Patricia Zambrano of IFPRI. The work in South Africa was done by Marnus Gouse of the University of Pretoria, the leading analyst of transgenic crops in South Africa. It was a great privilege to have been able to work with all of these people.

The analysis required more than farm-level fieldwork, however. One of the principal concerns about transgenic cotton is its agronomic performance. The press is full of reports of miracles and disasters, but we required a thorough, objective review of the scientific literature. The project was very fortunate to secure the services of Yves Carrière of the Department of Entomology at the University of Arizona and his colleagues Ann M. Showalter, Shannon Heuberger and Bruce E. Tabashnik. Their own involvement in research on transgenic cotton contributed to an exceptionally thorough technical review.

The project was also concerned with gathering basic statistics on the experience with transgenic cotton in all eight of the countries growing the crop at the time the project began. We were able to rely on local experts to provide us with this information, and thanks go to: Paul Clark, Gary Fitt, Marnus Gouse, Ruifa Hu, José Martinez-Carrillo, Reinaldo Muñoz, Bharat Ramaswami and Lorena Ruiz. In addition, a number of people were kind enough to provide additional information or help clarify particular issues, including John Chambers, Pedro Duran Ferman, Sumit Guha, Paul Heisey, James Larson, Barbara Meredith, Colin Poulton, Ijaz Ahmad Rao, Paul Sawyer and Allan Thiago. Terry Townsend and Rafiq Chaudhry at the International Cotton Advisory Committee (ICAC) provided a forum for discussion of the project and access to the ICAC's data and experience. Finally, a personal word of thanks goes to some people who have helped me understand cotton and entomology: Keshav Kranthi, Sandhya Kranthi, Derek Russell and Atul Sharma.

In an area as controversial as transgenic crops it probably goes without saying that the conclusions expressed in this book are the responsibility of the authors alone and should not necessarily be linked to the institutions that sponsored and supported the work or to the many kind people who provided advice along the way.

Robert Tripp

Abbreviations

AC	Advisory Committee
AMS	Agricultural Marketing Service (USA)
API	arrowhead proteinase inhibitor
Bt	*Bacillus thuringiensis*
CAAS	Chinese Academy of Agricultural Sciences
CBC	China's Biosafety Committee
CCAP	Center for Chinese Agricultural Policy
CED	Corporation for Economic Development (South Africa)
CIRAD	Centre de Coopération Internationale en Recherche Agronomique pour le Développement
CpTI	cowpea trypsin inhibitor
CRI	Cotton Research Institute (China)
CSD	Cotton Seed Distributors (Australia)
CSIRO	Commonwealth Scientific and Industrial Research Organization (Australia)
DoA	Department of Agriculture (South Africa)
D&PL	Delta and Pine Land
GM	genetically modified
GMO	genetically modified organism
GSSC	Gujarat State Seed Corporation
ha	hectare
IBR	Institute of Biotechnology Research (China)
ICA	Colombian Agricultural Institute
IFPRI	International Food Policy Research Institute
IIT	Indian Institute of Technology
IPM	integrated pest management
IPP	Institute of Plant Protection (China)
IPRs	intellectual property rights
IRM	insecticide resistance management
LecGNA2	snowdrop lectin gene
MCC	Makhathini Cotton (Pty) Ltd (South Africa)
MGP	minimum guaranteed price
MMB	Mahyco Monsanto Biotech Ltd. (India)

MNC	multinational corporation
MOA	Ministry of Agriculture
MOST	Ministry of Science and Technology (China)
mt	metric ton
ng	nanogram
NGO	non-governmental organization
NSC	National Seed Corporation (China)
OLS	ordinary least squares
PAAS	provincial academy of agricultural science (China)
PCR	polymerase chain reaction
PVP	plant variety protection
RR	Roundup Ready (Monsanto trademark)
SAGENE	South African Committee for Genetic Experimentation
SOE	state-owned enterprise
SSA	Sub-Saharan Africa
STK	South Africa Development Trust Corporation
UP	University of Pretoria
UPOV	Union for the Protection of New Varieties of Plants
USDA	United States Department of Agriculture
Vip	vegetative insecticidal protein
WTO	World Trade Organization

Foreword

Feeding the world with scarce resources in an environment increasingly affected by climate change is one of our most important global challenges. It must be addressed in a way that meets a second challenge – helping millions lift themselves out of poverty in the process of agricultural development. Despite its importance to two-thirds of the world's population (and 80 per cent of the population in Sub-Saharan Africa), agricultural development has experienced a systematic decline in funding over the past 40 years. While the global context has seen decades of low commodity prices, we have recently experienced a sharp spike in food prices with mixed implications for the world's poor. Food riots in the face of rising prices and immediate political responses, such as export bans, have jolted policymakers into recalling that price volatility in agriculture is an ever-present challenge. It affects the livelihoods of millions, threatens the ability of billions to escape hunger, and imperils political and social stability. Of course a global financial crisis adds insult to injury and can easily undermine this newly found political will to invest in agriculture. Nevertheless, the current state of global crisis has breathed new life into arguments to support agricultural development and has brought calls such as those for a new Green Revolution for Africa.

The biotechnology industry has quickly capitalized on this changing scenario and claims that it offers solutions to these challenges. News on breakthroughs in transgenic crop research, from drought tolerance to increasing yield potential, reaches us almost daily. However, decisions about the use of this technology are highly politicized and polarized between the proponents, who claim the science is safe and can offer solutions to productivity declines, land scarcity and harsh climatic conditions; and opponents, who question the moral and ethical responsibility being exercised by companies developing transgenic seeds and point to the lack of understanding of the environmental and health impacts of gene manipulation. Concerns from climate change to food and energy prices only serve to intensify the debates and underline the urgency of taking decisions around the future of genetically modified organisms (GMOs).

While both camps clash in the emotionally charged and politicized game of agricultural development, resource-poor farmers continue to face tough challenges and must make decisions about what to plant and how to make a sustainable livelihood.

Sustainability means that they can securely feed their families, send their children to school, meet their families healthcare needs, maintain their access to land and continue to make a living by farming. Resource-poor farmers constantly consider what seed they should plant and for some, transgenic seed is one option. Policy-makers in developing countries face the challenges of feeding populations and enabling growth in the agricultural sector in the context of volatile commodity and food prices, scarce financial and national resources, environmental degradation, increasing climatic pressures and globalization. They have to make tough decisions on where to invest scarce financial resources in the agricultural sector. Investing in transgenic crops is one of many options. Donor countries must understand the challenges confronting developing countries when providing assistance for the agricultural sector, and they must decide which competing voices or interests should inform their decisions.

In the context of declining productivity, volatile commodity prices, unfair trading rules and practices, donor pressures and conditionalities, and competing public opinions, how do policymakers decide to approve the commercial adoption of transgenic crops? How do transgenic seeds reach a Malian farmer trying to get the most from the land to sustain the household, and how does he or she make decisions around the possible use of the technology? These questions weighed on our minds at Oxfam as we worked with cotton producer associations in West Africa. In our work with West African cotton farmers to highlight the injustices in the international trading system and to shift the balance of power in the cotton value chain towards cotton producers, we could not ignore the pressure that existed to take decisions on establishing biosafety regulations to pave the way for the commercial adoption of transgenic cotton. Providing advice in this area seemed a daunting task given the very limited availability of rigorous assessments of the impacts of adopting this new technology.

In light of these questions, Oxfam proposed a study to assess the socio-economic impacts of the adoption of Bt cotton for resource-poor farmers by conducting case studies of its use by smallholders in a number of developing countries that had several years of experience with the technology – namely, China, Colombia, India and South Africa. The Rockefeller Foundation funded the research and a two-year project ensued. The goal was to produce a rigorous piece of research, located outside the polarized debate on GMOs, that stakeholders in West Africa could refer to in their decisions about the adoption of Bt cotton.

Will the calls for a Green Revolution for Africa ring hollow for cotton farmers in West Africa? The potential impact of such a strategy is threatened if we do not remember that the first Green Revolution benefited from the presence of solid institutions which supported its implementation, and even then, significant numbers of farmers and rural communities were left out. The strong emphasis on a science-based solution, without attention to the broader agricultural context, led to outcomes that did not always benefit resource-poor farmers.

A pro-poor strategy would put resource-poor farmers first and build an institutional architecture that keeps the farmer at the centre of all key processes. It would start with farmer knowledge and preferences, rather than breeders' knowledge and preferences. It would give equal weight to indigenous knowledge and to science-based knowledge. It would acknowledge the importance of issues like agrarian structure, food preferences and taste, the role of women in the agricultural system and power asymmetries in local and national markets. It would recognize and address the serious institutional deficits that confront poor farmers as a consequence of two decades of deleterious liberalization policies. It would recognize both the positive and negative aspects of the ascendance of private sector interests in the agricultural sector and their implications for poverty and global food security. It would champion the notion that governments should support appropriate institutional mechanisms to maintain a public domain for agricultural technology, and ensure that there is a strong and robust supply chain delivering high-quality technological solutions into that public domain. And, finally, it would emphasize values like sustainability, equity, inclusion, and coverage in its assessments of success.

This book makes an empirically based contribution to understanding the importance of the institutional elements of a pro-poor strategy towards biotechnology and the challenges of its specific design and implementation in different contexts. As a result of the efforts of a team of researchers, it offers an account of resource-poor farmers' experiences with the option of transgenic cotton, along with national governments' efforts to facilitate its adoption. It asks the question, what do resource-poor farmers need in order to take advantage of and benefit from the adoption of this technology? And it points to the requisite institutions for capturing the benefits of this technology. Likewise, it highlights that deficiencies in these institutions can impede the equitable utilization of the technology. Such shortcomings constitute the primary reason for caution in assessing the poverty-reducing potential of transgenic crops.

This study makes a case for shifting the focus of our assessment of transgenic crops away from seeing them merely as a technical solution and instead acknowledging the institutional challenges that determine the way in which a technology is utilized. We need to examine how a technology is generated, the nature of resource-poor farmers' participation in input and credit markets, the access of farmers to information and education, and the responsiveness of regulatory regimes to farmers' concerns. The case studies offer testaments to the need to devote more attention to the development of local institutions that support public and private capacity for technology generation; technology delivery through markets, extension and regulations; and farmer capacities to demand services, participate in markets and comprehend the technology they are using. Finally, the assessment proposes some key principles for policymakers and donors as they consider how to support the development of biotechnology. The capacity of farmers to make their voices heard features at the core of these principles.

An innovation such as a transgenic crop is not simply a technical solution; it is an intervention with social, economic and political consequences. This study argues that the polarized discussions on transgenic crops often fail to acknowledge the importance of the context of technology utilization. We risk the livelihoods of resource-poor farmers if we neglect the critical foundation of sound local institutions.

Ray Offenheiser
President
Oxfam America

Kimberly Pfeifer
Head of Research
Oxfam America

1 Biotechnology and agricultural development

Robert Tripp

Introduction

Under a clear November sky, a group of West African farmers takes a break from harvesting their cotton. The men survey the crop and dare to hope that the harvest will be better than last year, when a drought meant they were barely able to repay their loans for the expensive inputs used to produce cotton. The women participate in the harvest even though some of their own food crop fields still need attention and there are scores of tasks to be done at home. They need a good harvest, because cotton offers one of the few possibilities for earning the cash that is used to pay school fees and buy medicine and other essentials. In addition to their concerns about the harvest and the price they will receive, these farmers now find themselves at the centre of a worldwide controversy about agricultural biotechnology. The news they get on the radio and in discussions with other farmers is difficult to interpret, and the debates mostly take place far away, but the farmers hear there is a new type of cotton that resists some insects and lowers their need to buy insecticides. Some people argue that this will help them save money and keep up with other cotton-producing countries, while others say that it will put them at the mercy of powerful foreign companies and untested technologies.

The controversy goes well beyond genetically modified (GM) cotton and West Africa, and it has fundamental implications for the role of agricultural technology in poverty reduction. This book examines the experience of GM cotton in developing countries and draws lessons about the relevance of agricultural biotechnology for resource-poor farmers.

The term biotechnology can refer to a wide range of techniques that use biological processes for practical ends, including such long-standing practices as fermentation. But the more common references to biotechnology are often limited to a series of recent advances in molecular biology. The capacity to understand and describe the genetic makeup of an organism and, increasingly, to be able to manipulate genetic material has tremendous implications for medicine, industry and agriculture. The discoveries of this rapidly growing field have elicited a mixture of wonder, hope and apprehension, ensuring that biotechnology will be a subject of discussion and debate for the foreseeable future. While some aspects of modern biotechnology are relatively uncontroversial, the techniques of genetic engineering, and particularly the transfer of genetic material from one

---

Box 1.1 Conflicting visions of genetic engineering

Traditional farming has always been based on genetic engineering. Every major crop plant and farm animal has been genetically engineered by selective breeding until it barely resembles the wild species from which it originated. Genetic engineering as the basis of the world economy is nothing new. What is new is the speed of the development…Before long we will have sequenced the genomes of the major crop plants, wheat and maize and rice, and after that will come trees. Within a few decades we will have achieved a deep understanding of the genome, an understanding that will allow us to breed trees that will turn sunlight into fuel and still preserve the diversity that makes natural forests beautiful…While we are genetically engineering trees to use sunlight efficiently to make fuel, we shall also be breeding trees that use sunlight to make other useful products, such as silicon chips for computers and silicon film for photovoltaic collectors. Economic forces will then move industries from cities to the country. Mining and manufacturing could be economically based on locally available solar energy, with genetically engineered creatures consuming and recycling the waste products.

Freeman Dyson (1999) *The Sun, the Genome, and the Internet*, pp. 70–71.

[W]e are undergoing a revolutionary transformation in our resource base, our mode of technology, and the way we organize economic and social activity. Not surprisingly, these changes are accompanied by a revised cosmological narrative. New theories about evolution, steeped in information theory and borrowing heavily from cutting-edge ideas in physics, chemistry and mathematics, are beginning to exert an increasing influence on the fields of evolutionary and developmental biology. Like Darwin's theory, the new ideas about evolution are already beginning to provide an account of nature's operating design that is remarkably compatible with the operational principles of the new technologies and the emerging new global order. … [I]t is essential that the new cosmological narrative be closely examined. Our failure to do so might effectively shut the window to any possible future debate on the particulars of the Biotech Century. That's because…once the revised ideas about evolution become gospel, debate becomes futile, as people will be convinced that genetic engineering technologies, practices and products are simply an amplification of nature's own operating principles and therefore both justifiable and inevitable.

Jeremy Rifkin (1998) *The Biotech Century*, p. 207.

---

organism to another, have been the focus of considerable contention. The breadth of opinion surrounding these techniques is exceptionally great (Box 1.1).

Many people in industrialized countries are sufficiently familiar with the concept of genetically modified organisms (GMOs) to at least offer an opinion on this complex subject. The degree of concern and attention is variable, however. Applications in medicine seem relatively well accepted. Several therapeutic proteins such as insulin and interferon are now regularly produced by GM bacteria, and vaccine for hepatitis B is manufactured using GM yeast cells (Han 2004). Applications in the food industry are also becoming commonplace; in cheese making, the enzyme chymosin produced by GM microorganisms is increasingly utilized in place of the traditional rennet (Adams and Moss 2008). News reports of the genetic manipulation of insects, trees, fish and mammals appear with increasing frequency, describing discoveries that are potentially life saving (mosquitoes unable to transmit the malaria parasite), profitable (trees that provide better pulp for paper making), frivolous (fluorescent tropical fish) and bewildering (goats whose milk contains spider silk), and these are usually met with relatively muted reaction. But no such complacency is evident when it comes to GM crops, which have always been at the centre of the controversy surrounding biotechnology.

It is not difficult to understand why transgenic crops attract considerable opposition. In North America and Europe, an increasingly urbanized population takes advantage of low food prices that are the result of industrial agriculture, but feels anxious about the demise of the family farm. In these circumstances, opportunities to defend the virtues of traditional farming are welcome, and the countryside offers strong symbolism in battles over globalization. In addition, there is measurable evidence of environmental damage caused by some modern farming techniques, compounded by several high-profile food scares, making consumers nervous about their industrialized food supply. The appearance of technology based on genetic manipulation and promoted by large chemical companies is not likely to make them feel any more confident, especially when the innovations (such as herbicide-tolerant varieties) are difficult to interpret or to recognize on the dinner table. And when the multinational corporations appear to be moving towards control of seed supply, concern can only grow.

But transgenic crops have also received considerable support. The majority of agricultural researchers and educators are favourably disposed to transgenic crops, although there are significant differences of opinion among them. Even though the current transgenic varieties are essentially confined to a few traits (particularly those expressing insect resistance or herbicide tolerance), there is evidence of positive environmental benefit, and agriculturalists look forward to a greatly expanded range of crop varieties that address some of farming's toughest problems, such as drought, as well as offering important consumer qualities such as nutritional content. The majority of farmers who have had access to transgenic crops have taken them up with enthusiasm. It is estimated that in 2007, 12 million farmers in 23 countries grew 114.3 million hectares of GM crops (James 2007).

Both sides battle for public opinion, and although the early examples of transgenic crops were those designed for, and grown in, industrialized countries, the debate quickly involved the implications for farmers in developing countries. At times the battle has taken on moralistic dimensions. Monsanto's slogan for a while was the pious 'Food, Health, Hope'; non-governmental organizations (NGOs) countered with campaigns such as Christian Aid's (1999) 'Selling Suicide'. Of course not everyone has seen the issue in such confrontational terms; more balanced reviews expressing varying degrees of support and caution about the new technology were produced by a number of organizations, including Oxfam (1999), The Nuffield Council on Bioethics (1999) and The Royal Society (2000). But the struggle to win public support is not likely to depend merely on the strength of evidence; the debate over GM crops obviously draws on much broader concerns than mere agricultural technology. A number of recent publications examine the way that the arguments in the debate over GM crops are constructed (Cook 2004; Panos 2005; Pearson 2006).

Despite the considerable emotion generated by the controversy, policymakers have to weigh the evidence (and the public's reaction to it) to make decisions about a nation's strategies towards GM crops. This is particularly challenging for developing countries, with diverse agricultural systems, pressing production needs, uneven records of serving their farming populations and often considerable susceptibility to the pressures of multinational corporations and international NGOs. Of course the circumstances vary greatly, and some countries such as India, China or Brazil have advanced technological capacity of their own and corresponding policy independence. But even here, the choices are not clear-cut; a recent study in India describes the commercial, political and technical forces that influence the intricate, and sometimes contradictory, policies at both state and national level that govern the promotion of transgenic crops (Scoones 2006). But as experience grows with transgenic crops in both developing and industrialized countries, there are increasing opportunities for assembling evidence that will be useful for the policy process.

There are at least two important types of evidence that policymakers need to consider in making decisions about transgenic crops. One set of information is the data available on what might be called the externalities of transgenic crops – their effects on the environment and human health and the status of corporate control of agricultural technology. The second set of information is the impact that transgenic crops have on farmers and the agricultural economy. Although we will see that there is a significant area of intersection between the two concerns, it is the second that occupies most of the attention of the present book, which is specifically focused on the experience of resource-poor farmers in developing countries with this new technology.

The book examines one example of agricultural biotechnology: transgenic, insect-resistant cotton. (The technology is introduced at the end of Chapter 2 and described more fully in Chapter 3.) It focuses on the performance of this technology in developing countries. Given the breadth of issues related to biotechnology and the depth of the controversy that the subject engenders, it is important to provide the reader with a clear view of the assumptions that motivate the presentation that follows. The study has been conducted with an appreciation that biotechnology may be able to make significant and positive contributions to agriculture, but with a willingness to incorporate new evidence and to examine the priority currently assigned to transgenic crops. The narrow focus will not allow sweeping judgements certifying that transgenic crops are good or bad, appropriate or inappropriate. Given the complex nature of the arguments surrounding biotechnology, decisions about its future must ultimately be made by well-informed citizens in appropriate political forums.

Moreover, in focusing on developing countries and resource-poor farmers we are compelled to recognize the many factors that contribute to promoting equitable agricultural development. In that context, it is worth asking whether the introduction of a technology (no matter how ground breaking) would bring about meaningful improvements unless appropriate policies and institutions are also in place. Although it is certainly legitimate to promote specific policies that directly affect the introduction of biotechnology (Paarlberg 2001, 2008; Fukuda-Parr 2007), our conviction is that a much broader set of considerations must be addressed if this, or any, agricultural technology is to realize its full potential. This is especially the case if we are concerned about the fate of resource-poor farmers and the reduction of rural poverty. Simplistic support or opposition for a technology can mislead policymakers and donors by promising straightforward solutions to complex problems. Hence the analysis in this book emphasizes that expectations and apprehensions about biotechnology's relation to agricultural growth should be examined in a broad context that includes factors such as the organization of small-scale farming, the conduct of agricultural input and output markets, and the governance of technology generation.

With those considerations in mind, the rest of this chapter reviews three elements that contribute to the context of decision making about agricultural biotechnology. First, we briefly consider the ways in which technology can be seen as a driver of agricultural change and the extent to which a 'revolutionary' idiom is useful. Second, we examine some of the major concerns about the relationship between transgenic crops and the environment, human health and corporate control. These are not issues that the book's country case studies can address in any detail, but it is useful to examine them in relation to other instances of technological change and the nature of the agricultural institutions that are the book's concern. Third, we set the scene for the focus of the rest of the book by outlining the issues that should be taken into account in assessing the impact of a technology on resource-poor farmers and the agricultural economy. That discussion will help steer a course for the remaining chapters that avoids the temptation to make broad judgements about biotechnology, but attempts to use an analysis of how technology performance is shaped by local institutions in order to identify practical implications for agricultural policy.

Are there agricultural technology revolutions?

By far the most familiar instance of recent agricultural change in developing countries is the Green Revolution, understandably leading to speculation about a possible 'gene revolution' with the introduction of transgenic crops (e.g. Wu and Butz 2004). But it is worth questioning the utility of seeing agricultural change in revolutionary terms and, to the extent that the Green Revolution is taken as a model for agricultural development, looking at some of its lessons.

Agricultural change

Historians argue about the extent to which major shifts in agricultural technology can be described as revolutions. Mokyr's (1990) extensive review of technological change and economic growth recognizes that progress can come from both sudden 'macroinventions' and sequences of 'microinventions', but that in the case of agriculture, 'undramatic, cumulative, barely perceptible improvements led to increased productivity' (ibid: 294). This is neither to say that the pattern of growth in agricultural production has been a smooth, gentle curve, nor that particularly important innovations cannot be identified. For instance, the emergence of the three field system, the inclusion of legumes in rotations and the development of stronger ploughs all contributed to agricultural growth in medieval Europe. But as Grigg (1982) points out, attempts to define historical agricultural revolutions often suffer from disagreement on the most appropriate measures and a dearth of accurate data.

Even with evidence of increases in output or productivity over a given period, attribution to particular technologies is often made difficult by the relatively slow and uneven spread of many agricultural innovations, the fact that the efficacy of a new input often depends on the availability of other technologies or skills and the role of institutions in providing access to an innovation or incentives for its use. Overton (1996) discusses the problems in defining the periods and contributors to agricultural revolution in England. His analysis emphasizes that although the strongest period of growth (roughly 1750–1850) benefited significantly from technologies such as turnips and clover (contributing to soil fertility management) and mechanical innovations such as the seed drill, these were known and used before that period and their adoption was not, as legends insist, in response to proselytizing innovators such as 'Turnip' Townshend and Jethro Tull. In addition, the analysis shows the close link between technical change and institutional transformation, particularly in markets and land tenure.

The use of artificial fertilizer is a good example of the complex sources of innovation and the nature of diffusion. In nineteenth-century Europe the maintenance of soil fertility by rotations and manures was increasingly supplemented by imports of guano and mineral nitrates, but the major breakthrough came with the development of an industrial process to fix atmospheric nitrogen. The discovery of the Haber–Bosch process in the early twentieth century facilitated both increased agricultural yields and the production of explosives for war-time Germany (Leigh 2004). The discovery stimulated the expansion of the fertilizer industry after the First World War, but its growth was relatively slow, with four million tons of artificial fertilizer produced in 1940. The following decades saw a stronger expansion, with 40 million tons in use by 1965 and 140 million tons by 1990 (McNeill 2000).

Plant breeding is a technology of more ancient vintage, and farmers have been selecting superior plants as a source of next season's seed since the beginning of agriculture. Even before the rediscovery of Mendel's work on plant genetics in the early twentieth century, the development of improved plant varieties played an important role in agricultural advance. Olmstead and Rhode (2002) show how the continual selection and adaptation of new wheat varieties in the nineteenth-century USA, combined with crop management innovations to keep pests and weeds at bay, made as important a contribution to productivity growth as the much more visible advances in farm mechanization. Certainly the most revolutionary breakthrough in plant breeding (before biotechnology) was the discovery of hybrid vigour and the development of hybrid maize in the 1930s. The adoption of hybrid maize in the USA is the textbook case of rapid and sustained technology uptake, but the speed and extent of adoption varied significantly across regions of the country because of relative profitability and the presence of institutions (public research stations and private seed enterprises) that were needed to adapt and deliver the innovation (Griliches 1957). The steady growth in US maize yields from the 1930s into the 1980s can be linked not only to hybrid adoption but also to increased fertilizer use, the widespread adoption of herbicides and the fact that maize growing was curtailed in many less productive environments (Evans 1993). In addition, maize breeding continued to deliver consistent, year-to-year improvement in the yield potential of the varieties that were being offered to farmers (Duvick 1992).

The Green Revolution

Plant varieties and fertilizer were the key technological elements of the Green Revolution, which is the model of rapid agricultural change in developing countries that is most often put forward when discussing how to address Africa's farming crisis or, as we have seen, the promotion of biotechnology. The term is now used very loosely, but its original conception was in reference to the period in the late 1960s and early 1970s when short-stature, fertilizer-responsive varieties of wheat and rice were introduced to large parts of Asia (and a few other areas, such as Mexican and Turkish wheat production). The adoption of the technology led to significant yield increases in the participating countries and a marked reduction in their reliance on food imports and food aid. The immediate aftermath of the strategy also saw a number of critical studies that pointed to inequalities in access to the technology and trends towards concentration of rural resources (e.g. Frankel 1971; Griffin 1975). Several longitudinal studies have demonstrated more equitable results (Hazell and Ramasamy 1991; Lanjouw and Stern 1993), although either blaming or giving credit to a specific agricultural technology for outcomes observed in the midst of changes in population, labour opportunities and the wider economy is a risky business (Rigg 1989). The situation is perhaps best summed up by the observation (made nearly two decades ago) that the Green Revolution has been responsible for

> massive rises in yields of staple food crops eaten, grown and worked mainly by poor people. There have been positive effects on employment and on the availability, cheapness, and security of food. Yet there have been only delayed, scanty, and sometimes faltering and imperceptible improvements in the lot of the poor.
>
> (Lipton with Longhurst 1989: 5)

The strategy denominated the Green Revolution was unarguably responsible for very significant increases in food production within a relatively short space of time, but it is worth examining the nature of the revolution. The lynchpin of the strategy was varieties that would respond to additional amounts of fertilizer and whose short, stiff straw kept them from lodging as a result of the increased weight of grain. The rapid development of rice and wheat varieties with these character-istics suitable for Asian farming environments is one of the greatest accomplish-ments of modern plant breeding. But this revolution, like most others, had antecedents. The germplasm that provided the wheat dwarfing genes came from Japan and other Asian sources and had been known for some time. Nineteenth-century Japanese farmers had developed short, fertilizer-responsive rice varieties, and new techniques were spread through farmer associations and state institutions (Francks 1984). Short-stature wheat varieties had been available in the USA since the early 1940s and the growth in US wheat yields over the next four decades paralleled the gradual adoption of these varieties (and the increased use of fertil-izer); in this sense the USA experienced its own Green Revolution, albeit of a less dramatic nature (Dalrymple 1988).

In the Asian Green Revolution, the increased yields were the result of the per-formance of the new varieties and fertilizer, but usually also reliable irrigation (and in the case of rice, at least in the early years, insecticides to counteract the increased pest attack on susceptible rice varieties often grown outside the tradi-tional cropping season). Thus the technology required a coordinated supply of inputs, credit and extension and, in the case of irrigation, expansion of public systems or additional private investment. The organization of the supporting institutions, education and finance infrastructure was as important an achieve-ment as the technology itself. A recent analysis of the Green Revolution that seeks lessons for Africa concludes that we should see the changes that took place in Asia as the product of a 'state-driven, market-mediated and small-farmer based strategy to increase the national self-sufficiency in food grains' (Djurfeldt *et al.* 2005: 3). The process unfolded in a political environment that saw increasing food imports and unstable international grain markets; threats to national security (with India and Pakistan on the verge of war); food riots and prospects of famine. Although the political responses may have been motivated by self-preservation, and relied heavily on state resources, they usually also saw the private sector playing an important role in input and output marketing.

Food shortages and other agricultural challenges are increasingly on the minds of politicians of developing countries today, and there are discussions of the need for the coordinated policy changes that characterized the Green Revolution. But it can be misleading to see such changes solely through the lens of new technology (and the measures devised for its immediate diffusion). Appropriate technologies need to be harnessed to sufficiently well-defined goals to enlist coherent policy support. The Green Revolution is not only an outstanding example of the contribution of agricultural technology to develop-ment, it is also a major instance in which political commitment played a large role in technological change. Most historical instances of significant agricul-tural change were less obviously policy driven, but many featured support of one kind or another from the governments of the day, and most shared other characteristics. Rather than a single innovation, they were sets of technologies interacting over time and space to produce increases in yields and productivity; they responded, and in turn contributed, to changes in the wider economy; and they depended on the concomitant evolution of institutions. When this argument is applied to transgenic crops, biotechnology may be seen less as a revolutionary vanguard and more as part of a complex puzzle. This shift in focus does not diminish the potential importance of transgenic crops, but urges examination of the broader technological environment and the institutions that support agricultural change. This does not challenge the sentiment that transgenic crops can be considered a ground-breaking technology, but it questions whether the idiom of revolution is usefully attached to particular technologies and pushed forward to confront the complex challenges of agricultural development. Some of these issues will be outlined in the following text and they will be a major focus of the remainder of the book.

What is different about transgenic crops?

This section addresses two sets of issues related to the use of transgenic crops. They constitute some of the major concerns expressed by the technology's critics. The two areas of interest are biological (principally environmental and food safety concerns) and economic (mostly related to the commercial control of agricultural biotechnology). The issues arising from these concerns are often seen as distinguishing features of the new technology, justifying opposition or at least requiring an adequate response. Neither of these technical areas can be directly addressed in the type of studies that form the core of this book, but the performance of the institutions and policies that may address these concerns are often evident as we examine the utilization of the technology. This section attempts to introduce these concerns, set them in a wider context, and identify appropriate institutional responses. The section looks briefly at: environment and agriculture; the processes of creating transgenic crops; biodiversity and environmental pollution; food safety; and the corporate control of plant breeding.

Environment and agriculture

Agriculture is, by definition, a disturbance to the environment. Farming activity has transformed the earth's landscape, removing forests, redirecting rivers, draining marshland and creating large areas of economic activity and emotional attachment that we call 'the countryside'. Recent analysis suggests that early farming activities produced enough greenhouse gases to fortuitously counteract what otherwise would have been a cooling trend, resulting in the earth's relative climatic stability in the pre-industrial era (Ruddiman 2005). Industrial activity has since outstripped agriculture as a contributor to global warming, but it is estimated that modern farming activities are still responsible for about 14 per cent of greenhouse gas emissions (with deforestation contributing a further 18 per cent) (House of Lords 2005). Farming has also led to soil erosion and land degradation, and evidence of these problems and their consequences is available from earliest times

(Denevan 1992). Agricultural intensification has been responsible for a simplification of the landscape and has contributed to a loss of diversity; the preponderance of human food supply is now based on about 20 crops. Agricultural intensification has also depended on increasing use of fertilizers and manures. Nitrates in runoff waters are a serious health hazard, and nitrate and phosphate pollution of fresh water bodies (eutrophication) leads to the growth of algae and other invasive organisms that choke fish and plant life (Conway 1997).

Other agricultural inputs can have unintended effects, with the health and environmental consequences of pesticide misuse at the top of the list (Pretty 2005). In addition, attempts to control pests are usually met by response and adaptation. Synthetic pesticides have been responsible for the destruction of natural enemies and have favoured selection for insecticide resistance. Even organic farmers using sprays of the bacterial spores of *Bacillus thuringiensis* (Bt) have encouraged the emergence of resistant strains of diamondback moth (American Academy of Microbiology 2002). Plant pathogens cause severe losses; the Romans sacrificed to the god Robigus to protect them from wheat rust (Peterson 2001), and in more recent times plant breeders have devoted considerable effort to developing plant varieties with resistance. But despite considerable success in plant breeding, the pathogens often mutate to break down the resistance, calling forth further research (Slusarenko *et al.* 2000). Weeds compete with crops for nutrients and moisture and are the target of a range of cultivation practices. But cultivation can lead to changes in weed populations, which evolve to mimic the crops they grow with and adapt to changing tillage practices (Radosevich *et al.* 1997). The more recent use of herbicides has led to many instances of herbicide-tolerant weeds. These externalities and consequences of new agricultural technology have elicited a wide range of responses to balance the trade-offs, limit the damage and seek alternatives. The responses include the further development of new technology, the establishment of legal and regulatory mechanisms and the promotion of alternative farming strategies.

The creation of transgenic crops

Before reviewing some of the specific concerns about biotechnology, it is useful to consider the process of genetic modification itself. The debate about biotechnology often involves divisions of opinion about how 'different' transgenic crops are. The earliest farmers made significant changes to plant genomes by selecting those plant types that met their requirements for harvesting and food preparation, and their descendants became more skilled in these selection practices. Modern plant breeding is little more than a century old and includes techniques that allow the directed transfer of pollen in order to combine the useful characteristics of individual plants. These techniques mimic those that occur in nature and are confined to the improvement of a single species, but more recently techniques such as embryo rescue have allowed the development of many interspecific and intergeneric hybrids that would not otherwise have survived the artificial fertilization process (Sharma 1995), providing, for instance, genes from wild grasses to improve the disease resistance of wheat. Mutation breeding has also evolved in the past 50 years, where seed is exposed to radiation or chemical mutagens and then screened to identify useful characteristics from the resulting chromosomal rearrangements and genetic deletion and modification. Well over a thousand varieties of cereals and legumes produced by mutation breeding have been released worldwide (Gupta 1998).

As the techniques of plant breeding become more sophisticated, allowing ever greater freedom from the processes that normally direct plant evolution, there are arguments about nature and its boundaries. The methods of genetic transformation extend the boundaries, and the dispute, even further. In one method, a plasmid (a small piece of DNA) incorporating a 'construct' of a few alien genes is incorporated in a bacterium that has the capacity to insert its own genes into a plant genome and this is incubated with tissue from the target plant. In another method, a plasmid is coated onto small particles of metal and shot into the target plant tissue at high velocity. (See Chapter 3 for a more complete description of transformation methods.) Cook (2004) has correctly argued that labelling a certain portion of the continuum of plant breeding techniques as 'natural' or 'unnatural' is not useful, although one can certainly understand how some people might draw a line at these latest discoveries. But whether or not transgenic plants are deemed (subjectively) unnatural, it remains to decide (as objectively as possible) if they are safe and useful.

Biodiversity and the environment

One of the principal concerns about the safety of transgenic crops is their impact on biodiversity. There are several issues here. One concern is that the spread of transgenic varieties may lead to a reduction in the number and diversity of crop varieties grown. This has been an issue debated at least since the Green Revolution, when modern varieties replaced a large number of traditional varieties, and a single variety could take the place of several landraces found in dispersed localities. There is the fear that popular transgenic varieties could do the same thing. However, the relationship between the adoption of modern varieties and diversity loss is far from straightforward. A study by Brush (1992) showed no general pattern of varietal instability with the introduction of modern varieties of potato, wheat and rice in the centres of origin of those crops. Smale (1997) examined data for wheat and found little evidence to support the hypothesis of diversity decline. In European countries the proportion of area held by the dominant wheat cultivar has actually decreased over the past 50 years; and there is evidence that a single cultivar may have had a more dominant role in Punjab *before* the Green Revolution.

There are a number of mechanisms that can help counteract any deterioration in plant genetic diversity. Local varieties that are displaced are not necessarily 'lost' if they find their way to genebanks, and the use of molecular markers and other tools of biotechnology greatly expands plant breeders' capacities to take advantage of these materials (Tanksley and McCouch 1997). Programs that promote in-situ variety conservation also make important contributions (Smale 2006).

More careful analysis of the benefits and costs of increasing crop genetic diversity and assessing high-priority risks is also required (Heisey *et al.* 1997). But this is not to say that we should be complacent about potential threats to genetic diversity from the introduction of new crop varieties. The pressures of commercial agriculture act to limit diversity in breeding programs and increase the risk of depending on a narrow genetic base (Wilkes 1994). It is not clear what effect biotechnology will have on this pattern. The experience with transgenic crops is very preliminary, but in the USA the technology has stimulated the development of hundreds of new varieties, with little evidence of a decline in diversity, although the problem of reliance on a narrow range of breeding materials that characterizes conventional plant breeding is also evident for transgenic crops (e.g. Sneller 2003).

Another concern regarding transgenic crops is the possibility that they will cross with wild crop relatives, leading either to the demise of certain species or the alteration of wild plant ecology. Genetic interchange between crop species and their wild relatives is a reality, and the effects can be seen on both sides of the exchange. Commercial sugar beet seed producers must go to great lengths to ensure that wild sea beet pollen does not contaminate their fields, which would lead to an unharvestable crop. The more prevalent concern about contamination of the wild by the cultivated is illustrated by the fact that wild rice in Taiwan has been virtually wiped out over the past century due to cross-pollination from conventional rice cultivation (Ellstrand 2003). Thus the fear that transgenic crops may cause the extinction of wild relatives is in principal little different from the challenge of protecting wild species from conventional crop varieties.

On the other hand, a transgene could confer certain properties favouring the new hybrid. One of the principal concerns is the creation of 'superweeds' resistant to specific herbicides. This is indeed a possibility and such selection pressure is already in evidence from the use of herbicides, even with conventional crop varieties. Transgenic, herbicide-tolerant varieties add an additional threat, but so do the herbicide-tolerant varieties already commercially available that are the products of conventional plant breeding. Transgenic virus-resistant or insect-resistant varieties could cross with wild species to yield hybrids with a competitive advantage that might alter plant ecology, but again this threat exists for conventionally bred varieties as well. For instance, two squash varieties resistant to the same viruses have been developed and released almost simultaneously in the USA; one was conventionally bred and the other was transgenic [National Research Council (NRC) 2002]. Thus the need for vigilance extends well beyond transgenic crops.

> Genetic engineering has the potential to create *certain* phenotypes that will be much more problematic than the average product of plant breeding, just as plant breeding has the potential to create *certain* phenotypes that will be much more problematic than the average product of genetic engineering.
>
> (Ellstrand 2003: 186, emphasis in original)

Similarly, a review of US regulation found that '[n]ontransgenic crop breeding techniques have the potential to introduce genes and genetic variation into crops that equal or surpass the novelty associated with recombinant DNA techniques' (NRC 2002: 254).

Food safety

Another area of concern for transgenic crops is food safety. A particular focus of attention has been the fact that most current transgenic crops contain a 'marker' gene (used in the process of transformation but not required for the performance of the end product) that confers resistance to a certain class of antibiotic. The fear is that this resistance could be transferred to bacteria in the gut of humans or animals consuming the GM food. No evidence of such a transfer has been uncovered, but considerable progress has been made in identifying alternative marker strategies.

In addition, there are concerns that transgenic crops might contain novel allergens or other harmful substances (Goodman *et al.* 2008). But conventional breeding may occasionally develop unsafe products as well, especially in plant species that produce their own toxins for pest protection. A promising virus- and blight-resistant potato variety with excellent consumer qualities had to be withdrawn from the market when found to contain unacceptably high levels of poisonous glycoalkaloids (Zitnak and Johnston 1970). The challenges of managing food safety in the face of changing technology are not confined to plant breeding, as the growing problem of aflatoxin contamination of stored grain in developing countries attests (e.g. Shephard 2003).

Regulatory agencies pay close attention to these issues, but public opinion and preferences play an important role in the acceptance of something like GM food. The contrast between general consumer acceptance of GM food in the USA and the greater opposition in Europe has been the source of much discussion. Explanations include differences in awareness, trust in regulators, commercial interests, the influence of pressure groups and cultural predispositions (Zechendorf 1998; Tiberghien 2007). The answer probably lies in a combination of these factors, especially when one considers the considerable heterogeneity in European (and US) opinions on the subject. Culture surely plays a part, as illustrated by the differences between UK and French markets for green beans produced in Africa. The UK system has included strict control and traceability by large supermarkets, making it difficult for smallholders to comply and biasing towards sourcing produce from large farms using wage labour. The French system, on the other hand, is more directed towards peasant culture and small grocers, and this in turn is more compatible with support for smallholder African farmers. The differences can be partially explained by a particular French vision of the countryside that emphasizes the importance of peasant expertise and hence finds consumers more forgiving of inconsistencies in African produce. The same vision means that French consumers are more disposed to small-scale production than to organic agriculture, and less tolerant of GM food (Freidberg 2004). African green beans are a long way from transgenic crops, but the example illustrates the importance of seeing regulatory regimes in the broadest possible context and emphasizes that any society or group chooses what it wishes to identify as risks (Douglas and Wildavsky 1983).

Regulation

We have seen that transgenic crops share many of the types of risks presented by conventional agricultural technology. This is not to say that they are equivalent, but rather that the regulation of biotechnology needs to be seen in a broader institutional environment. Countries require more general regulatory capacity for managing the environmental and public health consequences of agricultural production.

The specific biosafety regulation that needs to be in place before a country attempts to use transgenic crops offers a number of challenges (Persley *et al.* 1993; Birner and Linacre 2008). The task is particularly complex because environmental, public health and agricultural agencies all can make claims for regulatory responsibilities related to transgenic crops. The USA has the most extensive experience to date in the regulation of transgenic crops, and a review by the NRC is instructive (NRC 2002). It concludes that while the regulation of transgenic crops enforces higher environmental standards than conventional technology, there is also a need for better definition of agency responsibilities for technologies such as insect-resistant crops, increasing rigour in assessment and higher staffing levels.

National regulatory systems responsible for addressing biosafety find themselves in the midst of a battle featuring two phrases that supposedly represent regulatory ideals, 'the precautionary principle' (on the one side) and 'science-based regulation' (on the other). It may be debated whether these phrases represent useful protocols or are merely empty slogans. The fact remains that regulatory regimes are necessarily imperfect, subject to various influences and continually in need of review and amendment. Regulation 'is a contested political resource' (Harriss-White 1996: 38). While we would hope that the regulatory process will involve the highest level of technical and scientific knowledge and will be conducted in the most transparent manner possible, the establishment of new regulatory regimes for a particularly controversial technology offers many opportunities for competing interest groups. Strong opposition from international and local NGOs can result in strategies calling for exceptionally stringent regulation or more study, further delaying the deployment of GM crops (Paarlberg 2001, 2008). Corporate power also exerts its influence and pursues more lenient treatment of GM crops; the US Department of Justice fined Monsanto $1 million for bribing officials in Indonesia to bypass environmental impact studies for its transgenic cotton (US Dept. of Justice 2005).

This book does not address the technical or organizational details of biosafety regulation in developing countries, but the case studies examine some of the ways that more general regulatory performance affects the abilities of smallholders to use transgenic crops and, in turn, identifies how rural institutions affect the nature of the regulatory process.

Corporate control of technology

Besides environmental and health issues, the other major concern about transgenic crops is the possibility of increasing corporate control of agricultural technology and food production (Tansey and Rajotte 2008). This concern has at least two important elements: intellectual property rights (IPRs) and corporate concentration.

Throughout much of the twentieth century plant breeders complained they were not afforded the same protection for their discoveries as other inventors, who had access to patents. Because a new plant variety could be freely multiplied and distributed, it was difficult for plant breeders to earn financial rewards for their work. Much plant breeding was done by public entities, and private seed companies depended on reputation and the fact that commercial farmers increasingly found it worthwhile to use purchased rather than saved seed (Tripp 2001a). The discovery of hybrid vigour was a major boost to the private seed industry because saved hybrid seed performs less well, encouraging farmers to return each year for fresh seed. More recently, systems for 'plant variety protection' have been established in many countries, and several other mechanisms are also available to help gain greater control over the use of new plant varieties. (See Chapter 5 for more discussion on IPRs related to transgenic crops.) The availability and utilization of these mechanisms varies between countries, but there are two issues that merit emphasis. First, it is important to distinguish various dimensions of protection. Probably the most understandable type of control allows the plant breeder to designate which company or companies can multiply and sell the seed. A more disputed issue is the extent to which a variety can be used by other breeding programs. And certainly the most controversial issue is the extent to which farmers can save seed of the protected variety. Second, the concerns and mechanisms for plant variety protection significantly predate the advent of biotechnology; transgenic varieties bring some added complications to the arena, but much of their governance is subject to the same instruments (and the same controversy) that affect conventional plant varieties.

Although the mechanisms governing farmer access to seed may be relatively familiar, the advent of biotechnology has engendered significant new controversy over the control of the underlying technology. The issue of 'patenting life' is widely debated and of course extends well beyond agriculture. The extent to which individual genes can be patented in a particular country, and the nature of those patents, is a controversial issue, and resolution cannot be expected soon. In agricultural biotechnology there is the possibility to patent particular genes, methods of modifying them, the ways in which they are inserted in plants, the methods used for regeneration and other tools and processes. An analysis of transgenic, pro-vitamin A 'Golden Rice' identified up to 44 different patents that could be in force, depending on the country where the variety was introduced (Kryder *et al.* 2000). In the early years of biotechnology, exceptionally broad claims were attempted (such as rights to all GM cotton), leading to calls for reforming the patent system in light of the new technology that was emerging (Barton 2000). The implications of biotechnology patents for access to innovations in developing countries deserve attention if there is any hope that such technology will address the goal of poverty reduction (Taylor and Cayford 2003). As with other technologies, it is necessary to steer a course between rewarding innovation and guarding against monopoly, and there are justifiable fears that the new technology is in too few hands.

Thus concerns about IPRs in biotechnology lead directly to the issue of corporate concentration. Until fairly recently, the seed industries in industrialized countries have included a mixture of small and large firms. Although there are some economies of scale in conventional seed production, small companies can efficiently serve local niches. In 1995, more than 300 companies were selling maize seed in the USA, although 7 companies accounted for 70 per cent of the market, a figure that had been fairly constant for 20 years (Duvick 1998). Although some chemical, oil and food companies began to explore links with seed companies in the 1970s, it was not until the 1980s when agrochemical companies conducting biotechnology research began to enter the seed market. Many of the emerging transgenic varieties were either linked to the companies' chemicals (herbicides) or could replace them (insecticides and fungicides). But the biotechnology companies came to understand that their innovations needed to be delivered in the best possible varieties. The story is told that when Monsanto made its (unsuccessful) bid to merge with Pioneer (the largest US seed company), the response was, 'Congratulations! You've got a gene! Guess what? We've got fifty thousand genes!...Without our varieties, your gene isn't worth a thing...' (Charles 2001: 119). But as transgenic crops became a reality, most seed companies found that they needed access to the capital and expertise of the life science industry giants, and takeovers became more common.

Not all of these ventures were successful, but the resulting acquisition and merger process left a much-reduced field. Srinivasan (2003) has shown that although the seed industry is still relatively fragmented at the global level, considerable concentration (measured by variety ownership) is evident for major crops in individual countries. Fernandez-Cornejo (2004) has shown how the market shares of the four largest firms in the maize, soybean and cotton seed industries in the USA have increased over the past two decades. Much of the concentration of variety ownership has come about through mergers and acquisitions. Similarly, King and Schimmelpfennig (2005) calculated that 70 per cent of the agricultural biotechnology patents held by the top six firms in the USA (which together hold more than 40 per cent of all such patents) are obtained not through parent company research but through mergers and acquisitions. Thus there are clear trends towards control of plant breeding and biotechnology in industrialized countries through consolidation, and similar trends are appearing in developing countries (Srinivasan 2003). The implications for competitiveness, incentives for research, and farmer access to technology will become evident in the coming years.

It should be clear that neither the biological nor the economic issues that contribute to the controversy about transgenic crops are necessarily unique to biotechnology. Their familiarity does not make them any less important, however, and they deserve careful attention. But these issues must be understood within the broader context of the governance of agricultural technology and the politics of agriculture. The same perspective is useful in examining the potential impact of the technology on smallholder farmers.

How do we assess a technology in relation to poverty reduction?

Although it may be possible to ask general questions about environment, health and corporate control for transgenic crops, it is more difficult to ask such broad questions about impacts of the technology on smallholders. Such questions are usually asked about specific technologies in particular circumstances. A comprehensive analysis of such impacts for a transgenic crop would be a daunting task. As Smale *et al.* (2006a) point out in a thorough review of the literature, it would be necessary to include an assessment of outcomes on farmers, consumers, the industries associated with the commodity, and trade. The research reported in this book pursues a narrower set of objectives by focusing almost exclusively on farm-level issues.

These issues have attracted more attention for transgenic crops than perhaps for any other agricultural technology. For instance, the Cartagena Protocol on Biosafety authorizes national policymakers to consider socio-economic impacts when considering the use of transgenic crops (Box 1.2). But the boundaries of 'socio-economic' are not delineated, leaving the way open for a wide range of interpretations.

This section proposes a set of concerns that should be considered in assessing technology from the farmer's perspective. It includes a review of factors related to on-farm technology performance, but also examines how the impact of biotechnology

---

Box 1.2   Socio-economic impact and the Cartagena Protocol on Biosafety

The Cartagena Protocol on Biosafety is a supplementary agreement to the Convention on Biological Diversity. The principal aim of the agreement is to ensure that the introduction of the products of biotechnology ('living modified organisms'), including transgenic crop varieties, is done in such a way as to protect biological diversity. Under the agreement, countries can choose to restrict the import and use of specific transgenic crops in accordance with their assessment of the potential impact. Article 26 of the Protocol allows countries to include socio-economic considerations in their decisions. Although this is aimed principally at the protection of the biological resources and biodiversity in areas inhabited by local communities, it may be extended to considerations of local traditions, knowledge and practices. A number of national biosafety laws incorporate these interests. For instance, the draft of the National Biosafety Framework of the Philippines includes the provision that 'the socio-economic, ethical and cultural benefits and risks, of modern biotechnology to the Philippines and its citizens, and in particular on small farmers, indigenous peoples, women, small and medium enterprises and the domestic scientific community, shall be taken into account' (Fransen *et al.* 2005).

on the institutions of research, input markets and information provision in turn affects farmer control of technology and the capacity for equitable technology development and delivery.

Technology performance

Even when we confine our interests to resource-poor farmers, delimiting the populations and issues of relevance to a particular agricultural technology is not necessarily straightforward. There is a growing appreciation of the fact that many rural households described as 'farmers' in fact earn their living from a range of activities, and agriculture may not be the principal source of income or the highest priority for attention (Ellis 1998). It is well known that economic growth is accompanied by a decline in the proportion of the population dependent on farming, and a major challenge for rural development policy is to find the right balance among: supporting those households that can earn a decent income as smallholders; helping those rural households who will continue to count on some subsistence production for at least the near future; and providing exit strategies that allow those with too few resources to find alternative, secure sources of income (de Janvry and Sadoulet 2000). At the very least, we must recognize that 'the small farmer' is far from a homogeneous class in terms of interests or resources.

Even when a specific segment of the farming population is identified as a potential beneficiary for technology development, differences in resources and conditions can lead to variable outcomes. There are many factors that determine patterns of adoption for a new technology. It is usual that those with more resources (including education and skills) are most likely to be the first to invest in new technology. Rogers' (1995) comprehensive review of the literature on the diffusion of innovations concluded that the better-off are almost inevitably more likely to be early adopters. Such early adopters usually earn 'innovators' rents' by being able to take advantage of increased production before it is reflected in declining crop price. An examination of experience with so-called 'low external input' technology, presumably more attuned to the needs of the poorest farming households, has shown the same pattern of adoption favouring the better-resourced (Tripp 2006). These are reminders that technology per se is an imperfect tool for redressing underlying conditions of significant inequality in access to resources.

Nevertheless, it is possible to develop technology that is more likely to be of wide access and that is compatible with the conditions of resource-poor farmers. Farmers will be attracted to technology that provides acceptable yield increments (or yield stability) in return for additional investment (in purchased inputs and/or their own labour), or that saves time or money. Farmers are usually able to assess these advantages for themselves, sometimes using criteria that researchers may not initially consider. In Pakistan, farmers choose cotton and wheat varieties not to maximize the returns on an individual crop enterprise (as extension agents sometimes urge) but rather to maximize returns to the cropping rotation; they may not get optimal wheat yields because of late planting but this allows them an extra picking from the preceding cotton crop (Byerlee *et al.* 1987). Attempts to explain the widespread and enthusiastic uptake of transgenic, herbicide-tolerant soybeans in the USA have found that the varieties offer little in the way of yield advantage or cost savings. Instead, farmers emphasize the simplicity and flexibility of the technology as its major attractions (Fernandez-Cornejo and McBride 2002).

As farmers are often more skilled than researchers at assessing which technologies are appropriate for their conditions, we might ask why it is necessary to look in detail at the performance of a technology such as transgenic cotton. If large numbers of farmers take up the technology, it is probably profitable; if they reject or abandon it, there is probably a good reason. In fact, the argument to 'let the farmers decide' is voiced by the biotechnology industry in India, where adoption of transgenic cotton has grown rapidly (Stone 2004). There is much sense in this point of view (although large corporations tend to be inconsistent defenders of smallholder capabilities), and it contrasts, paradoxically, with the opposition from NGOs who usually extol the wisdom of farmers' ('traditional') choices and practices but worry about farmers being misled by transgenic crops.

But there are good reasons to look carefully at technology performance, even when farmers are eager adopters. First, farmers are not infallible. In the early 1900s, maize farmers in the USA sought seed of varieties that won annual 'corn shows' for the size and uniformity of their ears, believing these would give the highest yields. The popularity of these contests waned only when it was shown that the winners were not necessarily the most productive varieties (Wallace and Brown 1988). Second, farmers can only make choices based on the information at hand; if this is insufficient, their choices may be flawed. For instance, farmers' lack of capacity to test alternatives for pest control may lead them to over-invest in what they see as risk-reducing pesticides. Third, technologies that provide attractive short-term returns may have negative externalities over the long run; the pesticide treadmill is one of the more prominent examples. Fourth, it is important to recognize that a technology need only be marginally superior in order to achieve widespread uptake; there is a distinction between a technology's prevalence and its relative importance (Edgerton 2006). Fifth, farmers' mere adoption of a technology does not indicate that they are necessarily empowered to make best use of it, to adapt it to their own conditions or to know where to turn when something goes wrong. Thus we need to look carefully at the institutions that provide information and that support the generation and delivery of technology.

Farmers' control of technology

The relevant institutions that determine the choice of technology available to a farmer include agricultural research and extension, markets for input delivery and the regulatory regimes that govern those markets. The nature of research and the efficiency with which information is provided determine the pace, direction and equity of technological change in agriculture. When innovation relies on physical inputs, regulatory systems often provide information unavailable through normal market exchange. The governance of these systems of information provision is as important for transgenic crops as it is for conventional technology.

The ability to understand and control a technology is an important factor in determining the impact on resource-poor farmers. Farmers' control over a technology is determined by the quality of information available regarding its characteristics, information about relevant alternatives, and opportunities to test and adapt the technology to local conditions. Neither states nor markets have been particularly successful at supporting opportunities for farmers to master new technology. Since at least the time of the Green Revolution, states have often provided extension advice and credit based on a rigidly determined 'package of practices', attempting to exploit the synergisms of component technologies (seed, fertilizer, pesticide) but not allowing farmers the capacity to adjust or experiment, and often paying little attention to the actual conditions under which the package was to be used. Despite the demonstration that it is often possible for farmers to adopt a package in incremental steps (Byerlee and Hesse de Polanco 1986), many public programs for technology promotion still follow this top-down strategy. There are few systems of public agricultural extension that cover significant areas, are financially viable and are able to strengthen farmers' capacities to adapt and innovate.

The development of any kind of viable public extension system is further challenged by lack of financial support from governments and donors and the increasingly prominent role of the private sector in technology provision. Although in earlier times inputs such as seed, fertilizer and pesticides were often supplied through government programs, most input provision is now handled by private firms and distributors. The public sector is still heavily involved in plant breeding, but even here privately developed crop varieties are increasingly common in developing countries (and the norm in the industrialized world) and seed provision is increasingly in private hands rather than with public seed enterprises (Tripp 2001a). There are a number of advantages to the development of such markets for agricultural inputs, but they serve the needs of smallholders only if they provide adequate information. Unfortunately, there is good evidence that resource-poor farmers often do not have even the most basic information about the crop varieties they are growing. Many farmers using modern varieties of food staples are unable to give their names; in one instance more than 40 per cent of Philippine farmers claiming to be growing a disease-resistant rice variety were mistaken (Tripp 2001b). Similarly, when rice varieties resistant to brown plant hopper were developed and made available, farmers continued to use high amounts of insecticide (Rola and Pingali 1993).

Institutional capacity

Building farmers' skills and control over technology depends on the development of public and private agricultural research and extension, transparent and equitable input markets, and a responsive regulatory system. Such development is in the hands of national policymakers.

Public agricultural research and extension will continue to be important for smallholders and it is imperative that there is an appropriate division of responsibilities, and collaboration, with the private sector (Byerlee and Echeverria 2002).

The determination of public research priorities is exceptionally complex and inevitably balances various interests, but it is important to develop mechanisms that make research and extension more responsive to the needs of smallholders.

Most transgenic crops (and associated inputs) will be developed and delivered by the private sector. If they are to serve the needs of smallholders, policies must be in place that ensure competitive markets for seed companies and other input suppliers. This requires the emergence of local enterprises, business ethics and reputations that support transparent markets. In the case of seed supply, viable mechanisms for establishing adequate property rights for plant varieties also need to be in place.

Equitable and trustworthy input markets will also depend on adequate regulatory mechanisms. Much of the debate about transgenic crops revolves around biosafety regulation. While this is undoubtedly important, more basic regulatory challenges stand in the way of farmers' ability to take advantage of new technology. These include the mechanisms by which new plant varieties and other innovations are approved for release and sale and the regulations governing the quality of seed and chemical inputs on the market. Regulation is a difficult subject, but it is a mistake to see it as simply the exercise of control over market activities by a third party agency. Farmers need access to reliable information about the identity and quality of the inputs they purchase. Regulatory systems respond to information deficiencies, and there are various ways of overcoming these weaknesses (Tripp 1997). The development of institutions that promote broad-based regulation is a particular challenge to modern agriculture.

Summary

Agricultural biotechnology is a controversial subject mostly because of debates regarding the performance and potential of transgenic crops. The divisions of opinion are so wide, and the social, economic and environmental arguments are so complex that no single treatment of the subject is likely to be comprehensive or achieve consensus. Nevertheless, the subject deserves careful attention, and one of the most urgent themes is related to the place of transgenic crops in developing countries and their potential impact on resource-poor farmers. This book seeks to contribute to an understanding of the issues by focusing on the most widespread example to date of the use of transgenic crops in developing countries, insect-resistant cotton.

Commentators and authors have adopted various approaches in addressing this subject. The image of revolution is frequently used by the technology's champions to characterize the potential impact such crops might have for farmers in developing countries. Although generally supportive of the new technology, this book will adopt a different approach. While not denying the novelty of transgenic crops, we emphasize that many of the economic, political and environmental challenges raised by the new technology are similar to those raised by more conventional technology. This stance is not meant to detract from the urgency of addressing technology-specific concerns but rather to underline the value of looking at the broader policies and institutions that govern technology generation for agricultural development.

Agricultural history has been punctuated by periods of fairly rapid technological change which may merit the term 'revolution', and biotechnology may occasion similar transformations, but there is value in recognizing the fact that single technologies are rarely responsible, by themselves, for bringing about significant agricultural advance. Technological change is usually more iterative and complex, and its impact on smallholders depends on the performance of institutions that govern access to markets, land and other resources. In addition, farmers' ability to take control of a technology and incorporate it in their production system depends on the responsiveness of the institutions responsible for carrying out research, providing information and offering a regulatory framework for input and output markets. These are the very institutions that are at the centre of debates about biotechnology, emphasizing that the relatively narrow concern of the impact of transgenic crop varieties should be approached by looking at many of the policies and institutions that govern broader agricultural development.

The book is organized in the following way. Chapter 2 provides an introduction to cotton, briefly reviewing the history of its cultivation, the institutional factors that determine production practices, the governance of technology generation and the development of transgenic, insect-resistant cotton. Chapter 3 provides a review of the agronomic literature on the types, performance and sustainability of transgenic, insect-resistant cotton. Chapter 4 summarizes the literature on the farm-level impact of the introduction of transgenic cotton, focusing on yields, costs and variability of outcomes. Chapter 5 looks at the institutional correlates of the introduction of transgenic cotton, with particular emphasis on the seed and input industry, intellectual property regimes, input delivery and farmers' access to information.

The second part of the book is devoted to original case studies that examine the performance of transgenic cotton in developing countries. Chapter 6 reviews the data available about transgenic cotton in China but concentrates on the results of a study that examines cotton farmers' input choices. Chapter 7 reports a comprehensive study of the experience with transgenic cotton in two contrasting areas of India: Gujarat and Maharashtra. Chapter 8 summarizes a recent study of the performance of transgenic cotton in Colombia's two major cotton-growing regions. Chapter 9 provides a thorough review of the experience of smallholder cotton in South Africa.

Chapter 10 provides a summary of the results from the case studies and discusses more general implications for policies and programs in support of smallholder agriculture in developing countries.

2 Cotton production and technology

Robert Tripp

If genetic engineering is a technology fraught with controversy and symbolism, it would be difficult to find a more perfectly matched crop than cotton. Cotton cultivation has been at the heart of some of the world's most inequitable regimes and is a subject of debates regarding environmental pollution, peasant exploitation and the injustices of world trading systems; at the same time, cotton is a natural fibre whose cultivation can allow farmers in developing countries to take advantage of domestic and international markets and to achieve productive livelihoods. Just as the previous chapter tried to situate the subject of genetic engineering within broader concerns of agricultural policies and institutions, this chapter will try to identify those aspects of cotton cultivation that are major factors in the governance of cotton technology generation and use.

This chapter begins with a very brief review of the history of cotton cultivation and its potential contribution to livelihoods in developing countries. This is followed by an examination of some of the specific characteristics of cotton cultivation that help determine the type of technology available to farmers, in particular access to markets, labour and input credit. The discussion then shifts to review specific aspects of cotton production technology, particularly variety development, seed provision and crop management, with particular emphasis on insect control. The concluding section introduces the technological innovation that will be the subject of the remainder of the book: transgenic, insect-resistant cotton.

Cotton and development

Cotton has been grown and used for textiles in both the Old and New World for several millennia. As the value of cotton cloth was recognized and it became an increasingly important item of trade from the sixteenth century, the expansion of cotton cultivation became central to meeting the demands of commerce and empire. Cotton's unusual biological background and wide dispersal meant not only that there was widespread experience in growing cotton, but also that there were exceptional opportunities for the exchange of cultivation technology in order to improve the productivity of what was becoming one of the world's most important industrial crops (see Box 2.1). In 2005 the world produced more than 25 million metric tons of cotton fibre on about 33 million hectares of land, the majority in developing countries.

Box 2.1 The distribution and development of cotton

Unlike most major crops, cotton plants evolved independently in both the New and Old Worlds. Although the genus *Gossypium* includes nearly 50 species, only four are cultivated. The New World species (*G. hirsutum* and *G. barbadense*) are tetraploids, with twice the number of chromosomes as the Old World diploid species (*G. herbaceum* and *G. arboreum*), apparently due to the chance mating of an ancient New World diploid and an Old World cotton whose seed probably floated across the ocean to the South American continent between one and two million years ago.

All the early types of cotton, both wild and cultivated, were shrubs or small trees that flowered during the short days of the tropical dry season. The spread of cotton to more temperate areas required cultivators to select plant types whose flowering was not determined by day length, and the development of annual rather than perennial types helped adapt the crop to an ever wider range of environments. Although there are important differences among the four cultivated species, there is also great variability within each of them. In addition, although cotton is classed as self-pollinating, there is enough cross-pollination so that early cotton fields exhibited considerable diversity and plasticity, allowing cultivators to select new types and adapt the crop to new environments.

The earliest evidence of cotton cultivation and weaving is from South Asia, but it was also an important crop for many civilizations in Africa and America. There was a growing demand for cotton in an industrializing Europe and an interest in establishing new sources of the raw material. The movement and exchange of species of cotton between regions, combined with considerable experimentation, led to a gradual but uneven spread of American upland (*G. hirsutum*) varieties. Most of the cotton production in colonial Africa was based on New World upland cotton, and by the 1930s upland varieties were widely grown in China, but India relied mostly on a wide range of Old World varieties until after Independence.

One of the most interesting cases of the movement of cotton germplasm involves the New World *G. barbadense*. Examples of this species that were grown in the Caribbean (where they were probably brought by early explorers or merchants from the South American mainland) apparently crossed with wild or cultivated *G. hirsutum* to produce a type of cotton with exceptionally long fibre. Examples were brought from the Bahamas to the coastal southern USA, where planters developed Sea Island cotton. Although it was not suitable for inland areas, Sea Island cotton remained an important crop and commanded a higher price than the more common upland cotton. Seed of Sea Island cotton was taken to the Mediterranean, Asia and elsewhere in the hopes that its high-quality fibre could be produced more widely. Although the exact details are unclear, examples of *G. barbadense* began to be tested in Egypt and the varieties that emerged became the basis of high-quality Egyptian cotton production from the mid-nineteenth century onwards. In the early twentieth century, seed of Egyptian cotton was brought to Arizona by the US Department of Agriculture and further breeding and selection developed the Pima varieties that are still important in the US Southwest. Shortly afterwards these Pima varieties were brought to Peru, close to where the species had originated many centuries earlier. These varieties are still an important part of Peruvian cotton production, growing alongside native *G. barbadense* types with lower fibre quality. In the meantime, the Sea Island cotton industry in the southern USA was destroyed by changes in the agricultural economy and the predations of the boll weevil.

Sources: Chao (1977), Stephens (1975), Ware (1936), Wendel (1989).

The analysis of transgenic cotton's performance is part of a wider concern to explore how cotton cultivation can contribute to providing dignified and sustainable livelihoods that help farmers escape from poverty in the twenty-first century. Unfortunately, much of the history of cotton cultivation offers little immediate encouragement for that challenge.

India's textile industry attracted the attentions of the East India Company from the seventeenth century, and as the relationship shifted from trade to colonial domination, and as England's own textile manufacturing demanded ever larger supplies of raw material, India's cotton cultivation was transformed. The central Indian district of Berar had been a cotton and textile producer for centuries, but as the handloom industry declined and most cotton production was destined for export, the region suffered widespread indebtedness and a series of famines, caused more by colonial rigidities than lack of productivity (Satya 1997). The demand for cotton was also a driving force of many colonial regimes in Africa, often leading to the enforced cultivation of cotton and the disruption of traditional economies and farming systems (Isaacman and Roberts 1995).

Cotton delivered economic prosperity to the recently independent USA based on the immoral practice of plantation slavery. After the Civil War, sharecropping became a dominant mode of production, and James Agee's description of tenant families provides a moving insight on poverty during the Depression. Of the relationship with cotton he found that

> … a tenant can feel, toward that crop, toward each plant in it, toward all that work, what he and all grown women too appear to feel, a particular automatism, a quiet, apathetic, and inarticulate yet deeply vindictive hatred, and at the same time utter hopelessness, and the deepest of their anxieties and of their hopes…

> (Agee and Evans 1965: 327)

Large-scale cotton production has also had serious environmental consequences. The expansion of cotton in the nineteenth-century USA led to widespread erosion and soil exhaustion (Stoll 2002). The technology of more recent times has caused additional damage. About a quarter of the world's insecticide use is devoted to cotton and half of the pesticides in developing countries are used on cotton, including several of those classified by the World Health Organization as 'highly hazardous' (Kooistra *et al.* 2006).

Modern cotton production is the subject of many accounts of rural injustice. The irrigated cultivation of cotton in Uzbekistan, a legacy of Stalinist policies, has caused the Aral Sea to shrink to one-third its former size, causes water shortages and widespread pollution, and forces a large proportion of the rural population to work as impoverished sharecroppers on state collectives (Pope 2005). In the minds of many newspaper readers, cotton production in contemporary India is linked to what seems an epidemic of rural indebtedness and suicide, although the extent to which this tragedy is directly linked to cotton cultivation, or even agriculture in general, is open to discussion (Mohanty 2005).

Critics of modern agriculture often cite such experiences in defence of the traditional production systems that existed before colonialism and globalization. It is possible to imagine more benign, small-scale cotton production in the distant past, but it is not easy to find examples. Mexican commoners were required to deliver huge quantities of cloth as tribute to their Aztec rulers (Berdan 1987), and West African slaves toiling on the cotton plantations of the Sokoto Caliphate (Lovejoy 1978) or indebted Indian farmers struggling to meet the revenue demands of Mughal emperors and landlords (Habib 1999) challenge sentimental notions about independent cotton-cultivating peasantries. Small-scale farming has not often been a profitable occupation throughout history, and the production of a crop like cotton that is mostly destined for commerce has placed additional burdens on peasantries ruled by local despots or colonial regimes.

However, a realistic assessment of the history of cotton cultivation and its consequences for resource-poor farmers must be tempered by an appreciation of the potential contributions of cotton for rural development. As cotton cultivation spread in Song Dynasty China, a poet asked:

> Why has heaven been so generous to Fujian
> As to give them a good plant like cotton?
> … if they harvest a thousand cotton plants
> Then the rich need not worry about want.
>
> (Xie Fangde cited in Sadao 1984: 21)

When there is equitable access to resources and good governance a cash crop like cotton may offer farmers real opportunities. For instance, when farmers are able to choose their own cropping patterns and practices, and when local agricultural markets function adequately, the competition between food crops and cash crops is much less likely to cause hardship. Studies in Côte d'Ivoire and Zimbabwe have shown a positive synergism between cotton cultivation, on the one hand, and food production and household nutrition, on the other, as the income and experience from cotton production are applied to the rest of the farm (Sahn 1990; Govereh and Jayne 1999). In West Africa, many cotton-producing regions have also experienced significant growth in cereal production because of the development of input provision and the emphasis on agricultural innovation (OECD 2006).

The fact that cotton production can be rewarded for achieving quality standards provides incentives for the type of careful management that may be one of the few advantages small-scale producers have to offer. Beyond providing an important source of cash income, cotton cultivation can strengthen rural institutions. Cotton production demands considerable planning and attention to detail. Bingen (1998) argues that the 'industrial-type discipline' required of smallholder cotton farmers in West Africa has been the stimulus for the emergence of successful farmer unions in Mali and Benin, and cotton cultivation has performed a similar role in developing rural political consciousness in Côte d'Ivoire (Bassett 2001).

Cotton's processing, transport and by-product industries create significant opportunities for rural employment. Where countries have their own textile industries, spinning, weaving, manufacture and marketing bring additional employment. Despite competition from the Lancashire mills and colonial restrictions on India's export of textiles, the local industry survived and prospered. Although local entrepreneurs had established spinning mills in Bombay by 1856, most weaving was still done by handlooms. This remained the case until after Independence when small-scale power looms were introduced, an enterprise of such scope and importance that it accounted for 20 per cent of India's wage labour by 1997 (Farnie 2004). A particularly remarkable instance of economic transition is found in the town of Tiruppur, south India, which dominates the national production of cotton knitwear. Much of the industry is run by members of the Gounder agrarian caste who, as peasants in the early twentieth century, took advantage of the demand for long-staple cotton to establish a productive local trade and used their farming profits (and experience in managing hired labour) to establish their own workshops and mills for the knitwear industry (Chari 2004).

Although continually threatened by man-made fibres, demand for cotton remains strong, and the crop offers opportunities for improving the livelihoods of many developing-country farmers, who produce about two-thirds of the world's crop. Millions of rural households are involved in cotton production worldwide, the majority in developing countries.

In recent years by far the most visible issue with respect to cotton cultivation in developing countries has been the relationship between low international prices and domestic support to cotton production, particularly that offered by the USA and EU to their growers (Baffes 2005). Brazil has received a favourable ruling from the World Trade Organization (WTO) in its case against US cotton subsidies, and a group of West African cotton-producing countries has filed a case with the WTO asking for the removal of producer support by the USA, EU and China. There are various estimates of the potential impact of the removal of such subsidies on smallholder farmers, particularly in Africa (Baffes 2005; Oxfam

2002), but the issue has captured public attention as an example of how protection of agriculture by industrialized countries can affect the livelihoods of producers in developing countries. A study in Benin estimated that a 40 per cent drop in cotton prices (such as occurred in 2002) causes an 8 per cent rise in rural poverty in Benin, where cotton accounts for 22 per cent of the gross value of crop production (Minot and Daniels 2005). However, a fair price for output must be complemented by efficient production practices, and our attention now turns to the organization of cotton cultivation.

How cotton is grown

An analysis of cotton production requires an understanding of the nature of the textile industry and the demands that it places on producers. Although cotton cultivation was originally part of household- or community-level textile production, as markets have expanded there has been an increasing division of labour. In sixteenth- and seventeenth-century China, for instance, some of the more isolated cotton-growing communities were self-sufficient; 'where the roads did not permit peddlers and merchants to pass, the men tilled the soil and the women wove cloth' (Dietrich 1972: 127). In early Mughal India, cotton was grown and ginned by peasants, cleaned or carded by itinerant labourers, and spun into yarn by peasant households before being sold to weavers (Habib 1999). But increased specialization was soon evident; in the seventeenth century, cotton grown on the Deccan plateau was transported to the coast in bullock carts where it was purchased by merchants who organized the production of yarn by spinners and then contracted weavers specializing in particular types of cloth (Brennig 1998).

In nineteenth-century West Africa, two production systems were superimposed. One fulfilled household needs, and the cotton was grown intercropped with food grains and spun and woven within the domestic unit. But demand for cloth and the expansion of trade encouraged more commercially-oriented farmers to dedicate large fields to monocropped cotton (Roberts 1996).

Today, cotton producers around the world are part of an exceptionally sophisticated and highly differentiated textile industry. The division of labour and specialization in the textile industry has important implications for the organization of cotton production and the nature of cotton technology. This section examines a few of the most important factors that determine how farmers are able to use technology, and the following section looks more specifically at cotton production technology itself. The organizational factors examined here include the quality and type of cotton grown, labour recruitment and input credit. The possibility of growing different types of cotton for a range of end uses means that it is important that farmers be able to meet specific quality demands. The fact that textiles are internationally traded (and more than one-third of cotton production itself enters international trade) makes significant demands on the efficient deployment of labour for cotton production. And efficiency in cotton production is increasingly associated with access to a range of expensive inputs whose provision to thousands of small growers presents particular challenges. It will be useful to briefly review the types of institutions that mediate cotton farmers' access to differentiated markets, labour supply and credit.

Fibre quality

Cotton quality has long been an important determinant of production technology. Different cotton varieties produce fibre that can be distinguished by staple length, fineness, colour and other parameters that determine its uses and its price. These qualities have traditionally been judged by merchants whose skills were based on years of experience. Cotton grading is now increasingly done in laboratories, often using sophisticated instrumentation. Advanced grading systems offer more objective assessment and can provide stronger incentives to farmers to produce cotton of particular characteristics.

Farmers should be able to earn a premium depending on the cleanliness and uniformity of their cotton, but this presumes that adequate institutions are in place to manage the grading. In Mali, farmers are theoretically paid for first or second quality cotton, but the village collection procedures do not allow individual farmers to be identified with their produce, and storage, transport and ginning procedures further reduce the possibility of a just reward for higher quality cotton (Bingen 2006). A recent analysis of cotton production in sub-Saharan Africa shows that improving fibre cleanliness and reducing contamination offers one of the most significant opportunities for higher producer prices (World Bank, forthcoming). However, the achievement of such gains is related to both improved management of cotton marketing and effective producer organization.

The assurance of high-quality cotton usually requires some type of authority, but this also raises the danger of excessive control. There have been numerous instances where political authorities attempt to maintain the quality and uniformity of the crop. One of the most common strategies is to mandate the choice of variety. Beginning in 1911, a number of state extension services in the USA began to promote a 'one-cultivar community plan' that would ensure uniform quality by establishing a single cotton variety for each community. By 1948 nearly half of the US cotton area was managed in this way (Smith *et al.* 1999) but the practice gradually disappeared, with the exception of a few areas such as California's San Joaquin Valley (Constantine *et al.* 1994).

Egypt's decision to establish its reputation for high-quality cotton was accompanied by a state program that ensured that seed of designated cotton varieties was multiplied and distributed not only to large landowners, but also to the peasants whose preference for saved seed might threaten the purity of the crop of their larger neighbours (Goldberg 2004).

But often the authority of the state has been more coercive. In colonial Côte d'Ivoire, farmers resisted the sole cropping of the new cotton varieties introduced by the administration, preferring to intercrop their traditional varieties. But when they sold their local cotton at the ginnery, the authorities arranged to heat the seed (so that it would not germinate) before returning it to the farmer, thus ensuring a transition to the mandated variety (Bassett 2001). The history of cotton production in nineteenth-century India includes many instances of colonial authorities trying to enforce the sowing of cotton varieties that met the needs of the British textile industry. Farmers often found that any premium for quality was negated by lower yields of the new American *hirsutum* varieties that were being promoted (Guha 2007).

In these cases, the aims of the state and of the farmers do not necessarily coincide. A more recent example is the state-managed cotton production system in Mali, where farmer organizations have successfully opposed the introduction of varieties with higher ginning percentages (an advantage to the industry) but lower yields (and hence lower incomes for growers) (Bingen 1998).

Labour

Cotton and textiles have long been items of local and international trade and this places particular pressure on the efficiency of production. Cotton is a labour-intensive crop and the recruitment and organization of labour helps determine the efficiency of production. Technology has an impact on labour organization and, conversely, the availability of labour influences the type of technology that farmers use. The expansion of cotton production has been responsible for the emergence of particular patterns of land tenure and labour recruitment. In Ming China, large landholders produced cotton using bondservants or wage labour, but the inefficiency of the system caused them to shift towards reliance on tenant farmers (Chao 1977).

In Egypt, Goldberg (2004) argues that much of the efficiency of early twentieth-century cotton production was due to an exceptionally high reliance on child labour. The use of child labour is one of the issues of concern regarding the impacts of cotton cultivation on public health in contemporary Uzbekistan (Carley 1989). The problem of child labour has come to the fore recently in India, in the production of hybrid cotton seed. India and China are the only countries that use significant amounts of hybrid cotton, in part because of the high labour component in its seed production. Hybrid seed production relies on careful hand-pollination, requiring large amounts of skilled field labour that can be deployed at precise times. In India seed companies keep production costs low by employing female children at very low wage rates, a practice that has led to protests and calls for reform (Venkateshwarlu and Da Corta 2001).

The spread of cotton cash cropping among smallholders in Africa has occasioned changes in labour patterns. Farmers in Côte d'Ivoire have made significant changes to traditional social organization to accommodate cotton's demand for labour; the changes include new types of labour mobilization within communities (particularly reciprocal labour groups), greater flexibility in the definition of culturally prescribed rest days, increased female household labour, and the adoption of new technology (particularly ox ploughs and herbicides) (Bassett 2001).

The labour requirements of cotton cultivation have played an overwhelming part in technology generation for the crop, and the mechanization of cotton production in industrialized countries is a good example. In the USA, the shift from mules to tractors in cotton farming took place gradually, as appropriate technology and economic conditions encouraged the increasing use of mechanical power for cultivation, weeding and eventually harvest (Day 1967). Cotton harvesting remained a manual task in the USA until well after the Second World War, when a combination of public and private research led to the development of mechanical harvesters. The adoption of the new harvesting technology was rapid in the West (on its large, productive farms) and more gradual in the South, where its eventual uptake was one of the major factors in the demise of the sharecropping system (Heinicke and Grove 2005).

Even variety choice is affected by labour. Contemporary China probably has the most labour-intensive cotton cultivation in the world; one study estimated over 400 person-days per hectare invested in the crop (Pemsl 2006). There is increasing use of hybrid cotton seed, in part because these varieties can be planted at lower densities (saving labour) and fit well into cropping systems relying on transplanting (Xu and Fok 2007). The varieties found in African cotton systems that flower and produce a crop over an extended period of time are compatible with a shortage of labour and the staggering of the harvesting period (Hillocks 2005). On the other hand, varieties that allow harvest at a single time are a solution to the labour problem in industrialized countries where mechanical harvesting is available.

Input credit

In addition to having access to adequate labour, smallholder cotton growers need to acquire the necessary production inputs. In many instances, credit is the major constraint. The type of credit available often plays a large role in determining what inputs are available to farmers, and the incentives of the credit supplier (whose principal returns may be derived from the interest charged, the inputs sold or the cotton produced) are a major factor in defining the type of technology employed by farmers.

After the US Civil War, cotton farmers and tenants depended on merchants to supply credit for household goods and, increasingly, for production inputs such as fertilizer (often proprietary mixtures of rock phosphate and various animal manures) (Earle 1992). In many areas, input merchants moved to acquire cotton gins as well, and merchant power was exercised through a crop lien system providing legal possession of the crop while it was still in the field. In some cases a merchant could command a territorial monopoly, but when several merchants operated in the same location some farmers could exploit these competing credit sources (Hahn 1983).

Cotton production in India has long depended on external capital. A description from the early nineteenth century illustrates the plight of the peasant. 'He is always in his banker's books, as deep in proportion to his means, as his European master, and can do nothing without aid. The brokers, or cotton cleaners, or gin-house men are the middlemen between the chetty [merchant] and the ryot [peasant]' (Royle 1851: 37).

In contemporary Peru, small farmers' inability to get loans at reasonable interest rates for cotton production has led them into a relationship with larger farmers. The latter (many of whom no longer grow cotton) have the necessary contacts with credit sources to be able to arrange loans for the small farmers, who organize themselves into groups and pay the large farmer partner a 25 per cent share of their production in return for the loan administration service (Escobal *et al.* 2000).

In Pakistan's Sindh Province, there is a tied input provision system, where the middlemen who purchase cotton from farmers to sell to spinning mills also provide loans for inputs. Some of the middlemen offer credit simply to ensure themselves adequate cotton supplies, while others are also in the input business. The majority of the cotton farmers depend on these seasonal loans, and close communication among the middlemen ensures that farmers do not try to default (Stockbridge *et al.* 1998).

In colonial Africa, governments attempted various strategies for input provision. In Tanzania, cooperatives were established to provide credit, inputs and ploughing services and they also had a marketing monopoly. After independence, the cooperatives also gained a monopoly on ginning and came under government control. The cooperatives suffered from mismanagement and lack of capital and their decline paralleled that of the country's cotton output. More recently, farmer cooperatives have been reorganized, making them voluntary and internally accountable (Gibbon 1998).

Lack of alternative credit sources for cotton production in several Anglophone African countries has led to the establishment of outgrower schemes with tied contracts. Ginning companies provide inputs on loan to farmers, who are expected to deliver their harvest in return. These systems require a fine balance; excessive competition encourages farmers to default on their loans by selling their cotton to a rival ginnery; controlling the market by limiting the number of ginneries or providing territorial concessions can help reduce side-selling, but heavy-handed coordination or monopolies can result in lower prices paid to farmers (Poulton *et al.* 2004; World Bank, forthcoming).

The same dilemmas are currently the subject of intense debate regarding the filière system of Francophone West Africa in which national parastatal cotton enterprises follow an 'administered monopoly' model, with a legal monopoly on input provision and a monopsony on cotton purchase from farmers. Most of the parastatals also have a monopoly on ginning, marketing and export of lint and seeds. Critics argue that better management would be more likely where private input suppliers and ginners could compete, and a few of these countries have already taken partial steps in this direction (Baffes 2005).

The role of institutions

The organization of cotton production for ensuring quality, deploying labour and accessing credit illustrates how institutions evolve in response to the requirements of a particular commodity. This evolution involves the state, markets, the industry and farmers in a continually shifting balance of power and initiative. The state may at times play a coercive role by, for instance, mandating the cultivation of certain types of cotton or endorsing the privileges of a landlord class. But the state can also help provide regulations to ensure good quality production and supply credit. These positive roles are often diminished, however, by lax management, and market institutions may prove to be more efficient. But markets bring their own drawbacks, as when merchants take advantage of farmers or when farmers are able to be free riders in an overly competitive credit market. The cotton industry itself may take an interest in regulating the market, to provide mechanisms that help maintain quality or ensure access to credit. Finally, farm-level organization helps determine the way that labour is deployed and technology is used and, when farmers have voice, puts pressure on state and market institutions to provide more effective service. The same interplay of states, markets and farmers determines the evolution of cotton production technology.

Cotton production technology

The focus of this book, transgenic cotton, is an innovation in production technology. To understand its impact and implications, we need to understand the institutions related to technology development, provision and regulation. This section briefly examines several areas related to transgenic cotton, including variety development and selection; seed provision and regulation; and crop management, with emphasis on insect control.

Cotton variety development

The fact that various species of cotton evolved independently in the Old and New Worlds means that there were many opportunities to exchange, test and adapt varieties in the various cotton-growing regions (see Box 2.1). India's early pre-eminence in cotton textiles was aided by trade links between western India and Persia, allowing for the interchange of distinct types of cotton (Hutchinson *et al.* 1947). Although American upland (*hirsutum*) cotton eventually became the dominant type grown commercially, planters in the early USA experimented with varieties from the Mediterranean, Southeast Asia and China (Gray 1933). The exchange, borrowing, and at times theft, of germplasm was paralleled by similar interchange in textile technology, providing an interesting backdrop to today's battles over intellectual property rights (Box 2.2).

For centuries farmers have selected, improved and adapted cotton varieties to suit their needs. Much of this work has been aimed at ensuring that cotton can be grown in specific circumstances of climate, soils and production technology. As with most cases of plant improvement, such changes often involve trade-offs (Fryxell 1979). Initial domestication selected for larger fruits and larger seeds, although this made the plant less hardy. Early cultivators selected types whose seed was amenable to hand ginning, often at the cost of lower reproductive efficiency. The demands of the Industrial Revolution called for higher yields and more uniform fibre, and the resulting monoculture increased susceptibility to pests and diseases. In twentieth-century plant breeding, selection for resistance to pests such as boll weevil often entailed a sacrifice in fibre quality, and selection

Box 2.2 Cotton and intellectual property

One of the major concerns about agricultural biotechnology is the use of intellectual property protection and its potential effect on local options and development possibilities. Disputes over intellectual property are not new to the cotton industry.

As colourful Indian cotton chintz became popular in Europe from the mid-seventeenth century, textile printers searched in vain for techniques that would make their dyes permanent, to compete with the superior imported cloth. Indian artisans had developed these skills over the centuries and passed them as closely guarded secrets from one generation to the next. It was not until 1742 that a French cleric working on the Coromandel coast convinced some of his converts to share the secrets, with the understanding that he would not divulge them; he promptly broke his promise and published the details, ending the monopoly of the Indian dyers (Yafa 2005).

The increasing cotton production in the USA led to pressure to develop more efficient ways of separating the fibre from the seed than the various roller gins that were in use. A young mechanic, Eli Whitney, developed a new design that greatly enhanced productivity. He was granted a patent in 1794 and rather than license the design to other manufacturers, he and his business partner hoped to establish ginning facilities where they would collect a toll on all cotton ginned. But the proposed toll proved too high for growers, the original gin design admitted many possible modifications, and soon a range of inventors were hard at work and offering their machinery to cotton growers. Whitney was unable to defend his patent and ended up concluding that, '[a]n invention can be so valuable as to be worthless to the inventor' (Green 1956: 94).

English spinning and weaving technology dominated world textile manufacturing by the late eighteenth century and its owners protected the secrets from potential rivals. Early American industrial spies were occasionally able to carry away bits of machinery falsely labelled as agricultural equipment, but a major coup was achieved when Francis Cabot Lowell, an American businessman, visited Manchester in 1810. His business contacts allowed him the courtesy of visits to spinning and weaving facilities, but his hosts did not recognize that Lowell harboured an ambition to establish a textile industry in his native New England. Mechanical aptitude and a photographic memory (and most probably notes that escaped customs officers' scrutiny) allowed Lowell to return to Massachusetts with enough information to establish his textile industry (Yafa 2005).

The ownership of crop varieties has long been a controversial subject, and the search for new varieties of cotton to plant in nineteenth-century USA included cases of piracy. Mexico was the source of most of the germplasm for the upland varieties that eventually became dominant (Moore 1956). Seeds of the varieties that made a particularly important contribution were obtained (according to one version of the story) in 1806 by a US diplomat in Mexico City who smuggled them out of the county stuffed in dolls (Collings 1926).

for increased fibre strength (to compete with synthetic fibres) frequently implied a trade-off with yield.

Farmers throughout history have invested in selecting cotton varieties that meet their needs, and have thought carefully about the trade-offs involved in those selections. In the face of pressures from the colonial authorities to grow high-quality 'Oomra' (*arboreum*) cotton, Indian farmers turned instead to the *herbaceum* types that were easier to cultivate and higher yielding (Satya 1997), leaving the authorities to complain about 'the triumph of high yield in low grade' (Watt 1907: 133). When pressure was exerted to grow American (*hirsutum*) types, which generally performed poorly in Indian conditions, the relatively few success stories were due to a combination of good experimentation, adequate environment and innovative farmers, as in the case of the variety denominated 'Dharwar-American' (Royle 1851; Guha 2007). On the other hand, when new varieties are introduced with superior traits, farmers are quick to take advantage. In the early twentieth century, French colonial authorities were disappointed by the low exports of the long-staple cotton they had introduced to West Africa; local spinners had recognized its advantages and most of the harvest was diverted to the production of handicraft textiles (Roberts 1996).

In the antebellum USA there was continual experimentation to find better adapted and more productive types of cotton. Plantation owners at first selected their varieties by choosing the best-looking seed, but soon began selection on the basis of plant type, and the products of their informal breeding efforts became available with distinguishing brand names such as Banana, Cluster and Pomegranate (Moore 1956). The development of new varieties continued after the Civil War, and there was apparently rapid turnover; of the 58 cotton varieties listed in a census in 1880, only 6 remained in cultivation by 1895 (Ware 1936).

Cotton is partially cross-pollinated (from 5 to 30 per cent), mostly by bees (at least until the advent of widespread insecticide use). This allowed considerable opportunity for local selection and adaptation. The early varieties were in fact mixed, heterozygous populations with considerable plasticity and potential for genetic change (Poehlman and Sleper 1995). On the other hand, this variability meant that cotton growers had to constantly renew their planting material and beware of deterioration.

By the late nineteenth century, scientific plant breeding was able to contribute to the development of cotton varieties. Cotton breeding has been done by private individuals (farmers, and later seed companies) and by public institutions. In the USA much cotton breeding was first done by large farmers and then by private seed companies, but the US Department of Agriculture and state agricultural experiment stations made important contributions, and there was often close collaboration between the public researchers and private seed companies. Public research was especially important in addressing pests and diseases. By the late nineteenth century wilt disease was a major problem for US cotton producers, prompting a widespread search for resistant varieties. The arrival of the boll weevil in the USA in the early twentieth century wiped out much of the productive, long-season cotton that had been grown and led to the development of earlier-maturing varieties that could better resist the pest (Ware 1936). From the 1970s, the industry association, Cotton Incorporated, was able to use grower check-off funds to support public cotton breeding at state research stations (Jacobson and Smith 2001).

Public investments in plant breeding were important elsewhere as well. In China, the adaptation of *hirsutum* cultivars in the 1920s was led by the University of Nanking, whose program produced a successful variety known as 'Million Dollar' (May and Lege 1999). An Agricultural Society was established in Egypt in 1898 to support cotton production, and this was followed by the creation of the Department of Agriculture in 1910, with the support of large landowners. The Department (later Ministry) was crucial in developing new varieties and ensuring the high and uniform quality of Egyptian cotton (Goldberg 2004). The extensive cotton breeding efforts in India during the colonial period were eventually coordinated under the Indian Central Cotton Committee which took responsibility for funding research. More recently, breeding conducted under the Indian Council of Agricultural Research has been responsible for an exceptionally wide range of new varieties and for the world's first use of cotton hybrids (Basu *et al.* 1990). The availability of these hybrids was a stimulus for the development of the private cotton seed industry in India. Public cotton breeding in Brazil in the 1960s was responsible for halting the spread of wilt disease and provides a well-documented example of the high social returns possible from investment in public research (Ayer and Schuh 1972).

Seed provision

Advances in plant breeding are of little use, however, without a mechanism for delivering seed of the new varieties. Economic depression in the USA from 1837 to 1849 caused cotton farmers to search for the most productive varieties, and this was an incentive for a nascent seed industry to spread the latest innovations, but also an opportunity to make a fast buck. Some businesses imported seed of untested varieties from other countries for sale to gullible farmers, and a number of planters branded and marketed chance mutations they had found in their fields, most of which had no advantages over the varieties already available. Newspapers and agricultural periodicals of the time were full of letters denouncing these charlatans. Meanwhile, some farmers performed a real service. Henry W. Vick, a Mississippi plantation owner, initiated a system of breeding and variety selection that was responsible for some of the most productive cotton varieties available before the Civil War. But other planters were able to multiply this seed and sell it, often under different names, so Vick received little credit or profit from his efforts (Moore 1956). It was not until the early twentieth century that the nomenclature of US cotton varieties was rationalized, a move that coincided with more formal regulation of the seed market (Ware 1936).

Seed of cotton is somewhat more difficult to save from season to season than seed of most field crops, as some type of mechanical separation of the seed from the fibre is required. This means that farmers must either reserve and buy back a portion of their seed from the ginnery or have access to small hand-turned gins that allow home processing of the seed. Such seed, even if it is the product of a single harvest, may be quite variable because cotton is an indeterminate crop, where seed development is not synchronous but rather spread over a period of time. Another factor in favour of commercial seed is the fact that ginned seed of most cotton varieties is still covered by fuzz (known as linters) which is removed in most commercial seed operations (usually by acid treatment) in order to increase germination percentage, control seed-borne disease and facilitate mechanical planting. Despite the difficulties with farm-saved cotton seed and the increasing investment in formal breeding and seed production, only 5 per cent of the cotton seed planted in the USA by 1933 was produced by companies or government agencies. The rest was 'gin-run' seed, reclaimed by the farmer after the ginning of the crop or purchased from neighbours (Smith *et al.* 1999).

Today, formal seed production by private and public entities accounts for the majority of farmers' cotton seed. In the USA and much of Latin America seed is produced and sold by private companies, while in Australia most cotton seed is produced by a grower-owned company. Although commercial seed enterprises may provide the majority of cotton seed in industrialized agriculture, seed saving is not uncommon; as recently as 1997, 20 per cent of the cotton grown in the USA (and 39 per cent grown in Texas) was from homegrown seed (Brooks 2001). In much of West Africa seed is provided by parastatal enterprises and farmers have little incentive to save seed. In China cotton seed is provided by formal seed companies, but many farmers also save seed (see Chapter 6). India's strong public seed system has been largely replaced by private companies, driven by the opportunity to sell hybrid seed, which farmers have difficulty saving (see Chapter 7). Until the advent of hybrids, however, there was considerable seed saving; more than half of the cotton sown in India's Punjab was from farm-saved seed as recently as the 1990s (Sidhu 1999).

Crop management

Cotton production technology is of course not limited to variety selection and plant breeding. Both farmers and researchers have been responsible for the development of a wide range of crop management techniques suited to specific circumstances and conditions. In many areas of China, limited land availability and access to irrigation encourages exceptionally intensive management of the cotton crop. Farmers often grow and then transplant cotton seedlings (which allows earlier crop establishment), prune vegetative branches, use plastic mulch and employ large quantities of external inputs, often including 3–400 kg of synthetic fertilizer per hectare. As labour shortages become more of a problem for Chinese farmers, research is seeking ways to modify this crop management system to cut costs (Dong *et al.* 2005).

At the other extreme, cotton farmers in drought-prone areas with greater land resources may practice much more extensive crop management. In South Africa, small-scale cotton farmers use little or no fertilizer (see Chapter 9). Changes in crop management can offer important opportunities for improving the productivity of cotton farming. A study in Mali indicated possibilities for significant yield gains if farmers provided better management of their current resources, including more timely thinning, weeding, insect control and fertilizer application (Fok 2003). Such deficiencies are often due to both labour constraints and lack of information about crop management.

The development of crop management technology is a continuous process. An example is provided by soil and weed management in the USA. An increasing proportion of cotton land is planted under some type of conservation tillage system, which helps prevent erosion and reduces the number of times that machinery must enter the field, lowering costs and reducing the risk of soil compaction. Much of the movement towards conservation tillage has been promoted by public research and extension but also depends on the development of herbicides by the chemical industry. The development of herbicide-tolerant transgenic cotton varieties has made conservation tillage even more feasible. A study in Mississippi showed gains in efficiency over the past decade due to better tillage and weed management, including the increasing use of new planting patterns developed by public research such as 'skip-row', where input savings are achieved by wider distance between cotton rows, facilitated by improved weed control (Thompson *et al.* 2007). An alternative for plant spacing, known as 'ultra narrow row' (Boquet 2005) significantly increases planting density but uses fewer inputs per plant and can also contribute to soil conservation. The development of this system relies on public crop management research as well as the investment of commercial firms to develop appropriate harvesting machinery.

Insect control

One of the major management problems facing contemporary cotton production is the susceptibility of the crop to attack by a wide range of insect pests (Box 2.3). Insect pests have become a much more important problem for cotton cultivation as extensive areas of cotton have been planted, often without rotation. In the 1940s the discovery that DDT could be used as an insecticide brought temporary respite from the boll weevil in the USA and was followed by the development of many other chemicals for insect control. The widespread use of chemical insecticides for cotton throughout the world has been responsible for helping farmers produce higher yields but is also the source of many problems, particularly in developing countries. The availability and promotion of cheap, broad spectrum insecticides has led to high dependence, which in turn has promoted the emergence of insecticide resistance in a number of pests and the decline or disappearance of many of the natural enemies of cotton pests that formerly helped maintain an ecological balance. In addition, the misuse of insecticides has been responsible for the illness and deaths of many cotton farmers and labourers and is the source of significant environmental pollution (Kooistra *et al.* 2006).

Box 2.3 Cotton insects

Cotton is subject to damage by an extraordinarily wide range of insect pests. Various cotton-growing ecologies may be affected by different pests and the damage varies as well by season and pest control regime. The following is a very brief introduction to some of the major insect pests of cotton.

Lepidoptera

The caterpillars of certain moths feed on various parts of the cotton plant. Many of those referred to as bollworms or budworms are controlled (wholly or partially) by current types of transgenic cotton.

- The **American bollworm** (*Helicoverpa armigera*) is also known by other names, such as corn earworm and tomato worm. It feeds particularly on cotton buds and bolls. Despite the name, it is not found in the New World. It is a major pest of cotton in countries such as India, China and Australia.
- The **cotton bollworm** (*Heliothis zea*) is a New World insect and a major pest of cotton in the USA. A related species (*Helicoverpa gelotopoeon*) is more important in South America.
- The **pink bollworm** (*Pectinophora gossypiella*) originated in the Old World but is now a major cotton pest all over the world.
- The **spotted bollworm** or **spiny bollworm** (*Earias* spp.) is a serious cotton pest in many parts of Asia, Africa and Australia.
- The **red bollworm** (*Diparopsis* spp.) is largely confined to Africa.
- The **tobacco budworm** (*Heliothis viriscens*), a New World insect, feeds on many cotton plant parts and was one of the principal targets (along with pink bollworm and cotton bollworm) for the original versions of transgenic cotton in the USA.
- **Cotton leafworm** (called **tobacco leafworm** in India) (*Spodoptera litura*) is an Old World pest that feeds on cotton leaves.
- **Fall armyworm** (*Spodoptera frugiperda*) is a New World pest feeding on many parts of the cotton plant.

Hemiptera

The *Hemiptera* are insects with mouthparts adapted to piercing and sucking and many of them damage the cotton plant by sucking sap from the leaves or other parts of the plant.

- **Cotton stainers** or **cotton bugs** (*Dysdercus* spp.) include many species throughout the world that feed on developing and ripe cotton seeds. The lint from such seeds is often stained brown. A related family of insects, the **stink bugs** (*Pentatomidae*), cause some damage to cotton in the USA.

(Continued)

Box 2.3 (Continued)

- **Jassids** (*Empoasca* spp.) are Old World insects that suck sap from the leaves of the cotton plant.
- **Whitefly** (*Bemisia tabaci*) is widely distributed. It is a very small insect that sucks sap from leaves and is also responsible for the transmission of leaf curl virus disease.
- **Mirid bugs** (*Lygus* spp.) are found throughout the world and feed on young buds and bolls of the growing cotton plant.
- **Cotton aphids** (*Aphis gossypii*) are very widely distributed and cause most damage in the early stages of crop growth.

Coleoptera

- The **boll weevil** (*Anthonomus grandis*) is the major example of a beetle that damages cotton. Adults feed on cotton leaves and buds and the female lays its eggs in the young bud; the larvae feed within the boll and the adult emerges to continue feeding. It apparently originated in Mexico and migrated to the USA in the late nineteenth century; it is still limited to the Americas.

Another problem for the use of synthetic insecticides is the regulation of the input industry. China has allowed pesticides to be sold by trade name only, and a single chemical may be marketed under hundreds of different names (Anon. 2008a). India's pesticide manufacturing industry features many small formulators and myriad products that can be difficult to regulate (Matthews 1993). This is a challenge to farmers who wish to distinguish between trusted and fraudulent input sources. The liberalization of cotton input systems in Africa is responsible for a growth in the availability of dangerous and sometimes poor quality products (Williamson 2003).

Integrated pest management

There are no easy answers to the challenge of insect control in cotton. Safer and better-targeted chemicals are being developed, but they are often more expensive and in any case do not entirely resolve the health and ecological risks associated with insecticide use. In addition, insect control technologies must be location specific, responding to the problems of particular areas and production systems. For instance, within the USA there is considerable variation in practices and problems. In the early 1990s, the majority of Texas cotton fields received less than one insecticide application per season, while some high-input systems in the Southeast used up to 12 applications (Luttrell 1994).

A significant amount of effort has been devoted to crop management techniques known as integrated pest management (IPM). IPM strategies for cotton require farmers to make more careful assessment of pest populations, reduce (or in some cases eliminate) insecticide use, utilize various crop management techniques to control insects and take advantage of biological insect control products.

One example of a successful IPM effort has been the control of the boll weevil in much of the USA. After DDT was banned, other insecticides were used, but the insect soon developed resistance. Effective IPM for the boll weevil only became possible in the 1970s when researchers discovered and were able to synthesize a weevil pheromone. The pheromone is used as bait in traps that attract the weevil, although this alone is not sufficient to effect control. Government agencies, universities and the cotton industry all collaborated in developing a comprehensive control program. Before it is introduced to a particular area, farmers must vote on whether they are willing to participate; if they agree then all farmers are required to take part and they must contribute by paying a fee based on the size of their holding. The program varies somewhat by region, but generally includes spraying (by the government program) in the fall with a low dose of insecticide, to ensure that weevils do not survive over the winter. Weevil traps are set out in the spring and inspectors use these to assess remaining weevil populations and make decisions on additional sprayings. The experience has been that within a few seasons insecticide spraying can be effectively eliminated. The program has had considerable success and has been shown to yield an excellent economic return on the investment (Ahouissoussi *et al.* 1993; Haney *et al.* 1996). A recent study that asked US cotton farmers to identify those innovations that have had the biggest impact on production in the past decade found that the boll weevil eradication program was ranked as high as transgenic varieties (Marra and Martin 2007).

Syria has one of the most comprehensive cotton IPM programs in the world (ICAC 2004; Khouri 1997). Syrian cotton production previously depended on relatively high levels of pesticide use, and in order to control costs the government took steps to introduce and establish IPM. Although Syria's irrigated cotton yields are exceptionally high, less than 1 per cent of its cotton area was treated with insecticides in 2003. Cotton production is managed by the Ministry of Agriculture, which produces an annual plan indicating where cotton can be planted. The IPM strategy includes controlling insecticide availability; the establishment of threshold levels for insecticide use; early planting and a ban on insecticide use early in the season; monitoring with pheromone traps; and research on appropriate biocontrol agents for the Syrian environment.

State support and coordination for IPM is often essential, and appropriate incentives must be in place. For instance, policy changes in China included the requirement that extension offices should generate much of their own income. This led to contradictory incentives for the agents, who were partially dependent on pesticide sales sold through their offices, while at the same time supposedly acting as sources of information on IPM to help reduce pesticide use (Pray *et al.* 2001).

Although there has been considerable progress with IPM methods and techniques, they are generally information-intensive, involve learning and constant adjustment, and often require the intervention of entomologists or other specialists. As with the cases described earlier, they also often require coordination among farmers and the participation of various public and private institutions. They are thus not likely to spread rapidly among farmers without strong institutions to support the generation and management of knowledge (Cowan and Gunby 1996). Not only are there fewer incentives for the development of IPM, but anything that threatens the chemical industry cannot be expected to receive its wholehearted support. Although the general principles of IPM surely represent the only major hope for sustainable insect control in a crop such as cotton, the institutional challenges are formidable.

Technology and institutions

This brief review of cotton technology generation highlights the same interplay of farmers, the industry, markets and the state that we saw earlier for cotton production. Farmers have played an important part in technology development, including their earlier role in selecting appropriate varieties and their continuing contributions to crop management innovation. Technology development has been accelerated by state support, often with contributions from the industry itself. But the state is a reliable supplier of information and technology only when it is responsive to farmers' concerns and conditions and when there is an appropriate balance between providing authoritative advice and building farmers' capabilities for managing and adapting technology. As agricultural science has advanced, and intellectual property regimes have become more important, private research has played an increasingly dominant role in plant breeding and in crop management inputs. As markets for technology have developed, the state has usually provided regulation and oversight. Such regulation must promote commercial transparency and the development of farmer voice. The importance of finding the correct balance among the commercial input sector and farmers' interests is nowhere better illustrated than in the case of transgenic cotton.

Transgenic cotton

One way to address insect damage in cotton would be to seek resistant varieties through conventional plant breeding, but this has proven to be very difficult (Box 2.4). A major breakthrough in plant breeding for insect resistance in cotton was achieved only when it became possible to produce transgenic varieties.

An early target for plant genetic engineering was a series of soil organisms, *Bacillus thuringiensis* (Bt), that produced toxins specific to particular types of insect. Bt toxins had been known for a long time and were the basis of a number of commercial insect control products that were particularly popular with organic farmers. Researchers reasoned that if the appropriate Bt gene could be inserted within a plant, it could produce its own toxin and reduce the need for chemical insecticides. By the early 1980s, a number of public and private research entities were attempting to produce genetically engineered tobacco plants containing a Bt gene. (Tobacco was the most common target in the early research simply because it was one of the easiest plants to transform.) At the same time, there was

---

Box 2.4 Plant breeding for insect resistance

Plant breeding would appear to be an option for achieving insect control, but insect-resistant crop varieties usually have been much more difficult to develop than those for disease resistance. Insects often have less specialized nutritional habits than the microorganisms that cause plant disease, and are able to attack various crops. In addition, because insects reproduce sexually, genetic variability affords many opportunities for developing resistance to plant defence mechanisms (Briggs and Knowles 1967). There are three basic options for seeking insect-resistant varieties (Dent 2000). First, plants may have biochemical or morphological properties that discourage initial infestation as a source of food or as a site for egg laying. Second, once a plant is colonized, it may resist by interfering with the insect's development or survival. Third, some varieties may be able to better tolerate an established insect infestation without losing yield or vigour. However, it is quite difficult to identify such characteristics or to test for their effects during a plant breeding program, and the properties responsible for resistance may also have side effects.

A relevant example of these challenges is research that has developed types of cotton with high resistance to several *Heliothene* species, pests that are also targeted by Bt cotton. Cotton varieties with an absence of extrafloral nectar glands, fewer trichomes (leaf hairs) and high levels of the chemical gossypol in the flower buds exhibit very high resistance to *Heliothene* attack (Lukefahr *et al.* 1975). But all of these properties present significant trade-offs. The nectar glands are often associated with the cotton plant's ability to resist other insects (by rewarding their predators). Higher trichome density helps ward of aphid attack. Gossypol is a toxin that limits the use of cotton seed in food and feed, and breeders often seek to reduce its presence. Thus each of the characters that helps confer resistance to *Heliothenes* presents serious drawbacks for a conventional plant breeding program.

---

increased pressure to patent the genes that coded for various strains of the Bt toxin. Early successes were registered at Washington University in St. Louis and at Plant Genetic Systems, a private firm in Belgium. But although it was possible to demonstrate the presence of the Bt gene in the transformed plants, its insecticidal performance was very modest. A major breakthrough came in the laboratories of Monsanto in 1988, where it was discovered that the bacterial gene needed to be 'codon modified' so that its genetic code was more compatible with that of plant systems. Once this was done, the transgenic plants exhibited significant insecticidal activity (Charles 2001).

When it was shown that genetic modification of plants using Bt genes was possible, the development of Bt cotton varieties became a high priority. (Various Bt toxins have also been used for the development of transgenic varieties of maize, potato, and several other crops.) Bt toxins active against several species of moths whose caterpillars attack various parts of the cotton plant (see Box 2.3) received first attention because one species (the tobacco budworm) was a growing problem for US cotton fields, where the insect was developing resistance to synthetic pyrethroid insecticides. In the early 1990s it was estimated that tobacco budworm and cotton bollworm together caused about one-third of the insect loss in US cotton and were responsible for more than one-third of insecticide use (Luttrell 1994).

By 1990 Monsanto had the first experimental varieties of Bt cotton available for testing. Although Monsanto had developed methods for producing transgenic plants able to express Bt toxins, they needed access to adequate cotton varieties if they were to convert the technology into a commercial success. In 1993, Monsanto signed an agreement with Delta and Pine Land (D&PL), a Mississippi company that controlled 70 per cent of the cotton seed market in the USA. Delta and Pine's dominance in the cotton seed market was not a product of corporate ruthlessness but rather a circumstance of the demise of several family-owned cotton seed companies in a market that had not been, until the advent of transgenic cotton, particularly profitable (Charles 2001). The first commercial plantings of Bt cotton took place in 1996 in the USA, Mexico and Australia.

In the USA, and most other countries, Monsanto's first Bt cotton varieties were sold with the trademark 'Bollgard'. Since that time, several other types of transgenic, insect-resistant cotton have become commercially available. (More information on the technology is found in Chapter 3.) The utilization of transgenes for insect-resistant cotton in those countries with at least several years of experience with the technology is summarized in Table 2.1.

The other major instance of transgenic cotton technology is herbicide tolerance. Herbicides have been used for many years in industrialized countries, and increasingly in developing countries (Naylor 1994) to control weeds. Many herbicides are broad spectrum, killing a wide range of plants, and thus must be used before planting or by protecting the standing crop from contact. Herbicide tolerance was another early target for genetic engineering, with the goal of transgenic varieties that could withstand applications of particular herbicides. Monsanto placed particular attention on developing transgenic varieties tolerant to its popular herbicide 'Roundup'. In 1996 Monsanto released its first varieties of 'Roundup-Ready' soybean and a year later it was able to offer 'Roundup-Ready' cotton in the USA. Since that time several other herbicide-tolerant transgenic cottons have been developed. In addition, there are cotton varieties with both insect resistance and herbicide tolerance, often referred to as 'stacked' varieties. In industrialized agriculture, herbicide tolerance is the most important transgenic trait currently in use. Where stacked cotton varieties are available they are often more widely used than single-trait varieties. In Australia, South Africa and the USA only a minority of farmers still use single-trait, insect-resistant cotton varieties.

Because insect resistance is the trait of most interest to smallholders, this book concentrates on insect-resistant cotton. Tables 2.2 and 2.3 summarize the status of transgenic cotton in countries that have used the technology for at least five

Table 2.1 Cotton insect-resistance transgenes available commercially, 2007

Country	Transgene[1]	Owner	First year commercially available in country	Proportion of insect-resistant cotton with this transgene (%)
China[2]	*cry1Ac* ('Bollgard')	Monsanto	1997	10
	cry1A	CAAS/Biocentury	1997	77
	cry1A + CpTI	CAAS/Biocentury	1999	12
	cry1Ac + API[3]	CAS/Henan Biotech Kerun Limited Company	2003	1
India	*cry1Ac* ('Bollgard')	Monsanto	2002	70
	cry1Ac+cry2Ab ('Bollgard II')	Monsanto	2006	24
	cry1A	CAAS/Biocentury	2006	2
	cry1Ac ('Event 1')	IIT, Kharagpur + JK Seeds	2006	4
Argentina	*cry1Ac* ('Bollgard')	Monsanto	1998	100
Colombia	*cry1Ac* ('Bollgard')	Monsanto	2002	100
Mexico	*cry1Ac* ('Bollgard')	Monsanto	1996	100
South Africa	*cry1Ac* ('Bollgard')	Monsanto	1997	100
Australia	*cry1Ac* ('Ingard')	Monsanto	1996	0
	cry1Ac+cry2Ab ('Bollgard II')	Monsanto	2004	100
USA[4]	*cry1Ac* ('Bollgard')	Monsanto	1996	52
	cry1Ac+cry2Ab ('Bollgard II')	Monsanto	2003	46
	cry1Ac+cry1F ('Widestrike')	Dow	2005	2

Source: National statistics and estimates collected by country consultants.

Notes
1 For more information on specific transgenes, see Chapter 3.
2 China estimates are for 2006, based on extension statistics published by MOA and biosafety certificates approved by MOA.
3 'API' is 'arrowhead proteinase inhibitor'; see Guo *et al.* (2003).
4 USA is for upland cotton only, calculated from data in AMS (Agricultural Marketing Service), 2007.

Table 2.2 Area of cotton planted, in hectares, by type (and per cent of total cotton area), 2007

Country	Insect-resistant (only) transgenic cotton	Herbicide-resistant (only) transgenic cotton	'Stacked' insect- and herbicide-resistant transgenic cotton	Conventional cotton	Total cotton area (hectares)
China	3,830,000 (69%)	—	—	1,717,000 (31%)	5,547,000
India	6,475,000 (73%)	—	—	2,428,000 (27%)	8,903,000
Argentina[1]	91,000 (22%)	239,000 (57%)	—	86,880 (21%)	416,880
Colombia[1]	19,943 (43%)	458 (1%)	482 (1%)	25,414 (55%)	46,297
Mexico	19,399 (17%)	4239 (4%)	34,981 (32%)	52,395 (47%)	111,014
South Africa[1]	909 (8%)	455 (4%)	9204 (81%)	795 (7%)	11,363
Australia	19,655 (12%)	15,625 (10%)	112,033 (68%)	17,188 (10%)	164,501
USA[2]	27,009 (1%)	827,692 (19%)	3,240,633 (74%)	260,941 (6%)	4,356,275

Source: National statistics and estimates collected by country consultants. (Includes estimates of legal and illegal planting.)

Notes
1 Argentina, Colombia and South Africa are 2006/07 season.
2 USA is for upland cotton only, calculated from data in AMS (Agricultural Marketing Service), 2007. A different set of estimates is provided in NASS (2007).

years. In addition, transgenic cotton was approved for sale in Brazil in 2006; it is estimated that 120,000 ha of Bt cotton were planted that year and 500,000 ha in 2007 (James 2007). Burkina Faso planted about 15,000 ha of Bt cotton in 2008 in experimental and seed production plots to prepare for its official release in 2009. In addition to those countries where Bt cotton is legally cultivated, the technology has spread to a number of countries where transgenic crops are not sanctioned. It is widely believed that a significant proportion of Pakistan's cotton area in 2007 was planted to illegal Bt cotton, and one observer estimates that 60–85 per cent of Thailand's cotton is Bt varieties smuggled from China (Napompeth 2007).

Summary

Cotton cultivation has been an important economic activity in both the Old and New Worlds for thousands of years. As textile industries grew and became more

Table 2.3 Area in hectares (and per cent of total cotton area) planted with transgenic, insect-resistant cotton, (single trait or stacked), by year

Country	2004	2005	2006	2007
China	3,700,000	3,300,000	3,500,000	3,830,000
	(66%)	(65%)	(66%)	(69%)
India	1,307,000	3,247,000	5,423,000	6,475,000
	(16%)	(38%)	(65%)	(73%)
Argentina	54,000	51,000	25,000	91,000
	(20%)	(13%)	(8%)	(22%)
Colombia	11,436	25,910	23,691	20,883
	(17%)	(35%)	(42%)	(45%)
Mexico	65,231	79,824	54,750	58,619
	(60%)	(61%)	(47%)	(53%)
South Africa	28,932	13,275	14,310	10,113
	(81%)	(61%)	(79%)	(89%)
Australia	58,057	214,662	247,295	131,688
	(29%)	(70%)	(78%)	(80%)
USA[1]	2,903,836	3,465,461	4,019,620	3,267,642
	(54%)	(61%)	(66%)	(75%)

Source: National statistics and estimates collected by country consultants. (Includes estimates of legal and illegal planting.)

Note
1 USA is for upland cotton only, based on data from AMS (Agricultural Marketing Service), various years.

specialized, increasing demands were placed on cotton production. Where farmers benefit from equitable political and economic regimes, cotton cultivation offers opportunities for rural development. But the viability of smallholder cotton production in such circumstances depends to a considerable extent on the provision of adequate technology, which in turn depends on a range of institutions, including public and private research, input and credit markets, regulatory and intellectual property regimes, information provision, and farmer organization. Policies in support of agricultural development must envision a strategy that draws on these institutions.

Cotton technology development was initially the province of innovative farmers, who selected superior varieties and devised improved methods of crop management. By the late nineteenth century publicly supported agricultural research began to contribute to technology generation, and this was complemented by private investments in plant breeding and later in the development of crop management inputs. The extent to which these research innovations benefit smallholders is related to the responsiveness of public research institutions and the transparency and efficiency of private input markets. Both input and output markets are usually subject to some type of regulation, but regulatory regimes can be constituted in a manner that promotes the interests of the politically powerful or they can be more supportive of farmer concerns. Agricultural technology is increasingly subject to intellectual property rights, which need to strike a balance that provides adequate incentives for innovation while protecting farmers' interests. Similarly, the provision of information by public extension needs to be managed to strike a balance between providing authoritative technical advice, on the one hand, and building farmer skills and capacities, on the other. The extent to which new technology can serve the needs of smallholders thus depends on various dimensions of farmer control, reflected in the effectiveness of public research, the equitability of markets, the reflection of farmer interests in regulatory regimes, and the capacity of farmers to demand and utilize new information.

Control of technology is a function of the balance of power among public institutions, private enterprises and farmers. This balance is subject to realignment with the advent of transgenic crops and deserves careful attention. Certainly the most interesting example to date for developing countries is transgenic, insect-resistant cotton. Most cotton farmers are already dependent on input markets for seed, fertilizers and pesticides, so we can see how transgenic cotton affects existing input provision systems. Insect control is one of the most intractable problems facing cotton farmers, and it is important to understand how they adapt the innovation to their production systems. Chapter 3 looks more closely at the technology itself and Chapters 4 and 5 examine the literature on the first several years of transgenic cotton cultivation. The rest of the book provides updates on more recent experience with the technology.

3 Development, agronomic performance and sustainability of transgenic cotton for insect control

Ann M. Showalter, Shannon Heuberger, Bruce E. Tabashnik and Yves Carrière

This chapter summarizes the methods used to develop transgenic cotton for insect control; discusses the major factors related to its agronomic performance; and describes the resistance management strategies used to enhance its sustainability. [See Showalter *et al.* (forthcoming) for a more comprehensive review.] An understanding of the technology's underlying biological characteristics is necessary to interpret the economic and institutional consequences of transgenic cotton described in subsequent chapters.

Several factors merit attention to understand how the biological characteristics of transgenic cotton affect the performance and impact of the technology. First, this chapter examines the processes of transgene transfer and plant breeding used to create transgenic cotton varieties. Second, it reviews the insecticidal toxins used in transgenic cotton and explains their efficacy against common cotton pests. Third, the chapter explores some of the factors that determine the expression and effectiveness of these toxins in different genetic backgrounds and environmental conditions. Fourth, it reviews some of the implications of insecticidal transgenic cotton for crop management. Finally, the chapter outlines the rationale for insect resistance management in the deployment of transgenic cotton and discusses options for enhancing sustainability of the technology.

Development of transgenic cotton cultivars

The development of transgenic cotton cultivars is similar to conventional cotton breeding, with the exception of the steps involved in the insertion of foreign DNA. This section describes the primary techniques currently used to transform cotton and the subsequent plant breeding steps required to produce commercial cultivars.

Insertion of foreign DNA into cotton

The process that distinguishes transgenic cotton from conventional cotton is the insertion of DNA from a different organism into the recipient plant's genome. The inserted DNA, or transgenic DNA, generally consists of three main parts: a gene of interest, a promoter, and a marker gene. The gene of interest produces a novel trait that could not be developed through conventional plant breeding [e.g. the production of an insecticidal protein from the bacterium *Bacillus thuringiensis* (Bt)]. However, insertion of this gene alone would not reliably produce the desired trait without the promoter, a regulatory sequence of DNA that determines the location, timing and quantity of gene expression. Promoters can be constitutive (active in all parts of the plant at all times), tissue-specific or inducible (active during certain developmental stages or in response to environmental stimuli). The third part of transgenic DNA is a marker gene, which produces a selectable characteristic (e.g. resistance to an antibiotic or herbicide). Expression of the marker gene signifies that the gene of interest has been successfully transferred to the plant's genome.

Many techniques for transforming plants are available, but the development of most commercial transgenic cotton cultivars has been achieved using one of three methods: *Agrobacterium*-mediated transformation, particle bombardment or the pollen-tube pathway (Potrykus *et al.* 1998; Xue *et al.* 2006). *Agrobacterium*-mediated transformation is the most widely used technique. It uses the natural ability of the plant pathogen *Agrobacterium tumefaciens* to transfer a circular piece of DNA called a plasmid into a plant's genome. To transform cotton, scientists create a plasmid containing the desired transgenic DNA (transgene together with promoter and marker genes) that is absorbed by the bacterium. Plant tissue or cell cultures are inoculated with the *Agrobacterium*, which transfers the transgenic DNA to the plant's genome. Inoculated plant tissue in which the marker gene is expressed is selected and allowed to regenerate into a whole cotton plant.

The second transformation technique is called particle bombardment. Like *Agrobacterium*-mediated transformation, particle bombardment requires plant cell or tissue cultures. However, instead of using a bacterium to transfer DNA, this technique uses ballistics. DNA-coated micro-projectiles are inserted into plant cells at high velocities using an instrument called a 'gene gun'. Once the transgenic DNA enters the cell, it is absorbed into the recipient plant's genome. Plant tissues expressing the marker gene are selected and grown into whole plants.

The third technique, the pollen-tube pathway, is distinct from the previous methods because it does not require cell or tissue cultures. Flowering cotton plants are allowed to self-pollinate. The plant produces a pollen tube from the tip of the pistil to the ovule. Sperm produced by the pollen grain travels down the pollen tube to an ovule where the egg is located. Next, the ovary, which contains the ovules, is exposed by removing the petals, and a solution containing transgenic DNA is injected into the ovary. The DNA travels down the pollen tube to the ovule and is absorbed into the genome of the developing cotton embryo (Zhou *et al.* 1983). When the ovules mature into seeds, the seeds are planted and selected for successful transgene integration.

Each of these transformation techniques has advantages and disadvantages. *Agrobacterium*-mediated transformation and particle bombardment are both established and accepted techniques that have been used successfully to create many transgenic cotton cultivars. These techniques have consistently produced transgenic plants in which the transgene is expressed in subsequent generations. The biggest drawback to these techniques is the required use of cell or tissue cultures for transformation. Most cotton cultivars cannot regenerate from these cultures, and many scientists choose the American 'Coker' cultivar as the recipient plant because it readily regenerates (Smith *et al.* 2004). In contrast, any cotton cultivar can be transformed using the pollen-tube pathway, because regeneration is not required. In addition, the pollen-tube pathway does not require a marker gene for the selection process. Because the method is applied to individual plant embryos as opposed to millions of cells, techniques such as PCR and Southern blot analysis can be used to check if a plant has been successfully transformed. Although the pollen-tube pathway has been used in Chinese biotechnology (Xue *et al.* 2006), this technique remains controversial because results are often inconsistent or irreproducible (Twyman *et al.* 2002; Xue *et al.* 2006).

Development of commercial cultivars and hybrids

After whole transgenic cotton plants have been regenerated from tissue (*Agrobacterium*-mediated or particle bombardment) or grown from seed (pollen-tube pathway), a rigorous selection process is undertaken to identify plants with good agronomic characteristics and the highest and most consistent levels of transgene expression. The most suitable transgenic plants are typically allowed to self-fertilize for a few generations to ensure that inheritance of the transgene is predictable and transgene expression remains stable (Skinner *et al.* 2004). During this stage, plant breeders may also select individuals with particularly good agronomic characteristics. Another goal of the self-fertilization process is to produce cotton plants that are homozygous for the transgene locus (i.e. that have two copies of the transgene at the same locus). Homozygous plants are sometimes called 'true breeding'. The end result of this selection process is a true-breeding transgenic cultivar.

This true-breeding cultivar is rarely commercially useful in cotton plants transformed using the *Agrobacterium*-mediated or ballistic techniques, because of its Coker genetic background (Smith *et al.* 2004). To develop a commercial transgenic cultivar and eliminate the Coker genetic background, a series of backcrosses are conducted. This begins when the transgenic Coker line is crossed with an established commercial cultivar. The initial progeny express the transgene and contain many Coker genes that may be undesirable. To eliminate these genes, the progeny are backcrossed with the commercial parent cultivar. Because backcrossing dilutes the proportion of Coker genes that comprise the plant's genome, the genetic background of the progeny contains fewer Coker genes with each successive backcross. For example, ignoring genes linked to the transgene (i.e. genes on the same chromosome as the insertion site), about 98 per cent of the Coker genes are replaced by genes of the commercial cultivar after five generations of backcrossing. Thus, backcrossing for 5–10 generations eliminates nearly all Coker genes and produces a transgenic cultivar that is similar to the commercial cultivar (Duck and Evola 1997). However, with an average of three backcrosses to produce some commercial transgenic cultivars (Bowman *et al.* 2003), more Coker genes are preserved.

The next step is to self-fertilize plants that bear the transgene and retain progeny homozygous for the transgene. This yields a true-breeding commercial transgenic cultivar, which is important because all of the progeny produced by a homozygous transgenic individual will contain a copy of the transgene even if the other parent is not transgenic.

If the goal is to develop transgenic cotton hybrids, an additional step is required. The true-breeding commercial transgenic cultivar (as described earlier) is crossed with a different, non-transgenic cultivar to produce hybrid seed. Until recently, commercial production of cotton hybrids was difficult to achieve. Because cotton plants mainly self-fertilize, they must be hand-pollinated to produce hybrids, a process that is labour-intensive and potentially uneconomical. Recent advances in breeding (e.g. inducing male sterility and fertility) have improved the efficiency of this process (Zhang *et al.* 2000; Dong *et al.* 2004). Despite these difficulties, hybrid cotton can be a valuable option for growers because hybrids are often more vigorous than either of their parental cultivars.

Cultivar and hybrid seed production

True-breeding commercial transgenic cultivars are grown throughout the world. Seed companies maintain pure lines of their varieties and grow them in carefully monitored fields to obtain subsequent generations of high-quality commercial seed. Most cotton farmers buy or are provided fresh seed each year. Those who save the seed of cotton varieties from their own fields are usually able to preserve the qualities of the variety, although varietal purity may decline after a few seasons if cross-pollination with other cotton varieties occurs and off-types are not removed (Heuberger *et al.* 2008a, b; Showalter *et al.* forthcoming).

Hybrid transgenic cotton is only grown in a few countries, most notably India and China. To produce fresh supplies of hybrid seed, seed companies must maintain both parental cultivars and cross those cultivars each year. If the seeds from a hybrid crop are saved after harvest, they are unlikely to perform as well as the hybrids themselves, because the progeny of the hybrids will exhibit high genetic and phenotypic variation. Hybrid transgenic cotton plants contain one copy of the transgene, which implies that approximately 25 per cent of seeds from interbred hybrid individuals will not carry the transgene. Thus, saved seed from transgenic hybrid plants will not provide the same level of protection against insects as the previous year's hybrids (Kranthi *et al.* 2005). To avoid these problems, hybrid seed should be obtained from seed companies each season to ensure high performance.

Description and efficacy of transgenic toxins available in cotton

Most of the early transgenic cotton cultivars produced Bt toxins Cry1Ac or Cry1A for insect control. However, several other toxins are available for use in cotton, and the range of available transgenic cotton cultivars and hybrids is expanding. Each toxin is produced by a different transgene and offers protection from some of the most economically important cotton pests. This section describes the various available toxins (and associated transgenes) and discusses differences in their efficacy.

Types of insecticidal transgenes

Many genes have been investigated for their insecticidal properties, but only nine are commercially available or may soon become available in transgenic cotton cultivars (Table 3.1). These genes and the toxins they produce can be grouped into four categories: Bt crystalline δ-endotoxins, Bt vegetative insecticidal proteins, proteinase inhibitors and lectins.

Crystalline (Cry) toxins from the soil bacterium Bt have been the most extensively studied and used in transgenics. After activation by insect proteases in the insect midgut, Bt proteins bind to receptors in the midgut (Schnepf *et al.* 1998). Such binding leads to the formation of pores in the midgut membrane that ultimately cause cell lysis and insect death. Five *cry* genes (*cry1A*, *cry1Ac*, *cry2Ab*, *cry1F* and *cry1EC*) are commercially available or nearly commercialized in cotton. While *cry1A* designates a family of toxins, *cry1A* is also used to describe a fusion of *cry1Ac* and *cry1Ab* genes used in some Chinese cultivars (Huang *et al.* 2002a; Dong *et al.* 2004).

The second group of toxins, vegetative insecticidal proteins (Vip), is also derived from Bt. Vip toxins affect insects in a manner similar to that of Cry proteins. However, they bind to different receptors on midgut cells (Lee *et al.* 2003). No cultivars with Vip toxins are currently available to growers.

The third group of toxins used in cotton transgenics includes protease inhibitors, which are derived from plants. Protease inhibitors inactivate the enzymes that digest proteins in an insect's gut. This leads to amino acid deficiencies that cause delayed development and insect death (Hilder *et al.* 1989). The cowpea trypsin inhibitor (CpTI) is one protease inhibitor that has been successfully introduced into transgenic cotton in China and is available commercially.

The final group of toxins currently used in cotton transgenics is lectins. Like protease inhibitors, lectins are found in many plant species. The exact mode of action of these toxins remains uncertain, although lectins are known to bind to the carbohydrate receptors on insect midgut cells and impair gut function and iron metabolism (Tinjuangjun 2002). In India, cotton with the snowdrop lectin gene (*LecGNA 2*) has been planted for research trials but has not been commercially released (Table 3.1; Jayaraman 2004a; James 2006).

As Table 3.1 indicates, in some cases two toxins are combined for deployment in transgenic cultivars. The most widely used examples include the combination of Cry1Ac and Cry2Ab in Monsanto's 'Bollgard II' and the combination of Cry1A and CpTI in many Chinese transgenic cotton cultivars.

Efficacy of transgenic toxins against insect pests

More than 1300 arthropod pests attack cotton around the world (Matthews and Tunstall 1994). The toxins described above are each effective against only a small number of these pests. We focus on the most economically important cotton pests, as efficacy data are available for most of them, particularly the ones found in the United States, India and China. Information on the efficacy of transgenic cotton is much more extensive for older cultivars than newer ones. Although efficacy

Table 3.1 Characteristics of transgenic cotton cultivars for insect control commercialized or in development

Protein(s)	Product name (developer)[1]	Date of release	Promoter	Marker gene	Transformation technique	Event(s)
Cry1Ac	Bollgard (Monsanto)	1996[2]	CaMV35S[3]	nptII[4] aad[4]	Agrobacterium-mediated (Coker 312)[3]	MON531[4] MON757 MON1076
Cry1Ac	NA[5] (IIT Kharagpur)	2006[2]	NA	NA	NA	Event 1[2]
Cry1Ac	NA (NBRI)	Not released	NA	NA	NA	NA
Cry1Ac + Cry2Ab	Bollgard II (Monsanto)	2002[2]	CaMV35S[6]	uidA[7]	Particle bombardment (DP50B)[6]	15985[7]
Cry1Ac + Cry1F	Widestrike (Dow Agrosciences)	2004[2]	d mas 2[8] ubiquitin 1[8]	pat[8]	Agrobacterium-mediated (Germain's Acala GC510)[8,9]	DAS-21Ø23-5 X DAS-24236-5[2]
Cry1A[10]	various (CAAS and others)	1997[2]	NA	NA	Agrobacterium-mediated, pollen-tube pathway (various)[11,12]	various
Cry1A + CpTI	sGK321 (CAAS)	1999[2]	NA	NA	Pollen-tube pathway (Shiyuan 321)[11]	sGK321[11]
Cry1EC	NA (NBRI)	Not released	CaMV35S[13]	nptII[13]	Agrobacterium-mediated (Coker 312)[13]	NA

Vip3A + Cry1Ab	VipCot (Syngenta)	Not released	Actin-2[14,15]	aph4[15,16]	Agrobacterium-mediated (Coker 312)[14,15,17]	Cot102 X Cot67B[18]
LecGNA 2	NA (CPMB)	Not released	NA	NA	NA	NA

Notes

1 Developers: IIT = Indian Institute of Technology; NBRI = National Botanical Research Institute (India); CAAS = Chinese Academy of Agricultural Sciences; CPMB = Centre for Plant Molecular Biology (India).
2 James 2006.
3 Perlak et al. 1990.
4 AgBios GM Database 2005a.
5 NA indicates that information was not available.
6 Greenplate et al. 2003.
7 AgBios GM Database 2005b.
8 AgBios GM Database 2005c.
9 Widestrike was created by crossing two transgenic cultivars (281-24-236 and 3006-210-23), which each contain one transgene.
10 Cry1A refers to a fusion between the cry1Ac and cry1ab gene.
11 Zhang et al. 2000.
12 Huang et al. 2002b.
13 Singh et al. 2004.
14 Llewellyn et al. 2007.
15 Information is available for the Cot102 parent cultivar only.
16 AgBios GM Database 2005d.
17 VipCot was created by crossing two transgenic cultivars (Cot102 and Cot67B), which each contain one transgene.
18 Kurtz et al. 2007.

Table 3.2 Efficacy of transgenic cotton cultivars against key cotton pests based on corrected per cent mortality

Pest species	Bollgard	Bollgard II	Widestrike	VipCot	Cry1EC	LecGNA 2
Helicoverpa spp.	Low–High[1,2,3]	Moderate– High[1,3]	—	High[4,5]	—	Low[6]
Heliothis virescens	High[7]	—	—	High[4,5]	—	—
Pectinophora gossypiella	High[7,8]	—	—	High[5]	—	—
Spodoptera spp.	Low[3,7,9]	Low– High[3,9]	Low– High[10,11]	—	High[12]	—
Aphids	No effect[13]	—	No effect[14]	—	—	—
Mirids	—	—	No effect[14]	—	—	—
Mites	No effect[13]	—	—	—	—	—

Corrected per cent mortality on transgenic cotton was calculated using Abbot's formula: $100 \times [(\%$ mortality transgenic / % mortality non-transgenic) / $(100 - \%$ mortality non-transgenic)]. Corrected per cent mortality values were rounded to the nearest per cent and assigned to the following categories: high = ≥90%; moderate = 60–89 %; low = <60%; no effect = transgenic cotton had no effect on the pest. Cultivars Cry1A and sGK321 are not included because mortality data were not available. Similarly, *Earias* spp., *Diparopsis* spp., jassids, whiteflies and thrips were excluded.

1 Llewellyn *et al.* 2007.
2 Adamczyk *et al.* 2001a.
3 Stewart *et al.* 2001.
4 Kurtz *et al.* 2007.
5 O'Reilly *et al.* 2007.
6 Shukla *et al.* 2005.
7 Jech and Henneberry 2005.
8 Henneberry *et al.* 2001.
9 Chitkowski *et al.* 2003.
10 Adamczyk and Gore 2004.
11 Willrich *et al.* 2005.
12 Singh *et al.* 2004.
13 MacIntosh *et al.* 1990.
14 United States Environmental Protection Agency 2005a.

can be quantified in many ways, we focus on studies that measure mortality using bioassays (Table 3.2) and studies that compare densities of insect populations between transgenic and non-transgenic plots or fields (Table 3.3). Bioassays are more easily conducted than field experiments and provide controlled estimates of efficacy. However, field studies of pest densities may be more representative of the control farmers can expect. The summaries presented in Tables 3.2 and 3.3 are drawn from a broad review of the literature (Showalter *et al.* forthcoming). The estimates of efficacy presented in Tables 3.2 and 3.3 and discussed in the following text often vary because of differences among studies and methods.

Most transgenic cultivars target caterpillars, which are the larvae of lepidopteran pests, including bollworms, *Helicoverpa* spp.; tobacco budworm, *Heliothis virescens*; pink bollworm, *Pectinophora gossypiella*; spiny/spotted

Table 3.3 Efficacy of transgenic cotton cultivars against key cotton pests based on the corrected per cent reduction of field pest density

Pest species	Bollgard	Bollgard II	Widestrike	VipCot	CryIA
Helicoverpa spp.	Low–High[1,2,3,4,5]	High[3,4,5]	Moderate–High[6]	High[7]	Low–High[2]
Heliothis virescens	High[8]	High[8]	High[6]	High[7]	—
Pectinophora gossypiella	Low–High[5,9,10,11,12]	High[9]	High[6]	—	Moderate–High[11]
Spodoptera spp.	Low–Moderate[4,8]	Moderate–High[4,8]	Moderate[13]	—	—
Jassids	—	—	—	No effect[14]	—
Aphids	—	—	—	No effect[14]	—
Whitefly	No effect[12]	—	—	No effect[14]	—
Mirids	No effect[12]	—	—	No effect[14]	—
Thrips	No effect[12]	—	—	No effect[14]	—
Mites	—	—	—	No effect[14]	—

Corrected per cent reduction of insect density in fields of transgenic cotton compared to fields of non-transgenic cotton was calculated using Abbot's formula: $100 \times (1 -$ insect density in transgenic field / insect density in non-transgenic field). Corrected per cent reduction in insect density was rounded to the nearest per cent and assigned to the following categories: high = ≥90%; moderate = 60–89 %; low = <60%; no effect = transgenic cotton had no effect on pest density. Cultivars sGK321, Cry1EC and LecGNA2 are not included because field density data were not available. Similarly, *Earias* spp. and *Diparopsis* spp. were excluded.

Notes
 1 Wu *et al.* 2003.
 2 Wan *et al.* 2005.
 3 Jackson *et al.* 2003.
 4 Chitkowski *et al.* 2003.
 5 Udikeri *et al.* 2007.
 6 United States Environmental Protection Agency 2005b.
 7 Kurtz *et al.* 2007.
 8 Adamczyk *et al.* 2001b.
 9 Marchosky *et al.* 2001.
10 Tabashnik *et al.* 2000.
11 Wan *et al.* 2004.
12 Wilson *et al.* 1992.
13 Adamczyk and Gore 2004.
14 Whitehouse *et al.* 2007 – results for Cot102 only.

bollworms, *Earias* spp.; and red bollworms, *Diparopsis* spp. In many countries, these species are the most economically important cotton pests (Hearn and Fitt 1992; Matthews and Tunstall 1994). Most of these insects are moderately to highly susceptible to the Cry toxins found in Bollgard, Bollgard II, Widestrike and Chinese Cry1A cultivars. However, the efficacy of Cry toxins is generally less against *Helicoverpa* spp. than the other insects in this group. Cotton with the Vip toxin (VipCot) provides moderate to high levels of protection against bollworms and budworms, while the recently developed LecGNA 2 cotton cultivar, which targets pests other than bollworms and budworm (see following text), offers little protection against *Helicoverpa* spp. Several bollworm species in the genera *Earias* and *Diparopsis*, which are important pests in parts of Asia and Africa, have not been tested for their susceptibility to the toxins in most transgenic cultivars.

Armyworms (*Spodoptera* spp.; Lepidoptera: Noctuidae) are close relatives of bollworms and can be important pests of cotton in certain parts of the world (Hearn and Fitt 1992; Matthews and Tunstall 1994). These insects are poorly to moderately controlled by the toxins found in Bollgard and Chinese Cry1A cultivars (Tables 3.2 and 3.3). However, newer transgenic cultivars such as Bollgard II, Widestrike and VipCot were designed to confer greater protection against armyworms. Cotton plants producing Cry1EC, a synthetic hybrid between Cry1E and Cry1C, were developed specifically to target armyworms. Cry1EC cotton killed all of the *Spodoptera litura* tested. Currently, no data are available on the efficacy of CpTI or LecGNA 2 against armyworms.

The remaining important cotton pests include the aphids, jassids, leafhoppers, mirids, mites, stink bugs, thrips and whiteflies. The importance of these pests in cotton agriculture varies regionally. These cotton pests are unaffected by the Bt toxins in Bollgard, Widestrike and VipCot. Indeed, studies of the efficacy of transgenic cultivars are rarely published for these pests, which are usually considered non-target arthropods (Wolfenbarger *et al.* 2008). However, LecGNA 2, which produces lectins, targets aphids.

Factors affecting transgene expression

Not only does efficacy vary among the many transgenic toxins available in cotton, but the transgene expression and performance of each cultivar can vary as well. Since the introduction of commercial transgenic cotton, several researchers have noted seasonal and spatial variation in transgenic toxin concentration of these cotton plants. Two types of factors cause this variation: traits of the plants themselves and environmental conditions. Most research on the factors affecting transgenic cotton performance has been conducted on Bollgard (Cry1Ac) cotton, and unless stated otherwise, the following discussion describes observations of Bollgard cotton.

Characteristics of transgenic cultivars

Variability in transgene expression, toxin levels and efficacy can be attributed to differences among cultivars, variation over the growing season and differences among parts of the cotton plant. Although it is not yet clear how the variation in toxicity affects yield, Bt toxin concentration is positively associated with efficacy against *Helicoverpa armigera* and *Helicoverpa zea* (Adamczyk *et al.* 2001a; Olsen *et al.* 2005). Therefore, Bt varieties and hybrids with higher toxin concentrations probably produce higher yields and greater reductions in insecticide use than cultivars with lower toxin concentrations in areas where these bollworms are key pests.

The genetic background of a Bt cultivar affects the amount of toxin produced by the cotton plant (Sachs *et al.* 1998; Adamczyk and Meredith 2004). Some Bt cultivars and hybrids contain as much as seven times more Cry1Ac than other Bt cultivars, although most varieties differ by less than two-fold (Sachs *et al.* 1998; Adamczyk *et al.* 2001a; Adamczyk and Meredith 2004; Chen *et al.* 2005a, 2005b; Kranthi *et al.* 2005, Olsen *et al.* 2005). However, the mechanisms underlying the interaction between a cultivar's genetic background, transgene expression and toxin concentration remain unclear. Plants with different genetic backgrounds may vary in transcription factors that are involved in *cry1Ac* expression. Cry1Ac concentrations in cotton also may be affected by nitrogen metabolism, overall protein production and interactions with other toxins (see following text), which may vary among cultivars because of their genetic background.

In addition, some Bt cultivars lose their toxicity over the growing season up to14 times faster than others (Sachs *et al.* 1998; Adamczyk *et al.* 2001a; Chen *et al.* 2005a, 2005b; Kranthi *et al.* 2005). The efficacy of Bt cultivars and hybrids can decline over the growing season because of decreasing concentrations of Cry1Ac (Adamczyk *et al.* 2001a; Bird and Akhurst 2005; Kranthi *et al.* 2005; Olsen *et al.* 2005). Cry1Ac concentrations in the vegetative plant tissues usually begin to drop as the cotton plants start producing flowers and bolls, and toxin concentrations during the reproductive stage are as low as one-fifteenth the concentration before reproduction (Sachs *et al.* 1998; Adamczyk *et al.* 2001a; Bird and Akhurst 2005; Chen *et al.* 2005a, 2005b; Olsen *et al.* 2005). However, the seasonal decline in toxin concentrations varies widely among cultivars (Sachs *et al.* 1998; Adamczyk *et al.* 2001a; Kranthi *et al.* 2005). Some cultivars lose as little as 5 per cent of their toxicity, while others lose as much as 99 per cent during the growing season (Sachs *et al.* 1998; Chen *et al.* 2005a, 2005b; Wan *et al.* 2005). Cultivars showing large reductions in Cry1Ac concentration over the growing season become more susceptible to insect damage, particularly from insects with only moderate susceptibility to Cry1Ac such as *Helicoverpa* spp. (Olsen and Daly 2000; Adamczyk *et al.* 2001a; Kranthi *et al.* 2005; Olsen *et al.* 2005). Toxin concentrations in Bollgard II and VipCot do not change in the same way as for Cry1Ac in Bollgard (Adamczyk *et al.* 2001b; Llewellyn *et al.* 2007). Cry2Ab concentrations in Bollgard II cotton tend to spike in mid-season before declining (Adamczyk *et al.* 2001b), while concentrations of Vip3A remain relatively stable throughout the season (Llewellyn *et al.* 2007). Despite the more consistent Vip3A concentrations, transgenic plants producing this toxin lose some of their efficacy against *H. armigera* during mid-season (Llewellyn *et al.* 2007).

The seasonal reduction in Cry1Ac concentration in Bt cotton could be caused by a variety of factors. For instance, reductions in Bt toxin production as plants age may result from a decline in overall protein production (Sachs *et al.* 1998; Chen *et al.* 2005a; Olsen *et al.* 2005). Reduced protein production is likely an effect of changes in nitrogen metabolism that occur as the plant shifts more nutrient resources to its reproductive tissues (Chen *et al.* 2005a). Some phytochemicals produced by cotton plants may directly interfere with the efficacy of Bt toxins (Olsen and Daly 2000). Concentrations of condensed tannins, which are anti-herbivory protein-binding molecules, increase in cotton as the plant develops (Zummo *et al.* 1984). These tannins can interfere with Cry1Ac efficacy by deterring insect feeding or binding to Cry1Ac (Navon *et al.* 1993; Olsen *et al.* 1998).

Finally, Cry1Ac concentration varies among plant parts in transgenic cotton (Adamczyk *et al.* 2001a; Kranthi *et al.* 2005; Wan *et al.* 2005). Leaves typically contain 1.8–19 times more Cry1A or Cry1Ac than reproductive parts such as squares, flowers and bolls (Adamczyk *et al.* 2001a; Kranthi *et al.* 2005). Toxin levels in the fruit wall of newly formed bolls are particularly low and may sink below the concentration necessary for adequate protection against *Helicoverpa* spp. during the growing season (Adamczyk *et al.* 2001a; Kranthi *et al.* 2005). It remains unclear why different tissues produce different levels of Bt proteins, although the possible explanations are likely to be related to the fact that plant tissues have different functions that require specific proteins, and the type and level of gene expression varies widely among tissues.

Although many of the details concerning variability in Cry1Ac expression and toxin content remain unknown, it is clear that the genetic background of a transgenic plant plays a significant role in Bt toxin production and efficacy against insect pests. For this reason, careful plant breeding and testing are necessary to optimize the efficacy of transgenic cotton. Not only should breeders rigorously select the genetic background of their transgenic cotton plants, but these plants also should undergo stringent laboratory and field testing to ensure optimal transgene expression and efficacy under local growing conditions.

Environmental factors

Several environmental factors are known to affect Bt toxin concentrations in cotton (reviewed by Dong and Li 2007), but many others have yet to be examined. Here we describe two of the more well-studied environmental factors that affect Bt concentrations in cotton: nitrogen and temperature.

Nitrogen is an important component of amino acids, which are the building blocks of proteins, including Bt toxins. Therefore, nitrogen availability could affect Bt toxin production. Although this hypothesis has not been fully evaluated, Bt cotton (Cry1Ac and Cry1A) had significantly higher (19–36 per cent) leaf nitrogen content than conventional isogenic cultivars, suggesting a higher uptake of nitrogen in Bt cotton than in conventional cotton (Coviella *et al.* 2002; Chen *et al.* 2005a). Furthermore, increasing nitrogen fertilizer raised concentrations of Bt toxins (Coviella *et al.* 2002), and the seasonal decline in Cry1Ac concentration was somewhat mitigated by nitrogen fertilizer (Pettigrew and Adamczyk 2006). Cry1A cotton plants may also have more active nitrogen metabolisms (using nitrogen more effectively to generate amino acids and proteins) than isogenic conventional cultivars (Chen *et al.* 2005a).

It remains unclear how the insertion of *cry1A* or *cry1Ac* genes into the cotton genome may cause higher nitrogen contents and metabolisms. Chen *et al.* (2005a) suggested that the transgenes may indirectly cause greater vegetative growth at the expense of reproductive output because the plant's natural balance between nitrogen and carbohydrate metabolisms is changed as a result of Bt toxin production. However, more research is needed to fully explore the consequences of these potential differences in nitrogen requirements between Bt and non-Bt cotton. For instance, it is not known if the relative performance of Bt cotton is maintained across the range of soil nitrogen contents typically encountered in developing countries, or if the applications of nitrogen fertilizer that result in higher toxin concentrations and more vegetative growth affect yield.

Temperature can also alter the concentration and efficacy of Cry1A and Cry1Ac in transgenic cotton. Leaves collected from pre-flowering Bollgard plants grown at high temperatures (22–32°C) were significantly more toxic to *H. armigera* than leaves from plants grown at low temperatures (14–24°C) (Olsen *et al.* 2005). The Cry1Ac concentration in leaves did not differ between plants exposed to high and low temperatures, which indicates that some other trait affected efficacy. However, Chen *et al.* (2005b) observed a significant decline in Cry1A concentration in plants exposed to short bursts of high temperatures (37°C) compared to plants maintained at constant temperatures (25–32°C). The reduction in Cry1A also paralleled a decline in amino acid synthesis and an increase in protein degradation, suggesting that high temperatures disrupt nitrogen metabolism in transgenic cotton plants. These results under high temperatures are not necessarily contradictory. Changes in temperature may have primarily affected the production of the plant's natural defences at moderate temperatures (below 32°C), while higher temperatures (37°C) may have stressed the plants and changed their nitrogen metabolism. It remains unclear whether high temperatures could, under some conditions, reduce the efficacy of Bt toxins to the extent that yields are significantly affected. However, studies conducted under the high-input cotton growing systems of the Sonoran desert in Arizona where temperatures are often above 40°C suggest that high temperatures do not impair performance of Bt cotton (Tabashnik *et al.* 2000; Cattaneo *et al.* 2006).

Management of transgenic cotton

Like any other agricultural technology, transgenic cotton must be integrated within existing farming environments and crop management practices, and this may require adjustments in crop management. This section examines several relevant examples of the implications of variable pest pressure on the performance of transgenic cotton, the consequences of reduced insecticide use on non-target pests and the need for further research on the performance of transgenic cotton under marginal growing conditions.

Performance under variable pest pressure

Because transgenic cotton is only effective against some pests and efficacy against a pest may range from modest to high, it follows that the performance and value of transgenic cotton will depend on the abundance of pests. For any pest, levels of infestation vary annually, which can affect the performance of the technology. For example, the variability of *H. armigera* populations in India has been one of the explanations for reported variation in Bt cotton performance. Higher bollworm infestations usually occur with increased rainfall, and years with higher bollworm infestations typically result in greater yield gains of Bt hybrids versus conventional cultivars (Qaim 2003; Qaim *et al.* 2006; Sharma and Pampapathy 2006). Rain renders insecticides less effective by washing off plants, giving Bt cotton an extra advantage over conventional cotton under rainy conditions. On the other hand, in years of low bollworm infestations, the number of larvae on unsprayed Bt plants can be similar to numbers on conventional cotton. Although Bt cultivars receive less bollworm damage to squares and bolls than non-Bt cotton, the difference in yield between Bt and non-Bt cultivars may be reduced in years of low infestations (Sharma and Pampapathy 2006).

Consequences for non-target pests

In addition to variation in target pest pressure, the performance of transgenic cotton can be affected by changes in management practices that affect non-target pests. Reduced insecticide use on transgenic cotton that targets pests such as bollworms may at times increase problems caused by other pests that are also controlled by these insecticides. For example, significant reduction in the use of synthetic insecticides in transgenic cotton favoured outbreaks of mirids and leafhoppers in China (Wu *et al.* 2002; Men *et al.* 2005). Before the introduction of Bt cotton these had been relatively minor pests that had been controlled by the same synthetic insecticides sprayed to control *H. armigera*. Similarly in South Africa, Kirsten and Gouse (2003) noted an increase in jassids on Bt cotton, possibly as a result of reduced insecticidal sprays for bollworms. Lower use of insecticides in Bt cotton was proposed as one factor that explains higher stink bug damage in some southern states of the USA (Greene *et al.* 2001). Other factors include a reduction of insecticide applications following the successful boll weevil eradication, the new availability of more specific insecticides for the control of lepidopteran pests and change in crop diversity that has increased the population density of stink bugs regionally (Greene *et al.* 2006).

Conversely, reduced insecticide use in Bt cotton can have positive consequences for the control of pests whose predators were formerly impacted by these insecticides. When non-transgenic cotton was treated with more insecticides than transgenic cotton, some studies showed lower density of natural enemies in non-transgenic cotton (Naranjo 2005; Whitehouse *et al.* 2005; Wu and Guo 2005; Sisterson *et al.* 2007; Wolfenbarger *et al.* 2008). However, the abundance of non-target arthropods did not always differ between Bt and non-Bt cotton in such situations (Cattaneo *et al.* 2006; Marvier *et al.* 2007). In some cases of increased predator abundance, predation rates were higher in Bt than non-Bt cotton (Head *et al.* 2005). For example in China, a reduction in insecticide use in transgenic cotton was associated with greater predator abundance and better control of the cotton aphid in the middle and end of the growing season (Wu and Guo 2003).

In addition, the overuse of synthetic insecticides, especially where these have become easily available and are often provided at subsidized prices, has led to the evolution of insecticide resistance. This occurred in China in the early 1990s with increasing use of insecticides to control *H. armigera* (Huang *et al.* 2002a). However, studies conducted after the introduction of Bt cotton in northern China showed a significant decline in resistance levels (Wu *et al.* 2005). This return to susceptibility was likely facilitated by the high availability of refuges provided by non-cotton crops where *H. armigera* could breed. The resulting increase in insecticide efficacy has increased growers' ability to control *H. armigera*.

After the introduction of Bt cotton in southern Tamaulipas, Mexico, *H. virescens* showed a similar return to susceptibility (Terán-Vargas *et al.* 2005). In the early 1990s, pyrethroids were regularly used for the control of this pest in cotton. By 1995, *H. virescens* had become highly resistant to many types of pyrethroids and control failures occurred. However, high adoption of Bt cotton from 1996 to 2001 coupled with low use of pyrethroids in cotton and other *H. virescens* host crops restored susceptibility to pyrethroids.

Nonetheless, deployment of Bt cotton does not always result in reversals of resistance to synthetic insecticides. For example, widespread cultivation of Bt cotton in Louisiana did not change the high levels of resistance to pyrethroids in *H. virescens* and *H. zea* (Bagwell *et al.* 2001). Stability of resistance in this case may be partially explained by scarcity of refuges, as pyrethroids were widely used in other crops attacked by these pests (e.g. maize, sorghum and soybean). In several regions of Texas, *H. zea* resistance to pyrethroids increased significantly after deployment of Bt cotton (Pietrantonio *et al.* 2007).

Performance under marginal growing conditions

In addition to the implications of transgenic cotton for pest control practices, characteristics of the technology deserve attention because of their possible interaction with other aspects of crop management.

When a new technology such as transgenic cotton is introduced in developing countries, one of the primary concerns is its performance under the marginal conditions and limited resources of smallholder farmers. For instance, controversy has occurred about the performance of Bt cotton in some regions of India. The problems reported with the performance of Bt cotton in regions such as Andhra Pradesh (Qayum and Sakkhari 2005) could result from specific environmental conditions or patterns of insecticide use. Soil fertility and water availability are common problems for cotton growers in many regions of India, including Andhra Pradesh (Jayaraman 2002; Qaim 2003). Farmers in these regions typically experience lower yields for both Bt and non-Bt cotton than farmers in more favourable regions (Qaim 2003; Qaim *et al.* 2006). In addition, Andhra Pradesh cotton farmers typically use more insecticides than farmers in other areas and thus may not lose as much of their yield to insect damage (Qaim *et al.* 2006). These differences in crop management and resources need to be considered when examining differential performance of transgenic cotton.

Recent research indicates that aspects of Bt cotton may have significant implications for crop management in marginal environments. Because Bt hybrids

typically experience less boll loss due to insect damage than their non-Bt counterparts, they generally provide higher yields (Hebbar *et al.* 2007a). The higher
yields are the result of synchronized boll development and earlier crop maturity,
as the plant is able to protect the developing bolls from insect attack (Hofs *et al.*
2006c, 2006d). However, if conditions such as water deficit limit the ability of
the plants to support this more rapid boll production, this could affect the performance of Bt cultivars (Hebbar *et al.* 2007b). The rapid maturity and early senes-
cence of the crop may not be optimal for moisture-stressed environments. Thus
more research is warranted on crop management requirements for transgenic
cotton under marginal growing conditions.

In addition, the evidence for higher nitrogen metabolism in Bt than non-Bt
cultivars (Coviella *et al.* 2002; Chen *et al.* 2005a; Pettigrew and Adamczyk 2006)
that was cited in the previous section implies the need for further investigation on
optimum fertilizer management for transgenic cotton.

Sustainability: Resistance management in transgenic cotton

Just as insects can evolve resistance to synthetic insecticides through repeated
exposure, they may also evolve resistance to transgenic cotton. Resistance to a
transgenic toxin is defined as a genetically based decrease in the frequency of
individuals susceptible to the toxin in a population that has been previously
exposed to the toxin (Tabashnik 1994a). The potential for this type of resistance
with the increasing cultivation of transgenic crops is one of the most debated top-
ics in agricultural biotechnology. Laboratory studies have shown that populations
of several insect pests can evolve resistance to commercially available Bt crops
(Tabashnik *et al.* 2000; Bird and Akhurst 2004; Jackson *et al.* 2004; Huang *et al.*
2007; Mahon *et al.* 2007), indicating that many species have the potential to
evolve resistance in the field.

Tabashnik *et al.* (2003) found no evidence of evolved target pest resistance to
transgenic cotton during the first five years of commercial use. Monitoring results
obtained by measuring field-derived lines of *H. armigera* from each of four
regions in India show consistent increases in the LC50 (the concentration of toxin
required to kill 50 per cent of a population) of Cry1Ac after the introduction of
Bt cotton (Gujar *et al.* 2007). However, these studies did not test a laboratory-
susceptible line simultaneously with the putative resistant lines, and the observed
decrease in resistance could also have been caused by decreasing potency of the
toxin used in bioassays over time. Similarly, increases in growth rate on Cry1Ac
diet were observed from 2002 to 2005 in *H. armigera* lines collected in the Anci
and Xijian counties of China (Li *et al.* 2007), but because no susceptible line from
the laboratory was tested simultaneously with the field-derived lines, these
increases could have been due to temporal changes in testing conditions.

Extensive published monitoring data provide no convincing evidence that resis-
tance to Bt crops has evolved in field populations of *H. armigera, H. virescens,
Ostrinia nubilalis, P. gossypiella* and *Sesamia nonagrioides* in Australia, China,
Spain and the USA (Tabashnik *et al.* 2008). However, a recent review of monitoring

data shows that field-evolved resistance to Cry1Ac cotton has been documented in some populations of *H. zea* from Arkansas and Mississippi (Tabashnik *et al.* 2008). Thus, after 12 years of commercial use of Bt cotton, one key pest has evolved resistance to Bt cotton in the field (*H. zea*), and equivocal evidence indicates that a second key pest (*H. armigera*) may be in the process of doing so. This chapter does not explicitly discuss resistance monitoring or remediation methods, but critical aspects of resistance management have been addressed in several recent publications (Tabashnik *et al.* 2000, 2006; Venette *et al.* 2000; Carrière *et al.* 2001; Fitt *et al.* 2004).

This section focuses on refuge management as a means of managing the evolution of pest resistance to transgenic cotton. It outlines the basic rationale of the refuge strategy and provides some specific examples that have been put into practice.

The refuge strategy

The refuge strategy is commonly used worldwide to delay the evolution of pest resistance to Bt toxins in transgenic cotton. The strategy requires that refuges of non-transgenic host plants be planted in or near transgenic cotton fields to promote the survival of susceptible pests (United States Environmental Protection Agency 2001; Carrière *et al.* 2005a; Tabashnik and Carrière 2008). A critical condition for success of the refuge strategy is that abundant susceptible insects from refuges mate with the rare resistant individuals surviving on transgenic cotton. Refuges can be provided in transgenic cotton fields by planting one or more sets of rows of a non-transgenic host plant in a transgenic field, planting a single row of a non-transgenic host in alternation with rows of transgenic cotton, or planting transgenic and non-transgenic seed randomly in a field. However, the choice between internal and external refuges has been based on the mobility of the larvae of targeted pests. Internal refuges have been used to manage resistance in pests with sedentary larvae (e.g. *P. gossypiella*) (Carrière *et al.* 2001, 2005a), but have been avoided when pests have mobile larvae that can easily move between cotton plants (e.g. *H. armigera* and *H. zea*) (Gore *et al.* 2002; Men *et al.* 2005).

Refuge strategies are based on understanding the inheritance of resistance. Transgenic cotton cultivars produce concentrations of Bt toxins that are extremely effective against some pests (e.g. *H. virescens* and *P. gossypiella*), but are only moderately effective against others (e.g. *H. armigera* and *H. zea*). For highly susceptible pests, even if there are many alleles that slightly increase resistance to Bt toxins in insect populations, these alleles rarely occur together in one individual and enable it to survive on transgenic cotton. On the other hand, individuals that carry one or a few alleles with major effects on resistance could survive on transgenic cotton (McKenzie 1996). Accordingly, it is expected that a single gene with major effects confers resistance to Bt crops producing one toxin, an assumption that was supported in several pests (e.g. Morin *et al.* 2003; Li *et al.* 2005). Furthermore, we assume for simplicity that such a resistance gene has two alleles (*r* for resistance; *s* for susceptibility). If resistance is inherited as a recessive trait, *rs* individuals do not survive on transgenic cotton but *rr* individuals do. In other words, hybrid offspring bearing one resistance allele and one susceptibility allele are killed by transgenic cotton. When nearly all resistant insects that survive on transgenic cotton produce hybrid offspring that are killed by that crop, the heritability of resistance (i.e. the resemblance between resistant parents and their offspring) is low, which delays the evolution of resistance (Gould 1998; Carrière *et al.* 2004a; Sisterson *et al.* 2004; Tabashnik *et al.* 2004; Tabashnik and Carrière 2008).

The refuge strategy is based on the general principle that the dominance of resistance depends on the dose of the transgenic toxin (Carrière *et al.* 2004a). Resistance is often dominant when the dose of a toxin is low, but recessive when the dose of a toxin is high (Tabashnik *et al.* 2004). This means *rs* insects survive at low but not high toxin concentrations. Accordingly, Bt toxin genes incorporated in transgenic cotton have been modified to produce high concentrations of Bt toxins (Mendelsohn *et al.* 2003). The high concentrations of transgenic toxins are expected to result in recessive resistance in some but not all target pests (Tabashnik and Carrière 2008; Tabashnik *et al.* 2008).

In pests highly susceptible to Bt toxins, toxin concentrations in Bt cotton are high enough to render resistance recessive. Thus, resistance evolution is expected to be substantially delayed in the presence of relatively small refuges (e.g. ≥5 per cent) (Gould 1998; Tabashnik *et al.* 2008). However, in pests less susceptible to Bt toxins, resistance to Bt cotton is not fully recessive, and refuges >50 per cent may be required to efficiently delay the evolution of resistance (Tabashnik *et al.* 2008).

The pyramid strategy

Use of plants producing two distinct toxins to delay pest resistance is called the pyramid strategy. The most widespread current example is Bollgard II, which produces Cry1Ac and Cry2Ab. The pyramid strategy is expected to be most effective when: the majority of susceptible pests are killed by the transgenic crop, resistance to each toxin is recessive, refuges are present and selection with either of the toxins does not cause cross-resistance to the other (Gould 1998; Roush 1998; Zhao *et al.* 2005). It is assumed that two genes, each with two alleles (*r1* and *s1*; *r2* and *s2*), confer resistance to Bt crops producing two toxins that act independently. This strategy is based on the principle that individuals with resistance alleles are killed on two-toxin plants as long as they have a susceptibility allele at either of the two resistance loci, a phenomenon called 'redundant killing' (Gould 1998; Roush 1998). For example, when resistance to each toxin is recessive, individuals with genotypes *r1r1 s2r2* and *s1r1 r2r2* would survive on single-toxin plants producing toxin 1 and 2, respectively. However, these individuals would be killed on plants producing both toxins.

Cross-resistance reduces the efficacy of the pyramid strategy because it diminishes redundant killing. Cross-resistance occurs when a genetically based decrease in susceptibility to one toxin also decreases susceptibility to other toxins. Toxins combined in cultivars are usually chosen because they have different structures and bind to different target sites in the larval midgut, two factors expected to minimize the risk of cross-resistance (Ferré and Van Rie 2002). Strong cross-resistance between toxins produced by Bt cotton does not appear common (Tabashnik *et al.* 2002; Ferré and Van Rie 2002). However, cross-resistance between Cry1Ac and Cry2Aa was documented in some populations of *H. virescens* (Gould *et al.* 1992; Jurat-Fuentes *et al.* 2003) and *H. zea* (Burd *et al.* 2003). Significant cross-resistance between other Bt toxins was also found in populations of other pests (Moar *et al.* 1995; Zhao *et al.* 2001). Thus it is uncertain whether cross-resistance will significantly affect efficacy of the pyramid strategy in the field.

Fitness costs

Fitness is a relative measure of the average contribution of one genotype to the next generation compared to that of another genotype. Fitness costs occur when fitness in refuges is lower for individuals with resistance alleles than for individuals without resistance alleles (Gassman *et al.* 2009). Costs result from indirect effects of resistance alleles, where resistance alleles increase fitness on transgenic crops but decrease fitness in the absence of transgenic toxins. Because costs select against resistance in refuges, the evolution of resistance can be delayed substantially or even reversed when there are fitness costs and refuges are present (Carrière and Tabashnik 2001; Tabashnik *et al.* 2005; Gould *et al.* 2006).

If resistance is recessive, individuals heterozygous for resistance are killed by transgenic crops and survive only in refuges. The fitness of these heterozygous individuals relative to that of susceptible individuals in refuges is a key determinant of resistance evolution. If the fitness of the heterozygotes in refuges is lower than that of normal individuals, then this can strongly favour a decrease in resistance through selection in refuges, even though the rare resistant individuals are favoured by selection in transgenic fields (Carrière and Tabashnik 2001; Tabashnik *et al.* 2005; Gould *et al.* 2006). With large refuges, recessive costs can also significantly delay or reverse the evolution of resistance (Carrière and Tabashnik 2001; Tabashnik *et al.* 2005; Gould *et al.* 2006).

Fortunately, resistance to Bt toxins is usually associated with fitness costs (Tabashnik 1994a; Ferré and Van Rie 2002, Carrière *et al.* 2006, Gassmann *et al.* 2009). The magnitude and dominance of costs associated with Bt resistance seem to be frequently affected by environmental conditions, such as variation between host plants (Carrière *et al.* 2005a; Janmaat and Myers 2005; Raymond *et al.* 2006; Bird and Akhurst 2007), competition for mates (Higginson *et al.* 2005), crowding (Raymond *et al.* 2005) and natural enemies (Gassmann *et al.* 2006). This creates an opportunity to manipulate costs to enhance the success of the refuge strategy. Further study assessing the magnitude and dominance of costs on different host plants or in the presence of natural enemies could improve resistance management through manipulation of refuge quality (Tabashnik and Carrière 2008; Gassmann *et al.* 2009).

Seed contamination

The complexities of refuge management point to another potential concern, the use of impure seed. In many countries farmers save seed to plant the next season, and because of cross-pollination from other fields and other factors, the seed may be contaminated (Heuberger *et al.*, 2008a, b; Showalter *et al.* forthcoming). Even when farmers purchase seed, it may not be purely transgenic or non-transgenic if the seed company's management of its production plots has been inadequate. An additional source of concern is the fact that when farmers are provided with non-transgenic seed to plant as a separate refuge, they may use it to fill gaps caused by poor germination or emergence of their transgenic crop, thus unwittingly planting an internal refuge when an external one is required. More research is needed to evaluate the effect of seed mixtures on resistance to transgenic cotton (Tabashnik 1994b; Carrière *et al.* 2004a; Fitt *et al.* 2004; Showalter *et al.* forthcoming). Similarly, while the effect of contamination of external refuges by transgenic cotton has been explored theoretically (Heuberger *et al.* 2008a), the implication for resistance management of simultaneous contamination of transgenic and non-transgenic cotton requires further investigation (Showalter *et al.* forthcoming).

Refuge deployment decisions

Decisions about refuge deployment are based on characteristics of the pest, the transgenic cotton cultivar, the pest-cultivar interaction and the agroecosystem, as well as possibilities for applying additional pest control measures (Gould 1998; Carrière *et al.* 2004a; Fitt *et al.* 2004; Tabashnik and Carrière 2008; Tabashnik *et al.* 2008). Sedentary pests require an internal refuge when larvae are sedentary, or an external refuge at a distance smaller than the dispersal distance of the pest (Carrière *et al.* 2004b; Sisterson *et al.* 2005). Choices must also be made about the crop used in the refuge. Refuges of non-transgenic cotton are required to delay resistance in insects feeding exclusively on cotton, while other crops not producing the same transgenic toxin as cotton, or non-cultivated plants, may provide refuges for pests that feed on many hosts. However, if a non-cotton refuge is used, similar timing of adult emergence in refuges and transgenic cotton fields is critical to increase matings between individuals from refuges and resistant individuals surviving on transgenic crops (Baker *et al.* 2008). Because factors influencing refuge deployment often change across regions, strategies used to manage resistance in specific pests are likely to differ geographically, as illustrated in the following text.

Pink bollworm in Arizona and China

In Arizona, Cry1Ac cotton was the primary tool for controlling pink bollworm from 1996 until 2006, when an eradication program that also included the release of sterile moths was introduced (Carrière *et al.* 2001, 2005b; Antilla 2006). In what follows, we outline the refuge requirements used in Arizona before 2006 and compare this to the situation in China.

Although pink bollworm moths can disperse over long distances, movement is usually limited in the presence of suitable cotton plants (Carrière *et al.* 2001,

2004b). In Arizona, pink bollworm is an ecological specialist on cotton, and Bt cotton kills virtually 100 per cent of susceptible insects (Tabashnik *et al.* 2000; Carrière *et al.* 2003, 2006). Pink bollworm resistance to Cry1Ac cotton is fully recessive (Carrière *et al.* 2006). The United States Environmental Protection Agency required a minimum refuge area of 5 per cent of the area of each Bt cotton field for the management of resistance (Carrière *et al.* 2005b). Arizona farmers often used external refuges but also planted in-field refuges with a single non-Bt cotton row for every six to ten rows of Bt cotton. Bt cotton use reached 84 per cent of cotton acreage in some regions and compliance to the refuge strategy ranged from 70 to 100 per cent of Bt cotton fields across regions (Carrière *et al.* 2005b). The frequency of pink bollworm resistance to Bt cotton declined from 1997 to 2006 in Arizona (Tabashnik *et al.* 2005, 2006).

Pink bollworm is also an ecological specialist on cotton in the Changjiang River region of China (Wu and Guo 2005). Several Bt cotton cultivars producing Cry1A, Cry1A + CpTI, or Cry1Ac have been used in that region since 1999. However, in contrast to Arizona, larval density of susceptible pink bollworm on unsprayed Bt cotton may only be decreased by 73–89 per cent compared to the density on unsprayed non-Bt cotton at the end of the growing season (Wan *et al.* 2004). High survival at the end of the growing season indicates that resistance to Bt cotton in pink bollworm is unlikely to be recessive in the Changjiang River region. This suggests that large refuges of non-Bt cotton would be needed to significantly delay pink bollworm resistance to Bt cotton, but a refuge strategy has not been explicitly implemented in that region (Wu and Guo 2005).

H. armigera in Australia, China and West Africa

Because larvae from *H. armigera* can easily move between plants, availability of external refuges has been considered important for managing resistance in this key pest. The identification of appropriate external refuges depends on the characteristics of local farming environments, as illustrated in examples from Australia, China and West Africa.

Crops other than cotton provide refuges for *H. armigera* in Australia (Fitt 1989; Sequeira and Playford 2001; Baker *et al.* 2008). However, bollworm populations rapidly evolved resistance to synthetic insecticides sprayed mainly on cotton, suggesting that refuges were too rare to substantially delay evolution of resistance to the insecticides (Fitt 1989; Fitt and Daly 1990). This prompted a cautious approach for the use of Bt cotton producing the Cry1Ac toxin, which was restricted to 30 per cent of cotton area in Australia from 1996 to 2004 (Downes *et al.* 2007; Baker *et al.* 2008). Cotton producing Cry1Ac and Cry2Ab (Bollgard II) was introduced in 2004 and replaced Cry1Ac cotton by 2005. The minimum refuge size for management of *H. armigera* resistance to two-toxin cotton became as low as 5 per cent after 2005 (Downes *et al.* 2007; Baker *et al.* 2008). Refuge requirements for Bollgard II depend on the type of crops planted in refuges and their capacity to produce susceptible moths (Baker *et al.* 2008). There is no evidence that *H. armigera* resistance to Cry1Ac and Cry2Ab increased in Australia between 2003 and

2006, although the frequency of recessive alleles conferring high resistance to Cry2Ab seems high compared to frequency of alleles conferring resistance to Cry1Ac (Downes *et al.* 2007).

As in Australia, populations of *H. armigera* exploiting cotton in China evolved resistance to synthetic insecticides. Such resistance occurred even if crops other than cotton received few insecticide sprays and were estimated to provide a 95 per cent refuge for cotton (Wu and Guo 2005). This indicates that refuges of non-Bt cotton could be required to significantly delay resistance to Bt cotton. However, key parameters affecting resistance (e.g. dominance of resistance, intensity of selection for resistance) may differ between synthetic insecticides and Bt cotton. Moreover, farmers apply synthetic insecticides at the end of the growing season to minimize *H. zea* survival on Bt cotton (Wu *et al.* 2005), which could help in making resistance to Bt cotton recessive by killing Bt-resistant individuals. Because large non-cotton refuges are available, it was suggested that non-Bt cotton refuges are not required to delay the evolution of *H. armigera* resistance to Bt cotton in China (Wu and Guo 2005). Monitoring of resistance from 1997 to 2006 indicated no increase in resistance to Cry1Ac in China (Wu 2007; but see Li *et al.* 2007). However, Wu (2007) proposed that more stringent resistance management measures could be needed to delay the evolution of *H. armigera* resistance to Bt cotton in the Yellow River region.

In West Africa, cotton is grown during the rainy season for 3–4 months when weeds sustaining *H. armigera* are rare compared to cotton (Nibouche *et al.* 2007). Vegetable crops suitable for *H. armigera* are uncommon and often distant from cotton fields. Nibouche *et al.* (2003, 2007) used simulation models to assess the area of external refuges of non-Bt cotton required to significantly delay resistance to Bt cotton in *H. armigera*. A period of 20 years before field failure of Bt cotton was deemed a significant delay. Taking into account the availability of non-cotton refuges and assuming relatively high survival of *H. armigera* on one- and two-toxin Bt cotton at the end of the growing season, they found that planting less than 25 per cent of the cotton cropping area with one- or two-toxin Bt cotton was required to significantly delay resistance evolution in West Africa. Such a low use of Bt cotton may not be practical for small farmers, especially if field trials demonstrate that Bt cotton can significantly improve farmer income. More research is needed to identify effective resistance management strategies in this environment (Showalter *et al.* forthcoming).

Summary

Transgenic cotton producing insecticidal toxins is a highly effective technology in the battle to control pest damage to cotton. Its effective deployment requires an understanding of the methods used for developing transgenic cultivars, the types and efficacies of available toxins, the factors that affect the expression of those toxins in different cultivars and environments, and the adjustments to crop management practices that may be required in some growing conditions. In addition, because insects are capable of evolving resistance to transgenic toxins, its deployment requires careful research to identify appropriate resistance management strategies.

The development of transgenic cultivars is a long process, requiring many steps of selection and testing. The process can produce cotton cultivars with a wide range of agronomic characteristics, but like all plant breeding efforts, transgenic cultivars must be targeted towards specific environments and conditions. A limited but growing number of toxins have been used in transgenic cultivars. Each toxin or combination of toxins targets specific types of insects, with various levels of efficacy. A toxin's efficacy is determined in part by several factors affecting transgene expression, which may vary temporally and among cultivars and plant parts. Transgene expression can also be affected by temperature or nitrogen availability. The performance of a transgenic cotton cultivar is influenced by the type and degree of pest pressure during the growing season. One of the benefits of transgenic cotton is that it usually allows farmers to use less synthetic insecticide. This can facilitate a resurgence in the natural predators of other pests or contribute to lowering insecticide resistance in target pest populations. However, reduced insecticide use can also allow secondary pests previously controlled by synthetic insecticides to become more prevalent.

Even when appropriate transgenic cultivars and crop management practices have been identified for local growing conditions, resistance management is needed to enhance the sustainability of the technology. The most common strategy for delaying evolution of insect resistance is the deployment of refuges of non-transgenic cotton or other suitable host crops. The design of appropriate refuge strategies depends on the biology of the target insect and the inheritance of its resistance to the toxin. This information is used to identify the type, size and crop composition of the refuge.

Overall, transgenic cotton can be very effective and, as with any new technology, care must be taken to appropriately integrate the technology into existing agricultural practices. Careful choice of cultivars is required to match local growing conditions, and appropriate transgenes need to be identified to target specific pest problems. Transgene expression and toxin efficacy in different genetic backgrounds, environments and crop management practices need to be more fully understood. The investment in developing and deploying appropriate transgenic cultivars must be matched by a commitment to design and implement resistance management strategies. Although much of the initial research on transgenic cotton may be done elsewhere, the ability to take full advantage of transgenic cotton cultivars depends on local research and technical capacities and on the availability of adequate information for farmers.

4 Transgenic cotton: Assessing economic performance in the field

Robert Tripp

The purpose of this chapter is to review information related to the performance of *Bacillus thuringiensis* (Bt) cotton during the early years of its cultivation in order to examine the impact on smallholder farmers. We will consider data on farm-level outcomes (yields, costs, pesticide use) and analyse adoption patterns. In Chapter 5 we will assess the nature of technology development, input markets, information provision and regulatory performance. Both chapters are based on a review of published literature and surveys of current usage of Bt cotton in the eight countries that have been growing the crop for at least five years.

Assessing the impact of a transgenic crop can be an exceptionally complex task, even if the analysis is focused, as it is here, on the implications for resource-poor farmers. Although it would appear a simple matter to compare the results (yields, income) of those farmers who use the new technology and those who don't, there are many complications. First, agricultural seasons are characterized by great variability (in rainfall, insect populations, etc.) so the results from any one year may not be representative. Second, the farmers who are the first to adopt a new technology may have other practices or resources that set them apart from their neighbours, making a side-by-side comparison problematic. Third, the adoption of a new technology may be so rapid that there are few farmers left to serve as a control group; there are several instances where this is the case for Bt cotton. Fourth, a technology such as Bt cotton is not so much yield-enhancing as yield-protecting, and its efficacy will depend on the level of pest attack and the use of other pest control practices. All of these factors can be addressed to some extent by careful survey design and statistical methods, as well as by the use of as broad a range of data as possible. Nevertheless, we must be aware that this type of impact assessment is an imperfect process. In addition, the agronomic and genetic factors discussed in Chapter 3 may be responsible for significant differences in performance between Bt varieties, or may interact with differences in crop management.

Besides the problems of dealing with dynamic and variable farming practices and circumstances, there are other methodological problems in assessing farm-level technology impact (Smale *et al.* 2006a). These include: problems in sampling; reliance on partial budgets that do not provide a comprehensive assessment of all the factors that affect farm-level decision making and household welfare; inadequate treatment of externalities affecting the environment or health; and inadequate treatment of institutional factors affecting the provision of the technology or the marketing of outputs. The analysis provided in this book cannot hope to deal with all of these factors, although we will try to pay particular attention to institutional concerns in the following chapter.

Changes in yield and insecticide use

Although Bt cotton has only been available to farmers for a relatively short time, there have been a number of studies documenting the technology's impact. A recent review of the literature on Bt cotton in developing countries found 47 published studies from five countries that attempted to quantify impact (Smale *et al.* 2006b). Some of these publications examine the same sets of farmers, so the number of independent samples is less than 20. However, some of the data sets follow the same farmers over two or more years, adding important depth to the analyses. Taken together, these studies help provide insights into the performance of Bt cotton in its early years of adoption. This section discusses some of the findings available in this literature.

Technology can contribute to farm productivity by raising yields and/or lowering costs of production. Table 4.1 summarizes the results from a sample of the studies reported in the literature (including some from industrialized countries), comparing changes in yield and insecticide expenditure between users and non-users of Bt cotton. The table is far from complete and the examples have been chosen to illustrate a wide range of circumstances and types of study. This summary of the data should be treated with great caution, bearing in mind the difficulties discussed above related to assessing changes attributable to technology adoption. The variation in results is due both to significant differences in agronomic and economic conditions between the samples and the array of sampling and analytical techniques used in the studies. The examples in the table are largely from the early years of Bt use because in many countries widespread adoption of the technology has now made this type of comparison difficult or impossible. But the table is useful for illustrating the significant variation in outcomes between and within countries and between years. Despite this variability it is possible to point out several major features of the results reported so far.

The majority of the results indicate gains from the use of Bt cotton in terms of reduction in pesticide use and/or yield increase. As the Bt gene is meant to substitute for some insecticides we should expect that its adoption would result in lower insecticide use. This is true in almost all cases, although the magnitude of the reduction varies considerably across countries and years. In China, as well as the USA and Australia, the adoption of Bt cotton has resulted (in the initial years at least) in a marked reduction in insecticide use with only modest yield increase. Those instances where insecticide use does not fall may have varying explanations. In one case, the early adopters of Bt cotton in Maharashtra appear to be slightly better-resourced farmers who invested in additional inputs (irrigation and fertilizers, as well as insecticide) for the new seed (Narayanamoorthy and Kalamkar 2006). In contrast, a two-year study among a small sample of smallholders in South Africa

Table 4.1 Changes in yield and insecticide use with Bt cotton

Country	Location or farm type	Year	Change in yield (%)	Change in insecticide cost (%)	Ref.
China	2 Provinces	1999	+8	−82	Huang *et al.* 2002a
	3 Provinces	2000	+56	−56	
	5 Provinces	2001	+11	−58	
India	Karnataka, irrigated	2002	+13	−46[1]	Pemsl *et al.* 2004
	Karnataka, rainfed	2002	−2	−18[1]	
	Maharashtra	2002	+32	−44	Qaim *et al.* 2006
	Karnataka		+42	−49	
	Tamil Nadu		+43	−73	
	Andhra Pradesh		−3	−19	
	Maharashtra	2003	+52	+5	Narayanamoorthy and Kalamkar 2006
	Andhra Pradesh	2002	−35	−2	Qayum and Sakkhari 2005
		2003	+3	−12	
		2004	+5	−8	
Mexico	Comarca Lagunera	1997	+3	−73	Traxler *et al.* 2003
		1998	+17	−81	
South Africa	Smallholders	1998	+63	−53	Bennett *et al.* 2006
		1999	+85	−53	
		2000	+56	−48	
	Smallholders	1998	+4	−30	Gouse *et al.* 2005
		1999	+40	−36	
	Smallholders	2002	+15	+23	Hofs *et al.* 2006b
		2003	(average of both years)	−27	
	Large, irrigated	2000	+19	−56	Gouse *et al.* 2003
	Large, rainfed	2000	+14	−59	
Australia	Nationwide	1998	−8	−32	Fitt 2003
		2001	+5	−69	
USA	Average of 12 states	2004	+9	−47	Mullins *et al.* 2005

Note
1 Change in number of insecticide applications.

showed great variability in insecticide practices, probably reflecting to some degree farmers' inexperience with these inputs (Hofs *et al.* 2006b).

If farmers do not have the knowledge or resources to apply effective insecticides, the adoption of Bt cotton sometimes has as much (or more) of an impact on yields as it has on insecticide use. Qaim and Zilberman (2003) propose that the yield impact of a crop like Bt cotton will be highest in those regions of the world where chemical insect control alternatives are inadequate or not available. There are a number of instances in India where Bt cotton's major impact has been through yield increase rather than savings in insecticide costs, perhaps because farmers control regimes are inadequate, the available chemicals are of low quality or insects have developed resistance to some of the more commonly used products. Stone's (2007) fieldwork in Andhra Pradesh indicates that farmers approach the market for Bt cotton seed looking for yield increases rather than pesticide savings. Smaller farmers in the earlier studies in South Africa tended to register higher percentage yield gains from the adoption of Bt cotton than larger farmers, presumably because the Bt toxin provides more effective control than their previous insufficient use of insecticide. However, there are some gains for larger commercial farmers as well; Gouse *et al.* (2003) reported that large farmers spray for bollworm only after scouting, so some damage is already done before the insecticide is applied.

Comparisons of experiences with Bt cotton must also be seen in light of the significant variability in cotton management at the farm level. Cotton lint yields among small farmers in China are more than 1 mt/ha, while yields in India average less than half that, and South African smallholders may harvest less than 200 kg/ha of lint. (When comparing yields, it is important to distinguish between seed cotton yield, before ginning, and lint yield. Because of the weight of the seed, lint yield is only about one-third of seed cotton yield.)

These yield differences can be explained by the wide range of management practices and cotton-growing environments. Most Chinese cotton farmers have access to irrigation, use large quantities of inputs and practise labour-intensive management. Before the advent of Bt cotton, Chinese cotton farmers were spraying their fields as many as 20 times in a season. Fertilizer and insecticide use in India is also significant, but generally well below the Chinese levels, and only about one-third of the cotton area is irrigated. At the other extreme, small cotton farms in South Africa are mostly rainfed, rarely receive any fertilizer and the prevalence of labour migration means that nearly half are managed by households headed by women.

The reduction in pesticide use with the adoption of Bt cotton can be quite significant. In the mid-1990s insecticide use on cotton in China had become exceptionally high, principally because of increasingly futile attempts to control bollworm. Researchers estimate that by 2001 the adoption of Bt cotton was responsible for a reduction in pesticides of 80,000 mt (Huang *et al.* 2002a). Similarly, in some areas of Mexico the introduction of Bt cotton (combined with a successful boll weevil control program) saw a 80 per cent fall in insecticide use (Traxler and Godoy-Avila 2004).

Despite the significant reduction in insecticide application shown in several examples, it is difficult to use such comparisons between adopters and non-adopters to provide reliable quantification of the actual impact of the technology on input use and yield. Because insect control is a yield-protecting rather than yield-increasing technology, it is a challenge to analyse it in the way that one might assess the impact of a new variety or increased fertilizer application. Farmers resort to insect control only when there are problems, and these may vary across fields and years. One of the major challenges is what economists call endogeneity; some of the factors that determine yield are the same as those that determine whether a farmer chooses to use an insect control technology. Thus special analytical tools have been used to estimate the impact of Bt cotton. (See Chapter 8 for an example.)

Shankar and Thirtle (2005) use a damage control function to show that South African smallholders under-use insecticide and that in this case the Bt technology is more yield-increasing than pesticide-reducing. Similarly, Qaim and de Janvry (2005) use data from Argentina to predict that although Bt cotton should provide equivalent relative reductions in insecticide use for large and small farmers, the absolute insecticide reduction would be greater for larger farmers while the yield gains will be much more pronounced, in both relative and absolute terms, for smallholders. An analysis of Chinese data showed that Bt cotton was responsible for a 58 per cent reduction in pesticide use (Huang *et al.* 2002b). An analysis with US data controlled for differences in bollworm infestations, prices and boll weevil eradication programs (spraying for boll weevil is harmful to natural predators of the bollworm) showed that Bt cotton adoption was responsible for a reduction of between 0.67 and 2.3 insecticide applications (Frisvold 2004).

The reduction of insecticide use should have benefits for the farmers and labourers who have to work with these toxic chemicals, although demonstrating such an impact is not straightforward. One study showed that clinics serving smallholder farmers in South Africa have shown a reduction in cases of accidental pesticide poisoning (Bennett *et al.* 2006). In China, farmers who were early adopters of Bt cotton reported significantly fewer instances of pesticide-related health problems than those who used conventional varieties and applied higher quantities of pesticide (Huang *et al.* 2003).

Cost of the technology

The benefits of yield gains and reductions in pesticide use must be balanced against increases in seed price for Bt cotton. Owners of technology want to earn as much as possible from their innovations in order to recover their investments and allow further research and expansion. Until the advent of biotechnology, seed had never been an important part of the costs of production for cotton farmers in the USA. In the early 1990s a US cotton farmer was paying about $20 for seed but $250 or more for insect control for each hectare planted. After Delta and Pine Land (D&PL) entered into an agreement with Monsanto to produce and market Bt cotton seed, the company reasoned that farmers would be willing to pay much more for their seed if it saved them a portion of their insecticide costs and agreed a pricing structure with Monsanto that would bring the technology owners half of the gain and the growers the other half. However, despite the significant potential economic benefits for farmers, they realized that it would not be easy to suddenly increase the price of a bag of cotton seed by a factor of 4 or 5. The solution devised by Monsanto and D&PL was to charge the normal price for the seed but to levy a second charge, a 'technology fee', as a separate transaction that in effect licensed the gene to each farmer (Charles 2001). The calculation that farmers would be willing to buy the seed if the price reflected a roughly even division of benefits with the technology owner seemed to pay off in the USA. An analysis of the first several years of Bt cotton in the USA showed that indeed farmers and the technology owners shared the gains almost equally (43 per cent and 47 per cent, respectively), with consumers experiencing the rest of the gains because of lower cotton prices (Falck-Zepeda *et al.* 1999). Since that time there have been further changes to the way that US farmers pay for transgenic cotton (Box 4.1).

Seed price regimes for transgenic cotton in other countries have also exhibited some variation. As part of the promotion of Bt cotton in South Africa, smallhold-ers were originally charged a lower price for seed than large farmers. In Mexico, the technology fees vary by region, with those regions with fewer bollworm

---

Box 4.1 Seed price of transgenic cotton in the USA

Since the introduction of Bt cotton, the methods for charging technology fees in the USA have changed several times (Larson *et al.* 2007). Initially, Monsanto charged its technology fee for seed of transgenic maize, soybean and cotton on a per acre basis. In 2002, it began to charge a royalty directly to seed companies for its maize and soybean products and this was reflected in higher seed price, but it maintained the per acre fee for cotton so that farmers continued to make two separate payments. Beginning in 1998, the technology fee calculations became even more complex for cotton seed. They were differentiated by size of seed (cotton varieties differ somewhat in seed size) and by the average planting density in different parts of the country. Thus a charge based on area planted was converted to one based on amount of seed, encouraging farmers to economize on seeding rate. This was particularly detrimental to the method of planting known as 'ultra nar-row row', which relies on very high seeding rates. A compromise was made for farmers planting at these high densities and a maximum charge was established, but even so the incentives were to lower planting densities in response to the technology fee. In 2004, the major seed suppliers switched from selling seed by weight to using seed count. Where previously farmers bought 50 pound bags of seed (whose exact number of seeds depended on the variety), they now buy bags containing a specific number of seeds (e.g. 250,000) and the technology fee is charged per seed. An additional chal-lenge for understanding seed costs in the USA is that seed price and tech-nology fees for equivalent products may vary widely between regions, depending on market forces.

problems (and hence less incentive to buy the seed) paying a lower fee (Traxler and Godoy-Avila 2004). In Colombia, there is a difference in technology fee between the two major cotton-growing regions.

Monsanto's calculations on what the market would bear have not always been accurate, however. Early experience in Argentina showed that farmers were much less willing to accept the original formula of four times normal seed price, resulting in low adoption rates for the new technology, particularly among smaller farmers. An analysis of the benefits of the technology and farmers' willingness to pay indicated that a lower seed price for Bt cotton in Argentina would not only attract more users but would also provide higher profits to the seed company (Qaim and de Janvry 2003).

Probably the most controversial instance of Bt cotton seed pricing has been in India. Many Indian cotton farmers have been used to paying relatively high prices for cotton seed because of the prevalence of hybrids in the market. (Although hybrid seed price is high, the amount of hybrid seed needed to plant a hectare is much less than with conventional varieties.) Mahyco, the seed company that was Monsanto's partner in the development of transgenic cotton for India, introduced its Bt cotton hybrids by setting a price approximately four times that of conventional hybrid seed. In subsequent years, other companies that licensed the gene and marketed their own Bt hybrids charged the same price. There were numerous complaints about the high price and several state governments stepped in by threatening to ban the companies from operating if the charges were not reduced. In the 2006 season the state governments of Gujarat, Andhra Pradesh and Maharashtra put a price limit on Bt seed in their states (which became in effect a limit for the entire country). The result was an approximate halving of the price of Bt cotton seed.

There is a great diversity of Bt technology and cotton seed sources in China (public and private, legal and illegal) making it particularly difficult to unravel seed price. A study in Shandong Province in 2002 found a remarkable range of prices paid for Bt cotton seed. Although the official price for seed containing the Monsanto gene was approximately $10/kg, Bt cotton seed was available for as little as $2/kg. In addition, slightly over half of the farmers were planting farm-saved cotton seed (Pemsl 2006). More recent analysis shows a similar range of seed types and prices (Hu *et al.* 2006). (See Chapter 6 for further detail.)

Table 4.2 attempts to summarize recent data on cotton seed prices in eight countries growing Bt cotton. The table provides an idea of the considerable variability in seed price between (and often within) countries, but there are a number of limitations to using the table to make direct comparisons between prices of transgenic and conventional seed. For countries like the USA where seed price is set by location and there are many different varieties, technologies and companies to choose from, it is only possible to indicate a range of prices. An additional challenge to simple comparisons in the USA is that there is little conventional cotton grown in many parts of the country, and almost no transgenic cotton that only has insect resistance; the vast majority is 'stacked' to include herbicide tolerance. In the USA and Australia, where technology fees are still charged separately, calculations of per-kilogram seed price depend on estimates of planting

Table 4.2 Cost of conventional and Bt cotton seed (2007)

Country	Cost of conventional cotton seed (US$/kg)	Cost of Bt cotton seed (US$/kg)	Ratio of cost of Bt seed to cost of conventional seed	Notes
China	$1.11	$4.44	4.0	Very wide range of seed prices. These are average prices for conventional seed and legal Bt cotton seed. Illegal Bt seed is widely available for lower price
India	$19.94 (conventional hybrid)	$42.74 (hybrid, Bollgard I)	2.1	(Several companies sell conventional and Bt versions of the same variety)
		$62.68 (hybrid, Bollgard II)	3.1	Non-hybrid, conventional seed from public sector costs approx. $0.50/kg
Argentina	$2.00	$4.67	2.3	Conventional seed from public sector costs approx. $0.67/kg but usually planted at higher rate
Colombia	$6.52	$12.52 (Interior) $15.34 (Coast)	1.9–2.4	Other cotton seed available from private sector ($3.47/kg) and public sector ($2.85/kg)
Mexico	$5.10–$7.50	$15.85	2.1–3.1	
South Africa	$2.55	$7.20	2.8	
Australia	$4.92	$25.84 (Bollgard II)	5.3	Technology fee charged as $248/ha. (Assume seeding rate of 12 kg/ha)
USA	$4.50–$6.50	$7.50–$10.00	1.2–2.2	These are representative costs estimated from seed price and technology fees for several states. Figures are for Bollgard; technology fees for Bollgard II are somewhat higher

Source: Country consultants.

density. In most countries, there is a range of conventional cotton seed available, and the prices vary depending on its quality and provenance. Seed from public entities is often cheaper, but farmers may need to plant higher densities of lower quality seed to achieve an adequate plant population, thereby diminishing some of the cost advantage of the cheaper seed. The 'conventional seed' column in the table lists prices for seed that is as closely equivalent to the Bt seed as possible, although other (often cheaper) seed may also be available.

In general, the relative price of Bt cotton seed has declined somewhat since its introduction. In some countries companies have learned that it is more profitable to charge a lower technology fee and attract more customers. In India the government has established a price ceiling and in China the vast amount of illegal seed (as well as saved seed) limits companies' capacity to charge high prices. In some countries where herbicide-tolerant transgenic cotton is available this has proven to have a higher demand than Bt cotton. This popularity often attracts relatively higher technology fees; in the USA the technology fee for the 'Roundup Ready' (RR) trait is roughly twice than that for the Bt trait.

Comparisons of seed price between countries should also be made with caution. The very high prices in India are for hybrids, which require much lower planting rates than non-hybrid seed, so the impact on costs of production is not nearly as great as the seed price comparison would indicate. (India is the major user of hybrid cotton seed, but hybrid use is increasing in China.) Prices also reflect differences in production systems. Australian seed is expensive, but is planted at relatively low densities in irrigated fields with a low risk of crop loss. Many seed companies in the USA offer a type of insurance to purchasers of transgenic cotton seed; if they fail to establish their crop because of drought or other natural causes and need to replant, the company will only charge for the new seed but will not collect the technology fee a second time. In South Africa, Monsanto offers to refund the technology fee if the seed fails to germinate (see Chapter 9).

Net benefits

Farmers are paying a higher price for insect-resistant seed in return for a chance to lower their investment in chemical application (and often achieve more effective pest control), and net returns depend on the balance between the cost of the seed and the magnitude of insecticide saving and yield gains. An analysis of early experience in Argentina showed that while Bt cotton contributed to higher yields and lower insecticide expenditure, the high seed cost implied a doubling in total input costs. This helps explain why the differences in gross margins between adopters and non-adopters was not significant (and adoption rates were modest) (Qaim and de Janvry 2003). A study in four Indian states showed that although Bt cotton led to a significant decrease in insecticide expenditure, the high cost of the Bt seeds eliminated this saving. The majority of farmers experienced an increase in net revenues only because of higher yields from the Bt cotton (Qaim *et al.* 2006). Another study in Andhra Pradesh showed that Bt adopters used almost as much insecticide as other farmers and that in most cases the value of any yield increases was cancelled by the higher expenditure on seed, leading to net losses. (Qayum and Sakkhari 2005). The early Chinese studies of Bt cotton showed clear gains in net revenues for adopters, partly because of significant insecticide saving and partly because the Bt seed was only 50–75 per cent more costly than conventional seed. (Pray *et al.* 2001).

In the USA, one study showed that insecticide cost savings were more or less balanced by higher seed prices, so that farmers' net gain from the use of Bt cotton was largely due to modest increases in yield (Frisvold *et al.* 2006). Another study failed to demonstrate any clear economic advantage of genetically modified (GM) cotton (Bt, herbicide-tolerant or stacked) over conventional varieties. Researchers in the US state of Georgia planted 13–16 popular cotton varieties (GM and conventional) at two experimental sites each year from 2001 to 2004. Basic treatment of the varieties (such as fertilization) was uniform, but insect and weed control for each variety was managed according to extension recommendations, applying herbicides and insecticides when economic threshold levels were reached. Costs of all inputs and their application were balanced against the value of the yields. The RR varieties provided the lowest returns, and there were no marked differences in returns between Bt, stacked and conventional varieties. 'When considered as a whole, no transgenic technology system provided greater returns than a nontransgenic system in any year or location' (Jost *et al.* 2008: 50). The authors propose that Georgia farmers' preference for transgenic technologies may be linked to savings in management time not accounted for in the experimental budgets.

The study indicates that Bt cotton may offer benefits to farm management that are difficult to quantify. It is interesting to compare this experience with that of RR soybeans in the USA, the most widely and rapidly adopted of all transgenic crops, which farmers have embraced more for the simplicity and flexibility it offers to crop management rather than for any yield gains or cost saving (Fernandez-Cornejo and McBride 2002). In South Africa, larger cotton farmers who can afford the requisite inputs appreciate the managerial freedom that Bt cotton allows them while for smallholders, who cannot afford to use many inputs, the use of Bt cotton lessens the labour demands of fetching water and applying pesticide with a backpack sprayer (Gouse *et al.* 2003).

There are additional problems in assessing the net benefits from the use of Bt cotton. In small-farm environments it is sometimes difficult to assign an appropriate value to household labour, which may be an important component of the costs of production. An additional problem in assessing the performance of a new technology such as Bt cotton is the possible concomitant changes that farmers may make in their crop management. In the case of Bt cotton, we are trying to assess the impact of the adoption of an insect-resistant variety in the midst of a complex set of continuously changing crop management practices. If farmers pay more for a new type of seed they may also invest more in other inputs. There seem to be cases where this happens for Bt cotton. Early adopters in China tended to use more fertilizer (Huang *et al.* 2002b), and Chinese farmers who buy higher price Bt cotton seed spend more on pesticides than those who use lower price Bt seed (Pemsl 2006). At least some Bt cotton growers in India have invested more in fertilizer, manure and field labour than their neighbours growing conventional varieties (Qaim *et al.* 2006; Narayanamoorthy and Kalamkar 2006).

Variability of impact

It is particularly important to understand how a new technology like Bt cotton affects smaller or more vulnerable farmers. Even in the same growing environment, the extent and nature of impact may differ between different types of farmer, depending on their capacities to deal with climatic risk, differences in crop management and access to resources, and the extent to which the technology is targeted to particular conditions.

In countries such as Argentina and South Africa, where both large and small farmers have access to the technology, we have seen that differences in resources and management practices between the two groups may lead to different types of impact, with smaller farmers more likely to benefit from yield gains while larger farmers take advantage of cost savings from reduced insecticide use. In countries where virtually all farmers are smallholders it is often more difficult to explore these types of differences. An analysis of early adoption of Bt cotton in China indicated that there were few differences in adoption rates by farm size (Huang *et al.* 2002b); higher income groups adopted the new technology more completely but lower income groups gained relatively more (Pray *et al.* 2001).

Bt cotton seed is an investment that farmers must make at the beginning of the season, without knowing how rainfall or pest populations will affect their crop. Such risks are more difficult to bear for resource-poor farmers. A study based on data from Karnataka showed that given the relatively high price of Bt cotton seed and the great variability in cotton yields under smallholder management, growers would be economically better off to invest in prophylactic insecticide treatment than to purchase Bt seed (Pemsl *et al.* 2004). The risk of financial loss with Bt was particularly high for farmers without irrigation, and a subsequent study among this group found that the majority had ceased to plant Bt cotton, in part because the yields were unacceptably low (Malkarnekar *et al.* 2005). A larger study across four Indian states showed generally better economic performance for Bt cotton but still found that wide differences in productivity and growing conditions meant that a significant minority of farmers suffered net losses with the new technology (Qaim *et al.* 2006).

Although much of the variability in the economic impact of Bt cotton can be explained by differences in crop management, access to resources and the relative prices of seed and other inputs, there are also several environmental and biological factors that contribute to the variable performance of the technology.

Farming is dependent on the weather, and the contribution of any technology is affected by climatic conditions. In some of the cases reported in the literature, the year of a particular survey was unusually dry, cotton yields were low, and the advantages offered by Bt cotton were relatively modest. In other cases, rainfall was at or above normal, yields (and insect populations) were high, and Bt cotton showed a more marked advantage. In some cases high rainfall not only induces more insect pressure but also makes chemical control less effective by washing away the insecticide. Farmers have always had to cope with this kind of variability, but because Bt cotton is a technology that requires an investment before the season begins it can represent an additional source of uncertainty for farmers, particularly in areas that are subject to significant climatic variation.

Bt cotton is of course only effective against a narrow range of insects, and even for these there are variations in its effectiveness. For instance, there appear to be significant differences in the expression of the Bt toxin in various parts of the plant, especially later in the season, depending on the particular variety (Chapter 3). Thus farmers must still scout for damage and be prepared to apply additional pest control measures. This is a particular problem in China, where there are many Bt varieties and some of the seed is produced by unapproved companies or where farmers save seed for use the next season. One study documents wide variation in Bt expression in Chinese cotton varieties (with nearly 60 per cent of the samples below standard). It shows that the higher priced (and presumably better quality) seed tended to have higher expression, and warns that this variability lowers farmers' confidence in being able to reduce pesticide applications (Pemsl *et al.* 2005). This may be one of the reasons why many Bt cotton growers in China still use very high levels of pesticide (Pemsl *et al.* 2005; Yang *et al.* 2005b). (For further discussion see Chapter 6.)

The Bt gene responsible for producing the toxin in a transgenic cotton variety is of course only one of the genes that determines the performance of the variety. It is thus important to consider the broader genetic background of these varieties. Much of the controversy surrounding the introduction of Bt cotton in India was concerned with the agronomic properties of the few varieties that were originally brought to market. These were based on conventional hybrids from the seed company (Mahyco) that had not been widely grown for several years. There were concerns that the varieties had particular deficiencies, such as susceptibility to wilt disease, and that farmers seeking an insect-resistant variety would also be getting one that had other deficiencies (Bambawale *et al.* 2004). There is some evidence that this was the case, which helps explain the disappointing experiences in the first years in certain parts of India, where several conventional commercial varieties were able to compete with the transgenic varieties, despite their susceptibility to bollworm.

The influence of genetic background is also a consideration when the Bt variety is simply transferred from one country to another, but experience has been varied. In South Africa, the first Bt cotton variety to be imported from the USA did not perform particularly well, but subsequent varieties (both Bt and conventional) offered significant agronomic advantages over local commercial varieties, even without considering the presence of the Bt gene. Indeed, the changes in both conventional and Bt varieties may help explain some of the variation in results reported in different impact studies (Hofs *et al.* 2006d).

Farmers must always face trade-offs when choosing varieties and the situation with Bt cotton is no different. A similar situation occurred in the USA when Bt cotton was first introduced; the only Bt varieties available to Alabama farmers were from neighbouring states that had longer growing seasons, but farmers had suffered such severe losses to tobacco budworms the previous season that they were willing to accept a variety of less than optimal maturity (Charles 2001).

Sustainability

Our farm-level analysis of the economic performance of Bt cotton cannot deal with the complex biological circumstances that determine long-term sustainability, but some of the most important factors deserve brief mention here, including effects on secondary pests, refuge management and the impact on varietal diversity.

Many new agricultural technologies have wider consequences than might be expected. Synergies between different technologies may offer broader benefits or require that a new practice is accompanied by other modifications. Changes consequent to the adoption of a new technology may lead to further challenges. The continued use of Bt varieties, and the concomitant changes in pest control practices, may have a number of implications. Chapter 3 provided evidence of additional positive impacts from the use of Bt cotton in some environments, including increased control of non-target insects by natural enemies that had previously been killed by bollworm insecticides, and the lessening of insecticide resistance in target insects. On the other hand, the elimination of spraying for bollworm can lead to the resurgence of secondary insects earlier controlled by the bollworm chemicals. A recent report that caused considerable comment, documenting the growing amount of insecticides used by Bt cotton farmers in China, can be partially explained by this need to control the resurgent mirid bug population (Wang *et al.* 2006).

An issue of particular importance for Bt cotton is the challenge of resistance management and the priority of ensuring that Bt cotton is managed in such a way that the development of resistance to the toxin is kept to a minimum. The effectiveness of many conventional insecticides has been reduced or negated as insects have developed resistance to the chemicals and the same process is possible for Bt cotton. In order to retard the emergence of such resistance, various refuge policies have been put in place that require the planting of a certain portion of the field in conventional cotton, or the planting of other crops that are hosts for the same insects (Chapter 3). As technologies such as Bt cotton become more widely used, the necessity of countering the insects' ability to develop resistance becomes more important. The widespread use of a technology often results in lower cost, which may lead to less discriminating use of the technology, increasing the dangers of resistance. One such example is the fact that the technology fees for Bt cotton are decreasing in the USA, and there is a growing tendency to market stacked varieties containing several traits. This could mean that the technology is planted in places where it is not needed, increasing the risk of developing resistance (NRC 2002).

Table 4.3 summarizes current refuge policies in the countries growing Bt cotton. China is the only country that does not have a refuge requirement. The reasoning behind this decision is that cotton in China is grown on very small plots (where a separate refuge would be difficult to manage) and these are close to plots of other crops (such as maize or soybeans) that are alternative hosts for the bollworm. Most refuge policies involve non-transgenic cotton, but Australia allows a range of other

Table 4.3 Resistance management for Bt cotton

Country	Requirements for refuge	Responsibility for monitoring
China	No refuge requirement	
India	Official requirement is 20% conventional cotton, to be planted surrounding the field	The requisite amount of conventional seed is sold with the Bt seed, but it is not clear who is supposed to monitor compliance
Argentina	Farmers must plant 20% conventional cotton, treated	The technology owner is supposed to monitor compliance, but inspection is irregular
Colombia	20% treated or 5% untreated	Monsanto conducts field visits to assess compliance
Mexico	20% treated or 5% untreated	Monsanto conducts field visits to assess compliance
South Africa	Refuge required. 5% untreated is the most common	Monsanto provides refuge seed to smallholders and monitors refuge seed purchase by large farmers
Australia	Several refuge options are available (for Bollgard II), including the use of conventional cotton, pigeonpea, sorghum and maize. Most common refuge is 5% pigeonpea, untreated	Audits are conducted by agents who sell the technology licence. Each farm is visited up to three times
USA	Several options (for Bollgard), including 5% untreated cotton; 20% treated cotton; 5% embedded (treated in the same way as rest of field). For Bollgard II, refuge areas of other susceptible crops are allowed in certain states	The technology owners are responsible for monitoring

Source: Country consultants.

susceptible crops to be used as refuges and the USA has recently approved the use of non-cotton refuges in certain parts of the country for the 'Bollgard II' technology.

Establishing a resistance management policy and enforcing it are, of course, two different issues. In many countries the owner or licensee of the technology is responsible for ensuring that the refuge policy is enforced. This may be done by making farmers sign agreements that oblige them to plant a refuge and by conducting on-farm inspections. The extent to which the industry carries out such inspections varies; it appears that Australia has a particularly rigorous inspection regime. In countries where such measures are difficult, the monitoring (and compliance) is less in evidence. India has dealt with the refuge challenge by requiring that the seed company provide the farmer with the requisite amount of non-transgenic seed when purchasing Bt cotton, but there are few resources for monitoring compliance. In Argentina, much of the Bt cotton planted is farmer-saved (or obtained from the black market) and refuge requirements are impossible to enforce in such circumstances.

Another concern related to the sustainability of transgenic crops is their potential effect on crop biodiversity. It is possible that a few transgenic varieties might dominate a nation's cropping patterns, thereby lowering the resilience provided by wider diversity. It is too early in the experience with Bt cotton to come to any conclusions about its impact in this regard. One way of examining the question is to look at the numbers of cotton varieties that are available. In some countries, particularly those without their own cotton breeding and seed industries, there is a tendency to rely on a few imported varieties, but this was often the case before the advent of transgenic cotton as well. Colombia and South Africa both rely on the same D&PL variety ('NuOpal') as the source of their transgenic varieties. In China and India, on the other hand, the availability of transgenes for cotton has made the seed market even more competitive, with a large number of varieties on the market.

An examination of the first eight years of transgenic cotton in the USA showed only a slight drop in the total number of varieties (conventional and transgenic) available, and as the area planted to transgenic cotton has increased so too have the number of varieties, so that the average area per transgenic cotton variety has remained fairly constant at about 53,000 ha (Traxler 2007). Although this figure is small in relation to the total area of transgenic cotton planted in the USA, it masks considerable concentration and dominance by relatively few varieties. In 2007, seven transgenic cotton varieties (all but one of them stacked), accounted for more than 52 per cent of the cotton area in the USA; in the Southeast states, one variety accounted for more than 58 per cent of the area and in the South Central states three varieties accounted for 51 per cent of area (AMS 2007).

More detailed examination of the distribution and parentage of cotton varieties would be required before drawing conclusions regarding biodiversity impacts. A study reviewing cotton in the USA in the 25 years preceding the release of transgenic cotton, based on an analysis of the parentage of varieties and their planted area, showed a decline in diversity. A significant investment in plant breeding during that period was counterbalanced by the dominance of a few popular varieties and the high degree of relatedness among many of the major varieties (Van Esbroeck *et al.* 1998). A subsequent study showed that the availability of transgenic cotton technology has improved the situation somewhat, mostly because of the considerable increase in plant breeding and release of new varieties, but the reliance on a relatively small pool of breeding lines remains an underlying threat to field diversity (Bowman *et al.* 2003).

Summary

It is impossible to provide a simple assessment of the field-level impact of a technology such as Bt cotton. Its introduction to a wide range of farming environments, through many different commercial cotton varieties and seed provision strategies, has yielded various results. Although the technology has proven generally successful in providing additional protection against several important cotton pests, the implications of this performance have been variable. In situations where farmers had used large amounts of insecticide to control these pests, there was usually a significant reduction in expenditure and often a modest increase in yield. In situations where fewer resources were normally devoted to insect control the major impact was often an increase in yield, as the Bt toxin provided extra protection. Such gains are welcome, although the net economic impact depended to a great extent on the cost of the technology, and in cases where this was high the financial gains were sometimes less than might have been expected. As with most agricultural technologies, the impact of Bt cotton is also affected by variations in local conditions (e.g. pest populations, weather) and by various tradeoffs (such as those implied by the choice of particular varieties or pest control regimes). Nevertheless, the balance of the experience in those countries that have had the chance to test Bt cotton is that farmers have favoured the technology, often enthusiastically, and rates of adoption have increased over time.

These general observations are also relevant for the experience of resource-poor farmers, but some additional concerns deserve attention. Although Bt cotton can help make up for inadequate pest control practices, in situations where poor cotton management or unfavourable climate result in low yields, the impact of this technology will be modest or variable. Although the technology provides in-built resistance against certain insects, this protection must be purchased before planting; the higher the price, the riskier the decision for a resource-poor farmer. In addition, the technology must be provided in cotton varieties that are well adapted to farmers' conditions, and those farmers must have enough information to allow them to choose the most appropriate seed. They must also know the capabilities and limitations of the technology and be able to adjust their management practices accordingly; Bt cotton can be a valuable component of a crop protection strategy, but it cannot substitute for the skills and knowledge required to address broader pest management challenges.

The impact of Bt cotton on the productivity of smallholders thus depends to a considerable extent on the conditions under which the technology is made available to them. The local seed industry must be able to offer appropriate cotton varieties, and this requires access to plant breeding capacity and a supportive intellectual property regime. The industry must be sufficiently competitive so that resource-poor farmers can afford the technology. The input delivery system must be competitive and transparent and farmers must have access to sufficient information about the products on offer. And farmers' ability to integrate Bt cotton into their pest control strategies requires access to good quality crop management information and experience. These conditions are determined by local agricultural institutions, and Chapter 5 looks at how those institutions have contributed to the recent experience with Bt cotton.

5 Transgenic cotton and institutional performance

Robert Tripp

This book emphasizes that the impact of an innovation such as Bt cotton should not be assessed simply in terms of yields or production costs but also with respect to the interactions with the institutions that govern farmers' access to the technology. This chapter reviews the literature and presents other relevant information on the major institutional consequences of the early years of Bt cotton production. The issues examined include: the effect on the seed and input industry, the role of intellectual property regimes, the organization of input delivery and farmers' access to information for managing the new technology.

The seed and input industry

Transgenic technology has changed the seed industry in a number of ways. A particularly important issue is the potential distinction between the technology owner and the seed company. Most private seed companies employ their own plant breeders to develop new varieties, or arrange to contract with public or private breeding organizations for access to new varieties or germplasm. But a corporation that develops transgenic technology does not necessarily have any seed production capability and thus must decide how to deliver its innovations to farmers. It may sell or license the technology to seed companies, or establish or buy its own seed production capacity.

Monsanto developed the original Bt cotton technology, but it entered into a licensing arrangement with the Delta & Pine Land Company (D&PL). The original agreement set a price for D&PL's transgenic cotton seed and D&PL agreed to return 70 per cent of this user fee to Monsanto (Charles 2001). Monsanto also acquired a smaller US cotton seed company (Stoneville) in 1997 but sold it again in 1999 when it attempted to acquire D&PL. That bid was not successful and Monsanto reacquired Stoneville in 2004. In late 2006 Monsanto announced that it was to acquire D&PL for $1.5 billion and agreed to relinquish its ownership of Stoneville, which it sold to Bayer Crop Science in 2007. Monsanto has also licensed its 'Bollgard' technology to other seed companies in the USA, and in 2003 Monsanto introduced 'Bollgard II' and began licensing it. In 2005 Dow AgroSciences introduced its 'Widestrike' Bt technology which is currently marketed only by PhytoGen Seed Company, which is owned by Dow.

When introducing Bt cotton to Mexico, Colombia, Argentina and South Africa the alliance between D&PL and Monsanto provided its own (imported) Bt cotton varieties, usually in partnerships or joint ventures with local firms for seed distribution. In Australia, before the introduction of Bt cotton, most of the cotton breeding was in the hands of the public Commonwealth Scientific and Industrial Research Organization (CSIRO) and seed of the public varieties was produced and marketed by Cotton Seed Distributors (CSD), a grower-owned organization. The introduction of the first Bt varieties saw D&PL gain a significant share of the Australian cotton seed market, but CSIRO obtained the transgenic technology under licence and began to produce its own Bt varieties (marketed by CSD) which soon became dominant. It is interesting to note that the strategy for diffusion of Bt cotton in Burkina Faso (planned to begin in 2009) involves the incorporation of Monsanto's 'Bollgard II' transgene in several locally adapted cotton varieties, rather than the importation of foreign germplasm.

In China, Bt cotton technology was developed and promoted by public sector research as well as by Monsanto and D&PL. The Biotechnology Research Center of the Chinese Academy of Agricultural Sciences (CAAS) developed and patented its own Bt gene. CAAS produced a number of cotton varieties containing this gene but there was no clear precedent for marketing and controlling such varieties directly through the public (provincial and county) seed companies that dominated the market at that time. CAAS therefore formed a joint venture with a real estate company, called Biocentury, to market the seed through contracts with provincial seed companies. CAAS subsequently developed other transgenes for cotton which were also marketed through Biocentury.

D&PL began testing transgenic cotton in China in 1995 (in partnership with CAAS) and in 1996 D&PL, Monsanto and another investor formed a joint venture with the provincial seed company in Hebei Province, called Jidai, to market D&PL cotton varieties (Pray *et al.* 2001). A similar joint venture was later established with the provincial seed company of Anhui Province (Andai). D&PL was not allowed access to any Chinese cotton germplasm to do its own breeding in China and so had to rely on varieties that it imported. Although the only legitimate Chinese Bt cotton varieties are those licensed through Biocentury or D&PL (and approved for use in particular provinces), much of the Bt cotton currently grown in China is either the legitimate varieties produced by unauthorized companies or unauthorized varieties incorporating the CAAS or D&PL genes (see Chapter 6).

Indian public sector research has been responsible for a wide range of successful cotton varieties and the development of the world's first cotton hybrids. When national policy changed in the mid-1980s to allow the growth of the private seed sector, a number of domestic companies emerged, most of which concentrated on the breeding and marketing of seed for crops that could be produced as hybrids, including cotton. When Monsanto sought a partner in India for its Bt cotton business it chose the Maharashtra Hybrid Seed Company (Mahyco), India's largest seed company. It first purchased a 26 per cent share in Mahyco and then formed a joint partnership called Mahyco Monsanto Biotech Limited (MMB). Monsanto transferred a US Bt cotton variety to Mahyco for use in its breeding program and the company produced Bt versions of three Mahyco cotton hybrids that had been on the market earlier. These were released in 2002, and in 2004 MMB began licensing the Bt cotton gene to other Indian seed companies who have used it to produce their own Bt cotton hybrids. In 2006, several Indian seed companies began marketing Bt cotton varieties based on transgenes from two other sources, Biocentury (China) and the Indian Institute of Technology (see Table 2.1). In addition, MMB began licensing the 'Bollgard II' technology to several Indian seed companies in 2006. The evidence to date indicates that the entry of Bt technology has not affected the competitiveness of the Indian cotton seed market, with more than a dozen companies defending significant shares of the market (Murugkar *et al.* 2007)

Table 5.1 provides a summary of the status of cotton seed industries in the eight countries growing Bt cotton in 2007. The table includes information on the availability of conventional cotton varieties as well as transgenic varieties. In many countries official statistics are not available and some of the figures in the table are based on the best estimates of local observers. Nevertheless, the table provides a useful picture of the variability in Bt cotton seed provision in the countries where the crop is legally grown. In China and India the availability of various insect resistance transgenes has resulted in the conversion of many conventional varieties and the development of new transgenic ones. In India most of the major cotton seed companies have acquired access to transgenic technology and are using it to compete for market share; although conventional varieties are still sold, most companies are now concentrating on transgenic varieties. The situation in China is more complicated and poorly regulated markets have allowed a proliferation of legitimate and illegitimate seed producers marketing transgenic varieties. In Argentina, Colombia, Mexico and South Africa, the seed markets are much smaller and have traditionally included only a few companies. The market for transgenic cotton is monopolized by D&PL in these countries; although a few other companies sell seed of conventional varieties, D&PL now often controls those markets as well. In Australia, the new technology initially allowed D&PL to gain a significant share of the market, but once CSD acquired the technology its local plant breeding capacities allowed it to reassert its dominance in the market. In the USA, the licensing of the technology has allowed a number of seed companies to market transgenic varieties. Although D&PL maintains a large share of the market for varieties containing the 'Bollgard' gene, the market for 'Bollgard II' varieties includes a wider range of companies. For all cotton seed marketed in the USA, D&PL accounted for nearly 43 per cent of the acreage in 2007; the major competitors were Bayer CropScience (29 per cent) and Stoneville (15 per cent) (AMS 2007).

Intellectual property protection and the control of seed markets

Because most seed can be easily reproduced, seed companies are usually concerned about the possible appropriation of their varieties. As discussed in Chapter 1, there

Table 5.1 Cotton technology for insect resistance, seed companies and varieties (2007)

Country	Insect-resistance transgenes	Number of seed companies with access to transgene	Approx. number of varieties with this transgene (in single or stacked versions)	Market share of top company for this transgene (%)	Number of companies selling conventional cotton seed (and number of varieties)
China[1]	*cry1Ac*	2	3	N/A[2]	Many
	cry1A/CpTI	>20	6	N/A	companies
	cry1A	>20	53	N/A	(unknown
	cry1Ac/API	1	2	100	number of varieties)
India	*cry1Ac*	20	100	20	300+
	cry1Ac/cry2Ab	5	23	40	companies
	cry1A (China)	3	6	95	(600+
	cry1Ac(event 1)	1	8	100	varieties)
Argentina	*cry1Ac*	1	3	100 (D&PL)	2 companies (4 varieties)
Colombia	*cry1Ac*	1	2	100 (D&PL)	2 companies (8 varieties)
Mexico	*cry1Ac*	1	4	100 (D&PL)	2 companies (13 varieties)
South Africa	*cry1Ac*	1	5	100 (D&PL)	2 companies (2 varieties)
Australia	*cry1Ac/cry2Ab*	2	9	90 (CSD)	2 companies (9 varieties)
USA[3]	*cry1Ac*	5	21	89 (D&PL)	6
	cry1Ac/cry2Ab	9	49	39 (Bayer)	companies
	cry1Ac/cry1F	1	6	100 (Phytogen)	(16 varieties)

Source: Country consultants; estimates based on most reliable national data.

Notes
1   China estimates are for 2006; numbers of transgenic varieties are those officially registered.
2   N/A = information not available.
3   USA is for upland cotton only, based on data from AMS (Agricultural Marketing Service) 2007.

are three major concerns: the multiplication and sale of the variety by another company; the use of the variety by the breeding program of another company to produce a competing variety; and farmers' use of seed saved from the previous harvest. It is often impossible to limit all of these uses of a company's variety, but in the case of transgenic crops, with their high research investments, companies are eager to

Box 5.1 Transgenic crop varieties and intellectual property rights

There are a number of mechanisms that can be used to control access to transgenic crop varieties and provide intellectual property protection. Most of these mechanisms may also be used for conventional plant varieties.

Patents

The field of biotechnology is sufficiently new and unique that the applications and limitations of patent law are still being debated. For genetically modified crops, an obvious place to start is the transgene itself, but even here there are complications. Some countries do not recognize patents for genes. Even when gene patents are allowed, a transgenic crop offers significant challenges. In the first place, there may be distinct versions of the functional (e.g. insecticidal) gene. In addition, the functional gene must be combined with several other genes (in a 'construct') in order to perform in the plant, offering further possibilities for claims of innovation and rights to protection. Finally, the methods used for inserting the gene construct and regenerating viable plants are also the subject of patents. Patents on genes or constructs need to be distinguished from patents on plant varieties (see following text).

Plant variety protection

Plant varieties offer peculiar challenges to conventional patents and hence a system of 'plant variety protection' (PVP) was devised in the 1960s, well before the advent of biotechnology. All industrialized countries and a growing number of developing countries have established PVP systems (in part because all members of the World Trade Organization must have a PVP system, or its equivalent, in place by 2013). Many countries are members of UPOV (Union for the Protection of New Varieties of Plants) under one of its two major conventions (1978 and 1991). The details of PVP systems vary somewhat, but they all offer a plant breeder (public or private) the opportunity to protect a new variety for a period of 15–20 years. This protection allows the breeder to determine who can produce and sell seed of the variety. In some cases (as in the UPOV 1991 Convention) it can also prohibit farmers from saving seed for reuse. Although PVP systems may prohibit rival breeders from marketing a variety that is only slightly different ('essentially derived') from the protected variety, there are usually no restrictions on using the protected variety in a breeding program. A few countries (notably the USA) also recognize plant variety patents, which offer stricter control than PVP and effectively prohibit the use of the protected variety by other breeders.

Purchase agreements

An additional method that is sometimes used to prohibit farmer seed saving is purchase agreements, similar to those used for computer software. By opening the seed bag the purchaser agrees that the harvest will not be used or sold as seed.

Hybrids

A number of crop varieties may be produced as hybrid seed. Although the term hybrid may be used to simply denominate a cross between two varieties, a hybrid in this case is the product of a cross between two or more inbred lines which exhibits a yield advantage in hybrid vigour. Second-generation hybrid seed loses some of its yield potential, which discourages seed saving. In addition, the inbred parents are a form of trade secret which keeps competing companies from producing the same hybrid variety.

Seed laws

In addition to intellectual property right (IPR) instruments such as patents and PVP, there are other legal mechanisms for helping control the unauthorized use of plant varieties. National seed laws define *variety release procedures* that determine what varieties may be grown and *seed quality and certification standards* that regulate the type of seed that can be sold. In countries that have mandatory variety release regulations, no variety (transgenic or conventional) can be brought to market without being characterized and passing performance tests. Where mandatory seed certification is in place, a breeder can designate who has access to authorized source seed of a variety. This limits the possibilities for misappropriation of a variety by a competing company.

Source: World Bank 2006.

establish as much control as possible. The standard legal mechanisms available to the companies include intellectual property right (IPR) instruments [patents and plant variety protection (PVP)] and seed laws, and all of these mechanisms can be used to limit the use of Bt cotton seed. Box 5.1 outlines the major options for protecting seed from use by other companies' breeding programs, multiplication and sale by unauthorized seed companies, and reuse by farmers. Table 5.2 summarizes the status of gene patents, PVP legislation and laws affecting farmer seed saving in the countries that have been growing Bt cotton.

Although the use of gene patents has been one of the most controversial issues in the debate about agricultural biotechnology, such patents have played a variable role in the early life of Bt cotton. As Box 5.1 explains, there are various ways of protecting biotechnology innovations. Patents have been most important for

Table 5.2 Intellectual property rights and transgenic cotton

Country	Gene patents	Plant variety protection	Farmer seed saving
China	Transgenes can be patented. The *cry 1Ac* gene is not patented in China but *cry1A* is patented by CAAS	PVP under UPOV 1978 since 2000, but until recently cotton was not covered by PVP	Farmer seed saving is allowed for all cotton varieties
India	Patent law has been recently revised but not clear whether this will cover transgenes. No transgenes currently patented	New Plant Variety Protection and Farmers' Rights Act allows PVP; first certificates expected to be granted in 2009	Farmer seed saving is allowed for all cotton varieties (but note that majority are hybrids and seed is not saved)
Argentina	Transgenes can be patented	PVP under UPOV 1978 in force	Farmer seed saving is allowed but purchase agreements for Bt cotton prohibit seed saving. (These contracts are poorly enforced and the majority of Bt cotton is farm-saved or acquired from other farmers.)
Colombia	Genes cannot be patented but genetically modified organisms may be patented	PVP under UPOV 1978 in force since 1995	Farmers may save conventional cotton seed, but must seek permission. Farmers are not permitted to save seed of transgenic crop varieties
Mexico	Transgenes can be patented	PVP under UPOV 1978	Farmer seed saving is allowed but purchase agreements for Bt cotton prohibit seed saving
South Africa	Transgenes can be patented	PVP under UPOV 1978	Seed law allows conventional and transgenic seed to be saved, but Monsanto contract for transgenic cotton prohibits seed saving unless farmer pays the technology fee

Table 5.2 (Continued)

Country	Gene patents	Plant variety protection	Farmer seed saving
Australia	Transgenes can be patented	PVP under UPOV 1991	Plant variety protection prohibits farmers from saving seed of transgenic varieties
USA	Transgenes can be patented	PVP under UPOV 1991. Plant variety patents also used	Plant variety protection and user agreements prohibit farmers from saving seed of transgenic varieties

Source: Country consultants.

allowing the technology owners to keep their innovations from competitors. The relevant gene patents are recognized for Bt cotton in the USA and Australia and these are used to control technology licensing to other companies. Monsanto has also acquired patents for the Bt gene used in domestically marketed transgenic cotton in Argentina, although it has not licensed the gene to domestic companies. India's patent system has recently been reformed, but at the time of the introduction of Bt cotton it was not possible to patent plant genes. Despite the absence of any patents, MMB is able to license its Bt cotton genes to other seed companies because it owns the biosafety data required for variety approval and so in effect licenses the use of this data to its partners. In China, Monsanto acquired patents for some of its technology, but not for the Bt gene; CAAS, on the other hand, has patents for its two transgenic cotton constructs.

The effectiveness of the patent system in controlling use of Bt technology depends on enforcement capacity. Despite the fact that the technology is patented in Argentina, the majority of Bt cotton seed is farm-saved or acquired from other farmers, although there is no evidence of unauthorized seed companies marketing Bt cotton. China probably provides the best example of how lack of patent enforcement has contributed to (but is not the only reason for) the emergence of many unauthorized seed producers that market Bt cotton varieties. An analysis of Bt cotton varieties planted by farmers between 1999 and 2001 showed that more than 60 per cent of the purchased seed was from unauthorized sources, including copies of legal varieties, unapproved varieties and seed sold from various public seed sources such as extension stations (Hu *et al.* 2006). (See Chapter 6 for a more recent analysis.)

The major controversy involving the use of Bt cotton technology in India had its origin even before the Monsanto varieties were released in 2002. Navbharat, a small seed company in Gujarat, began marketing a cotton variety ('Navbharat 151') which was advertised as 'insect-resistant', but did not claim to be transgenic. It was not until 2001 when the variety withstood a particularly severe incidence of bollworm that suspicions were raised. The seed was tested and found to contain the Bt transgene. The government confiscated all Navbharat seed on the market (and threatened to destroy the standing crop in farmers' fields). The company's breeder claimed that the transgene must have appeared in his plots by accident, but most observers suspect that he had acquired some Bt cotton seed from another country, incorporated it in his breeding program, and quietly beat Monsanto to the market. He has been variously vilified for piracy and celebrated as the Robin Hood of biotechnology. Because the technology is not patented in India, the legal case against the company is based on violation of biosafety law [marketing unauthorized genetically modified (GM) seed]. Although this particular variety was eliminated, other illegal Bt cotton varieties appeared to compete with the authorized varieties in several Indian states and gained considerable popularity (Herring 2007; Jayaraman 2004b; Murugkar *et al.* 2007). (Chapter 7 provides an update on the use of illegal Bt cotton varieties in Gujarat.)

In countries where gene patents are not permitted, or where they are poorly enforced, a PVP system can offer control over the illegal multiplication and sale of a company's varieties. PVP allows a breeder to designate who is authorized to produce seed of a variety. China established a PVP system in 1999 but it did not include cotton in the original list of eligible crops, so none of the first Bt cotton varieties was eligible for this protection. (Cotton has recently been included within the Chinese PVP system.) India spent a long time debating and formulating a Plant Varieties and Farmers' Rights Act and implementation of the Act began in 2006. Even before the arrival of Bt cotton the seed industry suffered from problems of piracy. Several major companies complained that their most popular (non-transgenic) cotton varieties were regularly marketed (under different names) by small, fly-by-night firms. The new PVP legislation allows seed companies to take such competitors to court. It does not, however, keep farmers from saving seed of protected varieties (even of transgenic cotton), because the law recognizes farmers' rights to save seed.

A biological method for limiting seed saving which is relevant to Indian cotton is the use of hybrid technology. Farmers who grow hybrids usually buy fresh seed each season. Although hybrid technology is widely used for many field crops, its application to cotton has been limited by the very high labour requirements for hybrid cotton seed production. India was the first country to develop the technology and is the only country with a significant area in hybrid cotton (currently accounting for about two-thirds of cotton area), although hybrid cotton use is increasing in China. If a company is able to protect the parent inbreds in its seed multiplication plots, hybrid technology also functions as a type of trade secret that keeps other companies from copying a variety. However, such protection of seed production plots has proven difficult in India, leading to the problems of commercial theft described earlier (which can now be addressed by the new PVP law). All of the Bt cotton varieties sold in India are hybrids, including those made available to the northern states of Punjab and Haryana, which have traditionally favoured non-hybrid cotton varieties. This growing reliance on hybrids significantly limits the incentives for farmer seed saving. However, Indian public research is currently developing non-hybrid Bt cotton varieties; current Indian law would not stand in the way of farmers saving and reusing this seed, but the

PVP legislation would allow the public breeders to designate who was authorized to undertake commercial seed production of these varieties.

The PVP laws of many countries permit farmer seed saving, although there are often provisions that limit this to seed for on-farm use rather than for sale. There are, however, a number of ways of further restricting seed saving. One common method is the use of commercial contracts; the farmer may sign an agreement, or the seed may be sold with a legal notice regarding grower obligations that are in force once the package is opened. Once again, enforcement is the key. In Argentina, the seed distributor required farmers to sign a purchase agreement that prohibited seed saving, but they have had trouble enforcing this (Qaim and de Janvry 2003). Enforcing such agreements is easier when there is control over output marketing as well. In Mexico, farmers sign agreements prohibiting seed saving and obliging them to deliver their harvest to designated ginneries, where the disposal of cotton seed can be controlled (Traxler and Godoy-Avila 2004). In the USA, Monsanto has been particularly aggressive in pursuing violations, including the establishment of a telephone hotline where suspicious behaviour can be reported. The company has pursued several cases in court and in one instance a Tennessee farmer was fined nearly three million dollars and given a four-month jail sentence for 'saving' several tons of GM soybean and cotton seed.

Seed laws (which have been in place in many countries for a long time) provide another mechanism for controlling the unauthorized use of transgenic crop varieties. Table 5.3 summarizes seed laws in the Bt cotton-growing countries. These laws define which varieties and what type of seed can be sold. In India, private companies can market their own varieties without any official testing procedure (although transgenic varieties require testing by the relevant state and federal biosafety authorities). A new seed law is being debated that would require all field crop varieties to pass official performance tests before being allowed in the market. This would provide a mechanism for helping control the underground seed market, because only approved varieties could be sold. In countries where seed certification is mandatory, seed must be inspected by a third-party regulator during and after the multiplication process. In these cases, the inspection includes verification of the origin of the variety, and germplasm from unapproved sources is not permitted. Unlike PVP, which requires that the owner of the variety identify instances of misappropriation and bring the violator to court, seed laws are enforced by the state, so a well-managed system of registration and point-of-sale inspection can eliminate many instances of inappropriate seed marketing. But if the state does not invest in enforcement, then the seed laws do not perform their function. China has variety release regulations (any cotton variety offered for sale must be officially approved) and a licensing system for seed producers and traders, and basic enforcement of these laws would help control the illicit trade in Bt cotton seed.

Although biosafety regulations are necessary to control the deployment of transgenes and to ensure that they are being used safely, it should be clear that these regulations are not appropriate instruments for regulating seed markets or providing property rights for seed companies. Patent systems, PVP and seed laws are better suited to protecting seed companies from unwarranted competition.

Table 5.3 Seed regulations in countries growing transgenic cotton

Country	Seed certification	Variety testing
China	No requirement for seed certification	Variety testing and approval is carried out at the provincial level, but variable enforcement
India	Most states have seed certification agencies but certification is not mandatory and the majority of private sector seed is not certified	Private crop varieties do not have to pass agronomic tests before being marketed, but a new Seed Law is being debated that would make such tests mandatory for all new varieties
Argentina	Domestically produced seed must be certified, unless there is a shortage	Cotton Committee of National Seed Institute tests and approves new cotton varieties
Colombia	Domestically produced cotton seed is certified	New cotton varieties must pass performance tests before being released
Mexico	Seed certification is voluntary	New crop varieties are tested and approved by government research agency
South Africa	Seed certification is voluntary	No performance tests required for variety release
Australia	Seed must be certified	No performance tests required for variety release
USA	Seed certification is voluntary and most cotton seed is not certified	No performance tests required for variety release

Source: Country consultants.

Very strict PVP systems can also control farmer seed saving, but most developing countries recognize that controls on farmer seed saving are politically unwise and impossible to enforce.

The challenge is to devise institutions that reward technological innovation and protect a company's investment, while at the same time allowing widespread access to seed and guarding against monopolization of the technology. The balance is a fine one. There is very legitimate concern about the 'patent thicket' that restricts access to basic elements of biotechnology. But unrestricted use and multiplication of something like Bt cotton is not the answer either. High-priced seed limits access by farmers with few resources, but low-priced, poorly controlled seed brings its own problems. Hu *et al.* (2006) have described the lack of incentives for further technology development in China due to the inability to enforce any type of property rights for transgenic cotton. The proliferation of seed types whose identity is unknown is not only a disincentive to further innovation but also limits farmers' ability to make wise choices and to learn from farming experience. Resource-poor farmers are often most affected in such circumstances. In the case of Bt cotton, the spread of varieties with inadequate expression of the toxin can also threaten the very sustainability of the technology (see Chapter 3).

The answer is not to be found in comprehensive patenting regimes or the most restrictive forms of PVP, but rather in identifying acceptable compromises at the national level that provide sufficient incentives for technology development and a transparent seed market, on the one hand, but provide opportunities for the development of public and private research and the emergence of a diverse domestic seed industry that can address the needs of all farmers, on the other.

Input delivery

Chapter 2 discussed the importance of input provision for cotton farmers and described some of the ways that this is managed, including private input dealers, tied contracts with ginneries, parastatal organizations and farmer cooperatives or associations. The effectiveness of input provision, and the extent to which farmers are able to understand and take advantage of the inputs that are on offer, depends to some extent on the nature of the input industries themselves.

We have seen that there are some significant differences in markets for Bt cotton seed. In South Africa, Colombia, Argentina and Mexico there is only one company that provides transgenic cotton seed. The markets for Bt cotton seed in Australia, and particularly in the USA, are more diversified. In India and China the situation is much more complex; in both countries there are a number of legitimate companies supplying different varieties of Bt cotton, and this type of choice and competition is certainly a positive factor. On the other hand, there is also a significant amount of unauthorized and illegal production and sale of Bt cotton seed that brings some confusion and uncertainty to the market.

The nature of the pesticide industry is also relevant to our interest in Bt cotton, and again there is considerable variability. In many countries a few major chemical companies dominate the scene with branded products, but India and China provide a significant contrast. Indian policy in support of small business development has favoured small pesticide formulators. Local chemical companies that produce active ingredients must supply half their production to local formulators, and international companies selling in India must supply information about their products; until recently patents were only admissible for processes and not products, so local manufacture of products based on molecules patented elsewhere has been common. The large number of formulators leads to a profusion of different brands for the same chemical and, despite the fact that state regulatory agencies monitor the market, there are concerns about the quality of many of the products on sale (Matthews 1993). In China pesticide manufacture is also regulated at the provincial level and a plethora of products (often mixtures of two or more active ingredients) are available from a range of enterprises. A survey of 150 farmers in Shandong Province recorded 448 different pesticide products (the vast majority insecticides) used in Bt cotton fields; many were not officially registered and in 15 per cent of the cases the researchers were unable to even identify the active ingredients (Pemsl 2006). One of the problems is that until mid-2008 pesticide companies were not required to list the active ingredient(s) in pesticides, and farmers faced a pesticide market that included thousands of trade names (Anon. 2008a).

In the India and China cases, farmers obtain their seed and pesticides through input dealers of various types and sizes. Many of the dealers are small and poorly trained and may not be well qualified to manage inputs or offer advice to farmers. Matthews (1993) cites the case of one large town in coastal Andhra Pradesh where 250 pesticide retailers are in business. Many input sellers in rural China run very small operations and some are itinerant, going from village to village (see Chapter 6).

In some other cases, Bt cotton farmers belong to associations that arrange credit and provide advice on inputs. In Mexico, smallholder (*ejidatario*) farmers growing Bt cotton are organized in groups (which are in turn part of associations); a technician is assigned to each group and farmers apparently defer to his judgment on the selection of inputs (Traxler *et al.* 2003). In Colombia, cotton farmers must be affiliated to a growers' association and usually pay the fees of a private extension agent who approves their choice of inputs (see Chapter 8).

In South Africa, the smallholder Bt cotton growers in Makhatini Flats have received much attention in the literature. They are part of a 'show-piece' smallholder development scheme (Thirtle *et al.* 2003) and the area has a history of government credit programs for cotton, most of which have been poorly administered (Witt *et al.* 2006). Such programs offer few opportunities for farmers to choose inputs or learn from experience. (See Chapter 9.)

The way in which inputs are made available has implications for cotton farmers' understanding of, and control over, Bt technology. Farmers not only need to be able to recognize and select the most appropriate cotton variety but they also need to understand something about the nature of the Bt gene and how it can contribute to pest management strategies.

Farmers' access to information

Variety choice may be difficult, requiring the consideration of various trade-offs. We saw in Chapter 2 that there is no such thing as a perfect variety, and farmers must select those that come closest to their requirements. Information on variety characteristics may be available from extension agents, the commercial input system or the advice of other farmers. It is often the case that farmers rely heavily on the experience of their neighbours rather than formal sources of information, and the same pattern may hold true in the case of Bt cotton. A study in Andhra Pradesh found that 46 per cent of farmers claimed to have based their decision to purchase seed of Bt cotton on information obtained from other farmers while only 14 per cent relied on input dealers and 3 per cent on extension agents (Dev and Rao 2006).

A long-term study that follows decision making on Bt cotton in Andhra Pradesh has found that although farmers rely on information from each other in their choice of cotton varieties, the process is subject to fads and rumours rather than the product of careful experimentation, resulting in large shifts in the popularity of individual varieties from one season to the next (Stone 2007). The study shows that farmers are often unable to describe basic characteristics (such as maturity or moisture requirements) for the varieties that they have purchased. Of the villages in the survey, the one that seems to show more considered choice of cotton varieties is composed of settlers from another region who have somewhat higher levels of education and have been in the vanguard of innovations in commercial farming. Farmers in this village are also somewhat more likely to plant more than one variety, which is taken as evidence of experimentation. However, the mere act of planting several varieties does not necessarily indicate careful experimentation. A study of Bt cotton growers in Gujarat also examines the extent to which farmers grow more than one variety and finds sufficient diversity to argue that farmers are indeed experimenting (Roy *et al.* 2007). But the use of multiple cotton varieties is almost exactly the same in the Andhra Pradesh and Gujarat cases (slightly more than half and a quarter of farmers plant one or two varieties, respectively, and the remainder plant more than two). The issue of farmer experimentation with Bt varieties is examined in more detail in Chapter 7.

Farmers may follow the crowd or do their own investigation when an innovation such as Bt cotton appears. The Gujarat case provides an interesting example, as this was where the illegal Bt varieties first appeared in India and farmers had a chance to gain experience with them. Even after the release of the legal varieties, many farmers maintained loyalty to the underground varieties. It is difficult to establish firm evidence, but there is some indication that the early legal Bt varieties were not necessarily as well adapted to some local conditions as the illegal varieties (Roy *et al.* 2007). Prices of the illegal varieties were generally lower as well. On the other hand, a survey done in Gujarat indicated that the legal varieties provided higher gross margins for their growers, although the variability in input use and management skills among survey farmers makes it difficult to draw firm conclusions (Morse *et al.* 2005). (Further examination of legal and illegal varieties in Gujarat is provided in Chapter 7.)

Not only do farmers have to choose between conventional and Bt varieties, they also need to know the implications of their choice for pest management practices. We saw in Chapter 4 that there is some evidence to indicate that larger, more commercialized cotton farmers (in industrialized countries and elsewhere) tended to benefit from Bt cotton principally through savings in pesticide expenditure, while other farmers benefit more from yield gains. We have also seen that the complicated markets for insecticides (and the lack of extension advice) in both China and India surely contribute to misuse of the chemicals.

Differences in pest control practices are not only due to differences in farmer income or national input markets. Qaim (2003) shows that better educated farmers in India make fewer and more selective applications of pesticide. In Argentina, on the other hand, where many farmers under-invest in inputs, more education is correlated with higher pesticide use (Qaim and de Janvry 2005). Farmer knowledge is certainly a crucial element in the ability to use pesticides properly or to take best advantage of an innovation such as Bt cotton. It appears that some South African smallholders believed that Bt cotton provided protection against other insects besides bollworms and may have mistakenly changed their use of insecticides accordingly (Bennett *et al.* 2006; Hofs *et al.* 2006b). A study in South Africa showed that smallholders using conventional varieties sprayed more frequently than did farmers using Bt cotton, but the latter applied significantly higher doses of chemicals (Hofs *et al.* 2006b).

Farmers are generally badly served by the guidance made available to them through commercial pesticide markets and often have to contend with confusing or deceptive information. On the other hand, there are occasionally instances when farmers may be able to deceive the output market. The growing interest in organic cotton is at odds with any attempt to promote Bt cotton, as the rules of organic production do not allow the use of any transgenic seed. Nevertheless, it would appear that some Indian farmers participating in organic cotton production find it worthwhile to use Bt varieties, at least until a more rigorous monitoring system is put in place (Singh 2006; Roy *et al.* 2007). Similarly, the refuge management rules imposed on seed companies, which they are supposed to enforce, may be ignored by farmers, either because of lack of understanding or insufficient follow-up. In Andhra Pradesh, Stone (2004) found that even many seed dealers were unable to explain the rationale for the small packets of refuge seed they were obliged to sell along with the Bt cotton seed.

The imperfect nature of pesticide markets and farmer insect control practices, and the evidence that farmers have not been as efficient as they might be in taking advantage of Bt varieties, raises some larger questions. Pemsl (2006) addresses this problem by asking what counterfactual should be adopted in analysing the impact of Bt cotton. The contribution that Bt cotton has made to lowering insecticide use must be balanced against the recognition that this 'improvement' has generally taken place in the context of an expensive, badly managed, and hazardous set of pest control practices. The fact that Bt cotton has provided a temporary respite from this unacceptable situation should not allow us to believe that this (or similar quick fixes) will be enough to encourage safe and effective insect control in cotton in developing countries.

It is worth asking to what extent Bt cotton has been incorporated in efforts that promote integrated pest control strategies for smallholders. There has been considerable work exploring how insect-resistant GM crops can be used within an IPM framework to achieve more sustainable crop protection (Romeis *et al.* 2008). There are a few examples of such interest in China and India. There is government support for programs in insecticide resistance management (IRM) in several Indian states. The IRM programs provide guidance to farmers on how to manage insecticides to lower the probability of insects developing resistance to the chemicals, and this is being extended to include resistance to Bt (which is unlikely to be addressed by an ineffective refuge policy) (Kranthi *et al.* 2004). There is also some government support for IPM in cotton and there is evidence that the use of Bt cotton can be a useful compliment to this strategy (Bambawale *et al.* 2004). Similarly, there is evidence from China that Bt cotton can be effectively combined with other elements of an IPM program, where farmers are trained through farmer field schools (Yang *et al.* 2005a). But none of these efforts is being promoted (or evaluated) on a large enough scale, and introducing this type of knowledge and management skills to smallholders is a challenge that requires significant investment.

The level of attention necessary to reduce and rationalize pesticide use is illustrated by the fact that most Australian and US cotton farmers now depend on private consultants for their pest management decisions (Luttrell *et al.* 1994). A description of the crop scouting services employed by a 'small' farm of about 400 ha in Mississippi growing Bt cotton provides an example of the resources required. A consultant, who has a degree in entomology, makes frequent visits to the farmer's field, collects samples of the insects present in each part of the field, enters the data on a hand-held computer, prepares an analysis and provides information on insect levels and recommendations for control to the farmer (Helferich 2007).

Summary

Adequate institutions are required to support farmers' use of a new technology such as Bt cotton. The performance of such institutions determines the extent to which small farmers are able to gain access to, and gain some control over, the technology.

Transgenic technology must be incorporated into plant varieties well adapted to local conditions and this implies that plant breeding capacity must be available in the local public or private sector. Small countries with correspondingly limited seed markets face particular challenges and the experience to date with Bt cotton is that such countries may have to rely, at least initially, on varieties provided from elsewhere. Countries without a strong local seed industry will be less able to take advantage of Bt cotton and adapt it to local circumstances.

Competition among seed companies is important. In countries with large markets, technology owners have licensed the transgenes to various seed companies who incorporate them in their own varieties. The ability to license technology and maintain a competitive seed market depends on the existence of some type of intellectual property protection mechanisms or other regulation or legislation that prohibits unauthorized appropriation of the technology. There is a delicate balance, however, between providing enough protection so that innovators have adequate incentives and seed producers are not subject to unfair competition; and ensuring that the advantages of the initial technology provider are not converted into a monopoly.

Issues of regulation and competition are also relevant for input delivery. Input supply is particularly important for cotton farmers, and even though Bt technology may lower the use of insecticides, most cotton farmers still depend on external suppliers for a range of inputs. Such supply may be organized through the state, the private sector or various types of producer association. In all cases, adequate transparency and choice are required so that farmers have a range of options and opportunities to learn from experience in order to improve their production efficiency. The evidence to date indicates that the introduction of Bt cotton has not generally been accompanied by improvements in the provision of inputs for cotton farmers.

The performance of the seed sector, the adequacy of legal and regulatory systems, and the organization of input delivery mechanisms have an impact on the quality of information available to farmers. We have seen that cotton pest management is an exceptionally complex challenge and even though innovations such as transgenic insect resistance can make an important contribution, cotton farmers still need both opportunities to strengthen their own capacities and access to reliable advice. Again, there is little evidence that the initial introduction of Bt cotton has been accompanied by significant improvements on these fronts.

As we have seen, there are significant differences among the countries that use Bt cotton, and the rapidly growing use of the technology has had important interactions with local institutions. As this book is most concerned with the impact of transgenic cotton on smallholders, we must look in greater detail at the most recent developments in those countries where smallholders have experience with Bt cotton.

The following chapters (6–9) provide a summary of the recent experiences of smallholders growing Bt cotton in China, India, Colombia and South Africa. They provide further evidence of the role of local institutions in determining the effectiveness of new technology.

6 Farmers' seed and pest control management for Bt cotton in China

Jikun Huang, Ruijian Chen, Jianwei Mi, Ruifa Hu and Ellie Osir

Introduction

China's biotechnology program has grown into the largest such initiative in the developing world. A study by the Center for Chinese Agricultural Policy (CCAP) shows that the government's annual spending on agricultural biotechnology reached 1.65 billion yuan in 2004 (equivalent to US $199 million). The Chinese program has generated a wide array of new technologies. Genetically modified (GM) varieties of more than 20 crops have been approved for environmental release and/or field trials. By the end of 2006, China's Biosafety Committee (CBC) received more than 1500 applications and approved 1024 of these for trials or commercialization. Among this growing range of crops and technologies, *Bacillus thuringiensis* (Bt) cotton is the most prominent example.

Farmers were introduced to Bt cotton varieties in 1997, some containing a transgene developed by the Chinese Academy of Agricultural Sciences (CAAS) and others containing Monsanto's transgene. Bt cotton spread rapidly in Hebei, Shandong and Henan, in China's northern cotton belt. By 2001, it accounted for 99 per cent of the cotton area in Hebei and 97 per cent in Shandong. In Henan it covered 90 per cent of the cotton area by 2005. Bt cotton was introduced in 1998 in the southern provinces of Anhui and Jiangsu. By 2007, Bt cotton accounted for 85 per cent of total cotton area in Anhui and 92 per cent in Jiangsu. There are also small amounts of Bt cotton planted elsewhere including Xinjiang in the West where bollworm is not a serious problem and Bt cotton is not recommended. By 2007, Bt cotton cultivation had expanded to 3.8 million ha, accounting for about 69 per cent of cotton area. The cotton holdings in China are very small; a survey by CCAP in 2007 found the average size of cotton farms (including cotton and non-cotton land) was only 0.75, 0.67 and 0.50 ha in Shandong, Henan and Hebei, respectively. It is estimated that more than 7 million smallholder farmers grew Bt cotton in 2007 (Figure 6.1).

Previous studies have shown that Bt cotton has significantly raised cotton productivity and farmers' income. Farm-level surveys in northern China show that the adoption of Bt cotton has raised cotton yields and allowed farmers to reduce their insecticide use (Huang *et al.* 2002c, 2004). Moreover, farmers planting Bt

Figure 6.1 Principal cotton-growing provinces of China

cotton report fewer incidences of poisoning from insecticide applications (Huang *et al.* 2002c; Hossain *et al.* 2004).

Despite these large gains from Bt cotton, there are questions regarding farmers' ability to take full advantage of the technology. China's seed industry is growing and diversifying, and an increasing number of Bt cotton varieties are available, but it is not clear if the seed market is sufficiently transparent and well regulated to provide farmers with enough information about the products on offer. How do seed markets operate in China and how do they affect farmers' selection of Bt cotton varieties? Are there differences in the quality and performance of seed from different sources? How do farmers make decisions on the seeds they plant? Answers to these questions are important for policymakers interested in reforming China's seed sector.

Similar questions can be asked about the extent to which Bt cotton has allowed Chinese farmers to adopt more efficient insect control practices. Despite the fact that Bt cotton significantly reduces insecticide use, several studies show that farmers are still overusing insecticides to control cotton pests (Huang *et al.* 2002b; Pemsl *et al.* 2005). How do insecticide markets function and how do they affect farmers' purchasing habits? What are farmers' sources of information for making decisions on the type and amount of insecticide to be used? How do farmers decide to apply insecticides to control pests in their fields? Answers to these questions are required to enhance the extent to which Bt cotton can reduce insecticide use.

The goal of this chapter is to answer these questions about the seed and insecticide input sectors and their impact on Bt cotton practices. The chapter is organized as follows. The next section describes the data used in this chapter. The third section discusses the evolution of China's seed sector and particularly the cotton seed market. The fourth section examines farmers' seed practices, including seed purchasing, the nature of local seed markets, farmers' knowledge of varieties and the performance of different varieties in farmers' fields. The fifth section analyses the nature of the insecticide market, discusses issues related to insecticide choice and examines farmers' decisions regarding insecticide use. The last section concludes with a summary of major results and policy implications.

Data Sources

Five types of data are used in this study. The first type is drawn from national statistics on the seed and pesticide sectors.

The second data set used in this study is from a database established by CCAP in 1999 to follow the performance of GM crops in China. By 2006 the database included five rounds of intensive farm household surveys that focus on Bt cotton production. The surveys covered three provinces in 1999 and 2000, five provinces in 2001, six provinces in 2004 and four provinces in 2006. In this chapter we only use data from Hebei, Shandong, Henan and Anhui, where we have the most complete record in the same villages over different time periods. Counties, townships and villages in the sample were selected randomly. In each village 20–30 households were randomly selected, with the number of households based on the size of the village. Each farmer was interviewed by trained enumerators from CCAP's survey team for about two to three hours using standard enumeration techniques. In earlier years these data were used by researchers to assess the efficiency of Bt cotton relative to conventional cotton varieties in China (e.g. Huang *et al.* 2002b, 2002c, 2003; Pray *et al.* 2001, 2002). In recent years (when all farmers in the study villages had adopted Bt cotton) the database has been used to assess sustainability issues such as insect resistance, the importance of secondary insects and risks and information associated with farmers' insecticide use (e.g. Huang *et al.* 2007, 2008; Wang *et al.* 2009; Liu 2008).

The third data set is from a household survey in 2007. The CCAP survey teams revisited 12 villages that had been studied in at least three previous years, including four villages (from two counties) in each of Hebei, Shandong and Henan provinces. Twenty farm households in each village were randomly selected from those households that had been surveyed in the previous period, for a total of 240 farm households. In this study, a new and more intensive survey method was employed. The farmers were asked to keep a daily record of all activities on inputs and outputs of Bt cotton production and marketing. To ensure that farmers could correctly record each farming activity, particularly those related to insecticide purchasing and application, enumerators visited farmers four times in June,

July, August and October 2007 to check farmers' records and make any necessary corrections.

The fourth data set is related to input markets. The marketing survey data consist of two subsets on seed and pesticide markets, respectively, obtained in 2007. Both surveys covered the 12 villages where the primary household surveys were conducted in 2007. The marketing studies covered villages, townships and county capitals. (Provinces are divided into counties and counties into townships; there are 22–50 villages in each township in the sample.) Thus the 2007 input market survey covered 12 villages from nine townships in six counties of Hebei, Shandong and Henan provinces.

The Bt cotton seed market survey was conducted in April 2007, just before cotton planting season. The survey was conducted in all six county capitals, eight township headquarters (one township headquarter is also a county capital) and 12 villages. Our survey includes two parts. The first collected general information (e.g. registration capital, setup date, ownership, types of seeds) of all seed companies and seed dealers selling Bt cotton seeds in each of six county capitals. The second part was conducted for a randomly selected sample of 3–5 companies and seed dealers in each of six county capitals and 2–4 seed dealers in each of eight township headquarters, and all seed dealers selling cotton seeds in the villages. The information collected included the prices and quantities of cotton seeds sold, sources of seeds, other characteristics of the varieties for sale and other major business activities beyond cotton seed. In total we have 32 seed companies and 83 seed dealers in six county capitals, 48 seed dealers in eight township headquarters and 14 seed dealers in 12 villages.

The pesticide market survey was conducted in June 2007. We selected 10 shops in each county. All shops in our sample villages were included. Because there are usually only one or two shops selling pesticides in each village, we interviewed all shops in each village and then made up the total of 10 by random interviewing of shops in the township headquarters and county capitals. In total, we interviewed 60 insecticide sellers to collect information on the insecticide market.

The fifth data set is from studies on the type of Bt gene and Bt toxin expression in farmers' cotton varieties that were jointly conducted by the CCAP team and scientists from the Institute of Plant Protection (IPP) of CAAS. The principal purpose of these tests was to examine differences in the efficacy of Bt toxin expression among the cotton varieties that farmers were planting. The team collected seed samples of all varieties planted by 240 households in the 12 survey villages. DNA was extracted from each sample and compared with that of control samples. To ensure accuracy, the extraction process was replicated three times and each test was done twice. The study of Bt toxin expression was done to assess the quality of different Bt varieties. Leaf samples were taken from each of 814 plots. Samples from the second leaf below the growth point were taken from 20 randomly selected plants (from five locations in each plot) at three times in the season (June, July and August). Bt toxin expression in the leaf samples was assessed by scientists from IPP. Each test was repeated three times and the mean of the results was reported for each plot and time period.

The seed sector in China

Evolution of seed markets and policies

The national seed system began to take shape in the 1950s shortly after the establishment of the People's Republic of China. The basic organization remained fairly stable until the 1990s. The system included approximately 2200 county seed companies, 500 prefectural seed companies, 30 provincial seed companies and the National Seed Corporation (NSC). Each layer of the hierarchy had its own set of responsibilities. County seed companies arranged the production of commercial seed through local contract growers. Prefectural seed companies produced foundation seed, using basic seed provided by the provincial or prefectural research institutes responsible for plant breeding. Prefectural seed companies also produced and sold some commercial seed. Provincial seed companies and the NSC were primarily planning and coordinating bodies.

The county, prefecture and provincial state-owned enterprises (SOEs) dominated China's seed industry into the 1990s (Keeley 2003; Li and Yan 2005; Huang *et al.* 1999). In many counties only the local SOE was allowed to sell seeds of the major crops. In the typical case, a county SOE sold its seed through township agricultural extension agents. Indeed, during the 1990s agricultural extension agents earned a large share of their income from selling agricultural inputs, including seed. In addition, seed also flowed to farmers through other traditional, non-commercial channels, such as the cotton office (a state-designated monopoly cotton procurement agency that operated until the late 1990s) and seed production bases (villages or groups of villages that had contracts with the SOEs for the multiplication of their seed).

In the past decade the seed sector in China has undergone a significant transition. Since the mid-1990s the laws and policies that govern the seed industry have changed in such a way that a competitive, commercial seed industry has begun to evolve (Keeley 2003; Li and Yan 2005). New legislation has eliminated the monopoly positions of county, prefectural and provincial seed companies. Any entrepreneur who has access to the required minimum amount of capital and appropriate facilities can sell and produce seed. Private companies are allowed to sell seed (including any variety of GM or non-GM cotton) that was bred by public research institutes. New sources of investment have emerged in the industry, and domestic entrepreneurs have invested in private seed firms. Some of the traditional SOEs have transformed themselves into commercial firms. Although they are still few in number, foreign firms have also begun to invest in the seed industry.

Perhaps more than any other part of the seed industry, these changes have been particularly important for cotton. The government's recent policy efforts appear to have been effective in encouraging the development of a commercial seed industry for the marketing of Bt cotton. There have been three fundamental shifts in the structure of the cotton seed industry: the appearance of large commercial seed companies that operate at the regional or national level; the rise of private foreign firms (although they still play a somewhat limited role); and the emergence of small, private cotton seed firms everywhere in China. Any seed company with initial registered capital of more than 1 million yuan is allowed to produce, package and sell conventional seed, and companies with initial registered capital of 5 million yuan can produce hybrid seed. Shops that sell seeds are not required to meet any capital requirements.

There have also been significant changes in the sources of cotton varieties. Before the commercialization of the seed sector, the Cotton Research Institute (CRI) of CAAS was the largest cotton breeding institute in China and its varieties accounted for about half of the country's total cotton area. The other half of the cotton area was mostly covered by varieties from the provincial academies of agricultural sciences (PAAS) in major cotton production regions, as well as some local research institutes at prefecture level. After China started to commercialize its seed sector in the late 1990s, and particularly after the commercialization of Bt cotton in 1997, the share of CRI's cotton varieties began to fall. It is estimated that currently CRI's cotton varieties account for no more than one-third of the cotton area in China while varieties from the Institute of Biotechnology Research (IBR) of CAAS, PAAS, Monsanto and emerging domestic companies with their own plant breeding capacity (such as Biocentury and Origin) have been gaining ground.

Over the past several decades, Ministry of Agriculture officials have developed a number of rules and regulatory institutions to administer the seed industry. Under China's seed law, all plant varieties must be registered with the government before commercial production is allowed. Crop varieties typically undergo three years of multi-location testing under the supervision of research institutes and seed testing stations. Based on the results of these tests, a committee of officials, local agricultural scientists and seed experts selects promising seed varieties for release at the provincial level.

Domestic research institutes and companies can have access to Bt transgenes from IBR/CAAS by paying a small fee that allows them to incorporate the gene in their breeding programs. Monsanto's Bt transgene, on the other hand, is restricted to the two joint ventures (Jidai in Hebei and Andai in Anhui) that are authorized to sell Monsanto's seeds. Despite these regulations and restrictions, many unauthorized Bt cotton varieties have entered the market. Many provincial, prefectural and other local research institutes and private seed companies backcross commercially available seed to generate their own Bt cotton varieties. Some of these varieties, particularly in the early period of seed sector liberalization, did not even go through biosafety regulation procedures before they were brought to market.

Seed market distribution in the six sample counties

The impacts of these seed policy changes are clearly evident from our seed market survey. First, the SOE seed companies that once dominated China's seed industry have been replaced by many other seed companies. In Table 6.1, we consider those seed enterprises that have more than 1 million yuan registration capital as seed companies, and other enterprises as seed dealers. Based on this

Table 6.1 Number of seed companies and seed dealers selling Bt cotton seeds in 6 county capitals, 8 townships and 12 villages by the level of registration capital in 2007

Location and type of business	Seed companies		Seed dealers	
	Registration capital: more than 5 million yuan	Registration capital: 1–5 million yuan	Registration capital: less than 1 million yuan	Without registration capital
Six county capitals	15	17	42	41
SOE	2	0	0	0
Joint state-private	0	2	0	0
Collective	2	0	0	0
Private	11	15	42	41
Eight townships	0	0	19	29
Private	0	0	19	29
Twelve villages	0	0	0	14
Private	0	0	0	14

Source: CCAP 2007 market survey.

rule, we found that among 32 seed companies, there were only two SOEs. The majority of seed companies are owned by the private sector.

Second, China's seed market is dominated by many independent seed companies and seed dealers. For example, the seed market survey shows that there were 32 independent companies and 83 seed dealers selling Bt cotton seeds in the six county capitals in 2007. Thus there is an average of about five seed companies and 14 seed dealers selling Bt cotton seeds in each county capital. In the eight township head-quarters surveyed, we found 48 seed dealers selling Bt cotton seeds; these are mostly family businesses. Even most villages (except those very close to township headquarters) have a few shops selling seeds. Normally these shops sell many other products as well, including fertilizers, pesticides and groceries.

Third, most companies and all seed dealers are small and the market is very competitive. Among the seed companies, only 15 have registration capital of more than 5 million yuan and 17 have registration capital of 1–5 million yuan. Seed dealers have little or no registration capital.

Our survey revealed some important distinctions among the seed businesses. First, there are differences in scale and specialization. The businesses in the county capitals are always relatively large. They have an apartment or a room exclusively used for selling seeds. Some of them are agencies or branches of the large seed companies outside the county, although they also sell varieties from many other seed companies. In the township headquarters, shops often sell seeds of various crops and many also sell agricultural chemicals, machinery and other items. They also have a room or apartment that is used exclusively for business. Within the villages, seed dealers are more flexible. Most of them use one room of their house for selling seeds. There are also mobile shops (trucks selling seeds from relatively large

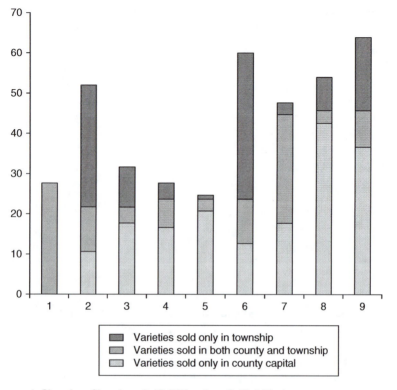

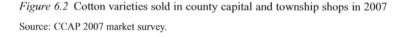

1: Shenzhou-Shenzhou; 2: Xinji-Wangkou; 3: Xinji-Mazhuang;
4: Xiajin-Xinshengdian; 5: Xiajin-Luanzhuang; 6: Liangshan-Yangying;
7: Taikang-Banqiao; 8: Fugou-Chaigang; 9: Fugou-Caoli.
(Note: Shenzhou township headquarters is also Shenzhou county capital.)

Figure 6.2 Cotton varieties sold in county capital and township shops in 2007
Source: CCAP 2007 market survey.

companies) that operate at the village level. Most of the village seed businesses in our survey are not registered and they are difficult to monitor.

Second, the seed businesses at different levels often sell different varieties. Our survey shows that shops in the county capitals normally sell more well-known varieties from large companies. Varieties produced by some small companies or that are not widely accepted by farmers have trouble finding outlets in county-level markets. These less well-known varieties are found more often at the sub-county level. Thus markets at different levels tend to feature different products (Figure 6.2).

Given the structure of the seed market discussed earlier, it is not surprising that there are many varieties available in the markets. Table 6.2 shows that on average each county capital shop sold more than five varieties of Bt cotton, ranging from

Table 6.2 Number of Bt cotton varieties sold in the shops located in county capitals in 2007

County	Average per shop	Max	Min	Total
Xinji	5.2	8	3	21
Shenzhou	6.3	7	5	26
Liangshan	8.5	12	4	23
Xiajin	3.0	5	2	23
Taikang	4.3	8	2	44
Fugou	4.5	8	2	45
Average	5.3	8	3	30

Source: CCAP 2007 market survey.

Table 6.3 Number of Bt cotton varieties sold in the shops located in townships in 2007

County	Township	Number of varieties per shop			Total number of varieties within a township
		Average	Max	Min	
Xinji	Ma Z	5.0	8	3	14
Xinji	Wang K	6.3	8	5	41
Xiajin	Luan Z	2.0	3	1	4
Xiajin	Xin S D	3.0	5	1	10
Taikang	Ban Q	4.8	8	2	30
Liangshan	Yang Y	16.2	24	11	45
Fugou	Chai G	6.5	7	6	11
Fugou	Cao L	8.5	12	5	27
Shenzhou	Shenzhou	6.3	7	5	26
Average		6.5	9.1	4.3	23

Source: CCAP 2007 market survey.

three in Xiajin to more than eight in Liangshan. On average, about 30 Bt cotton varieties are available in each county capital.

Although the number of Bt cotton varieties available in a township headquarters is less than that in a county capital, a similar range of varieties is sold in each shop. On the average, more than 6 varieties are available at each shop, and 23 varieties are available in the township headquarters (Table 6.3). The variations in variety number among townships reflect the size of township and the importance of local cotton production.

While we do not have systematic data to show the trend in types of Bt cotton varieties sold by each shop in different locations, our field surveys reveal that the varieties sold in each shop change over time. For example, one owner of a shop in Fugou county (Henan) told us that he had to introduce new varieties from large companies in Zhengzhou, the provincial capital, each year. Another shop owner told us that selling new varieties is much easier than selling the varieties that were sold in the previous year. This may be partly explained by farmers' seed practices, which will be discussed in the following text. As the local seed market is so competitive, dealers have to find a way of distinguishing the varieties sold in their shops, even if it is simply a difference in the packaging.

In summary, after the seed market reforms initiated in the mid-1990s, China's state cotton seed system has been decentralized and commercialized. The market is very competitive, unregulated and dominated by independent and small companies and seed dealers. The different market levels, ranging from the county capital to local townships and villages, often sell different varieties, and the number of varieties in the market is increasing. New varieties are more likely to come first to county-level markets before they move to township and village markets. There is no evidence of seed market consolidation; instead, China's seed market is still in the stage of expanding the number of players. Penetration of the seed market into local townships and villages may improve availability of seed for farmers, but given the large number of varieties available in each market and the frequent changes of varieties and trade names, ensuring good quality seeds for small farmers is a great challenge.

Regulation of GM crops and the performance of Bt cotton varieties

Since the early 1990s the government has made increasing attempts to regulate the plant biotechnology industry. In addition to normal seed regulation, further biosafety regulations have been imposed on all varieties generated from GM technologies and on the sale of GM seeds. The Ministry of Science and Technology (MOST) issued its first set of biosafety regulations in 1993. Following these regulations, the Ministry of Agriculture (MOA) issued the 'Implementation Measures for Agricultural Biological Engineering' in 1996. The MOA measures delineated the steps a firm must take to: get approval to do research on transgenic organisms; test GMOs outside of laboratories and greenhouses; and commercialize them. In recent years the policy and regulatory environment has become more stringent. In May 2001 the State Council decreed a new set of policy guidelines, 'Regulations on the Safety Administration of Agricultural GMOs', to replace the early regulations issued by MOST. The MOA also announced three new implementation regulations to replace their earlier rules. The new framework, which took effect in March 2002, greatly expanded the scope of regulation to include more detailed rules on biosafety management, trade and labelling of GM food products.

The MOA released another set of complementary regulations in 2004, largely in response to the problems of the proliferation of unapproved (and illegal) Bt cotton varieties in many areas of China's cotton producing areas in northern China and in the Yangtse River Basin. The strategy of the new regulations was two-fold. On the one hand, biosafety regulation procedures were made more comprehensive. For example, the MOA began to require that all newly developed GM varieties obtain a safety certificate before being allowed to enter regional variety trials (the last stage in the process by which crop varieties are certified for commercialization). Commercialization is permitted only after a review of data on yield and performance, and the variety owner must present a certificate that a variety is GM or non-GM. The tests are conducted in a series of MOA-designated testing institutes and organizations. On the other hand, the MOA also has sought to simplify the process of certification and approval. Any Bt cotton variety that has received a production safety certification (or commercialization certification) from one province can directly apply for a certificate from another province, as long as the provinces are within the same cotton ecological region. (China has three such regions.) In addition, the developers of any variety can apply for safety certificates in a province if the new variety was developed from a parent variety that already had been granted a safety certificate in the past.

The impact of the streamlined regulation procedures has been significant. In 2004, the number of Bt cotton varieties that applied for and received biosafety certificates soared. In total there were about 130 new commercialization certificates issued, far more than the total Bt cotton varieties released from commercialization in the previous years. Interestingly, nearly all of these new varieties were already being planted in farmers' fields at the time of approval.

Despite the increasing number of Bt cotton varieties approved by the CBC, our 2006 survey in four provinces in North China shows that there are still a large number of Bt cotton varieties adopted by farmers whose names are not in the list approved by CBC. Among 945 plots surveyed in 2006, 410 (about 44 per cent) contained varieties that were not in the CBC's approved list. We examined the names of these varieties and eliminated cases where we knew that the same variety was sold under different names; although there is still probably some duplication, we found 159 different named Bt cotton varieties in the 945 plots.

The explanations for the large number of non-approved varieties are complex. Our personal communications with some large seed companies indicate that there are several reasons for this phenomenon. First, dealers who want to avoid paying royalties or licence fees can use a new trade name for an existing Bt cotton variety that has been approved by CBC. Second, companies themselves have an incentive to create new names for their approved varieties in order to attract more customers. Finally, some small seed companies use approved varieties to backcross with their own germplasm to create new varieties that do not go through CBC's biosafety regulation procedures for approval. Unfortunately, it is not possible to quantify the share of non-approved varieties in each of these three categories.

The complexities of the Bt cotton seed market and uncertainties about variety origins are illustrated by the results of our genetic testing of seed samples from three provinces in northern China in 2007. Despite the unregulated nature of the market and the possibilities of fraud, only about 0.25 per cent of our sample did not contain a Bt transgene. Thus even the 'underground' seed market seems to maintain the basic insect-resistance technology in its products. There are two possible sources of Bt transgenes: several constructs developed by CAAS and the 'Bollgard' construct in Monsanto varieties. Although official Monsanto varieties accounted for about 10 per cent of our sample, the proportion of Bt cotton varieties tested containing Monsanto's Bt transgene was higher than that of Bt cotton varieties with a CAAS Bt transgene. This would indicate that there is considerable (and often unauthorized) use of commercial varieties in the plant breeding that develops new Bt cotton varieties. However, it is interesting to note that there

Table 6.4 Yield performance and insecticide use for Bt cotton varieties included and not included on China's Biosafety Committee approved list in 2006 and 2007

Year and type of variety	Number of plots	Yield, seed cotton (kg/ha)	Insecticide application to control bollworm(kg/ha)	Total insecticide use(kg/ha)
2006 in 4 provinces				
Varieties on CBC list	535	3376	7.4	21.5
Varieties not on list	410	3331	10.4	29.1
2007 in 3 provinces				
Varieties on CBC list	570	2941	7.6	19.3
Varieties not on list	244	2872	11.3	24.5

Source: CCAP 2006 and 2007 farm surveys.

Note: 4 provinces in 2006 are Hebei, Shandong, Henan and Anhui; 3 provinces in 2007 are Hebei, Shandong and Henan.

is no statistically significant difference in Bt expression or yield between varieties with the Monsanto or CAAS transgenes.

The analysis also shows that there are no significant differences in performance between approved and unapproved varieties. In order to examine quality differences between the varieties listed and not listed in CBC's approved varieties, we use yield, insecticide application and Bt toxin expression as indicators. Table 6.4 summarizes average figures for yield and insecticide use by farmers for these two groups of varieties in 2006 and 2007. It is interesting to note that in 2006 the average yield of varieties not approved by CBC (3331 kg/ha) was almost the same as the average yield of the approved ones (3376 kg/ha). The same results are also found in 2007. However, more analysis is needed to have a firm conclusion about the yield difference between these two groups of varieties because there are many factors simultaneously affecting cotton yield.

On the other hand, we find that farmers used about 30 per cent less insecticide to control bollworm in the plots planted with varieties on the CBC list than for those not on the list, and the difference is statistically significant at the 1 per cent level. One hypothesis is that some of the varieties not on the list might have been generated by backcrossing with approved varieties and may not have been subjected to sufficient testing to ensure adequate Bt toxin expression. However, the results from our laboratory test do not support this hypothesis. To test whether 'Not in CBC list' varieties have lower Bt toxin expression than that of 'In CBC list' ones, we examined Bt toxin expression for each of the varieties planted in each plot of farm fields in 240 households in 2007. A summary of results is presented in Table 6.5. Overall, the levels of Bt toxin expression for 'Not in CBC list' varieties are not significantly different from those of 'In CBC list' varieties. Indeed, we find 'Not in CBC list' varieties have a slightly higher Bt toxin expression than the others in Hebei and

Table 6.5 The level of Bt toxin expression, ng/g, by variety type and by location

Variety type and month of sample	Hebei	Shandong	Henan
In CBC list			
Average	987	888	991
June	1442	1325	1505
July	812	808	970
August	708	530	498
Not in CBC list			
Average	1084	928	954
June	1578	1383	1478
July	944	811	826
August	731	591	556

Source: CCAP 2007 farm survey.

Shandong, but not in Henan. (We also found that there is no significant difference in Bt toxin expression between the varieties with a CAAS gene and the varieties with the Monsanto gene.)

The results on Bt toxin expression seem to contradict the results on insecticide use presented in Table 6.4, where we found 'Not in CBC list' varieties received more insecticides. However, in another study, Huang *et al.* (2008) also revealed that, in general, there is no clear relationship between Bt toxin protein expression and insecticide use to control bollworm. There are no obvious differences in toxin expression among the classes of variety, but because there is so much uncertainty and confusion about variety identity, it is difficult to know how to do comparisons. One possibility is that these differences in insecticide practices among varieties may be partially explained by farmers' perceptions of the quality of the seed; this is explored later in the discussion of seed purchase.

Farmers' seed practices

The previous section discussed the expanding set of choices available to Chinese farmers who buy Bt cotton seed. The number of varieties (and variety names) is increasing. Some of the new varieties are officially approved but others are of uncertain origin. In such a competitive and unregulated market, farmers face significant transaction costs in identifying appropriate varieties. On the other side, the many small seed companies and dealers face high costs in trying to attract farmers' attention and convincing them of the quality of their products.

This section looks at farmers' seed practices in response to this type of market. It first discusses some further features of the seed market, including the use of hybrid seed and the issue of seed price. It then examines farmers' knowledge of seed companies and varieties, and it describes the patterns of variety use. Finally, it discusses farmers' seed saving and suggests some links between this practice and the nature of the seed market.

Seed price

There is a growing use of hybrid Bt cotton in China and a number of companies are investing in this technology. The hybrid seed price is 2–3 times that of conventional seed but its high yield potential and response to good management makes it an attractive alternative for some farmers (and the fact that it is planted at lower densities offsets much of the price difference). However, the current hybrid varieties are more suitable to the Yangzi River basin than they are to the Yellow River basin in the north, where colder weather affects hybrid production and exposes it to the risk of frost. For these and other reasons, the use of hybrid cotton seed varies greatly across China. Our survey in Anhui Province found that hybrid cotton adoption had reached 96 per cent. Some recently released hybrids have proven well adapted to certain parts of Henan, where the adoption rate is 26 per cent, but the use of hybrid cotton in Hebei and Shandong represents only 1–2 per cent of the cotton area. Our 2006 survey showed no significant differences in farm size, assets, farmer age or education between those farmers who used hybrid cotton and those who planted conventional varieties.

For non-hybrid varieties, seed price can affect farmers' choice of cotton variety, but the signals from the market are often difficult to interpret. Even for a given variety there may be a significant variation in seed price. Farmers understand that low-price seed may be of lower quality, but high price is not a guarantee of high quality. Figure 6.3 shows the variation in price among varieties, and within the same variety sold at different locations. The varieties in the figure are the nine most popular ones in the study villages. Varieties 1 and 8 are hybrids, which explain their higher price. The varieties with the greatest price variability (1–3, 7–9) are ones that are particularly well-known and produced by some of the largest and most reputable seed companies in the country. Varieties 4 and 5 were previously popular but are now being replaced by others.

There are several factors that may explain the variability in seed price. Variation in average prices among varieties can reflect differences in performance and demand. The significant price differences for the same variety are due to various factors. The seed of a variety from larger, well-established companies is usually priced higher than seed of the same variety produced by smaller companies (with or without authorization). Companies offering newer varieties with less reputation may need to set prices lower. In addition, prices vary along the retail chain; the price may be lower from a distributor in the county capital than from a dealer at the village level.

Seed purchase

Although it is possible for a cotton variety to establish its reputation among farmers, there are so many players in the seed market, and so little regulation, that it is rational behaviour for small firms to introduce new varieties, or give new names to old varieties, in order to try to capture farmers' attention. Such a strategy could backfire if farmers find that a particular company is not reliable, but this depends on farmers' familiarity with the seed industry. We explored farmers'

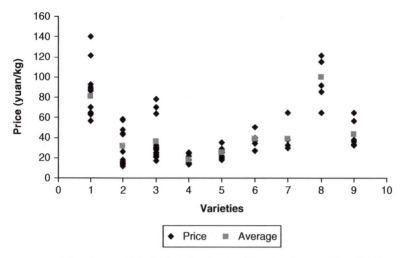

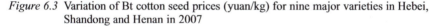

1: Lumianyan 15 (hybrid); 2: Lumianyan 21; 3: Lumianyan 28; 4: GK12;
5: Zhongmiansuo 23; 6: Jinmian 38; 7: Xinqiu 1; 8: Lumianyan 24 (hybrid);
9: Zhongzhimian 2.

Figure 6.3 Variation of Bt cotton seed prices (yuan/kg) for nine major varieties in Hebei, Shandong and Henan in 2007

Source: CCAP 2007 market survey.

knowledge of the seed market by asking them to name three seed companies that sell high-quality seed. Table 6.6 summarizes the responses. The top half of the table shows the responses when we accepted the name of any seed provider, even quasi-public entities such as the extension office; and the bottom half shows responses when we only accepted names of commercial enterprises. In both cases, the majority of farmers were not able to name a single seed company; only 3 per cent could give the names of three commercial seed enterprises.

On the other hand, farmers had somewhat better knowledge of cotton variety names. Almost every farmer could provide the names of several varieties (although some were described with local nicknames), and farmers were able to name the varieties they were planting that year (and could tell if they were hybrids or not), but could offer very little other information about them (such as their origin or whether they were approved), even though some of this informa-tion is available on the seed package.

The farmers in the 2006 survey planted an average of about two cotton variet-ies (Table 6.7). Nearly half the farmers planted only one variety, but more than 20 per cent planted three or more varieties, despite the fact that most cotton hold-ings are much less than a hectare.

Farmers often travel some distance to purchase seed, in many cases going to other parts of the township or even to the county capital and beyond to make their

Table 6.6 Farmers' knowledge about seed companies

Type of seed company	Knowledge	Number of farmers	Per cent
Any seed company (including those related to former public services such as the extension office)	Able to name 3 companies	11	5
	Able to name 2 companies	23	10
	Able to name 1 company	81	34
	Unable to name any company	125	52
Only private companies with no connection to public agricultural services	Able to name 3 companies	6	3
	Able to name 2 companies	11	5
	Able to name 1 company	55	23
	Unable to name any company	168	70

Source: CCAP 2007 farm survey.

Table 6.7 Number of varieties planted per household in Hebei, Shandong, Henan and Anhui in 2006

Number of varieties	Frequency	Per cent	Cum. per cent
7	1	0.3	0.3
6	2	0.6	0.9
5	6	1.9	2.8
4	14	4.4	7.2
3	49	15.3	22
2	99	30.9	53
1	149	46.6	100
Total	320	100	

Source: CCAP 2006 farm survey.

purchases (Table 6.8). The convenience of buying seed in the village must be balanced against the fact that seed dealers in larger towns offer a wider selection, and their varieties are more likely to be on the 'CBC Approved' list. The fact that farmers apply almost twice as much insecticide to cotton varieties from seed purchased in the village, compared to varieties of seed purchased in higher level markets, indicates that they may have less confidence in the seed that is available locally (Table 6.9).

Despite the large number of varieties available in the market, there is evidence that farmers in any particular village often buy the same varieties. We used our data set from 2006 to analyse variety use in 16 villages (Table 6.10). In all but four of the villages at least half of the farmers planted the most popular variety in part or all of their farms, but the identity of the most popular variety varied from village to village.

Table 6.8 The percentage of seed saved and purchased from shops located in different places in Hebei, Shandong and Henan, 2006

Province and county	(Save seed)	Within village	Out of village but within township	Out of township but within county	County capital	Outside the county
Henan-Taikang	(17)	19	50	0	8	6
Henan-Fugou	(14)	62	10	4	8	2
Shandong-Liangshan	(59)	21	15	0	3	2
Shandong-Xiajin	(26)	36	1	1	36	0
Hebei-Shenzhou	(58)	21	1	3	10	6
Hebei-Xinji	(58)	32	2	2	3	4

Source: CCAP 2006 farm survey.

Table 6.9 Insecticide use on cotton varieties from different seed markets

Seed source	Freq.	Per cent of plots with varieties on CBC list	Insecticide use (kg/ha)	t-test (t-value)
Purchased within farmer's own village	173	35	24.79	
Purchased in higher level markets	94	52	13.42	6.30[1]

Source: CCAP 2007 farm survey.

Note
1 Significant at 1%.

Seed saving

Although farmers in a village tend to prefer particular varieties, it would appear that the identity of the most popular variety in a village may change from year to year. We also asked the farmers in our 2007 sample how many years they had been planting each cotton variety (Table 6.11). In more than 62 per cent of the cases, this was the first year of planting the variety, indicating that there is a rapid turnover in varieties. Moreover, in those cases where farmers use a variety for more than one year it is often because they have saved the seed. The rate of seed saving (and acquiring saved seed from neighbours) is nearly 40 per cent. This use of farm-saved seed has remained fairly constant in the years we have been following the panel of cotton farmers. The principal exception is areas such as Henan where farmers have recently turned to the use of hybrid seed. Thus in many cases when a variety performs well the farmer will save the seed rather than risk having to identify it the following year in the seed market.

Farmers recognize that recycling seed eventually leads to a decline in seed quality, so this is only a short-term strategy. But if farmers save seed of good varieties for one or two seasons, our data show that they may not experience any decline in

Table 6.10 Adoption of popular Bt cotton varieties, by village, 2006

Province	Village	Name of most popular variety in village	Number of households (out of 20) that adopted most popular variety (in village)	On CBC list
Henan	Shizhuang	Shannong Fengkang 6	6	No
	Heyanzhang	Chun'aizao	9	No
	Dujia	Tongximian	12	No
	Gonghe	Shannong Fengkang 6	14	No
Shandong	Sunzhuang	Lumianyan 28	10	Yes
	Liuxianzhuang	Lumianyan 21	12	Yes
	Zhangzhai	Lumianyan 28	16	Yes
	Qianhuo	Jinmian 38	12	Yes
Hebei	Ximu	99B	17	Yes
	Dongmu	99B	17	Yes
	Mazhuang	Fengkangmian 1	16	No
	Dalisi	GK12	11	Yes
Anhui	Shiqiao	Wanza 3	10	No
	Xinfeng	Chuza 180	9	Yes
	Jiguan	Xiangza 3	17	Yes
	Xinnongcun	Xiangza 3	5	Yes

Source: CCAP 2006 farm survey.

Table 6.11 Number of years that farmers have planted cotton varieties used in 2007

Years	Freq.	Per cent	Cum.
1	355	62.4	62.4
2	149	26.4	88.6
3	41	7.2	95.8
4	16	2.8	98.6
5	2	0.4	99.0
6	5	0.8	99.8
10	1	0.2	100
Total	569	100	

Source: CCAP 2007 farm survey.

performance, and they may prefer their own seed supply to the confusing state of the formal seed market. Table 6.12 shows the yields and Bt toxin expression for pairs of matched varieties of the same names. It shows there is no yield difference between purchased and saved seed and only a modest decline in toxin expression.

Finally, we can test the hypothesis that although expanding seed markets and increasing seed availability in rural areas may increase farmers' opportunities to purchase seeds, the proliferation of seed types and variety names may increase search costs and have the opposite effect, encouraging farmers to save seeds that perform well in their fields. We test this by examining correlations between seed saving and (a) number of shops, (b) number of varieties.

Table 6.12 Yields and Bt toxin expression for saved and purchased seed of the same varieties

Type of seed	Yield, seed cotton (kg/ha)	t-value	Bt gene expression (ng/g)	t-value
Saved seed	2951.3	0.39	955.9	2.70[1]
Purchased seed	3003.8		1092.8	

Source: CCAP 2007 farm survey.

Note
1 Significant at 5%.

Table 6.13 Relationship between seed saving and (a) number of shops, (b) number of varieties in Hebei, Henan and Shandong in 2006 and 2007

Village environment	Level of commercial seed activity	Number of villages	2006 Seed saving rate %	t-value	2007 Seed saving rate %	t-value
(a) Number of shops	More than Median (34)	4	13	7.89[1]	11	6.38[1]
	Less than Median (34)	8	48		40	
(b) Number of varieties	More than Median (44)	7	44	1.65	40	3.44[1]
	Less than Median (44)	5	37		26	

Note
1 Significant at 1%.

The analysis, summarized in Table 6.13, supports our hypotheses. For example, when we divide the villages into two groups (above or below the median of total number of shops in village, township headquarters and county capital) we find that the average seed saving rate was much lower in those villages with access to more shops. This implies that farmers are more likely to participate in markets when more shops and dealers are available. On the other hand, when we divide the samples into two groups by the number of varieties available in the shops, the results show that farmers' seed saving rate is positively correlated with the number of varieties available in the local markets. A profusion of varieties in the market apparently encourages farmers to save seed of varieties that perform adequately.

Farmers' pest control practices

The principal contribution expected from Bt cotton is a reduction in the amount of insecticide used to control bollworm (and related species). In China, the technology's contribution in the early years of its introduction was nothing short of spectacular. In the early 1990s Chinese cotton farmers were using ever-increasing amounts of insecticide to control bollworm, while the insect was developing resistance to the chemicals that were available. Our work in 1999 showed that farmers planting Bt cotton were able to use 80 per cent less insecticide on their crop. Studies in subsequent years showed somewhat less, but still very significant, savings in insecticide use. The purpose of this section is to place farmers' pest control practices in a broader context. It first looks at the nature of the pesticide industry and local pesticide markets, then examines farmers' insecticide practices and finally reviews patterns of insecticide use and considers where further improvements could be made.

The pesticide market

Pesticide production and marketing in China was commercialized earlier than seed provision. The reform of the state-owned pesticide production and distribution system from the late 1980s not only improved the productivity of the sector, but also increased the availability of pesticides in rural areas. While the pesticide industry is dominated by many small companies, shops and dealers, the pesticide market is relatively more regulated than the seed market. For example, an insecticide company that wants to sell its products in the market should have a valid licence and its products should have sales permits. Moreover, key information such as ingredients, dose, target insects and producer information should be on the label. The demand for pesticide in China has increased over time due to rising pest pressures, falling real prices of pesticides and changing cropping patterns. Chemical pesticide use in agriculture (including insecticides, herbicides and fungicides) increased rapidly from the early 1990s and the amount of pesticide used nearly doubled between 1991 and 2006 (Figure 6.4). Several factors have contributed to this trend. First, increasing intensification of crop production has led to increasing pest pressure. A second factor is the growing importance of horticultural and other crops that require high levels of pesticide. Third, the increasing availability of pesticides and a fall in real pesticide prices have contributed to the rapid growth of pesticide use in China. The growth of domestic pesticide production has been higher than the growth of domestic consumption and China has become a net pesticide exporter in recent years.

It is interesting to note that the pattern of overall pesticide use presented in Figure 6.4 is very consistent with Bt cotton adoption. Cotton was one of the most intensive users of insecticide among major field crops. Despite cotton area being much lower than that of many other crops, the serious bollworm problem led to intensive use of insecticides; we estimate that cotton accounted for 15–20 per cent of total pesticides used in China in the early and mid-1990s. The decline in overall pesticide use in 2000 and 2001, and slow growth thereafter, is consistent with the pattern of Bt cotton adoption. After Bt cotton was approved for commercialization in 1997, Bt cotton area expanded rapidly to reach 45 per cent of total cotton area in 2001, reversing the demand for insecticides in the cotton sector. A moderate increase in total pesticide use resumed when Bt cotton adoption rate

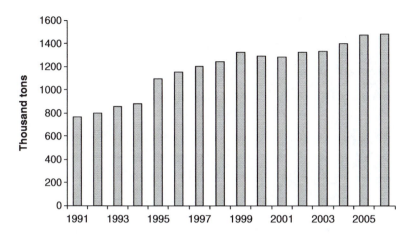

Figure 6.4 Chemical pesticides used in China, thousand tons, 1991–2006

reached its peak of about 65 per cent in 2004 and the reduction in cotton insecticide use could no longer counterbalance the increasing use of pesticides on other crops.

Most companies engaged in pesticide production are small and the local marketing channels are similar to those we found in the case of cotton seed. There are at least 2000 companies producing pesticides and hundreds of thousands of shops selling pesticides in rural China, ranging from the county capitals down to townships and villages. Many different products are available in these markets. During our field interviews, traders often told us that despite the wide range of trademarks and trade names in the market, the ingredients are often the same.

Our study of insecticide markets and farmers' pest control practices in three provinces in 2007 provided additional information to complement the data we had collected in previous years on insecticide management. Farmers purchase most of their insecticides in local villages and township headquarters. Unlike seed, there are no differences in the kind of insecticide sold in villages, townships and county capitals. In addition, the price differences for a given product are much less and are mainly determined by transportation costs. The market appears to be very competitive, with many small dealers trying to attract customers and earning profits of perhaps 5–10 per cent. Most of the pesticide retailers at the village level, and many at the township and county level, are not registered businesses.

Many insecticide sellers told us that there are too many products in the market and they do not have the opportunity to obtain detailed information about the products or their effects. Farmers also complained about insufficient information. Our data showed that on average there are 13 insecticide shops within 3 km of a farmer's home. On average, there are about 130 types of insecticide for cotton sold in each county, ranging from about 60 to nearly 300 (Table 6.14). The confusion over trademarks and trade names and the lack of enforcement is now being

Table 6.14 The number of pesticide shops and types of insecticides used in cotton in Hebei, Shandong and Henan, 2007

Province and county	Number of insecticide shops within 3 km of village (including in the village)	Number of cotton insecticide product names in each county[1]
Henan-Taikang	23	68
Henan-Fugou	8	51
Shandong-Liangshan	10	121
Shandong-Xiajin	14	130
Hebei-Shenzhou	8	194
Hebei-Xinji	15	210
Average	13	130

Source: CCAP 2007 market survey.

Note
1 These numbers were estimated by local officials. They probably underestimate the true number of products, especially from small companies.

Table 6.15 Number of insecticide company names recalled by farmers in Hebei, Shandong and Henan, 2007

Number of companies	Per cent of farmers
0	56
1	14
2	13
3	17

Source: CCAP 2007 farm survey.

addressed. An MOA rule mandates that pesticides must be sold by the name of their active ingredient beginning in mid-2008. This action should be an important step towards a well-functioning insecticide market.

Insecticide purchase

Until such regulations are established and enforced, however, farmers will have great difficulty in distinguishing among pesticide products. According to our survey, many farmers have no way of knowing whether one brand of insecticide is superior to another. More than half of the farmers were unable to give the name of a single insecticide company (Table 6.15). The similarity of the products and prices makes it impossible for farmers to distinguish among products, although we have no information regarding the actual variability in the quality of products in the market.

Because the pesticide market has penetrated into villages and there is not much difference in the types of pesticides sold in different markets, farmers purchase

Table 6.16 The percentage of insecticide purchased from shops located in different locations in Hebei, Shandong and Henan, 2007

Province and county	Within village	Out of village but within township	Out of township but within county	County capital	Outside the county
Henan-Taikang	15	83	0	2	0
Henan-Fugou	63	11	11	15	0
Shandong-Liangshan	62	23	4	10	1
Shandong-Xiajin	43	30	3	23	1
Hebei-Shenzhou	90	0	0	10	0
Hebei-Xinji	66	33	0	0	1
Average	57	30	3	10	0

Source: CCAP 2007 farm survey.

Table 6.17 Types of insecticide applied by farmers in Hebei, Shandong and Henan, 2007

Province-county	Types of insecticide (trade names) applied	Of which, types used for first time in 2007
Henan-Taikang	13	7
Henan-Fugou	13	6
Shandong-Liangshan	15	8
Shandong-Xiajin	10	4
Hebei-Shenzhou	15	8
Hebei-Xinji	16	6
Average	13	7

Source: CCAP 2007 farm survey.

most of their pesticides in their own village. According to our survey, 75–90 per cent of farmers purchased insecticide within their own townships and the majority within the village (Table 6.16). This purchasing pattern differs from what we found for seed (Table 6.8).

In the 2007 season the average farmer purchased 13 types of insecticide to control pests in the cotton field (Table 6.17). Farmers often mix several of these products together to control a specific pest. We were unable to learn whether such mixtures are the product of experience or are based on arbitrary decisions, but the opportunities for experimentation and learning are minimal, especially as it appears that more than half of the products that the farmer used were purchased for the first time. Such turnover is common, with the exception of a few products that seem to have a more stable market.

Farmers use various sources of information when choosing insecticides (Table 6.18). They most commonly rely on information from sellers and their previous experience. Advertising appears to have almost no effect on the decision.

Table 6.18 The most important source of farmers' information for selection of type of insecticide

Most important source of information	Per cent of farmers
Previous experience	35
Neighbours or relatives	8
The label	19
Sellers	36
Advertisement	2
Total	100

Source: CCAP 2007 farm survey.

Pest control practices

Tables 6.19 and 6.20 give detailed statistics for insecticide use in cotton fields from 1999 to 2006, based on our household surveys. The tables also give the insecticide practices recorded in our 2007 survey. All insecticide figures are in kg/ha of the commercial pesticide. Although we were not able to estimate the amount of active ingredient, we found a strong correlation between quantity and cost of insecticides, indicating that differences in the quantity of commercial product should provide a rough estimate of differences in active ingredient applied. The 2007 data are based on farmers' log books, while the data from previous years are based on recall at the end of the season, so the figures may not be strictly comparable, but we believe they tell much the same story.

Table 6.19 clearly shows the impact of Bt cotton on insecticide use to control bollworm. The introduction of Bt cotton led to a significant decline in the use of bollworm insecticide and while there is still some insecticide used to control bollworm in Bt cotton, particularly late in the season, this amount has remained fairly stable, although there is considerable variation among locations. According to Huang *et al.* (2002b), the cost saving in insecticide brought by Bt cotton is about 67 per cent. After several years of planting Bt cotton in China, the benefit of cost saving is still evident. For example, compared to the year before farmers began to plant Bt cotton, the cost saving in insecticide in 2006 is about 60 per cent (after we control for price changes). It is important to note that farmers who continued to grow conventional cotton varieties also reduced the amount of insecticide they used for bollworm. This is probably due to the reduction in pest numbers because of the widespread use of Bt varieties and the fact that lower chemical use reduced selection pressure and lowered the pest's genetic resistance to insecticides.

Bt cotton has been managed with a fairly stable (but still quite high level) application of insecticides. There has been a slight upward turn in insecticide use, particularly between 2001 and 2004, and the principal reason was the emergence of secondary pests such as the mirid bug (Table 6.20). Although part of this increase is probably related to the fact that mirids had previously been controlled by the

Table 6.19 Insecticide use (kg/ha) for all insects and for bollworm in Hebei, Shandong, Henan and Anhui, 1999–2007

	Insecticide for all insects						Insecticide for bollworm					
	1999	2000	2001	2004	2006	2007	1999	2000	2001	2004	2006	2007
Bt variety	**11.5**	**20.8**	**24.1**	**23.4**	**24.5**	**19.6**	**6.3**	**14.2**	**8.5**	**3.8**	**8.5**	**8.7**
Hebei-Xinji	5.7	21.5	16.7	30.6	36.3	39.4	2.0	14.7	9.8	2.9	19.4	24.9
Hebei-Shenzhou	5.6	5.7	—	—	18.9	17.7	2.1	3.1	—	—	7.8	9.3
Shandong-Xiajin	17.2	33.4	—	—	27.1	19.0	11.4	23.9	—	—	9.9	6.3
Shandong-Liangshan	15.4	20.9	19	10.8	11.2	9.6	8.5	14.5	8.2	3.2	5.3	3.6
Henan-Taikang	18.1[1]	24	13.3	27.6	19.9	15.7	11.0[1]	16.8	3.3	4.6	5.8	2.2
Henan-Fugou	9.5[1]	11.7	13.8	19.2	24.7	15.5	4.4[1]	6.3	4.4	3.3	7.8	3.9
Anhui-Dongzhi	—	—	46.5	28.6	27.5		—	—	—	8.5	3.5	3.8
Anhui-Wangjiang	—	—	45	30.6	30.6		—	—	17.5	8.2	8	
Non-Bt variety	**77.5**	**47.3**	**64.1**	**37.8**	**45.4**		**69.1**	**36.3**	**46.3**	**14.3**	**22.5**	
Hebei-Xinji	—	—	—	—	64.5		—	—	—	—	31.3	
Hebei-Shenzhou	—	—	—	—	—		—	—	—	—	—	
Shandong-Xiajin	77.5	—	—	—	—		69.1	—	—	—	—	
Shandong-Liangshan	—	—	—	—	33.5		—	—	—	—	24.7	
Henan-Taikang	54.5[1]	44.7	37.7	42.6	35.1		40.2a	33.2	27.5	16.3	15.2	
Henan-Fugou	56.5[1]	52.7	35.2	23.6	65.2		46.1a	42.6	27.3	7.2	32.8	
Anhui-Dongzhi	—	—	93.7	76.1	—		—	—	68.3	34.8	—	
Anhui-Wangjiang	—	—	82.6	30.5	—		—	—	57.2	12.1	—	

Source: CCAP farm surveys in 4 provinces of China, 1999-2006 and CCAP 2007 farm survey.

Notes: There were only a few observations for Non-Bt in 2006, and none in 2007.
1 Figures for Henan (1999) estimated from 2000 questionnaire.

Table 6.20 Insecticide use (kg/ha) for all other pests and mirids in Hebei, Shandong, Henan and Anhui, 1999–2007

	Insecticide for all pests other than bollworm						Insecticide for mirids					
	1999	2000	2001	2004	2006	2007	1999	2000	2001	2004	2006	2007
Bt variety	**5.2**	**6.5**	**15.6**	**19.6**	**16.0**	**10.9**	**0.0**	**0.0**	**0.3**	**7.1**	**6.5**	**4.9**
Hebei-Xinji	3.7	6.8	7.0	27.7	16.9	14.5	0.0	0.0	0.0	15.5	10.3	7.1
Hebei-Shenzhou	3.4	2.6	—	—	11.0	8.5	0.0	0.0	—	—	8.0	5.9
Shandong-Xiajin	5.8	9.5	—	—	17.2	12.6	0.0	0.0	0.0	—	8.1	3.9
Shandong-Liangshan	7.0	6.4	10.8	7.6	5.8	5.9	0.0	0.0	0.0	3.7	2.6	3.1
Henan-Taikang	7.1[1]	7.2	10.0	23.0	14.1	13.4	0.0[1]	0.0	1.0	11.4	6.4	4.6
Henan-Fugou	5.1[1]	5.3	9.4	15.9	16.9	11.6	0.0[1]	0.0	0.6	4.6	8.4	4.9
Anhui-Dongzhi	—	—	38.0	25.0	23.7		—	—	0.3	0.1	4.0	
Anhui-Wangjiang	—	—	27.5	22.3	22.5		—	—	0.5	0.1	5.7	
Non-Bt variety	**8.4**	**11.0**	**17.9**	**23.5**	**22.9**		**0.0**	**0.0**	**0.2**	**8.3**	**14.5**	
Hebei-Xinji	—	—	—	—	33.2		—	—	—	—	30.4	
Hebei-Shenzhou	—	—	—	—	—		—	—	—	—	—	
Shandong-Xiajin	8.4	—	—	—	—		0.0	—	—	—	—	
Shandong-Liangshan	—	—	—	—	8.8		—	—	—	—	5.3	
Henan-Taikang	5.2[1]	6.5	15.6	19.6	16.0		0.0[1]	0.0	0.3	7.1	6.5	
Henan-Fugou	3.7[1]	6.8	7.0	27.7	16.9		0.0[1]	0.0	0.0	15.5	10.3	
Anhui-Dongzhi	3.4	2.6	—	—	11.0		0.0	0.0	—	—	8.0	
Anhui-Wangjiang	5.8	9.3	—	—	17.2		0.0	0.0	—	—	8.1	

Source: CCAP farm surveys in 4 provinces of China, 1999-2006 and CCAP 2007 farm survey.

Notes: There were only a few observations for Non-Bt in 2006, and none in 2007.
1 Figures for Henan (1999) estimated from 2000 questionnaire.

chemicals used for bollworm, other factors are also important. We examined the question using a multivariate regression analysis and found that the rising level of secondary pests is not significantly related to the insecticide practices for bollworm, but rather that differences in temperature and rainfall explain 40–80 per cent of the variation of insecticide use for mirids (Wang *et al.* 2009).

Despite the significant drop in insecticide use in cotton over the past decade, farmers are still using very high levels of chemicals. An earlier analysis showed that Bt cotton growers' insecticide rates were 10 kg/ha higher than the optimum, and non-Bt growers were using an excess of 40 kg/ha (Huang *et al.* 2002b). These very high rates of chemical use are a function of both frequent spraying and high dosages. When we asked farmers in our 2007 sample about dosage, 91 per cent claimed that they used more insecticide than the recommendation on the label. Many use the label as a reference and adjust the dosage according to experience. Only 15 per cent of the farmers claimed to rely on the advice of the sellers regarding dosage. Almost all of the pesticide sellers we interviewed said that access to more technical information, in order to make recommendations to farmers, would be the principal factor that would help them gain more customers.

From the data collected during the 2007 survey we saw a great diversity among farmers. Significant differences existed not only among different locations, but also between farmers in the same village. Figures 6.5 and 6.6 give us an impression of the distribution of general insecticide use and insecticide use specifically for bollworm. To quantify the effects from different factors, we also did regression analysis. The results indicated that the county variable, which mainly accounts for weather conditions, explained 20 per cent of variation in insecticide use. When we added the village variable, which is mainly a proxy for some environmental conditions such as soil and cropping pattern, the R^2 of the model rose only slightly to 0.26. Those results confirm that much of the difference in insecticide use comes from differences among farmers in the same village.

These results would also reinforce the conclusion that it should be possible for farmers to significantly reduce their dependence on insecticides, but this requires education and training. We examined lack of information and risk preference as possible explanations for the overuse of insecticide, with the policy implication that we can further reduce insecticide use in Bt cotton through education and agricultural insurance.

To identify the impacts of technology information on insecticide use, we asked farmers a set of five questions covering knowledge about the characteristics of Bt technology and key aspects of pest control. We classified farmers into two groups: low score (0–2) and high score (3–5). Table 6.21 shows that there is considerable variation in knowledge among the farmers. The average farmer in the low-score group sprayed significantly more insecticide than farmers in the high score group. This result highlights the important role of training in pest control and verifies the importance of education.

We also tested the relationship between risk preference and insecticide use (Table 6.21). The farmers are classified into three groups according to the degree of their risk preferences (represented by the symbol σ). The risk preference was

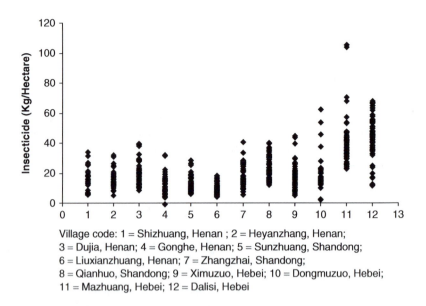

Figure 6.5 Insecticide application in sample villages, Henan, Shandong and Hebei, 2007

Source: CCAP 2007 farm survey.

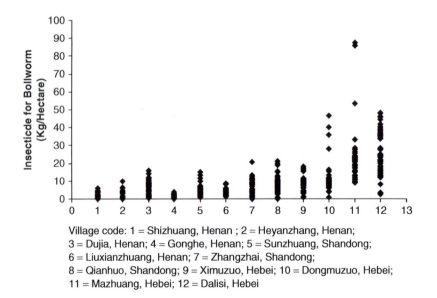

Figure 6.6 Insecticide application for bollworm in sample villages, Henan, Shandong and Hebei, 2007

Source: CCAP 2007 farm survey.

Table 6.21 Relationship between insecticide application (kg/ha) and (a) technology knowledge and (b) risk preference

	Number of plots	*Insecticide application*	*t-value*
Technology knowledge			
Low-score group (0–2)	461	25.9	
			5.02[1]
High-score group(3–5)	182	19.1	
Risk preference			
Group 1(0.05 ≤ σ ≤ 0.5)	363	24.5	
			0.21
Group 2(0.55 ≤ σ ≤ 1)	239	24.2	
			3.63[1]
Group 3(1.05 ≤ σ ≤ 1.5)	41	17.1	

Source: CCAP farm surveys in three provinces of China, 2006–2007.

Note
1 Significant at 1%.

measured using a series of dichotomous lotteries with varying probabilities to win a monetary prize, an experiment conducted in 2006. (For more detail on the design of the experiment, see Liu 2008). As shown in Table 6.21, group 1 is the lowest risk-taking group while group 3 is the highest one. The average insecticide application of group 1 is significantly higher than that of group 3. The results indicate that risk plays an important role in explaining farmers' pest-control behaviour.

Conclusions

Bt cotton has made a significant contribution to Chinese cotton production. Introduced at a time when bollworm damage and increasing insecticide use were threatening the future of the industry, the new technology provided effective pest control and allowed farmers to increase their productivity. The technology spread rapidly through those cotton-growing areas where it was most needed. But a decade after its introduction it is time to assess what has been learned and to identify policy priorities.

Bt cotton spread so rapidly because publicly available transgenes were available to seed companies while China was experiencing the emergence of the private seed sector. If Monsanto's joint ventures had been the only source of Bt seed then the technology would have spread more slowly, but public biotechnology research also provided Bt transgenes to plant breeding institutes and seed companies who incorporated them in new varieties. A large number of small- and medium-size companies ensured that seed was widely available. But both the multinational's and the public sector's technologies were used by many seed companies without authorization, and without compliance with China's seed and biosafety regulations. The short-term result for farmers has been largely positive, with wide availability and low seed price. But the seed market has become so complex that farmers have trouble identifying superior varieties and often prefer to save the seed of the varieties that perform well. In addition, neither private nor public research has sufficient incentives to introduce new technology if they feel that any licensing agreements will be violated in an unregulated seed market.

Privatization also benefited the pesticide sector, and Chinese farmers have wide access to products at low prices. But these low prices encourage over-use, and although Bt cotton greatly reduced the need for insecticide, there is evidence that farmers are still using more chemicals than they need to control pests. In addition, the unregulated use of trade names and (until recently) the lack of a requirement to describe an insecticide's active ingredients on the label mean that farmers have little ability to identify high-quality products or to learn from their experience.

These conditions help us identify several areas that deserve the attention of policymakers. First, reforming agricultural input markets is a high priority. Both seed and pesticide markets need to be made more transparent. China's seed and biosafety regulations were designed to support a competitive seed sector, but there has been little enforcement. Similarly, new regulations in the pesticide sector are well intentioned, but must be backed up by adequate enforcement. The unrestricted proliferation of seed and pesticide firms is not necessarily compatible with a competitive and efficient input market. It may be that further regulations are necessary, or that more restrictions are needed to control market entry, but investment in on-the-ground enforcement capacity for regulations already in place would be an important step forward.

In addition, it will be necessary to strengthen consumer capacities. Farmers find it difficult to identify reliable products in the input markets. The enforcement of regulations should put pressure on businesses to develop commercial reputations that help farmers recognize the seed or chemical companies that are in the market. Attention could also be given to helping input dealers acquire more information about their products so that they can advise their customers.

But it will not be possible to rely solely on a well-regulated private input market to provide sufficient information. The public extension and research services need to offer more information to farmers about the crop varieties and crop management technology that is available. Farmers should have more access to tests and demonstrations of new technology. The recent policy to stop extension agents earning part of their income from commercial activities in input and output markets is welcome and should be enforced in its implementation. In addressing complex problems such as pest control in cotton, extension stations need to be supported to help farmers learn how to take best advantage of agricultural input markets and to improve their own crop management skills.

7 India's experience with Bt cotton: Case studies from Gujarat and Maharashtra[1]

N. Lalitha, Bharat Ramaswami and P.K. Viswanathan

Introduction

India grows more *Bacillus thuringiensis* (Bt) cotton than any other country in the world. While this is partly a reflection of the fact that India is the world's largest cotton producer, it is also an indication of the rapid spread of the technology since it first became available in 2002. While India was cautious in introducing the technology, it has subsequently found wide acceptance among farmers.

Cotton is grown on 9.5 million ha by about 4–4.5 million farmers (with an average cotton holding of little more than 2 ha) in nine states in India. Although it has the largest cotton area, India's production has been characterized by relatively low yields, reflecting the marginal environments in which much cotton is grown, the fact that only about one-third of the crop has access to irrigation, and inadequate crop management. However, the introduction of Bt cotton has coincided with increasing cotton yields and production in the past few years.

In this chapter we are particularly interested in the seed and pesticide markets that help determine farmers' ability to take advantage of Bt cotton. The goal is to understand whether there are gaps in the information utilized by growers in making decisions about crop management. These gaps could arise because of market failures or deficiencies in other institutions such as government regulation, product testing and agricultural extension.

The chapter is based on a farm-level survey carried out during the 2007–08 cotton season in two states, Gujarat and Maharashtra. Although cotton is widely grown in India, these two states together accounted for 55 per cent of cotton output and 60 per cent of cotton area in 2007. In addition, they provide a useful contrast for the study; Gujarat is one of the more advanced cotton-growing states, with widespread access to irrigation, while Maharashtra is home to many of the most resource-poor cotton growers, farming on marginal land. An additional contrast is that Gujarat is the first place that unauthorized Bt cotton seed was sold, at least as early as 2001, before the release of the authorized varieties. Gujarat continues to have the highest concentration of unauthorized Bt cotton varieties and thus provides an interesting opportunity to follow the progress of an underground seed market.

1 We sincerely thank our research investigators who helped us collecting the primary data from farmers in both the states. Particularly we thank Ila Mehta, Devendra, Laljibhai, Bhimbhai and Prabhat who worked tirelessly in Gujarat. In Maharashtra we were ably assisted by Mr Atul Sharma and his team members Kishore, Promod, Mayur and Vaishali.

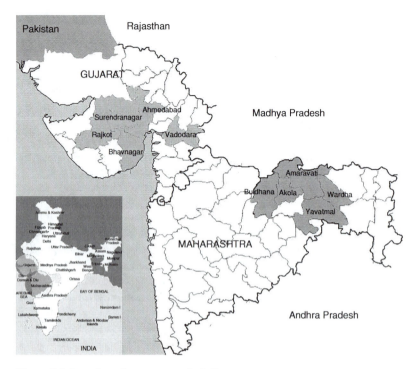

Figure 7.1 Location of survey areas in India

Note:
The northern border illustrated is a matter of dispute between India and Paksitan.

In Gujarat, the farm survey was carried out in five leading cotton-growing districts (Ahmedabad, Bhavnagar, Rajkot, Vadodara and Surendranagar) which together account for 65 per cent of cotton area in the state. This choice was partly determined by the fact that we had done an earlier study of cotton farmers in these districts in 2003–04 and could thus assess changes in the intervening years. The study in Maharashtra was done in traditional cotton-growing areas in the Vidarbha region, covering five districts (Wardha, Amaravati, Akola, Yavatmal and Buldhana) which together account for about 40 per cent of the cotton area in Maharashtra. The survey areas are indicated on the map in Figure 7.1.

In each district, approximately 40 cotton growers were randomly selected through a three-stage process. Within each district, four *talukas* (an administrative unit smaller than a district) were randomly selected and within each taluka, two villages were randomly sampled. The target was to sample five cotton growers within each village. In Maharashtra, the sample design accommodated more than five growers in some villages because of concerns over attrition during the length of the survey.

The study involved three visits to each farmer. The first visit took place shortly after planting and data collection focused on farm and household characteristics and current and historical variety choices. The second visit came during the growing season and focused on insect control practices, including a careful recording

Table 7.1 The study sample

District	No. of farmers interviewed	Total no. of cotton plots planted by sample farmers	No. of focus plots for study of insecticide use
Gujarat Districts			
1. Rajkot	40	108	89
2. Bhavnagar	40	115	85
3. Vadodara	40	89	75
4. Surendranagar	40	128	87
5. Ahmedabad	40	106	81
Total Gujarat	200	546	417
Maharashtra Districts			
1. Wardha	43	91	83
2. Amaravati	40	118	101
3. Akola	40	100	86
4. Yavatmal	43	77	69
5. Buldhana	39	88	83
Total Maharashtra	205	474	422

of all use of insecticide. (Farmers had been provided with notebooks during the first visit to help record their insecticide practices.) The final visit was shortly after harvest; it completed the inventory of insecticide use as well as collecting yield and other data. As many farmers have several plots of cotton, we recorded basic data about all the plots. However for detailed analysis on crop management, such as decision-making about seed choices, insecticide practices, harvesting and post-harvest management practices, we focused on a maximum of three plots for each farmer, choosing the largest plots that provided information about the range of variety types the farmer was growing. The basic characteristics of the sample farm households and holdings are summarized in Table 7.1.

The rest of the chapter is organized as follows: we first look at the utilization of Bt cotton by summarizing some of the most important characteristics of the cotton farmers in our sample and the nature of the Indian seed market, followed by an examination of the patterns of Bt cotton adoption and its impacts on yields. The next section looks more closely at how cotton farmers choose the seed they will plant; it reviews the types of Bt cotton available to farmers and then looks at the criteria they use in making seed choices. The following section examines how farmers use insecticides and the relationship between Bt technology and insecticide use. The chapter closes with some conclusions about the ability of farmers to take advantage of Bt technology.

The utilization of Bt cotton

The cotton farmers

Cotton is grown in contrasting environments in the two states. In the study districts of Gujarat, cotton is an important crop accounting for 27–51 per cent of cropped area. Other crops grown in these districts include groundnut, wheat, pearl millet and sesame. A few rows of crops such as maize, castor or mung beans are sometimes

Table 7.2 Sample farmer characteristics

District	Total cultivable area/farmer (ha)	Cotton area/farmer (ha)	Average no. cotton plots per farmer	% land irrigated	% total income from cotton
Gujarat					
1. Rajkot	6.11	3.40	2.2	79.5	70.38
2. Bhavnagar	8.86	6.19	2.5	77.9	78.62
3. Vadodara	8.46	4.67	2.0	91.4	62.63
4. Surendranagar	8.00	5.73	2.9	53.0	85.30
5. Ahmedabad	7.26	5.41	2.2	60.3	79.08
All districts	7.70	5.08	2.7	72.6	75.33
Maharashtra					
1. Wardha	7.15	2.10	2.1	56.54	40.35
2. Amaravati	4.41	2.11	2.7	32.16	55.58
3. Akola	8.27	2.54	2.5	51.25	34.63
4. Yavatmal	5.43	1.67	1.9	19.48	37.88
5. Buldhana	6.31	1.67	2.3	75.66	34.97
All districts	6.30	2.02	2.3	49.02	40.92

Source: Survey data.

sown intercropped in cotton fields. Cotton is planted in the month of June and most of it is harvested by December, but for some long-duration varieties the last picking may take place in March. Gujarat's cotton area has been expanding in recent years, rising from 1.7 million ha in 2001 to about 2.5 million ha in 2007.

In Maharashtra, on the other hand, cotton area has remained steady at about 3 million ha in the past decade. There is less irrigation than in Gujarat; other crops that are grown include wheat, sorghum, onions, pigeonpeas and pulses. Cotton area has recently been losing out to soybeans, which also enjoy greater policy support from the state government. Normally cotton is planted in the middle of June and harvested in the month of December. In Maharashtra cotton fields are often intercropped with occasional rows of pigeonpea, mung bean or black gram.

Table 7.2 summarizes some of the principal characteristics of the two state samples.

In both areas, cotton farmers buy all of their production inputs in shops located in nearby towns whose dealers represent seed and chemical companies. The only exception is fertilizer in Gujarat, where many farmers get fertilizer on credit through cooperative societies. All cotton farmers sell their seed cotton to private buyers who then deliver it to ginneries. The cotton is not graded at the time of purchase and farmers receive a standard price. Although the government declares a minimum support price, this has little influence on the prices paid for cotton procurement.

The cotton seed industry

Indian farmers have had access to a range of cotton varieties for many years. It is important to note that India was the first country in the world to commercialize cotton hybrids, the outcome of a public sector research program that led to the first cotton hybrid in 1970. Through the 1970s and 1980s the public sector agricultural research system released many location-specific hybrids whose seed was sold by state seed corporations. Although the first privately bred, proprietary hybrid was released in 1979, it was only in the 1990s that private sector efforts gained momentum. In 1996 hybrid varieties accounted for about 55 per cent of the total cotton area, but two-thirds of this was covered by public hybrids. By 2004, hybrids covered 6 million ha (two-thirds of the cotton area), of which 5 million ha were sown to proprietary hybrids (Murugkar *et al.* 2007). Hybrid cotton spread more rapidly in the southern and central zones of India than in the northern zone (e.g. Punjab), where the late maturity of most hybrids made them less compatible with local cropping systems, but the popularity of Bt cotton (combined with increased private breeding efforts) has meant that even states such as Punjab have now moved towards Bt hybrids.

Thus long before the advent of Bt cotton many cotton growers in India were familiar with hybrid seed and with the practice of purchasing seed from dealers each year. Nevertheless, the early experiences with Bt cotton in Gujarat and Maharashtra exhibit some important differences.

Gujarat is the home of the first cotton hybrid (H4), developed by the Gujarat Agricultural University and sold to farmers through the Gujarat State Seed Corporation (GSSC). H4 and its successors held sway among Gujarat cotton farmers for a long time, although proprietary hybrids also began making significant inroads.

Before the approval of the first Bt varieties from Mahyco Monsanto Biotech (MMB) in 2002, an unauthorized Bt cotton hybrid was discovered in farmers' fields in Gujarat. The discovery was made in 2001, but the variety may have been present even earlier. The unauthorized variety was NB151, a variety registered with the Gujarat government as a conventional hybrid and belonging to Navbharat Seeds, a firm based in Ahmedabad. Later investigation confirmed that the Bt gene in NB151 was the one developed by Monsanto and used in the approved varieties. After initial threats by the state government to destroy all fields with NB151, farmers were allowed to harvest and market their crop, but the company was barred from the cotton seed business and has been prosecuted for violating the biosafety laws.

Despite the ban on Navbharat, the unapproved Bt hybrids continue to be widely available and highly popular in Gujarat. Although the unapproved seed is particularly prevalent in Gujarat, it can be found to a lesser extent in some other states, including Andhra Pradesh and Punjab. It would appear that the breeding lines for the NB151 hybrid have been provided to a number of informal seed enterprises who produce the seed on farms in Andhra Pradesh and Gujarat. In the early years the variety was in such high demand that second generation (F2) seed of the hybrid was also sold. It was usually identified as such and sold for a lower price than the F1.

The unauthorized Bt varieties are hybrids, and because hybrid seed production requires organization, capital and specialized labour, unauthorized seed production and distribution is unlikely to be the outcome of individual acts of piracy (Ramaswami *et al.* forthcoming). Rather, the seed is produced through a loose network of seed growers (many of whom were former contract seed growers for Navbharat) and their agents. It is not clear how many people in this network obtained the Navbharat inbred parental lines, but their ownership seems fairly dispersed. As a result, there has been wide experimentation and the male parent (with the Bt gene) often has been crossed with different female lines producing a range of hybrids well adapted to local conditions.

Although the seed producers are careful not to advertise on a wide scale, the unauthorized seeds are sold under locally known brand names, or simply known as NB151. It may be sold as loose seed, but is more frequently packaged. Many of the packages superficially resemble those of legitimate brands, but the name and location of the seed company is absent and the package often includes a disclaimer stating that it does not contain commercial seed but is merely an opportunity for farmers to exchange seed among themselves. If the production and distribution of unauthorized seeds occurs through individual growers saving and exchanging seed, as allowed by Indian seed law, governments have limited powers to enforce biosafety laws. This loophole has allowed the state government to claim ignorance of the extent of unauthorized plantings, although seed law would allow inspectors to raid shops and seize at least the unauthorized seed sold in individual packets. For their part, unauthorized seed sellers try to soften their challenge to the law by taking care to mask their sales as seed exchange. The unauthorized seeds are sold without a bill of purchase. Although it is still not on display in any shop, some dealers are now willing to talk openly about it, as they have seen that the state government has not attempted to restrict the sale of what is still a very popular type of seed.

The immense popularity of the unapproved Bt hybrid in Gujarat captured a large part of the market previously in the hands of legitimate seed producers, both public and private. While hybrid cotton seed was previously 25 per cent of the turnover of the GSSC, this dropped to 5 per cent by 2003–04. Vikram Seeds, previously the leading private hybrid cotton seed provider in the state, lost most of its market, compounded by the fact that it was not among the first Indian companies to license the Bt gene for its own breeding program (Murugkar *et al.* 2007). It is only recently that legitimate seed companies with approved Bt cotton hybrids have begun to make an impression on the Gujarat market.

In addition, some farmers in Gujarat also grow local (*desi*) cotton. These are traditional varieties of *Gossypium arboreum* which are known for their drought tolerance and resistance to sucking pests. They tend to be planted on unirrigated land, usually by larger farmers, and they receive less intensive management than the hybrids.

The cotton seed situation in Maharashtra is somewhat more straightforward. Before the introduction of Bt cotton, many Indian seed companies had established a market share for their proprietary hybrids in the state. In addition, some public hybrids produced and sold by the Maharashtra State Seed Corporation were also popular. The original approved Bt varieties were only available from one company (Mahyco) and a few farmers began to plant them. Some unapproved seed was also available, but the authorities in Maharashtra have been quite strict in controlling the availability of such seed. Dealers say they would be closed down if they were found selling it, and no farmer in our Maharashtra sample claimed to

Table 7.3 Bt cotton adoption trends for sample farmers

Gujarat

	Aggregate cotton area (ha)	Aggregate Area under Bt cotton (ha)	Proportion of cotton area under Bt cotton
2003/04	737.25	394.33	0.54
2004/05	781.78	519.43	0.67
2005/06	879.76	704.86	0.80
2006/07	967.21	832.79	0.86
2007/08	1014.57	912.55	0.90

Maharashtra

	Aggregate cotton area (ha)	Aggregate Area under Bt cotton (ha)	Proportion of cotton area under Bt cotton
2003/04	376.92	6.48	0.02
2004/05	406.88	18.62	0.05
2005/06	414.17	65.59	0.16
2006/07	450.61	244.94	0.54
2007/08	414.57	300.81	0.73

Source: Survey data.

be growing unapproved Bt cotton. As the companies who had been providing conventional hybrids to Maharashtra farmers became able to license the Bt gene from Monsanto they were soon able to bring to market Bt versions of some of the varieties that farmers had been planting. In addition, other new Bt hybrids began to appear on the market in Maharashtra.

Adoption of Bt cotton

The trends in the adoption of Bt cotton are summarized in Table 7.3. In Gujarat, only 10 per cent of the sample area is under non-Bt cotton and almost all of this is *desi* varieties. The adoption of Bt cotton has occurred along with an increase in area under cotton, possibly because the yield advantages of Bt cotton are edging out other competing crops. In Maharashtra, area under cotton is levelling off and the adoption of Bt cotton lags behind Gujarat. The big jumps in adoption have occurred more recently than in Gujarat, in 2006 and 2007, corresponding to similar trends at the national level.

Another way to look at the adoption process is to compare the number of farmers that grow only Bt varieties, only conventional varieties, or both types of variety. Table 7.4 shows that in 2003–04, almost the entire sample in Maharashtra and nearly half the sample in Gujarat grew only non-Bt varieties. Since then, the situation has rapidly changed in both states. The number of growers with only non-Bt cotton has diminished to negligible levels in Gujarat and to only 30 growers in the Maharashtra sample. The rest of the farmers grow either only Bt cotton varieties or a combination of Bt and conventional varieties.

Table 7.4 Adoption trends by number of growers[1]

Year	Gujarat. No. of farmers growing:			Maharashtra. No. of farmers growing:		
	Only Bt	Bt and non-Bt	Only non-Bt	Only Bt	Bt and non-Bt	Only non-Bt
2003/04	102	10	69	3	0	169
2004/05	122	16	49	9	3	174
2005/06	160	12	25	29	17	142
2006/07	170	19	10	92	46	60
2007/08	174	21	4	134	42	30

Source: Survey data.

Note
1 A few sample farmers are not included in the earlier years because they were not able to clearly identify the varieties they were growing at that time.

Table 7.5 The diffusion of illegal seeds in Gujarat (sample area)

	Area under illegal seeds (ha)	Proportion of Bt cotton area under illegal varieties	No. of farmers growing only illegal Bt varieties	No. of farmers growing only legal Bt varieties	No. of farmers growing both legal and illegal Bt varieties
2003/04	304	0.77	81	23	8
2004/05	425	0.82	102	24	12
2005/06	481	0.68	106	43	23
2006/07	525	0.63	98	51	40
2007/08	535	0.59	100	62	34

Source: Survey data.

Table 7.5 shows that while the total area under unauthorized Bt seeds has increased in Gujarat, this phenomenon peaked in relative terms in 2004–05. Since then, the area under authorized Bt seeds has expanded much more rapidly, although by 2007–08 the proportion of Bt cotton area under unauthorized seeds was still greater than 50 per cent. The table also looks at the diffusion of unauthorized seeds by number of growers. In the early years, most Bt growers adopted unauthorized varieties. After 2004–05, while the number of unauthorized Bt growers has remained stagnant, the number of authorized Bt growers has grown. The early authorized Bt varieties did not necessarily have all the agronomic qualities of some of the conventional varieties, but starting in 2005 a much wider range of commercial Bt hybrid varieties became available. This may have played a role in the steadily increasing adoption of authorized Bt varieties in Gujarat.

Who adopts Bt cotton?

Because almost all farmers in Gujarat plant at least some Bt cotton, and the vast majority in Maharashtra do so, we have difficulty analysing differences between

Table 7.6 Adoption of Bt in Maharashtra

Farmer characteristics	Farmers who use some or all Bt	Farmers who use no Bt	Significance of difference[1]
No. of farmers	176	30	—
Average age	43.76	45.1	ns
Average education (years)	11.12	9.46	*
Average landholding (ha)	6.7	3.5	***
Average cotton holding (ha)	2.09	1.55	*
% income from cotton	39.7	46.7	ns

Source: Survey data.

Note
1 ns = not significant,
* significant at 10% level,
** significant at 5% level,
*** significant at 1% level.

Table 7.7 Differences between growers who use unapproved seed and others, Gujarat

Farmer characteristics	Farmers who use only unapproved varieties	Other Bt growers (who use some or all approved varieties	Significance of difference[1]
No. of farmers	100	96	—
Average age	46	46.8	ns
Average education	9	10.2	ns
Average landholding (ha)	6.68	8.91	**
Average irrigated landholding (ha)	4.11	7.26	***
Average cotton holding (ha)	4.94	5.24	ns
% income from cotton	82	69	***

Source: Survey data.

Note
1 ns = not significant,
** denotes significance at 5% level,
*** denotes significance at 1% level.

adopters and non-adopters of Bt. Table 7.6 compares the characteristics of those farmers in Maharashtra who plant no Bt cotton with those who plant some or all Bt cotton. The minority who do not use Bt cotton appear to have somewhat smaller landholdings and less area in cotton, although they depend as heavily on cotton for their incomes as do the adopting farmers.

For Gujarat, the most interesting comparison is between those who grow only unapproved Bt cotton varieties and those who plant at least some approved varieties (Table 7.7). The biggest difference is that the greater the extent of irrigated land and total area, the more likely it is that the grower does not use unapproved seeds. This possibly reflects the fact that households that have irrigation prefer to plant approved seeds. In addition, the greater the percentage of income from cotton, the greater the probability that a grower chooses unapproved seed. Thus it appears that smaller farmers with less irrigation and less diversified cropping systems continue to rely on unauthorized seed, perhaps because it is cheaper.

Cotton yields

Table 7.8 reports our sample median seed cotton yields in Gujarat and Maharashtra for 2005–07. (We use medians as opposed to averages because they are more robust to outliers and measurement errors. In most of the cases considered here the medians are close to, but lower than, area-weighted average yields.)

In both states median Bt cotton yields are higher than non-Bt cotton yields. In Gujarat the gap is large and statistically significant, but by the time of our survey there were very few non-Bt fields in Gujarat, and most of those were planted to *desi* cotton, which receives less management attention. For Gujarat we also examined the average yields for approved and unapproved Bt cotton varieties (Table 7.9). In all years, the yield for approved varieties is higher than that of unapproved varieties, although the difference in median yields is statistically significant only in 2006. This is a reversal of the situation in 2003–04 where our survey found unapproved varieties to generally outperform approved varieties (Table 7.10). The gap in yields between Bt and non-Bt hybrid cotton noted in the earlier survey is consistent with, and indeed helps explain, the rapid adoption of Bt varieties in Gujarat.

The gap between Bt and non-Bt cotton yields shown for Maharashtra in Table 7.8 is smaller than the gap noted for Gujarat (Table 7.10), which might also help explain the slower pace of adoption of Bt in that state. Yields are considerably lower in Maharashtra, in part because most cotton is grown without irrigation.

Figure 7.2 shows average seed cotton yields for Gujarat, Maharashtra and all India. It can be seen that that there is a fairly consistent upward trend beginning in 2002, which corresponds with the release of Bt cotton. The increase is particularly sharp in Gujarat, which is consistent with the rapid shifts towards Bt observed in our data. The yields seem to level off in Gujarat from 2005 (consistent with our survey results), which can be explained by the fact that by this time most of the growers had already shifted to Bt cotton and therefore this source of technological change was largely exhausted. In Maharashtra, average yields have risen in parallel with the shift to Bt cotton; the upward trend is not as sharp as in Gujarat, perhaps because of the slower pace of the shift to Bt cotton varieties, but is still continuing. The recent yield increase noted for India may have several explanations. For instance, there is some evidence that farmers often provide better management for the expensive new Bt varieties (e.g. Narayanamoorthy and Kalamkar 2006; Qaim *et al.* 2006). But a very substantial part of the increase is surely due to the improved production provided by the protection from insect damage offered by the Bt varieties that are now widely grown.

Table 7.8 Median seed cotton yields for sample farmers

Year	Gujarat						Maharashtra					
	Cotton yield (kg/ha)	No. of plots	Bt cotton yield (kg/ha)	No. of plots	Non-Bt cotton yield (kg/ha)	No. of plots	Cotton yield (kg/ha)	No. of plots	Bt cotton yield (kg/ha)	No. of plots	Non-Bt cotton yield (kg/ha)	No. of plots
2005/06	2058	328	2196	282	988	46	988	349	1235	63	988	285
2006/07	1966	403	2164	367	865	36	1186	426	1383	238	988	188
2007/08	1729	337	1801	315	988	22	1317	390	1376	310	1112	80

Source: Survey data.

Table 7.9 Yields of approved and unapproved varieties in Gujarat, 2005–07 (kg seed
cotton per hectare)

Gujarat	Approved varieties		Unapproved varieties	
	Cotton yield kg/ha	No. of plots	Cotton yield Kg/ha	No. of plots
2005/06	2470	87	2161	195
2006/07	2398	137	1976	230
2007/08	1801	177	1729	138

Source: Survey data.

Table 7.10 Yields of approved and unapproved varieties in Gujarat, 2003–04 (kg seed
cotton per hectare)

Type of variety	Desi	Non-Bt hybrid	Legal Bt	Illegal F1 Bt
Yield (kg/ha)	492	1613	2468	2836

Source: Ramaswami *et al.* (forthcoming).

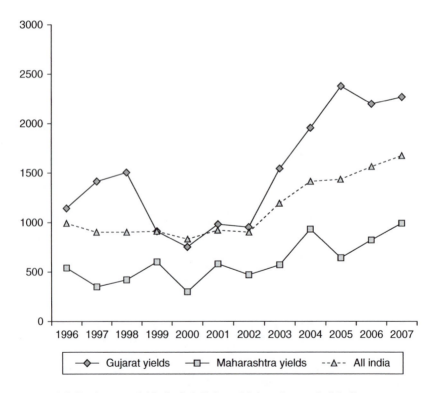

Figure 7.2 Seed cotton yields (kg/ha) Gujarat, Maharashtra and all India

Source: Cotton Advisory Board.

Seed choice

The cotton seed market

When the first approved Bt hybrids were brought to market, their price was four times that of conventional hybrids. Several state governments protested and established a maximum price for Bt seed (equivalent to approximately twice the price of conventional hybrid cotton seed), which turned into a national price cap. The unapproved seed originally sold for somewhat less than the approved seed (about three times the price of conventional hybrids), but because of competition from the many new approved Bt varieties that have been released the price of the unapproved seed has dropped drastically, to the point where it now sells for slightly less than conventional (non-Bt) hybrid cotton seed. In 2007, seed with Monsanto's 'Bollgard II' gene became available in hybrids produced by several Indian seed companies. The price was set at three times the conventional hybrid price, but in 2008 state governments again stepped in and limited the price to that of the other Bt varieties.

All seed of approved cotton hybrids (conventional and Bt) is sold in packets of 450 grams, calculated to be sufficient to plant 1 acre. The seeding rate for hybrid cotton is significantly less than that for conventional seed, so the high price of the hybrid is partially compensated by the low seeding rate. But the high price of hybrid seed presents an added risk to farmers in marginal environments subject to drought or flooding. Hybrid Bt cotton represents an investment of about US$40 per hectare. If an Indian farmer is able to demonstrate that purchased seed (of any crop) was of poor quality and did not germinate, he or she may be able to press for compensation, and consumer courts will hear such cases. But there is no mechanism for insuring against loss due to natural calamities. During our study we heard of a few cases where a company was willing to provide fresh seed of a Bt hybrid to a farmer who had lost the initial planting because of flooding, but this is unusual. In some cases in Gujarat, farmers with a poor initial plant stand of an approved Bt hybrid buy seed of an unapproved hybrid to fill in the gaps.

Farmers in both Gujarat and Maharashtra face a complex seed market that offers many choices. Table 7.11 provides an indication of this complexity by summarizing the aggregate number of distinct varieties reported by the farmers in our survey over the past five years. (The complete range of cotton varieties in these two states is of course wider than this, but these figures provide a useful estimation.) We distinguish between Bt and non-Bt varieties and in Gujarat we also show the number of distinct authorized and unauthorized varieties. We consider distinct varieties as those known by distinct names. If the same variety is called something different in another village or district it would enter in the survey as a distinct variety. This is a particular challenge for the unauthorized varieties and it is possible that many of these differ little from each other but are simply sold under different local names.

In both states farmers currently have at least 50–60 approved Bt hybrids to choose from, and this number has been growing steadily. On the other hand, the number of conventional hybrids grown by the sample farmers has been declining. The most remarkable difference between the two states comes from the unapproved varieties in Gujarat.

Table 7.11 Number of distinct varieties sown by sample farmers, 2003–07

Year	Gujarat					Maharashtra		
	No. of distinct varieties	No. of distinct Bt varieties	No. of distinct non-Bt varieties	No. of distinct authorized Bt varieties	No. of distinct unauthorized varieties	No. of distinct varieties	No. of distinct Bt varieties	No. of distinct non-Bt varieties
2003–04	79	56	21	13	43	62	4	57
2004–05	89	65	22	15	50	66	10	55
2005–06	116	103	12	27	76	90	20	68
2006–07	148	135	12	34	101	86	32	53
2007–08	190	180	9	54	126	98	62	36

Source: Survey data.

Table 7.12 Number of varieties grown by sample farmers

Year/ growers	Gujarat			Maharashtra		
	No. of distinct varieties per grower	No. of distinct Bt varieties per grower	No. of distinct non-Bt varieties per grower	No. of distinct varieties per grower	No. of distinct Bt varieties per grower	No. of distinct non-Bt varieties per grower
2003–04	1.31	0.83	0.50	1.63	0.03	1.71
No. of growers	199	181	181	201	172	172
2004–05	1.40	1.03	0.39	1.65	0.08	1.63
No. of growers	200	187	187	204	186	186
2005–06	1.62	1.40	0.22	1.80	0.34	1.52
No. of growers	200	197	197	204	188	188
2006–07	1.97	1.80	0.17	2.13	1.21	0.94
No. of growers	200	199	199	203	198	198
2007–08	2.50	2.37	0.13	2.29	1.72	0.57
No. of growers	200	199	199	206	206	206

Source: Survey data.

Table 7.12 presents the average number of distinct Bt and non-Bt varieties grown by cotton farmers in Gujarat and Maharashtra. (In some cases neither the grower nor the interviewer could identify the variety type grown in past years, so the number of farmers for which we have identifiable variety information is less than the total number of growers.) The table shows that (a) the average number of varieties grown by a cultivator is increasing over time and (b) in the last couple of years, cultivators on average grow two or more distinct varieties. The first trend may be regarded with some suspicion because the data are based on recall, but the second feature of the table is more robust and demonstrates that farmers either hedge their bets or experiment with some new varieties, or both. When we examine the proportion of farmers growing different numbers of varieties, the figures for Gujarat and Maharashtra are remarkably similar. About 30 per cent of farmers grow only one variety, another 30 per cent grow two varieties, and the remaining 40 per cent grows three or more varieties. The table also demonstrates a third feature – as the importance of Bt varieties has grown, farmers have also expanded their choices of Bt varieties.

With so many different varieties available, and the average farmer planting about two varieties, it is important to consider the patterns of farmers' seed choice. Farmers buy their seed each year from shops, each of which carries the stock of a certain number of seed companies. The companies may offer incentives to the dealers to promote their products, and often provide items such as calendars that can be given to farmers. In addition, there is a great deal of advertising propaganda promoting different brands. There is thus much opportunity for the manipulation of farmers' choices, and it is worthwhile to look in more detail at how these are determined.

Criteria for seed choice

A study of Bt cotton in Warangal District, Andhra Pradesh, describes how farmers 'face a frenzied turnover in the seed market (which they encourage with their penchant for new products), deceptiveness in seed brands...and a noisy and unreliable information environment' (Stone 2007: 76). We can use our survey data to examine how typical this description of faddish and uninformed behaviour is for cotton seed markets in other parts of India.

In order to understand the extent to which the cotton seed markets in our study sites are unstable, we examined the distribution of cotton varieties for the 2007 and 2006 seasons. In Maharashtra, 13 varieties account for 70 per cent of all the cotton area in the sample in 2007. Of these 13 varieties, 9 are Bt and 4 are conventional; all are private varieties except for one conventional variety sold by the state seed corporation. In the previous season (2006) the top 13 varieties in Maharashtra accounted for 71 per cent of cotton area in the sample. Only 3 of the top 13 from 2006 fail to appear in the top 13 the following year, and 2 of those are hovering just outside the top 13 rank.

The situation in Gujarat is somewhat more complicated, particularly because of the presence of many different names of unauthorized varieties. In 2007, the top 25 varieties covered 65 per cent of the sample area and the top 10 varieties account for 45 per cent of the area. In the previous year (2006) the top 25 varieties covered 74 per cent of the area and the top 10 accounted for 52 per cent of the area. The only new entry in the top 10 for 2007 was a recently released 'Bollgard II' variety. There is more change in the top 25 varieties between the two years in the Gujarat sample, but some of this is because the unauthorized varieties are described by so many different names. In addition, some farmers in Gujarat were less precise than their counterparts in Maharashtra in being able to name approved varieties.

This examination of the most popular varieties provides some evidence of stability in variety choice at the aggregate level, but we need to understand more about individual farmer choices. The analysis for Andhra Pradesh distinguishes seed choices based on farmer experimentation ('environmental learning') and those based on persuasion or imitation ('social learning') (Stone 2007). Although social learning can itself have a basis in environmental observations, the suggestion is that social learning is also likely to be subject to very many biases that may reflect social pressures rather than first-hand experience.

There is no straightforward method for identifying a farmer's planting practices as experimental. A minimum requirement is that the farmer plant more than one variety, and we have seen that in our samples approximately 70 per cent of

Table 7.13 Cumulative distribution of novice plantings, sample farmers

Less than x% of total novice plantings	Maharashtra	Gujarat
	Proportion of area under novice plantings	Proportion of area under novice plantings
1%	0.08	0.02
5%	0.12	0.07
10%	0.14	0.08
25%	0.20	0.15
50%	0.33	0.25
75%	0.50	0.40
90%	0.90	0.71
95%	1.00	1.00
99%	1.00	1.00

Source: Survey data.

the farmers are planting two or more cotton varieties. There are various reasons for growing more than one variety. For our entire sample we found a modest correlation between number of varieties and total cotton area, and a stronger correlation with number of plots, which would indicate that farmers may target varieties to the varying conditions of their different plots or take advantage of multiple plots to test different varieties.

It is natural to suppose, however, that growers who intend to experiment will allocate small areas to varieties that they intend to evaluate. Table 7.13 examines the area devoted to 'novice plantings', the term Stone uses for varieties planted for the first time. (In Maharashtra this accounts for 44 per cent of cotton land and in Gujarat it covers 41 per cent of the cotton area.) The table shows the cumulative distribution of novice plantings (measured as proportion of total cotton area) among individual growers. In Maharashtra, 50 per cent of novice plantings are allocated to plots less than 33 per cent of a farmer's total cotton area. In Gujarat, the median value is 25 per cent of total area. These figures are similar to a classic study of the adoption of hybrid maize in Iowa which found that farmers planted a median of 18–30 per cent of their total maize acreage to hybrid seed when they first tried it (Ryan and Gross 1943). However, they are vastly different from Stone's study in Andhra Pradesh which found that as many as 70 per cent of novice plantings occupied the entire cotton area.

A key implication of the environmental learning hypothesis is that growers maintain continuity in their variety choices over time. We have already seen that more than 50 per cent of cotton area is accounted for by varieties planted in the past history of the grower. Another implication of the environmental learning hypothesis is that current area allocations to varieties depend on the grower's experience with that variety. To test this effect we regress the area allocated to variety x on 4 dummies. The first dummy takes the value 1 if in 2007 variety x is in the second year of planting. The second dummy takes the value 1 if in 2007

Table 7.14 Varietal history and area allocation: Maharashtra[1]

Experience with variety	Coef.	Robust std. error	t	P>t
2nd year of planting	0.75	0.15	4.84	0.00
3rd year of planting	0.60	0.24	2.47	0.01
4th year of planting	1.90	1.06	1.79	0.08
5th year of planting	0.97	0.40	2.41	0.02
Total cotton area	0.21	0.04	6.07	0.00
Constant	1.73	0.11	15.63	0
R^2		0.38		
No of observations		474		

Source: Survey data.

Note
1 See text for explanation of variables.

Table 7.15 Varietal history and area allocation: Gujarat[1]

Experience with variety	Coef.	Robust std. error	t	P>t
2nd year of planting	1.18	0.44	2.69	0.01
3rd year of planting	1.56	0.62	2.53	0.01
4th year of planting	2.21	0.66	3.36	0.00
5th year of planting	2.31	0.67	3.43	0.00
Total cotton area	0.21	0.03	7.15	0.00
Constant	0.53	0.41	1.29	0.20
R^2		0.33		
No of observations		547		

Source: Survey data.

Note
1 See text for explanation of variables.

variety *x* is in the third year of planting. The third and fourth dummies are defined similarly. The constant term then represents the effect if the variety is planted in 2007 for the very first time. The results are shown in Tables 7.14 and 7.15 and clearly indicate that the area allocation to a particular variety increases with greater farmer experience with that variety. In Maharashtra the area allocation reaches its peak in the fourth year of planting, while in the Gujarat allocation the experience effect continues to increase through the fifth year. These results attest to the strength of the environmental learning hypothesis.

If experimental plantings are subtracted from novice plantings, the remainder represents plantings due to social learning. While it is difficult to quantify the importance of different sorts of social learning, it is possible to see how much of novice planting involves varieties that are market leaders. This can be called the 'imitation effect'. While such social learning could stem from a herd instinct and therefore need not have any basis in environmental learning, it would also seem that observing varieties in the fields of other farmers or demonstration plots, or

Table 7.16 Types of planting (novice, experimental and imitation) for sample farmers, 2007

	Maharashtra (%)	Gujarat (%)
Proportion of total cotton area that is planted with:		
a) varieties farmer has grown in previous seasons	56	59
b) 'novice plantings' (varieties farmer plants for first time)	44	41
Proportion of 'novice planting' area that is:		
c) 'experimental' (occupies less than 30% of total cotton area)	38	44
d) 'imitation' (planted with varieties that were among 13 most popular in 2006)	50	24
e) 'imitation' but not 'experimental' (i.e. planted in *more than* 30% of total cotton area)	34	14
f) 'experimental' plus 'imitation' (c + e)	72	58

Source: Survey data.

exchange of information with other growers, is a lot more probable with the varieties that are popular than with varieties that are highly localized. This is particularly compelling when there are a large number of varieties on offer.

We quantify the imitation effect in the following manner. In both states, we suppose that a novice planting in 2007 embodies an imitation effect if the variety belonged to the top 13 list in the 2006 season. Table 7.16 expresses estimates of the imitation effect as percentage of all novice planting area. The gross estimate (line d) is the proportion of novice planting area due to the imitation effect. In the net estimate (line e), the imitation effect is computed after removing experimental plantings (defined as those novice plantings that account for 30 per cent or less of total area). The imitation effect is much stronger in Maharashtra. To see why the imitation effect is lower in Gujarat, we looked at the 15 varieties that had the highest share of novice plantings. Ten of these were varieties that were not ranked among the popular set in 2006. And of these ten varieties, seven were approved Bt varieties. It therefore seems that Gujarat farmers are moving towards approved Bt varieties and hence it is likely that the ranking of market leaders will change in future years. Farmer experimentation and imitation effects together explain 72 per cent of novice plantings in Maharashtra and 58 per cent in Gujarat.

Information sources

A question in the survey asked growers about their information sources when a variety was first planted. Table 7.17 summarizes the sources of information for

Table 7.17 Sources of information about Bt cotton seeds (percentage responses)

Principal response[1]	Maharashtra	Gujarat		
		All	Approved	Unapproved
Neighbourhood farmer	15	45	31	56
Seed dealer	29	28	44	15
Seen variety in fields of others	25	14	7	20
Advertisements in media	9	2	5	0
Demonstration plots	11	1	0	1
Others	10	10	13	9

Source: Survey data.

Note
1 The answers to this question sometimes had multiple responses. The table is compiled based on the first response, but including second responses does not change the relative importance of different information sources.

Bt varieties. There is an interesting contrast between Gujarat and Maharashtra. Consultation with local farmers (and observations in nearby fields) is most important for Gujarat farmers using unapproved seeds. In contrast, they rely heavily on dealers' advice for the approved varieties. Local learning (from neighbouring farmers and observing the variety in other fields) is most important for Maharashtra farmers, although seed dealers also play an important role. Advertisements and demonstration plots hold comparatively little sway although their influence is much more in Maharashtra than in Gujarat. It would seem that dealers' direct advice is the primary channel for companies to influence seed choices.

A follow-up question asked growers if they were able to buy their preferred varieties and in the required quantities. This was meant to ascertain whether seed dealers manipulate choices by denying growers their preferred seeds. In more than 90 per cent of cases in Gujarat and Maharashtra, growers obtained their variety of choice and in quantities sufficient for their requirements.

Insect control

The insecticide market

Farmers buy insecticides from input dealers, often the same ones that sell them seed. Many of the insecticides on the market are out-of-patent chemicals that are manufactured by large firms as well as by small formulators. In addition, there are a few newer (and often more expensive) proprietary insecticides on the market. Many insecticides are fairly heavily advertised on billboards and posters. Most farmers in the sample purchased their insecticides with cash.

Despite the relatively large number of products on the market, farmers are usually able to identify the insecticides that they use. In some cases they know the

Table 7.18 Labour use for insecticide application and farm size

Farm size class[1]	Proportion of plots					
	Gujarat			Maharashtra		
	Self or family labour	Only hired labour	Both or other	Self or family labour	Only hired labour	Both or other
Marginal	59	36	5	47	46	7
Small	51	46	3	19	70	11
Medium	22	71	7	16	73	11
Large	25	75	0	–	–	–

Source: Survey data.

Note
1   Farm size classes are defined as: a) marginal: 0–1 ha, b) small: 1–2 ha, c) medium: 2 –10 ha, d) large: above 10 ha.

product by its chemical name (e.g. monocrotophos), although this may be provided by a number of different firms; in other cases farmers know a trademarked name, especially for newer products (e.g. 'Confidor'); and in other cases farmers only know a brand name (e.g. 'Tiger') without necessarily knowing the active ingredient.

When farmers were asked about their source of information when they first purchased a particular insecticide, the majority (60 per cent in Gujarat and 67 per cent in Maharashtra) said that they followed dealers' recommendations. The second most important source of information on insecticides was other farmers.

Farmers apply most of their insecticides by mixing the purchased powder or liquid with water in the tank of a backpack sprayer. Farmers also purchase other products that are applied to cotton as sprays, sometimes mixed with insecticides in the same sprayer tank. We collected data on foliar fertilizers, growth regulators and fungicides, but do not report those here.

Insecticide practices

Almost all of the farmers in our sample apply insecticides using backpack sprayers. In some cases the farmer or another family member does the spraying, while in other cases hired labour is used. In many of these latter instances, the labourers provide their own spraying equipment. Table 7.18 examines the relationship between farm size and hired labour for insecticide spraying and shows that larger farms more frequently delegate the task to hired labour.

There is a sharp difference between the two samples in the number of times that farmers spray their cotton with insecticide. The frequency distribution for the number of times a plot is sprayed with insecticides is shown in Tables 7.19 and 7.20. In Gujarat, the median number of sprays is seven while it is only three in Maharashtra.

Table 7.19 Number of insecticide sprays applied to fields (Gujarat)

No. of sprays	No. of plots	% of plots	Cumulative percent
0	18	4.3	4.3
1	6	1.4	5.8
2	8	1.9	7.7
3	29	7	14.6
4	36	8.6	23.3
5	43	10.3	33.6
6	52	12.5	46
7	50	12	58
8	66	15.8	73.9
9	53	12.7	86.6
10	17	4.1	90.6
11	2	0.5	91.1
12	12	2.9	94
13	7	1.7	95.7
14	5	1.2	96.9
15	12	2.9	99.8
20	1	0.2	100
Total	417	100	

Source: Survey data.

Table 7.20 Number of insecticide sprays applied to fields (Maharashtra)

No. of sprays	No. of plots	% of plots	Cumulative percent
0	18	4.33	4.33
1	16	3.85	8.17
2	72	17.31	25.48
3	166	39.90	65.38
4	92	22.12	87.50
5	36	8.65	96.15
6	14	3.37	99.52
12	2	0.48	100.00
Total	416	100	—

Source: Survey data.

One of the most important features of insecticide application for cotton in India is the frequency with which farmers mix two or more insecticides in the same tank. Entomologists caution strongly against this practice, but farmers either feel that the spraying will be more effective with several insecticides or wish to save time and labour by applying several products at once (sometimes targeted at different pests). In Gujarat the majority of farmers mix two or more insecticides in a single spraying, while in Maharashtra slightly less than half of the sprayings contain multiple insecticides (Table 7.21).

To understand if growers receive any guidance in the use of pesticides, we asked them whether their fields were visited by any outside agency such as extension

Table 7.21 Number of insecticides used in each spraying

No. of insecticides used in each spraying	Gujarat		Maharashtra	
	No. of sprays	(%)	No. of sprays	(%)
1	569	20.13	695	54.51
2	1483	52.48	461	36.16
3	622	22.01	88	6.90
4	118	4.18	23	1.80
5	22	0.78	2	0.16
6	9	0.32	6	0.47
7	3	0.11	0	0.00
Total	2826	100.00	1275	100.00

Source: Survey data.

officials, representatives from the state agriculture departments or pesticide companies. The answer was positive for only 8 per cent of the sample in Maharashtra and 16 per cent in Gujarat, and the most common category of visitors (47 and 40 per cent, respectively) were representatives of seed and pesticide companies. During interviews, many farmers noted their lack of information especially when dealing with new pests, and contact with the extension system was negligible for most of the growers in the sample. There are state programs that teach farmers principles of insecticide resistance management (IRM), but only about 5 per cent of farmers had heard about them and even fewer had participated.

Insecticide use on different types of variety

There are several ways to examine differences in insecticide practices for different varieties. The most straightforward method is to compare the number of insecticide sprayings per plot. In Maharashtra, there was little difference between the two types of variety; the average number of sprayings was 3.23 for Bt varieties and 3.35 for non-Bt varieties, and the distribution of sprayings over time was also similar for the two variety types.

In the survey, the farmer was asked to identify the pest(s) that were targeted in each spraying. In some cases the farmer gave two responses, but a preliminary analysis indicated that analysing only the first response did not lead to significantly different results. We classified the answers into bollworms (i.e. those *Lepidoptera* with some susceptibility to the Bollgard toxin), *Spodoptera*, sucking pests and others. Only one farmer in Maharashtra mentioned *Spodoptera* (as a secondary target), so we do not include this in our analysis for that state. Table 7.22 presents sprays by time period, primary target and type of variety. The table shows that in every time period, Bt cotton plots are sprayed more against sucking pests than non-Bt cotton plots. On the other hand, non-Bt cotton plots are sprayed more against bollworms than sucking pests. Aggregate numbers of sprays per plot are not much different between Bt and non-Bt plots.

Table 7.22 Insecticide sprays per plot, by pest and by time period: Maharashtra

Days after sowing	Pest target	Sprays per plot			Percentage of all sprays during period		
		Bt cotton	Non-Bt	All	Bt cotton	Non-Bt	All
1–30 days	Sucking pests	0.41	0.34	0.40	65.00	57.14	63.45
	Bollworms	0.06	0.13	0.07	9.00	22.45	11.65
	Others	0.13	0.07	0.12	20.50	12.24	18.88
	Unknown	0.03	0.05	0.04	5.50	8.16	6.02
	Total	0.63	0.60	0.63	100.00	100.00	100.00
31–60 days	Sucking pests	0.75	0.61	0.72	50.53	40.00	48.32
	Bollworms	0.28	0.39	0.30	18.90	25.60	20.30
	Others	0.25	0.27	0.26	16.99	17.60	17.11
	Unknown	0.20	0.26	0.21	13.59	16.80	14.26
	Total	1.49	1.52	1.50	100.00	100.00	100.00
61–90 days	Sucking pests	0.34	0.12	0.30	36.82	13.16	31.99
	Bollworms	0.31	0.44	0.33	32.77	47.37	35.75
	Others	0.12	0.27	0.15	13.18	28.95	16.40
	Unknown	0.16	0.10	0.15	17.23	10.53	15.86
	Total	0.94	0.93	0.93	100.00	100.00	100.00
91–120 days	Sucking pests	0.05	0.02	0.05	27.12	8.00	21.43
	Bollworms	0.07	0.20	0.10	38.98	64.00	46.43
	Others	0.01	0.02	0.01	5.08	8.00	5.95
	Unknown	0.05	0.06	0.06	28.81	20.00	26.19
	Total	0.19	0.30	0.21	100.00	100.00	100.00
Above 121 days	Sucking pests	0.003	0.00	0.00	23.08	0.00	23.08
	Bollworms	0.01	0.00	0.01	76.92	0.00	76.92
	Others	0.00	0.00	0.00	0.00	0.00	0.00
	Unknown	0.00	0.00	0.00	0.00	0.00	0.00
	Total	0.013	0.00	0.01	100.00	0.00	100.00
Entire season	Sucking pests	1.553	1.09	1.47	48.04	32.54	44.87
	Bollworms	0.73	1.16	0.81	22.58	34.63	24.67
	Others	0.51	0.63	0.54	15.77	18.81	16.45
	Unknown	0.44	0.47	0.46	13.61	14.03	14.01
	Total	3.23	3.35	3.28	100.00	100.00	100.00

Source: Survey data.

Because farmers often mix two or more insecticides in a single spraying, it is also possible to consider the number of 'insecticide applications', where each instance of insecticide in the tank gets counted as an application. Table 7.23 shows the insecticide applications per plot by variety and over the growing season. The number of applications is larger than the number of sprayings, as is to be expected. There is also a greater difference between Bt and non-Bt plots, suggesting that multiple insecticides are more common for the latter.

Table 7.23 Insecticide applications per plot: Maharashtra

Days after sowing	Bt plots	Non-Bt plots	All
1–30 days	0.84	0.96	0.87
31–60 days	2.11	2.67	2.23
61–90 days	1.58	1.55	1.57
91–120 days	0.36	0.50	0.39
121–150 days	0.00	0.00	0.00
151–180 days	0.00	0.00	0.00
181 days and above	0.01	0.00	0.01
Total	4.91	5.68	5.07

Source: Survey data.

Table 7.24 Insecticide use per ha against target pests in Maharashtra

Target pests	Bt plots			Non-Bt plots		
	Lt/ha	Kg/ha	Total	Lt/ha	Kg/ha	Total
Sucking pests	0.55	0.1	0.65	0.95	0.04	0.99
Bollworms	0.36	0.05	0.41	1.4	0.15	1.55
Others	0.17	0.03	0.2	0.54	0.04	0.58
Unknown	0.19	0.03	0.22	0.43	0.01	0.44
Total	1.28	0.22	1.5	3.32	0.24	3.56

Source: Survey data.

In addition, it is possible to compare the quantities of insecticide applied on cotton fields. Table 7.24 compares the quantities of liquid insecticides (in litres) and powdered insecticides (in kilograms) applied to the two types of variety. The differences between Bt and non-Bt plots are quite noticeable, and the major factor is the higher amount of insecticide used to control bollworm on the non-Bt plots. So although there is virtually no difference in the number of times farmers spray their Bt and non-Bt cotton, the non-Bt varieties tend to receive somewhat more insecticides per spraying and considerably higher total quantities of insecticide over the season. Further analysis is required to see to what extent these differences are reflected in the type of insecticides used for different varieties and the total costs of insect control.

In Gujarat the average number of sprayings per plot for approved Bt varieties (7.39) is only slightly higher than that for unapproved varieties (6.91), and the distributions over the season are also similar. Plots of the traditional *desi* varieties, which do not receive much insecticide, averaged 1.81 sprayings per season.

Table 7.25 shows sprays by time period, primary target and type of variety in Gujarat. Most of the sprays are against sucking pests. The proportion of sprays against bollworms is much less than in Maharashtra, but for all pests the number of sprays is higher in Gujarat. Plots with approved varieties receive more sprays against sucking pests and *Spodoptera* than plots with unapproved varieties.

Table 7.25 Insecticide sprays per plot, by pest and by time period, Gujarat

Days after sowing	Pest target	Sprays per plot				Percentage of all sprays during period			
		Approved Bt plots	Unapproved Bt plots	Non-Bt plots	All	Approved Bt plots	Unapproved Bt plots	Non-Bt plots	All
1–30 days	Sucking pests	0.24	0.22	0.15	0.22	72.73	56.47	44.44	61.74
	Bollworms	0.00	0.00	0.00	0.00	0.00	1.18	0.00	0.67
	Spodoptera	0.00	0.00	0.07	0.00	0.00	0.00	22.22	1.34
	Others	0.01	0.02	0.00	0.01	1.82	5.88	0.00	4.03
	Unknown	0.08	0.14	0.11	0.12	25.45	36.47	33.33	32.21
	Total	0.33	0.38	0.33	0.36	100.00	100.00	100.00	100.00
31–60 days	Sucking pests	1.70	1.48	0.37	1.50	82.42	71.62	62.50	76.00
	Bollworms	0.07	0.10	0.00	0.08	3.17	5.02	0.00	4.14
	Spodoptera	0.05	0.01	0.04	0.03	2.31	0.44	6.25	1.34
	Others	0.02	0.08	0.00	0.05	1.15	3.71	0.00	2.56
	Unknown	0.23	0.40	0.19	0.31	10.95	19.21	31.25	15.96
	Total	2.07	2.06	0.59	1.97	100.00	100.00	100.00	100.00
61–90 days	Sucking pests	1.97	1.74	0.37	1.75	77.88	74.28	83.33	75.99
	Bollworms	0.21	0.24	0.04	0.22	8.47	10.17	8.33	9.39
	Spodoptera	0.15	0.08	0.00	0.11	6.12	3.45	0.00	4.59
	Others	0.03	0.04	0.00	0.03	1.18	1.54	0.00	1.36
	Unknown	0.16	0.25	0.04	0.20	6.35	10.56	8.33	8.66
	Total	2.53	2.35	0.44	2.30	100.00	100.00	100.00	100.00
91–120 days	Sucking pests	1.33	1.09	2.00	1.14	77.78	75.16	88.89	76.58
	Bollworms	0.14	0.11	0.25	0.12	8.33	7.76	11.11	8.08
	Spodoptera	0.18	0.05	0.00	0.10	10.42	3.42	0.00	6.62
	Others	0.00	0.06	0.00	0.03	0.00	4.04	0.00	2.10
	Unknown	0.06	0.14	0.00	0.10	3.47	9.63	0.00	6.62
	Total	1.71	1.45	2.25	1.48	100.00	100.00	100.00	100.00

121 days and above	Sucking pests	0.65	0.52	0.75	0.56	86.7	77.6	100.0	83.6
	Bollworms	0.06	0.1	0	0.08	8.0	14.9	0.0	11.9
	Spodoptera	0.01	0.01	0	0.01	1.3	1.5	0.0	1.5
	Others	0.01	0	0	0	1.3	0.0	0.0	0.0
	Unknown	0.03	0.03	0	0.03	4.0	4.5	0.0	4.5
	Total	0.75	0.67	0.75	0.67	100.0	100.0	100.00	100.0
Entire season	Sucking pests	5.89	5.05	3.64	5.17	80	73	83	76
	Bollworms	0.48	0.55	0.29	0.5	6	8	7	7
	Spodoptera	0.39	0.15	0.11	0.25	5	2	3	4
	Others	0.07	0.2	0	0.12	1	3	0	2
	Unknown	0.56	0.96	0.34	0.76	8	14	7	11
	Total	7.39	6.91	4.38	6.8	100	100	100	100

Source: Survey data.

Table 7.26 Insecticide applications per plot, Gujarat

Days after sowing	Approved	Unapproved	Non-Bt	All
1–30 days	0.63	0.68	0.59	0.65
31–60 days	4.33	4.15	1.26	4.04
61–90 days	5.92	4.99	0.96	5.10
91–120 days	3.97	3.12	0.56	3.29
121–150 days	1.45	0.89	0.22	1.07
151–180 days	0.35	0.27	4.37	0.28
181days and above	0.08	0.09	1.30	0.08
Total	16.74	14.18	3.59	14.53

Source: Survey data.

Many Gujarat growers often use combinations of insecticides in a single spray, and Table 7.26 displays the insecticide applications per plot. The difference between approved and unapproved plots is proportionately greater for insecticide applications than for insecticide sprayings.

Table 7.27 examines the actual quantities of insecticide used by farmers growing the two types of variety. Gujarat presents an additional complication for measuring insecticide use because in a number of cases farmers purchased insecticide powder which they applied by hand, so the table includes three measures. Farmers using approved Bt varieties applied considerably higher quantities of insecticide than those planting unapproved varieties.

There are clear differences between Gujarat and Maharashtra in terms of the amount of insecticide applied to Bt cotton varieties. Insecticide practices vary markedly by season, so a single year's comparison is not definitive. But it would seem that Gujarat cotton farmers use significantly more insecticide than their counterparts in Maharashtra, and that this difference is not explained by variation in the types of cotton varieties planted. Whether pest pressure is greater in Gujarat, or relatively wealthier farmers with higher cotton yields choose to spend more on insecticide, is not clear.

The precise impact of Bt cotton on insecticide practices is difficult to assess from a single year's data. If we compare the Gujarat data from 2007 with results from our study in 2003 we find that the total number of sprayings has declined, for both approved and unapproved Bt varieties, by about one-third (Table 7.28). The difference is largely due to a decline in insecticide use for bollworm. It is not clear if this is due to declining bollworm populations, or farmers' increasing confidence in the efficacy of Bt varieties. We have no similar comparative data for Maharashtra, but anecdotal evidence as well as comparison with earlier studies in the same region indicates a decline in the number of sprayings per season, and this may be attributed to the spread of Bt cotton. The comparison between Bt and non-Bt varieties in Maharashtra shows that Bt growers currently spray as frequently as non-Bt growers, but tend to use less insecticides per spraying and considerably lower quantity of commercial products per spray. Further analysis is required to understand the significance of these differences, but the new technology's efficacy in controlling bollworm is clear.

Table 7.27 Insecticide use per ha against target pests in Gujarat

| Target pests | Approved Bt plots | | | | Unapproved Bt plots | | | |
	Lt/ha	kg/ha	Hand application kg/ha	Total	Lt/ha	kg/ha	Hand application kg/ha	Total
Sucking pests	2.70	1.53	1.11	5.35	1.87	1.13	1.51	4.51
Bollworms	0.34	0.09	0.00	0.43	0.18	0.12	0.09	0.39
Spodoptera	0.19	0.20	0.00	0.40	0.03	0.03	0.37	0.43
Others	0.02	0.05	0.00	0.07	0.07	0.04	0.09	0.20
Unknown	0.12	0.07	0.00	0.19	0.26	0.12	0.37	0.76
Total	3.37	1.94	1.11	6.43	2.42	1.44	2.43	6.29

Source: Survey data.

Table 7.28 Number of insecticide sprays per plot in Gujarat: 2003–04 versus 2007–08

Variety	Bollworms		Sucking pests		Others		Total	
	2003–04	2007–08	2003–04	2007–08	2003–04	2007–08	2003–04	2007–08
Approved Bt varieties	4.18	0.48	5.2	5.89	1.76	1.02	11.14	7.39
Unapproved Bt varieties	3	0.55	5.2	5.05	1.8	1.31	10.0	6.91

Source: Survey data and Ramaswami *et al.* (forthcoming).

The opinions of cotton farmers about Bt cotton generally support our data on yields and insecticide practices (Table 7.29). The majority of farmers believe that Bt cotton has contributed to higher yields, particularly in Gujarat. Most farmers believe the technology has lowered the use of insecticides for bollworm control. However, the majority of farmers in Gujarat believe that they have seen an increase in insecticide use for other pests since the uptake of Bt cotton; this opinion is not so strongly held in Maharashtra (where in any case insecticide use is more moderate). Most farmers in Gujarat associate Bt cotton with higher fertilizer use, which may simply be an indication of the improved management applied to the more expensive seed, but this opinion is in the minority in Maharashtra.

It will be interesting to follow the progress of the newly released 'Bollgard II' varieties that contain a combination of genes that are more effective against bollworm and also control *Spodoptera*. There are 21 plots in the Gujarat sample where farmers grow these new varieties. The sample is small and it is not possible to draw firm conclusions, but it is worthwhile examining this example of the early adoption of the new technology. Table 7.30 shows that the 'Bollgard II' growers are larger farmers with more irrigated area, which is not surprising for the first adopters of a more expensive variety. They also appear to use less insecticide than other Bt growers; whether this is because they are taking advantage of the new variety or because they normally use less insecticide is not certain.

Refuge management

Bt cotton seeds are sold in packets of 450 grams (supposedly sufficient for 1 acre) and they are accompanied by 150 gram packets of non-Bt seed to be planted as a refuge. The packet instructs the growers to sow the refuge seed along the borders of the Bt plot. In Maharashtra, compliance with the refuge requirement is fairly high, but not in Gujarat (for approved Bt varieties) (Table 7.31). Refuge seed is of course not sold for the unapproved seed and therefore the practice of planting a refuge is negligible for those varieties. In both states refuges are usually planted on borders, as recommended by the instructions.

Table 7.29 Farmers' opinions about Bt cotton

Effect of Bt cotton on:	Gujarat (%)	Maharashtra[1] (%)
Yield		
Increased	81.0	58.0
Decreased	9.5	26.4
No change	7.0	14.9
Don't know	2.5	0.6
Insecticide use for bollworm		
Increased	16.0	5.2
Decreased	75.5	78.2
No change	6.0	14.9
Don't know	2.5	1.7
Insecticide use for sucking pests		
Increased	80.0	51.1
Decreased	10.5	29.9
No change	7.0	17.8
Don't know	2.5	1.1
Insecticide use for other pests		
Increased	62.5	17.2
Decreased	21.5	40.8
No change	12.5	35.1
Don't know	3.5	6.9
Use of fertilizer		
Increased	80.5	39.7
Decreased	4.0	8.6
No change	13.0	51.1
Don't know	2.5	0.6

Source: Survey data.

Note
1 Only Bt growers.

Table 7.30 Characteristics of 'Bollgard II' growers in Gujarat

	Bollgard II growers	Other Bt growers
Number	19	177
Total cultivated area (ha)	10.9	7.3
Total irrigated area	9.7	5.3
No. of sprays per plot	5	7
No. of insecticide applications per plot	9.7	15

Source: Survey data.

Conclusions

Although debates about approval procedures and environmental concerns meant that India was relatively late in introducing Bt cotton, the subsequent diffusion of the technology has been very rapid. Farmers' willingness to pay a much higher price for the seed (and little evidence that farmers abandon the technology once

Table 7.31 Refuge management

Refuge practice	Gujarat[1]	Maharashtra
Bt plots reporting a refuge	61/223 = 27%	271/354 = 77%
% refuge as border	93%	88%
% refuge as block or separate plot	—	5%
% refuge as gap filler or mixed	4%	6%

Source: Survey data.

Note
1 Only for approved varieties.

they try it) indicates that the Bt hybrids contribute to cotton productivity. Our survey data support this conclusion.

One of the reasons that the technology was able to diffuse so rapidly throughout India's varied cotton-growing environments was the long tradition of public sector and, more recently, private sector plant breeding capacity. This meant that a very wide range of germplasm was available that could incorporate the insect-resistance transgene. One of the factors that contributed to the technology owner's decision to license the transgene to other seed companies was, paradoxically, an unauthorized plant breeding effort that demonstrated the importance of tailoring Bt varieties to particular environments.

Because India's cotton farmers had long experience with seed markets, and the majority were accustomed to buying commercial hybrid seed every year, the introduction of Bt hybrids did not require any major changes. Nevertheless, farmers' behaviour in Bt seed markets in the two states of this study exhibits important differences, determined in part by the character of the seed market before the entry of Bt and in part by state government policies on regulatory enforcement.

Cotton seed markets in Gujarat had been dominated by hybrids from the public seed corporation and a small number of private firms, none of which had immediate access to the Bt technology when it first became available for licensing. This vacuum was filled by the sale of unauthorized Bt varieties that had been developed in Gujarat, and the state government chose not to attempt control of this underground market. As a result, unauthorized varieties constituted the majority of Bt cotton area in Gujarat, and it is only recently that their dominance is declining in favour of seed from authorized companies. Although Gujarat has always been one of the more advanced cotton-producing states, its farmers are slightly behind in learning about what is currently available in the legitimate seed market.

In contrast, cotton farmers in Maharashtra had been served by a more diverse set of seed companies before the introduction of Bt technology, and many of those companies were able to bring Bt versions of their popular varieties to market quite quickly. At the same time, the state government adopted a much stricter policy of seed law enforcement, and the sale of unauthorized Bt varieties was discouraged. Because cotton farmers in Maharashtra are generally smaller and poorer than their counterparts in Gujarat, and because they did not have access to the unauthorized varieties, their adoption of Bt technology has been slower, but they have the advantage of facing a seed market that is less confusing than Gujarat's. In addition, they are more conscientious in following refuge requirements. The technology has now spread widely, even among resource-poor farmers, although the small minority who have not yet tried Bt cotton in Maharashtra appear to be those with smaller landholdings.

Cotton seed markets in both states offer farmers many (some would say too many) choices. Nevertheless, there is evidence that in both cases the majority of farmers' decisions to try new varieties are either taken in an attempt to experiment on a fraction of their land or to adopt a variety that has become generally popular in previous seasons. This is not to say that the situation is perfect. Despite the importance of a considerable number of commercial varieties in each state, there are also many lesser-known varieties about which it is difficult to get information. The underground market is particularly chaotic, with a profusion of names and nicknames to describe the products, and this seems to be related to somewhat less precision in the process of variety selection in Gujarat.

Although Bt cotton contributes to yield increases, its original purpose was to lower the requirements for insecticide use. The major differences in insecticide management found in the study are between states and not between variety types. Gujarat farmers used much more insecticide in 2007 than did their counterparts in Maharashtra. We have no evidence on the relative importance of pest pressure or farm management strategies in explaining these differences. The more modest differences in insect management between Bt and non-Bt varieties in Maharashtra is difficult to interpret. The Bt growers spray less frequently than the non-Bt growers for bollworm, but spray more often for sucking pests. On the other hand, the Bt growers make somewhat fewer total insecticide applications and use a considerably lower quantity of insecticides.

It is not clear to what degree the farmers' insecticide practices respond to actual pest pressure or are determined by custom, misinformation or influence from pesticide markets. What is clear is that farmers have many fewer resources and opportunities to test alternative pest management strategies (in contrast to their experimentation and information exchange related to variety choice). There is virtually no extension advice available to help farmers develop more efficient insect control practices, and most information about insecticides comes from dealers. Despite the widespread access to, and productivity contributions of, transgenic cotton, there are few mechanisms that allow farmers to learn how to use the new technology as part of a more rational approach to insect control.

8 The socio-economic impact of transgenic cotton in Colombia[1]

Patricia Zambrano, Luz Amparo Fonseca, Iván Cardona and Eduardo Magalhaes

Introduction

Colombia has a long tradition of growing cotton. In the 1970s cotton was the nation's second most important crop, after coffee, but its place in the rural economy gradually declined. The current annual production of about 45,000 mt of fibre is only one-quarter of the output registered in the days when cotton was at its peak. However, the Colombian government has recently placed renewed emphasis on the crop, recognizing cotton's important role in generating rural employment and its contribution to the country's textile, apparel and fashion industries.

Colombia has two distinct cotton-growing regions (Figure 8.1). About 60 per cent of the national harvest comes from the northwest of the country, on the Atlantic coast, where the crop is planted from July through October and harvested in January through March. The remaining 40 per cent of the cotton harvest is from the south-central interior of the country, where cotton is planted in February or March and harvested in July through September.

Phytosanitary regulations require that all farmers register their cotton plots with one of the local cotton associations, and almost all farmers are affiliated to one of them. An umbrella organization, the Colombian Cotton Confederation (CONALGODÓN), represents the majority of these producer organizations. It promotes the interests of cotton farmers and ginneries in discussions with the government and with others in the textile industry. It negotiates with the industry and the national government regarding the domestic price paid to farmers and it manages a fund based on a cotton production levy (0.5 per cent of the value of fibre and 1 per cent of the value of cotton seed) that is used to support research and development in the cotton sector and the provision of information. It also collects and analyses statistics on the national cotton sector and promotes the use of Colombian cotton.

1 We would like to acknowledge the contributions of: Lorena Ruiz, Coordinator of Basic Statistics at CONALGODÓN, for her outstanding support in data management; Latha Nagarajan; Eduardo Ramírez; CONALGODÓN's regional coordinators, Dario Viña and Adolfo Nuñez; and all the farmers that participated in our survey. We would also like to acknowledge financial support from OXFAM-America and from the Genetic Resources Policy for the Poor Project (GRP1) and its donors at the Environment and Protection Division of IFPRI.

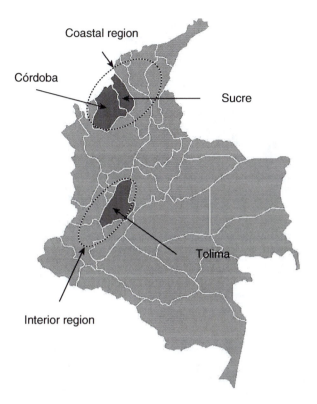

Figure 8.1 Colombia and cotton-growing regions

As part of its efforts to support the cotton sector, the Colombian government entered into discussions with Monsanto about the possibility of introducing transgenic cotton. Colombia has a biosafety framework and a Technical Committee for Biosafety has been in operation since 1998, under the leadership of ICA (Colombian Agricultural Institute), the government regulatory authority, with participation from other institutions such as the Ministry of Environment. ICA has a well-established seed regulatory framework and a system for plant variety protection which are quite effective for the country's major commercial crops. In addition to transgenic cotton, Colombia also grows two other genetically modified products, herbicide-tolerant maize and blue carnations.

Monsanto's 'Bollgard' cotton was approved for commercial release in Colombia in 2003 and first planted in 2004. Since that time its use has increased, as illustrated in Figure 8.2.

This chapter analyses the recent experience with Bt cotton. It is based partly on CONALGODÓN secondary data, but the majority of the chapter reports the results of farm-level surveys carried out during the 2007–08 seasons in the coastal and interior regions. On the coast, the survey was done in the department (*departamento*) of Córdoba, which accounts for the majority of coastal cotton production,

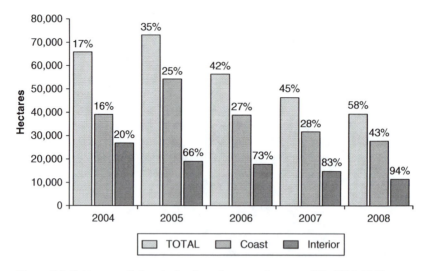

Figure 8.2 Cotton area (ha) and adoption of transgenic cotton (%), 2004–2008

Source: CONALGODÓN.

and the department of Sucre, which contributes a much lower share of the production but has a particularly high proportion of small-scale cotton farmers. The study also included the department of Tolima, which accounts for about 79 per cent of cotton production from the interior region (see Figure 8.1). The three departments account for more than 80 per cent of Colombia's cotton production.

The next section of this chapter introduces Colombia's cotton farmers and describes how they obtain their inputs. The following section examines the nature of Bt cotton adoption. The next section looks more closely at the economics of cotton production and uses this analysis to help explain adoption patterns. The final section presents some conclusions about the place of transgenic cotton in Colombia.

The organization of cotton production

Cotton sector support

Since 1999, when it became apparent that cotton production was declining because of the open-market policies of previous administrations, the Colombian government has adopted several policies to support the cotton sector. Traditionally, cotton had been a very important engine of the local economy, particularly in Tolima and Córdoba. Once cotton area started to dwindle as a response to low international prices there was a significant drop in productive activity and an increase in unemployment, creating additional public order challenges in already complicated areas. Given this situation, the government put in place several instruments to try to recover the sector. One of those instruments established a minimum guaranteed price (MGP). Currently this price is determined using

Table 8.1 Distribution of cotton area by size of holding

Department	Landholding class	Size of holding (ha)	% total cotton land in department
Tolima	Bottom 50%	1.0–5.0	8.6
	Top 50%	>5.0–342	91.4
Córdoba	Bottom 50%	0.1–2.9	10.5
	Top 50%	>2.9–586	90.5
Sucre	Bottom 50%	0.5–2.3	18.3
	Top 50%>	>2.3–91.1	81.7

Source: CONALGODÓN.

national cost of production data, gathered and analysed by CONALGODÓN. The government has agreed to maintain these arrangements until 2015 and in exchange cotton farmers have been committed to take several actions, including increasing their competitiveness, improving yields and helping open export markets for their product. CONALGODÓN is responsible for negotiating the seasonal MGP (calculated separately for coast and interior) with the government.

As part of the MGP policy, the government intervened to facilitate a negotiated price for domestic cotton buyers. This domestic price is established using a formula that takes into account the price that a domestic buyer would pay to import a ton of cotton. This is the price the textile industry pays to all cotton sellers. To account for fluctuations in the international market this price is updated monthly. The difference between the MGP and the price paid by the industry is covered by the government. (The farm-level economic analyses in this chapter use the MGP.)

Farmers and access to land

Two features of cotton farming deserve particular attention. First, the distribution of cotton land is markedly skewed; although the majority of cotton holdings are quite small, most of the production comes from a relatively few, larger holdings (Table 8.1). Second, much cotton production (even on larger plots) is carried out on rented land. About 67 per cent of cotton fields are rented in Colombia, and the practice is particularly marked in the interior of the country, where 80 per cent of cotton fields are on rented land. Cotton farming in Colombia is an uncertain venture, and many farmers do not necessarily grow cotton each year. Instead, they make judgements based on the profitability of the crop and the availability of land. Over the past three years there has been an average of about 5700 cotton farmers in Colombia.

Table 8.2 presents an overview of the three departments that are the focus of this study. (The data are derived from CONALGODÓN statistics and are for the entire departments, rather than for the study samples.) The table gives an idea of some of the differences among the departments in farm size and adoption of Bt cotton. The choice of cotton variety is determined to a significant degree by the

Table 8.2 Number of farmers and variety use, by department

	Tolima 2007			Córdoba 2007–08			Sucre 2007–08		
	Conv.	Bt	Total	Conv.	Bt	Total	Conv.	Bt	Total
Farmers (no.)	317	903	1220	2231	127	2358	291	183	474
Farmers (%)	26.0	74.0	100	94.6	5.4	100	61.4	38.6	100
Area planted (ha)	1998	9613	11,612	13,281	5774	19,055	904	675	1579
Area planted (%)	17.2	82.8	100	69.7	30.3	100	57.2	42.8	100
Hectares per farmer	6.3	10.6	9.5	6.0	45.5	8.1	3.1	3.7	3.3

Source: CONALGODÓN.

grower associations to which the farmers are affiliated because the associations are the sole providers of Bt cotton seed. Nevertheless, most farmers are able to select an association that will supply their choice of seed. Grower associations are a key element in the organization of Colombia's cotton production and deserve more careful examination.

The cotton grower associations

In order to grow cotton in Colombia, a farmer must register his or her plots with a local association (*agremiación*). Most farmers choose to affiliate with an association because it is the only way to get access to favourable credit. Aside from credit, associations provide inputs and other services, including ginning and marketing of the harvested cotton. The associations may take different forms. The most common is a business formed by a small number of partners, but there are also shareholding associations as well as cooperatives and other entities that act as cotton associations. But variations in the associations' legal form are often less important than the business model and motivations of the associations. While most associations in the interior region and Sucre tend to be well-established organizations that are under the control of cotton producers, in Córdoba there are many new associations that are established more as input intermediaries. This has lead to a proliferation of short-lived associations in Córdoba and has created opportunities for conflict of interest regarding the promotion of insecticides and other profitable inputs that might not always be the best options for farmers inscribed in these associations.

There are currently 58 cotton grower associations in Colombia. A farmer who is not happy with the service an association offers during one season can switch to a different one the following year, providing an alternative is available. Farmers inscribed in an association must register all their cotton plots and agree to deliver their entire harvest to the association. Table 8.3 summarizes the cotton area, membership and distribution of cotton associations. A relatively small number of larger associations dominate the distribution; the 14 per cent of associations that each has over 1500 ha represent more than half of the cotton area and about one-third of the cotton farmers.

Figure 8.3 outlines the types of organizations with which the associations establish relationships and the services the associations offer to their farmers. These include the facilitation of credit and the provision of inputs, as well as ginnery services. Depending on the region and the type of producer, the associations finance between 50 and 70 per cent of the total costs of a cotton farmer's production. The farmer is responsible for the remaining costs, by providing household labour and cash resources or by securing additional loans.

The majority of the credit offered through the associations is accessed from a special government program for farmers associations run by the Agrarian Bank (*Banco Agrario*); similar modalities are available for associations of maize, sorghum or rice growers. This type of credit has particular advantages, including access to collateral funds (up to 70 per cent of the total credit), a single transaction

Table 8.3 Cotton associations by area and number of farmers, 2008

Cotton area served (ha)	Number of associations			% of total associations	Area (ha)	% of total cotton area	Number of farmers	% of total cotton farmers
	Interior	Coast	Total					
<500	8	27	35	60.3	7390	16.0	1626	26.5
500–799	1	4	5	8.6	3556	7.7	471	7.7
800–999	0	4	4	6.9	3499	7.6	654	10.6
1000–1499	2	4	6	10.3	7201	15.6	1333	21.7
1500–3499	2	3	5	8.6	12,417	26.8	1302	21.2
3500–4600	1	2	3	5.2	12,235	26.4	755	12.3
TOTAL	14	44	58	100	46,298	100	6141	100

Source: CONALGODÓN.

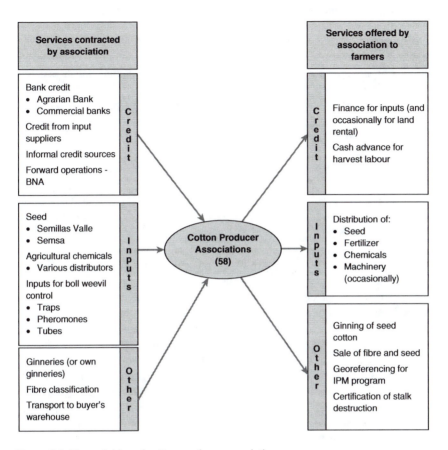

Figure 8.3 The activities of cotton producer associations

that covers multiple growers in the association and concessionary interest rates for small and medium growers. However, there is considerable paperwork associated with acquiring this type of loan and associations typically must acquire initial funds from more expensive sources until the Agrarian Bank's loan is disbursed. Although farmers must pay the cost of these initial loans, the overall package and its guarantees are much better than anything that could be obtained on the open credit market. The associations bear the risk of the loans and there is currently no efficient mechanism that would allow the restructuring of debts or provide insurance in cases where there are losses due to climatic or other environmental factors. (There is a program called *Ola Invernal*, but once a farmer or association uses it their creditworthiness is severely damaged, making it very difficult to access future loans.)

The credit line offered to farmers is available for inputs and labour for harvest, and occasionally other items as well, such as rental of machinery or land. For seed, fertilizer, and other chemicals each association has relations with a number of input supply firms. Most pesticides are the products of multinational firms and the fertilizers are supplied by a few Colombian firms. There are currently only two suppliers of cotton seed (see following text). Each association establishes relations with a number of input suppliers and farmers obtain the inputs at the association office. There is a tendency for the larger associations to act as cartels and set prices for their services.

Another major function of the association is to facilitate ginning. Associations either have their own gins or contract for ginning. Once the harvest is ginned, the association subtracts the credit charges, the association's commission, and various taxes and other charges and the remainder is paid to the farmer. There are 33 gins owned by 20 associations. The current national ginning capacity far exceeds the supply and although the official ginning charges are usually fixed by agreement there is intense competition to obtain as much cotton as possible. Associations without their own ginnery can seek the best price. In recent years a black market in seed cotton has emerged, where some associations have trouble policing their members and ensuring that they deliver their total harvest. Monsanto supervises the management of cotton seed from its transgenic varieties at the ginneries to ensure that none of it is appropriated illegally for planting purposes.

Smaller associations tend to have less access to credit and offer fewer services; many do not have their own ginnery. Some input distributors may not be willing to work directly with smaller associations, which may have to go through other associations for access to particular products (such as transgenic seed). Thus the smaller growers, with higher levels of poverty and illiteracy, are often seen as greater credit risks and their only choice may be to inscribe in a small association with limited facilities. If farmers are unable to inscribe in an association they occasionally may be able to obtain credit and inputs through an intermediary. The surveys found one case in Tolima where a number of resource-poor farmers were represented by an intermediary who was inscribed in an association. The intermediary obtained credit and inputs through the association and provided it to these farmers, charging an additional commission.

Another role of the associations is participation in a nationwide program for boll weevil control. Farmers are required to destroy their cotton stalks after harvest and the associations are authorized to retain up to 8 per cent of a farmer's cotton income to pay for the destruction if the farmer has not done so. There is a legal contract between the association and the phytosanitary authority that regulates both the retention and destruction of the stalks. The associations also monitor the dates before and after which cotton may be planted and the stalks must be destroyed. They also are required to participate in a control program for boll weevils that includes the use of traps as well as the distribution of tubes containing a pheromone attractant and insecticide. CONALGODÓN promotes these products and government phytosanitary regulations require the associations to enforce their use. CONALGODÓN distributes the traps and tubes at cost to associations.

Despite the promotion campaign and the phytosanitary regulations, the actual use of the tubes is only partially effective in the interior region and quite limited in the coastal region. The proportion of cotton area covered by the program in

2007 in the interior region was 65 per cent and only 12 per cent for the coastal region. Several factors have influenced this limited adoption. First, farmers are reluctant to use the tubes because of lack of visual evidence that they are effective in controlling boll weevils. The second factor is related to associations' effectiveness and interest in enforcing the use of the tubes among their farmers. Associations that are successful and well established, as most in the interior region, are better at enforcing the use of the tubes and they require their affiliates to buy these tubes. In the coastal area, where there are less well-organized associations, the enforcement is much lower and they are likely to ask the phytosanitary authority (ICA) for exemptions regarding these regulations. When the program first started and the tubes were freely distributed in order to promote their use, participation was high, but once the associations started charging, farmers began complaining about its effectiveness.

The associations are also required by ICA to georeference all inscribed cotton plots as this enables more precise control over the actual destruction of cotton stalks at the end of the season and it also allows them to make better cotton production estimates in order to control the unauthorized delivery of the cotton harvest to someone other than the association.

Access to seed and other inputs

Farmers who are active members of an association obtain most seed and chemical inputs through the association on credit. The choice of seed and inputs is usually decided by the farmer in consultation with a private extension agent. Until recently, all cotton farmers were required to hire an extension agent to provide advice throughout the season. Associations only disburse credit subject to the approval of their own extension agents' periodical assessments. These agents visit farmers' plots to inspect the development of the crop, and this helps explain why the vast majority of cotton farmers still follow the practice of hiring private extension agents. The average cost of extension for a season is about US$30 per hectare. Most of these private extension agents are independent of the associations, but they may have informal relationships and associations may recommend particular agents. A farmer is free to choose the agent and if not satisfied can seek another one the following year. Once there is a decision about initial inputs (e.g. seed and fertilizer) these are provided by the association.

The extension agent visits the farmer frequently during the season, inspects the field and recommends further inputs, such as insecticides. The farmer is only able to obtain these inputs through the association on the presentation of a written note from the extension agent. The extension agents have some flexibility in recommending particular insecticides, although they are expected to follow some general guidelines (such as a ban on organophospates during the first 60 days of the cropping season). The major insecticides used on cotton are out-of-patent products, such as methyl parathion and cypermethrin, but the input dealers also promote new and often safer (but generally more expensive) products. Hired labour is often used for spraying insecticide, even for quite small farms, and there are specialists who own their own backpack sprayers and hire themselves out to apply insecticide on the cotton fields.

The choice of seed is particularly interesting for our study. The major seed supplier until 2007 was a local firm, Semillas Valle, which was the exclusive representative for Delta and Pine Land (D&PL). Although the transgenic varieties commercialized in Colombia were owned by D&PL, the transgenes were the property of Monsanto. Once Monsanto finalized the acquisition of D&PL in 2007, the supply of what were DP&L varieties has opened to different agents, including some associations. Monsanto established a company in Colombia, Compañía Agrícola Colombiana Ltda, whose main activities regarding transgenic seeds are to promote and monitor their use. The other seed supplier is SEMSA, a company established by private agents, including some cotton associations, to distribute cotton varieties and other inputs. The seeds SEMSA provide are varieties developed by the Colombian public agricultural research institute, CORPOICA, plus an old D&PL conventional variety (DP90) that D&PL stopped distributing when their patent expired in the USA.

The seed choices available to Colombian cotton farmers are quite limited. Until 2007, the only transgenic (Bt) cotton was the D&PL variety NuOpal, the same variety that had the greatest initial success in South Africa; the seed of NuOpal is produced in South Africa and imported to Colombia. In 2007, several new transgenic cotton varieties were brought to the market, including DP 455 and DP 555, both of which are stacked varieties with Bt and 'Roundup' herbicide tolerance; and DP164, a stacked version that combines 'Bollgard II' (Monsanto's combination of Bt genes that provides protection against a wider range of *Lepidoptera*) and 'Roundup Flex' (that allows use of the herbicide later in the season). These three stacked varieties are all used in the USA (where together they accounted for more than 20 per cent of cotton area in 2007) and the seed is imported from there. A few farmers were able to plant these varieties in the coastal Region in 2007–08, but they were more widely available throughout the country in 2008–09.

Farmers sign a technology agreement when they buy Bt cotton seed. By law, any farmer growing Bt cotton must plant a refuge consisting of either 4 per cent of the area with a conventional variety and no control for *Lepidoptera*; or 20 per cent of the area with a conventional variety, with any type of insecticide allowed. Most farmers have opted for the '96-4' system. Although Monsanto hires inspectors to verify that Bt farmers comply with this requirement, it is difficult to assert that most small-scale farmers do in fact follow the rules for refuges. One of farmers' main complaints is the lack of information they receive from Monsanto regarding adequate practices for transgenic cotton.

Most farmers growing conventional cotton varieties use D&PL's Delta Opal variety (which is isogenic with NuOpal), although some use the old DP 90 or choose from among the public varieties that are available. There are seven CORPOICA cotton varieties, mostly bred for specific environments, but few are in active seed production and only a small minority of farmers use them.

Although in theory a farmer should be able to choose from among all available cotton varieties, the choice is sometimes constrained. This is especially true for

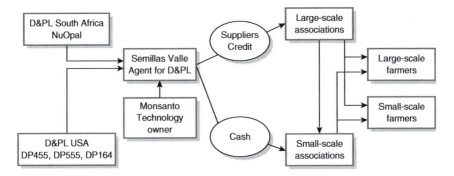

Figure 8.4 The commercialization channels for transgenic cotton seeds, 2007.

Bt cotton. Larger associations (with more prosperous farmer affiliates) have little trouble obtaining Bt cotton seed from the distributor on credit, but smaller associations may find that they must pay upfront or rely on contacts with larger associations. On the other side, some associations adopt the position that Bt cotton is too risky an investment for smaller growers and they will not support this choice. The flow of transgenic cotton seed is illustrated in Figure 8.4.

The behaviour of associations with respect to Bt cotton varies by region. The interior cotton production area is a more commercially oriented mechanized region, with access to irrigation. Associations in the department of Tolima are headed by farmers whose main interest is the production of cotton. All of them are willing to finance Bt cotton and a few of them have a policy of exclusively providing Bt (or other transgenic) seed. On the other hand, in the coastal department of Córdoba there is no access to irrigation and there is little mechanization. Some associations are headed by input intermediaries, rather than cotton producers, which explains the proliferation of short-lived associations that are unable or unwilling to finance the transgenic seed. Table 8.4 shows the variety use for the 31 associations that serve cotton farmers in Córdoba. Those associations in the top part of the table are ones that do not finance Bt cotton, while those on the bottom provide credit for transgenic seed. It can be seen that those associations that finance transgenic seed generally have a smaller number of affiliates, who tend to have larger farms. Within any association, the farmers who use Bt cotton usually have larger farms than those who plant conventional seed.

The farm-level surveys done in 2007 and 2008 provide more information about the adoption of Bt cotton, and we now turn to examine that data.

The adoption of Bt cotton

The areas of the study and the sample

A farm-level study of cotton growers was conducted in order to assess the experience with Bt cotton. The study included both the interior and coastal cotton

Table 8.4. Cotton associations in Córdoba by variety use, number of farmers and area

Association	All			Bt and Bt/RR cotton			Conventional cotton		
	Area (ha)	Farmers (no.)	Average size (ha/farmer)	Area (ha)	Farmers (no.)	Average size (ha/farmer)	Area (ha)	Farmers (no.)	Average size (ha/farmer)
Agrocultivos La Hormiga	57	27	2.1				57	27	2.1
Sagricor	29	12	2.4				29	12	2.4
Agrovet de la Costa	93	28	3.3				93	28	3.3
Agroinsumos El Paso	299	66	4.5				299	66	4.5
Alianza del Sinú Ltda	276	55	5.0				276	55	5.0
Coopiagros	2881	561	5.1				2881	561	5.1
Sinucampo	215	41	5.2				215	41	5.2
Servicampo	612	73	8.4				612	73	8.4
Agrosomena	1116	116	9.6				1116	116	9.6
Coagrince	729	57	12.8				729	57	12.8
Cultygan	442	3	147.5				442	3	147.5
Agropecuaria Casa Loma	254	1	254.0				254	1	254.0
Fibras del Sinú	627	139	4.5	49	11	4.5	576	128	4.5
Agricaribe	767	198	3.9	10	2	5.1	757	196	3.9
Sinuagro	315	98	3.2	28	5	5.5	287	93	3.1
Comersinú	37	13	2.9	24	4	6.1	13	9	1.4

Casa del Agricultor	115	35	3.3	14	1	13.7	101	34	3.0
Insumos Tierraltica	240	41	5.9	62	3	20.6	178	38	4.7
C.I Córdoba	1318	209	6.3	124	5	24.7	1195	204	5.9
Agrorepresentaciones	590	67	8.8	76	3	25.2	514	64	8.0
Comertol	512	40	12.8	428	15	28.6	83	26	3.2
Coagrocor	3182	214	14.9	1,964	67	29.3	1219	147	8.3
Inversiones SC Ltda.	1179	54	21.8	584	15	38.9	595	41	14.5
Comerfood	207	5	41.5	207	5	41.5			
Coopacor	195	74	2.6	47	1	46.5	149	73	2.0
Comercampo	629	127	5.0	47	1	46.7	583	126	4.6
Agro Av Ltda.	413	10	41.3	409	8	51.1	4	2	2.1
Producir del Sinú	77	11	7.0	52	1	51.6	25	10	2.5
Chaguí y Chaguí	265	4	66.2	265	4	66.2			
Manzur Aldana	115	1	114.6	115	1	114.6			
Proagrocor	2329	1	2328.6	2329	1	2328.6			
Total	**20,115**	**2368**	**8.5**	**6831**	**153**	**44.6**	**13,281**	**2231**	**6.0**

Soure: CONALGODÓN.

Table 8.5 Characteristics of the survey sample, by department

Variable	Tolima 2007		Córdoba 2007–08		Sucre 2007–08	
	Conv.	*Bt*	*Conv.*	*Bt*	*Conv.*	*Bt*
Number of farmers	59	72	78	55	57	43
% of total farmers in department growing this variety	*(18.6)*	*(8.0)*	*(3.5)*	*(43.3)*	*(19.6)*	*(23.5)*
Cotton area (ha)	221	607	349	503	156	142
% of total cotton area in department planted in this variety	*(11.0)*	*(6.3)*	*(2.6)*	*(8.7)*	*(17.2)*	*(21.1)*
Area per farmer (ha)	3.7	8.4	4.5	9.1	2.7	3.3

regions. It was conducted in Tolima and Córdoba, the two most important cotton-producing departments, and Sucre, with a relatively modest cotton area but an important participation of small-scale farmers. We have already mentioned the contrasts between the coastal (Córdoba and Sucre) and interior (Tolima) regions. Cotton planted on the coast is rain-fed and is harvested by hand; there is a scarcity of machinery such as precision planters. Plots in Córdoba are usually planted twice a year, mostly with maize in the first season, and cotton in the second. In Sucre, on the other hand, rainfall permits only a single season, so those who plant cotton are particularly dependent on this crop. In contrast, 85 per cent of cotton in Tolima is irrigated, 70 per cent of the harvest is done mechanically, and precision planters and other modern machinery are more easily available.

In selecting the sample for Tolima and Sucre, the major cotton-producing municipalities (*municipios*) of each department were selected and farmers were chosen randomly from these. Because the total number of Bt cotton plots was very low in Córdoba, the sampling strategy was modified for this department. Almost all farmers growing Bt cotton were included and a random sample of conventional cotton growers from the major growing municipalities was selected. Although the survey in the coastal region coincided with the first season when stacked cotton varieties were commercially introduced, the only transgenic variety included in the survey is NuOpal, as the number of farmers using other transgenic varieties was still very limited.

Table 8.5 shows the nature of the sample. A total of 131 farmers were surveyed in Tolima and 233 on the coast. The division between Bt and conventional growers in the sample is roughly equivalent to that of the population in Tolima and Sucre, but Bt growers are over-represented in the Córdoba sample.

Who adopts Bt cotton?

The discussion of cotton associations pointed to factors that make it more difficult for smaller, resource-poor farmers to get access to Bt cotton, and this is reflected in

Table 8.6 Landholding and land quality for sample farmers

Variable	Tolima 2007			Córdoba 2007–08			Sucre 2007–08	
	Conv.	Bt	Stat. sig.[1]	Conv.	Bt	Stat. sig.[1]	Conv.	Bt
Farm size								
Less than 3 ha (%)	66.1	47.2	**	67.9	34.5	***	71.9	69.8
Between 3 and 20 ha (%)	32.2	40.3	**	30.8	54.5	***	28.1	30.2
More than 50 ha (%)	1.7	12.5	**	1.3	10.9	***	0.0	0.0
Tenancy								
Own land (%)	28.8	23.6		50.0	36.4		29.8	34.9
Rented land (%)	71.2	76.4		50.0	63.6		70.2	65.1
Field characteristics								
Adequate texture (%)[2]	98.3	81.9	***	83.3	76.4		66.7	67.4
Adequate fertility (%)[3]	57.6	73.6	*	100.0	100.0		94.7	97.7
With irrigation (%)	37.3	87.5	***	2.6	5.5		1.8	0.0

Notes
1 Significance of differences at 90% (*), 95% (**) and 99% (***).
2 Based on self-assessment by farmers. In Tolima soils adequate for cotton are sandy loam; in the coastal region adequate soils are light or medium texture.
3 Based on self-assessment by farmer.

Table 8.5, which shows that the average cotton holding for Bt growers is roughly twice that of conventional seed users in Tolima and Córdoba; the difference is not nearly as pronounced in Sucre, where a number of associations representing small-scale growers have been more open in promoting the use of transgenic seed. Unlike their counterparts in Córdoba, Sucre associations have better access to credit from the Bt seed distributor. The seed distributor is less likely to extend credit to associations in Córdoba, given the characteristics of many of those associations described earlier. One important difference between Cordoba and Sucre is that the latter has no rotation crop after cotton. Cordoba rotates mainly with maize, whose harvest season tends to overlap with cotton-planting season. This creates competition for labour during this critical period and, as prices of maize increase, cotton tends to have less available hands to fully prepare the land for cotton planting. Many farmers and associations don't consider it worth planting costly seed under these conditions. Seeding rates can be reduced by using precision planters, but these require a clean plot and given the scarcity of labour at maize harvest in Córdoba this is difficult to achieve. In contrast, some associations in Sucre have precision planters, where they are easier to use because of the single-crop season in that department.

These differences are further illustrated in Table 8.6, which shows the use of varieties by farm size. The table shows that the distribution of variety use is not related to land tenure. In Tolima, the Bt cotton tends to be planted on better soils, where there is irrigation.

Table 8.7 Characteristics of cotton farmers in the sample – percentages

Characteristic	Tolima 2007			Córdoba 2007–08			Sucre 2007–08		
	Conv.	*Bt*	*Stat. sig.*[1]	*Conv.*	*Bt*	*Stat. sig.*[1]	*Conv.*	*Bt*	*Stat. sig.*[1]
Farmers who have planted cotton for 4 consecutive years	30.5	26.4		57.7	49.1		24.6	18.6	
Reason for planting Bt cotton the first time									
Reduce risk of loss to insects	n.a.	0.0		n.a.	45.6		n.a.	72.3	
Better yield	n.a.	52.0		n.a.	24.6		n.a.	8.5	
Save costs	n.a.	48.0		n.a.	22.8		n.a.	10.6	
Other	n.a.	0.0		n.a.	7.0		n.a.	8.5	
Source of first recommendation to plant Bt cotton									
Extension agent	n.a.	68.2		n.a.	50.9		n.a.	44.7	
Monsanto	n.a.	9.1		n.a.	33.3		n.a.	8.5	
Other farmers	n.a.	6.8		n.a.	10.5		n.a.	36.2	
Other	n.a.	15.9		n.a.	5.3		n.a.	10.6	
Opinion about current variety									
Excellent	2.2	2.2		7.7	40.7	***	3.5	4.7	**
Good	65.2	62.2		79.5	48.1	***	68.4	55.8	**
Average	28.3	33.3		10.3	9.3	***	26.3	20.9	**
Poor	4.3	2.2		2.6	1.9	***	1.8	18.6	**
Contract extension agent (%)	44.1[2]	97.2 ***		100.0	100.0		100.0	100.0	

Notes
1   Pair-wise t-tests and Pearson Chi-square tests show significant differences at 90% (*), 95% (**) and 99% (***).
2   Many small farmers in the Tolima sample are not affiliated with an association but obtain inputs through an intermediary.

Table 8.7 presents some of the characteristics of farmers who use conventional and transgenic cotton seed. There is not much difference in cotton-growing experience between the two types of farmers, and it is worth noting that in most cases only a minority of farmers have grown cotton for all of the past four years. Farmers' initial reason for growing Bt cotton differs between Tolima and the coast, with the former more interested in the possibility of additional yield and cost savings, while the latter are more concerned about risk reduction. In all three areas the contracted extension agent had an important role in the decision to plant Bt cotton. Monsanto representatives had more direct influence in Córdoba, perhaps because of a special, but very localized, extension community development program (*Campo Unido*) the firm supported there. In Sucre, farmer recommendations played a prominent role in the decision to adopt Bt cotton. Farmers who

Table 8.8 Household characteristics of sample farmers

Variable	Tolima 2007		Córdoba 2007–08		Sucre 2007–08	
	Conv.	Bt[1]	Conv.	Bt[1]	Conv.	Bt[1]
Means						
Number of household members	4.2	4.5	4.6	3.6***	4.5	4.3
Age of household head (yrs)	52.0	49.9	49.3	46.4*	49.4	50.5
Education (years)[2]	5.3	8.3***	8.2	10.1***	4.7	5.5
Head	*4.0*	*7.9****	*7.1*	*9.0***	*2.7*	*4.0*
Spouse	*4.5*	*8.2****	*7.0*	*9.0***	*2.9*	*4.3*
Farm income as % of total income	93.1	80.3***	68.8	64.0	81.8	74.0
Cotton income as % of total income	63.2	41.2***	41.9	38.2	52.4	47.2
Percentages						
Adequate housing (%)[3]	15.9	26.3	3.8	38.2***	7.0	11.6
Tractor ownership (%)	13.6	21.1	5.1	7.3	1.8	0.0
Ownership of livestock, poultry, fishponds, or orchards (%)	81.8	45.6***	4.4	43.6***	73.7	55.8*
Monthly household income (as % of legal minimum wage)						
< 110%	*81.8*	*10.5****	*33.8*	*29.1*	*54.4*	*44.2*
110–220%	*13.6*	*54.4****	*37.7*	*29.1*	*40.4*	*51.2*
>220%	*4.5*	*35.1****	*28.6*	*41.8*	*5.3*	*4.7*

Notes
1 Pair-wise t-tests and Pearson Chi-square tests show significant differences between Bt growers and non-Bt growers at 90% (*), 95% (**) and 99% (***).
2 Average education of all household members.
3 Adequacy of housing assessed by quality of structure, access to public services and location of kitchen and bathroom.

grew Bt cotton give it a generally good rating; the opinions are particularly high among the growers in Córdoba, while a minority of growers in Sucre are unhappy with the variety's performance.

Table 8.8 summarizes some of the economic characteristics of the farmers in the sample. The households growing Bt cotton tend to be slightly better off, with somewhat more education; the difference is most notable in Tolima (for household income) and Córdoba (for adequate housing). Cotton (and agriculture in general) tends to be a slightly lower component of total income for those who use Bt cotton. On the other hand, the conventional growers often have more diverse farming strategies, with livestock and other enterprises.

In summary, the early adopters of Bt cotton in Colombia tend to have some-what more and better resources. This is not surprising, and is typical of the adoption experience of most agricultural technologies. The use of Bt cotton in Colombia has steadily grown in the past four years. Questions about its further diffusion relate to the policies and capabilities of the cotton associations that provide access to inputs, and this in turn will depend to a considerable degree on the cost of the technology and its performance in the field. We now examine farm-level performance of the technology.

The economics of Bt cotton production

Costs and benefits of Bt cotton

The farm surveys conducted in 2007–08 collected detailed data on costs of production and yields for 170 farmers growing Bt cotton and 194 farmers growing conventional varieties. The data were analysed in order to provide the parameters used by Colombia's cotton farmers and industry to assess productivity, including total costs per hectare, yield of seed cotton per hectare, costs of production per ton of lint and benefits (or losses) per ton of lint. The results for the three departments in the survey are summarized in Table 8.9.

In each of the three cases, the Bt cotton growers obtained higher yields, higher benefits per hectare and lower costs of production per ton of fibre. However, in three of the six cases, the returns to farmers were negative (the conventional variety growers in Tolima and all growers in Sucre). Part of the explanation for the continuation of cotton cultivation in the face of apparent negative returns is the fact that some of the costs in Table 8.9 are opportunity costs. This is particularly the case for labour, as well as for some use of farmer-owned machinery and the cases where farmers own, rather than rent, their land. Farmers do not necessarily use market prices for these factors when assessing their returns, and hence may be willing to continue cultivating cotton, or switch between cotton and other crops depending on their experience.

There are also additional factors that explain the negative returns observed for Sucre and conventional farmers in Tolima. In Sucre, farmers experienced one of the most prolonged droughts of the past years during the growing season and then unseasonal rains, which affected both conventional and transgenic cotton fields. The data from conventional cotton farmers in Tolima are affected by the fact that many are not even members of an association, but rather are under the control of an intermediary who is the sole credit beneficiary for all inscribed plots and also receives discounted inputs from a well-established association. She provides inputs on demand (on a very small scale) and in exchange receives, weighs and pays for all cotton at the end of the season. Given this arrangement, farmers have difficulty accounting for their actual yields and expenses; the figures reported here are the best estimates available, but the lack of precision may partly account for the high reported losses.

Table 8.9 Costs of production and yields of sample cotton farmers, by variety and department

	Tolima			Córdoba			Sucre		
	Conv.	Bt	Stat. Sig.[1]	Conv.	Bt	Stat. Sig.[1]	Conv.	Bt	Stat. Sig.[1]
Costs of factors of production (Col$/ha)[2]									
Land	290,135	480,124	***	425,516	426,906		195,085	205,560	***
Labour	1,043,964	1,067,954	***	1,020,899	850,961	***	775,587	821,009	***
Machinery	276,935	391,974	***	71,458	88,690	**	140,901	145,475	***
Inputs	1,291,581	2,048,242		1,380,372	1,531,723		715,098	990,535	***
Seed	*192,528*	*353,119*	***	*299,047*	*542,688*	***	*154,149*	*377,902*	***
Insecticide	*241,356*	*398,956*	***	*347,557*	*290,458*		*155,961*	*183,853*	**
Fertilizer	*599,616*	*807,507*	***	*428,960*	*437,316*		*216,835*	*244,600*	*
Herbicide	*110,417*	*177,468*	***	*143,855*	*123,380*		*134,688*	*130,551*	
Other	*147,664*	*311,191*		*160,922*	*137,881*		*53,464*	*53,629*	
Fuel	135,552	191,676		34,292	42,562		67,618	69,813	
Transport	125,089	91,800		73,086	64,310		71,416	82,567	
Extension	38,728	58,524	***	53,080	58,403		69,534	69,122	
Indirect costs	88,236	132,141	***	119,808	119,808		55,418	55,418	
Interest	222,136	292,080	***	213,248	226,716	*	167,737	205,799	**
Total	**3,512,356**	**4,754,515**	***	**3,391,759**	**3,410,079**	**	**2,258,394**	**2,645,298**	*
Yields and benefits									
Yield of seed cotton (kg/ha)	1766	3089	***	2419	2652	**	1209	1425	*
Ginning and other costs (Col$/mt seed cotton)	237,010	237,735		282,085	260,883	***	246,653	250,774	

(Continued)

Table 8.9 (Continued)

	Tolima			Córdoba			Sucre		
	Conv.	Bt	Stat. Sig.[1]	Conv.	Bt	Stat. Sig.[1]	Conv.	Bt	Stat. Sig.[1]
Yield of fibre (kg/ha)	662	1,156		905	988		459	540	
Costs of production (Col$/mt fibre)	5,382,048	4,185,801		4,042,612	3,700,275		5,100,000	5,096,228	
Income (Col$/mt fibre)	4,451,439	4,457,693	***	4,315,303	4,330,216	***	4,310,995	4,345,045	***
Net benefit (Col$/mt fibre)	−930,609	271,892	***	272,692	629,941	*	−789,005	−751,183	

Notes
1 Differences significant at 10% (*), 5% (**) and 1% (***).
2 During 2007 US$1 was worth approximately Col$2,200.

It is notable that the total costs of production for Bt growers were significantly higher than those of the conventional growers (35 per cent in Tolima and 17 per cent in Sucre). Surprisingly, part of the difference in costs of production in these two departments was increased spending on insecticide; only in Córdoba did Bt growers spend less than the conventional growers on insecticides. Nevertheless, the overall statistics indicate that the adoption of Bt cotton has contributed to higher yields and lower costs per ton of fibre, despite higher production costs per hectare. But the variability among the results from three departments and the nature of changes in production costs deserve further examination.

Explaining differences in costs and performance

The discussion earlier in this chapter pointed to some differences between farmers who adopt Bt cotton and those who plant conventional varieties. The Bt growers tend to have somewhat better land and access to more resources. The policies and resources of the grower associations play a large role in determining access to transgenic seed, and smaller farmers are less likely to be affiliates of associations that promote or provide transgenic seed. Because smaller farmers are less likely to grow Bt cotton, their management conditions and practices are over-represented in the accounts for conventional cotton in Table 8.9, just as better-resourced farmers are over-represented in the accounts of Bt growers.

Such factors help to explain the rather remarkable differences in the costs and benefits for the Tolima sample. In general, the Bt growers are larger farmers. Three-quarters of the conventional growers in the Tolima sample are not directly affiliated to an association, but rather gain access to inputs and credit through an intermediary who charges them for this service and limits their access to the full range of inputs. The higher costs of production for Bt growers include: higher land rental (indicating better quality land), higher machinery costs (with access to better equipment, such as precision planters), and higher investment in fertilizers. All of these factors can contribute to higher yields. (Differences in seed and insecticide costs are treated in the following sub-section.)

One way to illustrate the effect of farm size and resources on production practices and outcomes is to examine Tolima farmers' experience by farm size. Table 8.10 shows costs of production, yields and costs per ton of seed cotton, by farm size. In all cases, the Bt growers have higher yields (and higher costs of production), but the results indicate that when small farmers have access to adequate resources and inputs they can do as well as larger farmers in growing Bt cotton. Attention should also be given to the medium-size growers of conventional cotton, who had excellent yields and achieved among the lowest costs per ton of seed cotton produced. On the other hand, two of the four large farmers who planted conventional seed were affected by bad weather, which led to low yields.

Another way to get an idea of the contribution of Bt cotton to the increased yields is to look at the 15 farmers in Tolima who grew at least one field with Bt cotton and one with conventional cotton. Although the sample size is small, the comparison will help to eliminate some of the factors related to the large average difference in resources between Bt growers and other farmers. Table 8.11 shows

Table 8.10 Costs of production and yield, by variety and farm size, Tolima

Production data	Type of seed		
	Conv.	*Bt*	*% diff. (Bt-Conv.)*
Small farmers (< 3 ha)			
Number of plots in sample[1]	39	34	
Cost of production (Col$/ha)	2,736,521	4,323,657	*58%*
Yield (kg/ha)	1299	2816	*117%*
Cost of production (Col$/mt fibre)	2,106,714	1,535,437	*−27%*
Médium farmers (3.1–10 ha)			
Number of plots in sample[1]	16	23	
Cost of production (Col$/ha)	3,755,817	4,850,450	*29%*
Yield (kg/ha)	2509	2846	*13%*
Cost of production (Col$/mt fibre)	1,496,860	1,704,379	*14%*
Large farmers (10.1–50 ha)			
Number of plots in sample[1]	4	15	
Cost of production (Col$/ha)	3,844,870	4,788,263	*25%*
Yield (kg/ha)	1195	3226	*170%*
Cost of production (Col$/mt fibre)	3,217,249	1,484,430	*−54%*

Note
1 Total plots is greater than number of farmers in sample because 15 farmers have at least one plot of conventional cotton and one plot of Bt cotton.

the total costs of production for the Bt plots is 15 per cent higher than for conventional plots and the yield advantage of the Bt cotton is 35 per cent. There is relatively little difference in land costs, and although there is still considerably higher investment in fertilizer, herbicides and other inputs for the Bt plots, the differences are not as marked as they are for the larger Tolima sample.

A challenge to understanding the specific contribution of Bt technology to higher yields is the fact that the farmers who adopt Bt also benefit from a number of other conditions, as discussed earlier. To isolate the effects of Bt cotton on yields we need to correct for endogeneity, the fact that some of the factors that contribute to higher yields are also the ones that determine the likelihood of adopting Bt technology.

One way to address endogeneity is to adopt a two-stage estimation, using instrumental variables. The conventional approach to identifying the determinants of yield is an ordinary least squares (OLS) regression, where yield is the dependent variable and there are a number of independent variables. But if these variables are not truly independent (meaning that the covariance between a given variable and the error term is not zero) then endogeniety occurs. In such cases it becomes necessary to first find a set of instrumental variables that are correlated with the independent variable but not with the error term. The first stage of the analysis is an OLS regression for the binary variable (adoption), and the second is an estimation of yields using the predicted adoption from the first stage.

The first step of the analysis for Tolima is to estimate an OLS regression for adoption. We hypothesize that farmers who adopt are those who have more

Table 8.11 Costs of production and yields for 15 Tolima farmers growing both conventional and Bt varieties

Cost of factors of production (Col$/ha)	Conventional	Bt
Land	343,534	371,899
Labour	1,077,125	1,099,531
Machinery	353,413	385,972
Inputs	1,529,786	2,046,925
Seed	*161,104*	*366,938*
Insecticide	*260,191*	*367,187*
Fertilizer	*757,870*	*867,483*
Herbicide	*137,029*	*171,756*
Other	*213,592*	*273,562*
Fuel	173,265	189,007
Transport	157,362	120,860
Extension	57,535	54,341
Indirect costs	159,278	142,453
Interest	251,911	295,264
Total costs (Col$/ha)	4,103,209	4,706,254
Seed cotton yields (kg/ha)	1958	2237
Cost of production (Col$/mt seed cotton)	2,095,496	1,784,907

assets, education, experience or income and are located in better lands (those where land quality is better and with access to irrigation). We also control for the fact that many farmers located on less favourable land must rely on an intermediary for inputs. As farmers' subjective estimations for land quality in our survey yielded poor results, we opted to use rent as a better proxy for land quality and irrigation. The results for this first stage are in Table 8.12. The significant variables that explain adoption in Tolima are plot size, number of boll weevil applications, cost of land and not relying on the intermediary. These results confirm our initial assessment that those who adopt tend to be the ones located on better land, use more insecticides for boll weevil and have bigger plots.

In the second stage, we take the predicted adoption that we estimate from the previous analysis and use it in the yield equation (Table 8.13). In this analysis, the variables that explain higher yields, aside from Bt adoption, are the ownership of a harvester and land rental (as opposed to ownership). In addition, a higher number of insecticide applications for boll weevil is associated with lower yield. All other specifications that we tried consistently yielded similar results. Rent is positively related to yields because farmers who rent try to find the best land possible, given a very active rental market. Many Tolima farmers report that they plant cotton only if they can find a 'good' plot. Farmers who own a harvester are likely to be more commercially oriented and better-off, so the variable serves as a general measure of wealth.

We also ran a two-stage analysis to examine the impact of Bt cotton on yields in the coastal region. Adoption has been much slower, particularly in Córdoba

Table 8.12 Tolima: first stage – OLS estimation for Bt adoption

Variable	Coefficient[1]	St. error	t-value
Plot size	0.012**	0.006	2.18
Owns harvester	−0.270	0.175	−1.54
Rents land	0.000	0.000	1.24
Cost of insecticides	−0.104	0.067	−1.56
Number of boll weevil applications	0.026**	0.013	2.06
Number of *Spodoptera* applications	−0.022	0.029	−0.76
Spodoptera incidence	0.027	0.085	0.32
Boll weevil incidence	0.025	0.104	0.24
Obtains inputs through intermediary	−0.298***	0.104	−2.85
Age of household head	0.003	0.003	0.96
Education of household head	−0.013	0.100	−0.13
Experience with Bt	−0.024	0.022	−1.08
Share of income in cotton	−0.027	0.195	−0.14
Whether farmer is in upper rank income	−0.207	0.171	−1.21
Cost of land (rent paid)	0.000***	0.000	5.17
Constant	0.090	0.236	−0.38

Note
1 Estimates significant at 10% (*), 5% (**) and 1% (***).

Table 8.13 Tolima: second-stage – yield estimation

	Coefficient[1]	St. error	z-value
Whether farmer adopts Bt	1990.132***	237.077	8.39
Plot size	−6.747	12.213	−0.55
Owns harvester	934.350**	476.093	1.96
Rents land	370.036**	177.092	2.09
Number of boll weevil applications	−67.443**	30.032	−2.25
Number of *Spodoptera* applications	60.066	68.458	0.88
Spodoptera incidence	188.727	245.228	0.77
Boll weevil incidence	233.837	264.566	0.88
Constant	770.919***	270.843	2.85

Notes: Estimations were obtained through generalized methods of moments to address heteroskedasticity.
1 Estimates significant at 10% (*), 5% (**) and 1% (***).

and we take this into account in our analysis. As some associations in Córdoba can be classified as non-adopters we also include a variable to account for this. As opposed to farmers in Tolima who expected higher yield from adoption, farmers in the coastal region said they favoured Bt cotton more as insurance against possible pest attack. To account for this we introduced a measurement of risk that could account for this behaviour. The measurement used was total debt over total

Table 8.14 Coast: first stage – OLS estimation for Bt adoption

	Coefficient[1]	St. error	t-value
Plot size	0.012301*	0.007	1.79
Córdoba	−0.32727**	0.119	−2.74
Rents land	−0.04413	0.073	−0.6
Labour cost	1.06E-07	0.000	0.62
Cost of land (rent paid)	1.12E-06***	0.000	2.47
Debt/assets	0.187167**	0.051	3.68
Adopting association	0.069799	0.067	1.04
Income rank	−0.06945	0.080	−0.87
Age head of household	8.91E-05	0.003	0.03
Education head of household	−0.01749	0.072	−0.24
Whether farmer is in upper rank income	−0.05615**	0.026	−2.12
Cost of land (rent paid)	0.363964***	0.128	2.85
Constant	0.209234	0.236	0.89

Note
1 Estimates significant at 10% (*), 5% (**) and 1% (***).

assets, and we expected the higher the exposure the more likely were farmers to adopt. The results are shown in Table 8.14.

These results confirm our initial assessments. Farmers in Córdoba are less likely to adopt, as confirmed by the national data. Farmers with larger size plots are more likely to adopt. What is not so straightforward is the significance of the income rank variable, which indicates that farmers in the lower rank are more likely to adopt. The plausible explanation is that of all cotton farmers in the coastal area, farmers in Sucre, most of them relatively small and resource-poor, are the ones who are adopting. As in Tolima, land rent, which we use as a proxy for land quality, is also significant in this adoption equation. The proxy we use for risk confirms that the higher the risk, the more likely are farmers to adopt.

We then used the predicted value of adoption to estimate the yield equation. Yield differences in the coastal region are not as striking as the ones in Tolima, but are still important. The results of the yield equation are in Table 8.15. Only two variables are significant, Córdoba farmers and labour cost. This again is consistent with the results presented in the descriptive statistics. Although most adopters are in Sucre, yields in Córdoba are higher, even when comparing conventional cotton results of Córdoba with those of Bt cotton in Sucre, so it is understandable that the coefficient for Córdoba is positive. The significance of labour costs also corresponds to the specific characteristics of the coastal region, where there is little or no mechanization and production is labour intensive from planting to harvesting. Those who can secure and pay for the required labour are likely to obtain higher yields. Contrary to Tolima, where higher yields are explained in good part by the fact that farmers adopt Bt, this variable is not significant for the coastal region, probably as the higher yields are more prevalent for farmers in Córdoba, where adoption is relatively low.

Table 8.15 Coast: second-stage – yield estimation

	Coefficient[1]	*St. error*	*z-value*
Whether farmer adopts Bt	149.4955	278.0916	0.54
Plot size	−0.08959	5.322546	−0.02
Córdoba	1131.224**	79.98952	14.14
Rents land	42.04999	73.50285	0.57
Labour cost	0.001138***	0.000211	5.39
Constant	288.8528***	178.2623	1.62

Notes: Estimations were obtained through generalized methods of moments to address heteroskedasticity.
1 Estimates significant at 10% (*), 5% (**) and 1% (***).

The weather also played an important role in determining outcomes on the coast. In Córdoba, a number of the plots sown to conventional varieties in 2007–08 were affected by excess rainfall and farmers had to invest additional resources in drainage. On the other hand, the results in Sucre must be seen in relation to a drought during the growing season that lasted more than one month, followed by unusually heavy rains. The results are a setback for Sucre farmers, where Bt cultivation has risen from 3 per cent of the area in 2004 to 48 per cent in 2008.

Differences in environmental conditions can affect the performance of any technology, and the risks are increased for new technologies that farmers have little experience with. Three stacked varieties of transgenic cotton have recently been introduced in Colombia. One of them appears to have experienced poor performance in Tolima in 2008, where many farmers complain that the variety DP 455 showed poor boll filling and appears to have significantly inferior yields to other conventional and transgenic varieties. The 2008 season in Tolima was unusually wet, with much less sunlight than average, and the initial hypothesis is that this weather was partly to blame for the variety's poor performance. Further study of the new stacked varieties is in order. It is likely that their improved insect resistance and compatibility with herbicides will eventually create a significant market for such varieties, but the recent experience underlines the importance of adequate testing and the availability of a range of technological options.

Seed and insecticide costs

Seed cost is strongly associated with variety choice. Transgenic seed is more than twice as expensive as conventional seed; the cost of the transgenic NuOpal in Colombia is equivalent to that of Bt cotton seed in the USA. Most of the sample farmers who grew conventional cotton planted the Delta Opal variety, except in Sucre, where many farmers grew the older DP 90 (which costs about 20 per cent less than Delta Opal). There is also some relation between seed price and grower associations; farmers affiliated with smaller associations often have to pay slightly higher prices for their transgenic seed.

Table 8.16 Seeding rate, by type of variety and farm size, Tolima

Farm size	Seeding rate (kg/ha)	
	Conventional	Bt
Small (<3 ha)	15	14
Medium (3–10 ha)	16	13
Large (>10 ha)	13	12

The high cost of transgenic seed has led to some changes in planting practices, as farmers try to reduce their seeding rates. The best way to do this is with
a precision planter, but these are not available everywhere, and affiliates of
larger associations are more likely to have access to this equipment. For small
farmers, one way to economize on seed is to return to planting by hand, a task
where women tend to have more participation. In drought-prone areas, particularly on the coast, the weather sometimes interferes with attempts to lower
seeding rates, as farmers may find that they need to replant part of their fields
if the initial rains have not been adequate. Table 8.16 shows seeding rate by
farm size in Tolima and illustrates that, in general, larger farmers are better able
to achieve lower seeding rates.

One of the most interesting features of the Colombia case is that the use of Bt
cotton is not associated with a significant reduction in insecticide use; indeed, in
many cases Bt growers spend more on insecticides than farmers growing conventional varieties. Table 8.17 summarizes insect control expenditure by type of
insect. Farmers reported the principal insect for which they made each insecticide
application, but a particular insecticide may control other insects as well. Thus the
classification reported in the table is not perfect, but provides a useful guide to
farmers' priorities for insect control.

Probably the most important determinant of insecticide use in Colombia is the
boll weevil, which is the major insect pest of cotton. Boll weevil control was the
largest single item in insecticide expenditure for growers of both Bt and conventional varieties. In all three departments in the study, the Bt growers spent more
on boll weevil control than the conventional growers, and the difference is particularly notable in Tolima. This is consistent with the generally greater resources
and ability to invest in crop management of those who plant the transgenic variety. This may also reflect the fact that when farmers don't apply insecticide to
control budworms and bollworms they inadvertently allow further boll weevil
development, which has to be controlled subsequently.

As we would expect, Bt growers spend very little on the control of *Lepidoptera*,
other than the fall armyworm (*Spodoptera*). The principal insects in Colombia that
are susceptible to the single Bt gene in 'Bollgard' cotton are the tobacco budworm
(*Heliothis virescens*), two types of pink bollworm (*Sacadodes* and *Pectinophora*)
and a type of cotton leafworm (*Alabama argillacea*). Pink bollworm had earlier

Table 8.17 Cost of insect control, by type of insect, cotton variety and department

Cost of insect control[1] (Col$/ha)	Tolima 2007		Córdoba 2007–08		Sucre 2007–08	
	Conv.	Bt	Conv.	Bt	Conv.	Bt
All insects	311,514	526,717	436,352	401,370	286,647	305,205
Budworm, bollworm, leafworm	90,540	3469	77,690	329	27,967	0
Boll weevil	96,748	240,711	188,536	239,637	210,709	233,613
Armyworm	86,994	170,787	143,961	94,301	1034	996
White fly	8381	69,321	15,841	53,519	827	0
Others	28,850	42,430	10,324	13,584	0	0

Note
1 Costs include insecticides and labour (or machinery) for application.

been a particular problem in Tolima, which helps to explain the high adoption rates for Bt in that department.

In some cases the insecticides used against boll weevil are partially effective against some *Lepidoptera*, so part of the investment in Bt cotton may be superfluous until more targeted boll weevil control is possible. Farmers sometimes mix two insecticides, in order to control several insects, which may be a further disincentive for the use of Bt cotton.

Thus the economic advantage of the Bt cotton does not derive from savings on insecticide, but rather from the increase in yield. At least part of this increase appears to be due to the superior protection against pests that the transgene provides. (Recall that in most cases the conventional growers are using the variety Delta Opal, which is isogenic with NuOpal, so yield differences cannot be attributed to different germplasm.)

Armyworm (*Spodoptera*) is not controlled by the version of Bt cotton originally introduced in Colombia (but is controlled by 'Bollgard II', which was a component of one of the stacked varieties introduced subsequently). Armyworm has also been a particular problem in Tolima, and the Bt users spent nearly twice as much as the conventional variety growers in controlling this pest. The opposite is true for Córdoba, where those with the conventional variety spent more on armyworm control. One possible explanation is that a number of the Bt growers in Córdoba used a new (and quite expensive) insecticide to control boll weevil that also has an effect on armyworm. This is another example of the difficulty in targeting insecticides to specific pests to achieve more rational pest control.

Conclusions

The farm-level survey carried out during the 2007–08 season in Colombia demonstrated that farmers using Bt cotton had higher yields than those using conventional varieties, and despite generally higher costs of production per hectare, their costs per ton of fibre were lower than those of conventional variety growers. It is not possible to attribute all of the productivity gains of Bt growers to the transgenic technology but it would certainly appear that it has made a positive contribution to those who have been able to use it.

The results of a single year's survey are not conclusive, given the many differences in production practices, economic resources and climatic conditions. Nevertheless, the higher productivity of farmers growing Bt cotton is evident across the three departments surveyed. In addition, the fact that farmers using the transgenic technology get generally higher yields is consistent with the results of smaller studies carried out in previous years by CONALGODÓN. However, the yield contributions of the Bt technology are much easier to demonstrate econometrically in the interior region than they are on the coast, where adoption is not as high and a number of other socio-economic and environmental factors played important roles in determining cotton yields during the year of the study.

The nature of the increased productivity is somewhat different from what might be expected. Rather than saving farmers significant investment in insecticides, the technology's principal advantage appears to be its yield enhancement, presumably by providing extra protection from insect attack. Despite this protection against certain insects, Bt growers in two out of the three departments surveyed spent more on insecticides than the farmers growing conventional varieties. Damage from other insects required high investment in chemical control. Much of this higher investment by Bt growers is simply a function of their superior resources and ability to acquire inputs, although some may be related to the fact that the chemical controls eliminated by Bt would have had some carryover effect on other insects, which eventually required attention. In addition, high insecticide application is part of the cotton-growing culture in Colombia, and the mere use of transgenic seeds has not yet made a significant change in this practice. Farmers' main complaint about the technology is precisely that the release of the new varieties has not been accompanied by knowledge transfer that would allow better management of these varieties.

The linkage between higher yields and additional investment is confirmed by our analysis of the adoption patterns for the technology. In the first place, the highest rates of adoption of Bt cotton are found in Tolima, which previously suffered the greatest incidence of pests controlled by Bt cotton, particularly pink bollworm and tobacco budworm. In addition, Tolima is the most economically advanced cotton-growing department, where the vast majority of farmers have access to irrigation and modern machinery. On the other hand, the coastal departments that have lower rates of adoption are characterized by rain-fed agriculture and less access to machinery.

These differences between departments are similar to differences noted between adopting and non-adopting farmers. The former tend to have more resources that can be devoted to cotton production, a better standard of living, more education and higher incomes. On the other hand, those farmers who grow conventional varieties tend to be from smaller, more diverse farms that depend to a somewhat greater extent on agriculture as a source of income.

Despite these differences, there are many cotton farmers with relatively small holdings who are taking advantage of Bt cotton. One of the most important factors is the position of the cotton producer association. These producer associations are an important part of Colombia's cotton sector, and their technical and financial capabilities can make an important difference in terms of access to Bt cotton. Those associations that are better organized, more stable and with better access to various sources of credit, are more likely to be able to offer access to Bt cotton. If a smallholder is affiliated to a strong association, this facilitates access to the technology, but many of these farmers are members of smaller and less stable producer associations. The larger associations may offer other advantages as well, such as access to precision seeders that allow farmers to lower the seeding rate for this expensive input. Access to credit is one of the most important challenges for farmers all over the world, and the strategy of grower associations in Colombia goes a long way towards addressing that problem. Attention to smallholders' needs requires strengthening those associations that serve this sector of the farming population.

Bt cotton should allow farmers to make a reduction in insecticide use, but this has not been the case. There are several explanations. One is the continuing presence of other pests, principally the boll weevil but also pests such as armyworm and white fly, which require insecticide applications. A second reason may be the absence of attention to strategies that can lower the dependence on insecticides. Most farmers follow the advice of private extension agents for their insecticide choices, as well as for most other aspects of crop management. Farmers cannot obtain insecticide on credit without the written permission of the extension agent. On the one hand, this system helps guide farmers' control measures and limits the possibility of using inappropriate products. On the other hand, the extension agent has no incentive to teach the farmer or build his or her crop management skills. In addition, the extension agent may be open to influence from input distributors who wish to promote their products. Although the extension agents must behave responsibly (and can be dismissed by the farmer), they also have incentives for recommending more (and more expensive) inputs. It must also be remembered that the association earns part of its income from input sales.

Thus further progress in achieving more rational insect control in Colombian cotton will depend on addressing several challenges. One is finding the right balance between the expert advice of private extension agents (who undoubtedly make a positive contribution) and the necessity of building farmers' own capacities to make judgements about pest control. A second is the challenge of ensuring that the associations that play such an important role in credit provision have incentives that direct them towards sharing the rewards with farmers for lower costs of production (and less dependence on environmentally hazardous chemicals), rather than relying on commissions from chemical sales to earn their profits. A third challenge is to strengthen the program for boll weevil control that must rely to a considerable extent on farmers' willingness to comply and collaborate, and on the committed support of producer associations.

Finally, the experience with Bt cotton in Colombia has provided an important new technology for cotton farmers, but has revealed weaknesses in farmers' access to seed and their lack of information about options. The transgenic seed requires a significant investment from farmers, and not all of them are able to afford the new varieties. The transgenic varieties are all imported; the company has become essentially a monopoly supplier of seed which allows it to maintain high prices. More important, despite some field days and meetings, most farmers do not have an adequate chance to learn about the advantages and disadvantages of new varieties. There is no independent mechanism that allows widespread testing and evaluation of the varieties offered to farmers. The recent problems with one of the new stacked varieties illustrate this weakness. In addition, there is little incentive to incorporate useful transgenes in locally adapted cotton varieties because of the small size of the market. This is of little interest to the technology owner, and in any case the public research service does not currently have the resources to be a partner in such an endeavour. With innovations such as grower associations and new ways of providing extension, there is certainly the possibility that the Colombian cotton sector could grow back towards its former importance. Transgenic cotton can make an important contribution here, but more choice, competition, and information for growers can help redress the current imbalance that finds farmers overly dependent on a single technology supplier.

9 Ten years of Bt cotton in South Africa: Putting the smallholder experience into context

Marnus Gouse

Introduction

In 1997 South Africa became the first country in Africa to commercially produce a genetically modified (GM) crop, insect-resistant (Bt) cotton. Even though both large-scale commercial farmers and small-scale, resource-poor farmers contribute to the cotton crop, the South African Bt cotton experience has been a subject of international interest because it presents the first case of smallholder GM crop adoption in Africa. Research describing this experience has focused on the Makhathini Flats in northern KwaZulu Natal, one of only two areas in South Africa where small-scale farmers have been producing cotton in a relatively sustainable manner for the past three decades. The majority of the literature has reported impressive adoption rates and positive economic returns, suggesting that South African smallholders benefited from the introduction of Bt cotton. However, some observers have questioned these claims by pointing out that smallholder cotton production in South Africa did not expand (indeed, the total South African cotton area drastically declined) and the programs that provided smallholders credit and extension advice failed after the introduction of the new technology.

This chapter endeavours to shed light on the South African Bt cotton experience and to explain the performance of the Bt technology in the historical, political and institutional context of the Makhathini Flats and, more broadly, the South African cotton sector. It begins with an introduction to the South African cotton sector, describes the introduction of Bt cotton and its impact on the seed industry, reviews studies analysing the farm-level impact of Bt cotton and examines the institutions that govern access to inputs and information for South African farmers.

The status of South Africa's cotton sector and government aspirations for smallholder cotton

Although there is a report that early sixteenth-century Portuguese explorers came across people at the southern tip of Africa who wore crude clothes made from a type of wild cotton, attempts at cotton production in South Africa were only initiated in the late seventeenth century with the establishment of the Cape Colony and the entry of the Dutch East India Company. The early experiences were less

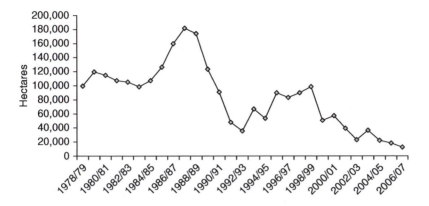

Figure 9.1 Cotton production area in South Africa

Source: Cotton SA.

than successful, and it was not until 1846 that an American missionary was able to produce cotton in the subtropical Amanzimtoti area in KwaZulu Natal, from seed he brought from the USA. Between 1860 and 1870 cotton was planted on a relatively large scale due to an increased demand for fibre created by the American Civil War, but after 1870 cotton production in South Africa came to a virtual halt and was only to be reinitiated at the start of the twentieth century.

Cotton was produced mainly in the Lowveld and Eastern Transvaal areas (Mpumalanga) and in 1913 an experiment station was founded in Rustenburg (now the Agricultural Research Council's Institute for Industrial Crops), in order to support farmers through cotton research. The cooperative movement in the cotton industry had its origin in Barberton in 1922 with the establishment of a farmers' cooperative and a ginnery. A number of other ginneries were erected but at the time South Africa had no infrastructure for spinning or weaving and the ginned fibre was exported, mainly to Liverpool. Cotton was produced under irrigation for the first time in 1927 in the Lower Orange River area and in 1939 cotton was officially declared an agricultural crop in order to be regulated under the Marketing Act of 1939. After the Second World War the South African textile industry started to develop and greatly benefited from the high import tariffs on textiles imposed by the government in 1963. By the late1980s the textile industry provided job opportunities to hundreds of thousands of workers.

Cotton production in South Africa peaked in the late 1980s and then declined as production shifted to other countries in southern Africa where smallholder farmers have a comparative advantage due to better climatic conditions and inexpensive land and labour (Figure 9.1). With relatively better prices for competing crops in South Africa, cotton production has decreased over the past few years to levels where a number of gins have had to close down and ginning companies have followed the shift in production to the other cotton-producing countries in the region.

Historically the South Africa cotton industry has been divided into adversarial camps of producers, commercial cotton ginners and spinners (Hobson and Le Roux 2005). Cotton policy was first formalized in 1974 with the establishment of the Cotton Board. In addition to keeping statistics and grading and classifying seed cotton and lint, the Cotton Board established seed cotton quotas for ginneries as well as the lint quotas to be allocated to textile firms. The Cotton Board also administered the purchasing price of seed cotton in the framework of the Cotton Marketing Committee. Under this regulated environment ginners made acceptable returns and spinners were able to avoid fluctuations in the international cotton price. However, cotton producers were dependent on commercial ginners for a fair seed cotton price. The Cotton Board was dissolved in 1997 under the Marketing of Agricultural Products Act (1996) as part of the liberalization of the agricultural sector. In the liberalized market, price setting, tariff barriers and protection mechanisms for local industries were diluted or removed, exposing producers and ginners to competition from farmers in neighbouring countries, a depressed world cotton price (due to support programs in large cotton-producing countries) and inexpensive textile imports.

After liberalization, the cotton industry pushed for the establishment of a non-profit organization to take over some of the functions of the Cotton Board. Cotton SA was established to provide information, stimulate production and cotton use, enhance marketability through research, offer training and quality standards and serve as an advisory body and industry forum.

Because of South Africa's political history, the country has a dualistic agricultural sector. Large-scale commercial farmers are predominantly white and the land they farm is privately owned, while smallholder farmers are generally black and produce on communal land. For many large-scale cotton producers, the crop is not the dominant farming enterprise. Enterprise choice is usually determined by rotation requirements, availability of irrigation water and the relative prices of competing crops. For the majority of smallholder cotton farmers in South Africa, the possibility of producing other crops is much more limited due to harsh climatic conditions and a lack of support services.

In 2001 the Department of Agriculture released the 'Strategic Plan for South African Agriculture' with the vision of 'a united and prosperous agricultural sector' and the strategic objective of 'equitable access and participation in a globally competitive, profitable and sustainable agricultural sector contributing to a better life for all' (DoA 2001). In support of the strategic plan, South Africa's cotton growers, in collaboration with private sector input suppliers, output processors and the National Department of Agriculture, developed a 'Strategic Plan for the South African Cotton Sector' with the following objectives.

- Increasing cotton output to a stable 370,000 bales of lint by 2007
- Broadening participation to enable emerging farmers to contribute on average 25 per cent of the national cotton crop by 2007 and 35 per cent by 2014
- Ensuring stability through ongoing commitment from all major players through forms of support and methods of operation that are affordable, internationally

acceptable (economically, socially and environmentally) and that do not compromise competitiveness

- Raising productivity by training at least 60 per cent of emerging farmers by 2007 and by improving research and extension services and technology transfer
- Expanding exports by value, diversity, country of destination and client base
- Accelerating the elimination of unfair competition through promoting regional and international cooperation and through more effective lobbying in international trade forums

Considering that South Africa's total cotton area decreased from about 56,600 ha in 2000–01 to about 11,360 in 2006–07, it is correct to conclude that the majority of these objectives were not met. While smallholders' contribution to cotton production rose from less than 5 per cent in 2000–01 to 20 per cent in 2005–06, this was due to a drastic decline in production by commercial farmers. This also indicates smallholders' lack of options, their inability to react to market signals and even indifference to cotton price at planting time.

By 2007 about 650 smallholders had attended training courses in cotton production. Courses were presented in four five-day modules during the production season. The training program covered a) soil preparation and planting, b) plant protection, pests, diseases and weeds, c) pre-harvest crop preparation, harvesting and grading and d) financial management. Even though the target of training 60 per cent of emerging farmers by 2007 was not met, it can be argued that substantial progress had been made despite a faltering sector, limited funds for training, and reluctance and difficulty for farmers (especially women) to attend week-long courses often far away from home. It can also be argued that it was the most viable smallholders who attended the courses and not the opportunistic producers who only react when credit and grants are available. This issue will be discussed in more detail later.

Cotton production areas in South Africa

Historically, cotton production by large-scale farmers took place in several production areas (see Figure 9.2). The most important dryland production areas are: the Springbok Flats in Limpopo Province (A) and in the Dwaalboom region in the North West Province (B). Irrigated cotton is produced around the towns of Marble Hall and Groblersdal and on the Loskop irrigation scheme in Mpumalanga Province (D), at Weipe in Limpopo Province (F) and in the Northern Cape and lower Orange River areas (E). (Some large-scale farmers in the Pongola district in northern KwaZulu Natal occasionally grow cotton as well.) The only areas with substantial smallholder cotton production are Tonga (Kangwane) in Mpumalanga (just north of Swaziland, bordering Mozambique) and the Makhathini Flats in northern KwaZulu Natal (C).

Cotton production has been dominated by the large-farm sector. In the 2000–01 season an estimated 300 large-scale farmers produced 95 per cent of the South African cotton crop (Gouse *et al.* 2003). But large-scale cotton farmers also grow other crops. Cotton farmers on the Loskop irrigation scheme also produce export

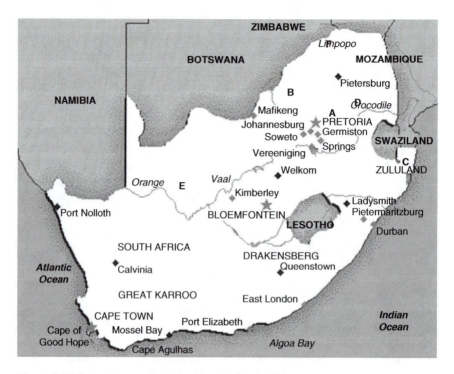

Figure 9.2 Main cotton production regions in South Africa

Note:
A – Springbok Flats, Settlers (Limpopo); B – Dwaalboom region (North West); C – Makhathini Flats (KZN); D – Loskop Irrigation Scheme and areas around Groblersdal and Marblehall (Mpumalanga); E – Northern Cape with production on the Vaalharts Irrigation Scheme and areas around the Orange River next to towns and cities like Douglas, Prieska, Luckhoff, Keimoes and Upington; F – Weipe (Limpopo).

table grapes, citrus, deciduous fruit and vegetables. The main crops of farmers in the Northern Cape are viticulture (for wine and export table grapes) and ground-nuts. Most farmers with irrigation in Mpumalanga and the Northern Cape rotate or substitute maize and cotton in the summer and produce wheat in the winter. On the Springbok Flats, cotton is rotated with maize and sunflower. Figure 9.1 shows that cotton production (by predominantly commercial farmers) has decreased significantly over the past couple of seasons. As other crops become relatively more profitable, cotton areas decrease. From Table 9.1 it can be seen that the drop in commercial cotton production was particularly marked in the Limpopo Province as well as in the North West. Most of these farmers replaced cotton with maize and sunflower.

Smallholder cotton farmers have far fewer options than large-scale farmers and they are still concentrated in a few areas. Despite various land reform projects attempting to settle small-scale farmers in established and potential cotton pro-duction areas, the traditional areas of Tonga and Makhathini Flats remain the

Table 9.1 Cotton production area by province

Area	2000–01 production season		2006–07 production season	
	Irrigation (ha)	Dryland (ha)	Irrigation (ha)	Dryland (ha)
Mpumalanga	9718	10	3165	591
Limpopo Province	4006	29351	1577	102
Northern Cape	2781	0	1123	0
KwaZulu Natal	528	3587	1030	1900
North West	208	5205	10	0
Orange River	1748	0	695	0
Eastern Cape	0	0	320	850
Total	18,989	38,153	7920	3443

major contributors to smallholder cotton production. In the past decade the total number of smallholder cotton producers has varied somewhat but generally amounted to a few thousand farmers. The vast majority of these farmers are situated on the Makhathini Flats, and their Bt cotton experience will be examined later in the chapter.

Bt cotton in South Africa

South Africa and GM crops

In 1989 the US seed company Delta and Pine Land (D&PL) applied to perform contained field trials with GM insect-resistant cotton in South Africa. This set in motion the South African biosafety process and initiated the first trials with GM crops on the African continent. The South African Committee for Genetic Experimentation (SAGENE) had been formed in 1979 to monitor and advise the National Department of Agriculture on the responsible development of genetically modified organisms (GMOs) through the provision of guidelines and the approval of research centres and projects. The approval for the commercial release of insect-resistant cotton and maize was done under the guidelines of SAGENE for the 1997–98 and 1998–99 seasons. South Africa's GMO Act of 1997 was approved by Parliament in June 1997 and entered into force in November 1999 when the regulations were published. In 1999 SAGENE was replaced by the Advisory Committee (AC) that was established under the GMO Act (Wolson and Gouse 2005). The Registrar of GMOs forwards submitted applications that comply with the provisions of the GMO Act to the AC. Successful applications are recommended to the decision-making body, the Executive Council, which includes officials of the departments of Agriculture, Health, Environment & Tourism, Trade & Industry, Labour, and Science & Technology; since the amendment of the Act in 2006 (in order to bring it in line with the Cartagena Protocol), the departments of Water Affairs & Forestry and Arts & Culture are also represented on the council.

Table 9.2 Percentage and estimated areas (hectares) planted to transgenic crops in South Africa

Crop	2002–03	2003–04	2004–05	2005–06	2006–07
Bt cotton %	70%	81%	60%	39%	8%
Bt cotton area	18,000	30,000	12,719	8420	1080
RR cotton %	12%	7%	30%	13%	4%
RR cotton area	3500	2500	6360	2805	540
Stacked cotton %	0	0	0	40%	81%
Stacked cotton area	0	0	0	8630	10,935
Bt yellow maize %	20%	27%	22%	18%	36%
Bt yellow maize area	197,000	250,000	249,000	107,000	391,000
Bt white maize %	3%	8%	8%	23%	35%
Bt white maize Area	55,000	175,000	142,000	221,000	552,000
RR yellow maize %	0	0	1%	11%	13%
RR yellow maize Area	0	0	14,000	68,000	137,000
RR white maize %	0	0	<1%	6%	10%
RR white maize area	0	0	5000	60,000	152,000
RR soybeans %	11%	35%	60%	59%	79%
RR soybean area	15,000	35,000	91,200	135,000	214,000

Source: Van Der Walt (personal communication) and author's own survey.

After approval of D&PL's application for field trials with Bt cotton in 1989–99 the company's involvement in South Africa increased. D&PL used South Africa as a location for winter field trials in the development of new varieties for the USA, and in 1995 approval was granted to produce Bt cotton seed in South Africa for sale in the USA. Hundreds of applications for permits to do glasshouse and field trials with GMOs have subsequently been reviewed. Crops for which field trial permits have been issued include maize, cotton, soybean, wheat, potato, sugarcane, strawberry, canola, tomato, apple and sweet potato.

South Africa became the first country in Africa to commercially produce transgenic crops with the release of Bt cotton for the 1997–98 season. Bt maize was approved for the 1998–99 season, but initially only transgenic yellow maize varieties were available and several years of plant breeding were required to produce acceptable South African white maize varieties (the type most commonly used for food). Herbicide-tolerant (RR) cotton and soybeans were made available for commercial production in the 2001–02 season and that season also saw the first white Bt maize plantings. RR maize seed was commercially released for the 2003–04 season while stacked-gene cotton (Bt plus RR) was released for the 2005–06 season and stacked-gene maize for the 2007–08 season. Table 9. 2 summarizes the areas planted under transgenic crops in South Africa for the most recent seasons. It is clear that Bt cotton has been very popular, reaching 81 per cent of total cotton area in 2003. The share decreased somewhat with the introduction of RR cotton but remained the more popular of the two. With the introduction of stacked cotton, Bt's share dropped considerably as farmers opted for cotton with both traits. In the 2006–07 season 93 per cent of the cotton plantings in South Africa were GM.

The cotton seed sector in South Africa, pre- and post-GM

In order to ensure a relatively homogenous cotton crop for the textile industry, Cotton SA (like its predecessor, the Cotton Board) makes seasonal variety recommendations for cotton production areas based on field trials (done by the Agricultural Research Council) focusing on characteristics such as yield, fibre qualities, adaptability and disease tolerance. Table 9.3 gives details of the cotton varieties delivered to gins each season since 1996–97 and also summarizes the deliveries for the previous 10 seasons. The cultivar percentages are indicated according to marketing seasons, i.e. the season following the planting season (cotton produced 1996–97 is marketed 1997–98). The first five entries are GM varieties. The table shows that varieties tend to achieve widespread use for a couple of seasons but are then replaced by new, better-adapted and higher yielding varieties. The growing dominance of GM cotton varieties since their introduction for sale in the 1998–99 marketing season is also clear from this table.

As the only GM cotton seed supplier in South Africa, D&PL was able to capture almost the entire cotton seed market. The initial uptake of the first Bt cotton varieties, NuCotn 35B and 37B, was less than spectacular, as the conventional varieties of Clark Cotton (Tetra, Sicala, HS 44, and Acala), Lonhro (Albacala), and a local cooperative (Acala OR3, developed by the National Department of Agriculture) were the most popular varieties. Before D&PL became more involved in the South African cotton seed market, Clark (the largest ginning company in South Africa at the time) also marketed the D&PL variety DP 90. NuCotn 37B was based on this DP 90 variety which had been popular previously but was losing market share to other varieties. NuCotn 35B was not well suited for most of the cotton areas in South Africa and very little seed was ever sold. Some commercial farmers were also cautious during the first seasons and wanted to test the new technology and see how ginners and the rest of the industry reacted. However, when the Bt gene was introduced into D&PL's popular OPAL variety (originally from Australia) adoption increased dramatically. NuOPAL (Bt), DeltaOPAL RR and NuOPAL RR (stacked) are all based on the DeltaOPAL germplasm.

With D&PL's monopoly on Bt cotton, Clark Cotton quickly lost its place as market leader. Figure 9.3 shows the market share of cotton seed companies over the past two decades, although Clark Cotton's share may be slightly underreported because they also sold and distributed seed for other smaller firms (Gouse *et al.* 2004). With field trials showing better bollworm control with Bt varieties, Cotton SA started including Bt cotton in their national cultivar recommendations. For the 2007–08 cotton production season, Cotton SA recommended eight cultivars for the country's eight cotton production regions. Some of the varieties are recommended for all eight areas but only two of the recommended cultivars are non-GM, DeltaOPAL and Acala OR3.

Table 9.3 Cultivars received at cotton gins the past 22 years according to marketing seasons

Cultivar	% last planted	Average 1986–1995	1996–97	1997–98	1998–99	1999–2000	2000–01	2001–02	2002–03	2003–04	2004–05	2005–06	2006–07	2007–08
NuOPAL RR		—	—	—	—	—	—	—	46.3%	81.3%	71.2%	64.6%	36.7%	89.2%
NuOPAL		—	—	—	—	—	—	—	—	2.6%	15.0%	10.6%	46.6%	4.4%
DeltaOPAL RR		—	—	—	—	—	—	—	—	—	—	—	0.8%	1.5%
NuCOTTN 35B/37B			—	—	—	6.7%	13.5%	27.2%	23.8%	—	—	—	—	—
DP5690RR			—	—	—	—	—	—	3.4%	—	—	—	—	—
DeltaOPAL		—	—	—	—	2.9%	24.0%	38.9%	19.2%	10.5%	10.0%	17.0%	15.1%	0.9%
TETRA	19.1% in 1994	8.6%	19.2%	14.8%	19.4%	16.4%	11.6%	5.7%	—	—	—	—	—	—
HS 44		—	—	—	12.9%	16.0%	1.6%	—	—	—	—	—	—	—
SICALA	19.5% in 1994	3.9%	25.8%	28.5%	19.6%	13.9%	19.8%	7.4%	—	—	—	—	—	—
ALBACALA	13.7% in 1994	14.5%	8.1%	19.8%	10.4%	10.4%	11.4%	5.7%	—	—	—	5.3%	—	—
DP 90	3.6% in 1994	7.6%	18.3%	13.9%	14.0%	9.1%	3.5%	—	—	—	—	—	—	—
SICALA V1		—	—	—	11.4%	8.2%	—	—	—	—	—	—	—	—
CS 189		—	—	—	—	3.5%	5.0%	9.0%	—	—	—	—	—	—
CA 223		—	—	—	1.5%	2.9%	—	—	—	—	—	—	—	—
ACALA	23.8% in 1994	41.5%	19.5%	14.7%	2.1%	2.1%	—	—	—	—	—	—	—	—
ACALA OR3	17.4% in 1994	9.8%	3.5%	5.3%	4.7%	2.0%	1.7%	2.4%	2.4%	1.3%	0.8%	0.9%	—	—
SIOKRA		—	—	—	—	2.0%	5.6%	1.5%	—	—	—	—	—	—
CS 85		—	—	—	1.1%	—	—	—	—	—	—	—	—	—
GAMMA	3% last planted in 1993	5.5%	1.1%	—	—	—	—	—	—	—	—	—	—	—
APLHA	5.7% last planted in 1991	2.0%	—	—	—	—	—	—	—	—	—	—	—	—

KNX 111	5% last planted in 1989	0.8%	—	—	—	—	—	—	—	—	—	—	—
McNAIR	2% last planted in 1987	0.4%	—	—	—	—	—	—	—	—	—	—	—
ALBAR	1% last planted in 1987	0.4%	—	—	—	—	—	—	—	—	—	—	—
REBEL	4% last planted in 1985	0.4%	—	—	—	—	—	—	—	—	—	—	—
DP 61/DP	3% last planted in 1986	1.4%	—	—	—	—	—	—	—	—	—	—	—
OTHER		3.2%	4.5%	3.0%	2.9%	3.9%	2.3%	2.2%	4.9%	4.3%	3.0%	1.6%	0.8%	4.0%

Source: Cotton SA.

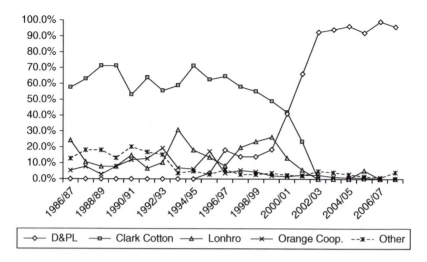

Figure 9.3 Market share of seed companies according to cotton delivered to gins per market season

Source: Cotton SA.

There is some concern in the cotton industry that most of the cotton seed currently sold and planted in South Africa belongs to one company and is based on the same germplasm. However, in an ailing industry profitable possibilities for additional seed companies are limited, and D&PL (which is now owned by Monsanto) has been able to deliver a high-quality product.

There has been some recent effort by D&PL to address the specific needs of smallholders. It has developed a hairy-leaf stacked-gene variety called DP Lebombo. Varieties with hairy leaves (widely planted in the rest of Africa) suffer less damage from sucking insects such as aphids and jassids. However large-scale farmers who use mechanized harvesters do not like hairy cotton varieties as the leaves stick to the cotton lint during the harvesting process. For smallholders (and some commercial farmers who harvest by hand), the hairy stacked-gene variety could offer a broader spectrum of insect control against bollworms and sucking insects, but trials have shown that it would require additional efforts to control white flies (*Aleyrodidea*) which flourish on the hairy leaves that supply protection against their predators.

Seed prices for GM cotton

The seed cost associated with Bt seed is comprised of the price paid to the seed supplier (D&PL) and the technology fee paid to Monsanto. Table 9.4 compares the conventional cotton seed prices with the price of Bt seed and indicates the technology

Table 9.4 Cotton seed prices and technology fees (Rands per 25 kg bag of seed)

Year	Seed cost DeltaOpal (conventional)	Seed cost NuOpal (Bt)	Bt technology fee	RR technology fee	Stacked technology fee
1997–98	120	—	—	—	—
1998–99	150	165	786.68	—	—
1999–2000	150	165	600	—	—
2000–01	170	190	600	—	—
2001–02	185	210	600	240	—
2002–03	215	250	600	300	—
2003–04	295	295	700	300	—
2004–05	350	350	700	350	—
2005–06	370	370	785	365	—
2006–07	390	390	785	365	1150
2007–08	410	410	785	365	1150
2008–09	430.50	430.50	785	365	1150

Source: D&PL.

fees for Bt, RR and the stacked gene (which is the sum of the fees for Bt and RR). Initially Bt seed itself was slightly more expensive than its conventional equivalent, which D&PL justified by the higher cost of producing the transgenic seed. Although the difference in price between Bt and conventional seed disappeared by 2003 it appears that the price of conventional seed has increased to the level of Bt and not vice versa. The cotton seed prices have generally followed the same trend as the national producer price index for farm requisites, but there was a significant jump in the prices for both conventional and Bt seed in the period 2002–04. The price for conventional seed almost tripled in dollar terms from 2002 to 2005 and one can argue that this was, at least in part, a symptom of D&PL's monopoly.

The Bt technology fee was adjusted downwards by about 24 per cent after the first season following farmer concerns that the technology was not affordable. The fee was then held constant at R600 (between about US$50 and 75 according to the fluctuating local currency) for the period 1999–2000 to 2002–03, after which it experienced a 12 per cent increase; indications are that the fee will stay fixed for the 2008–09 season.

There has been some innovation in the method of levying the technology fee in order to segment the market between rain-fed and irrigated farmers and large-scale and smallholder farmers. In the 1998 and 1999 seasons Monsanto introduced a system under which farmers could pay a technology fee based on the area planted and which differentiated between irrigated or rain-fed land. The system was meant to alleviate very high technology fees for farmers with irrigation who planted at higher densities. But this approach had limited success because farmers had to supply global positioning system coordinates for their fields and administration and monitoring costs for D&PL were high. The vast majority of large-scale farmers who planted Bt cotton over the past 10 years paid the technology fee according to the number of 25 kg bags of seed purchased.

In the 1999–2000 season smallholder farmers on the Makhathini Flats paid a technology fee of R230 for a 25 kg bag of seed compared to R600 by large-scale farmers. This lower fee may have been partly an effort by Monsanto to favour resource-poor farmers, but it also helped establish a market for GM cotton among small-scale producers which could be cited elsewhere in Africa. (Another reason for a lower technology fee for smallholders is that although most plant by hand at low seed rates, a minority of them (about 20 per cent) use a hired, mechanized planter which uses three times more seed per hectare.) In the first few years, the seed was sold through the sole gin and input supplier on the Makhathini Flats, Vunisa, and because there were no large farmers in the area it was possible to restrict access to the lower technology fee (Gouse 2007).

For the 2007–08 season, smallholders purchasing a 25 kg bag of seed paid the same Bt technology fee as a large-scale farmer. But many smallholders buy special 5 kg bags of NuOPAL; their cost is based on the usual seed price and technology fee but they include an additional 500 g of conventional seed for the refuge and the seed is treated with an insecticide. Larger farmers have to pay extra for refuge seed and seed treatment, but they can often claim a refund on the 14 per cent value added tax, so the expenditure on seed for commercial and smallholder farmers is very similar.

The Monsanto technology fee contract includes a clause stating that the fee will be returned to the farmer if the seed does not germinate due to adverse weather conditions. In an attempt to stimulate large-scale dryland cotton production for the 2007–08 season, D&PL and Monsanto revised this clause to include 30 per cent of the seed cost (in addition to the technology fee) if the seed does not germinate or the farmer was not able to establish a crop due to drought. If the crop was established but not harvested due to drought, only the technology fee would be returned. However, seed sales for the 2007–08 season indicate that this risk-limiting incentive has had little effect on cotton plantings. These guarantees were not available to smallholders, where factors such as minimal fertilizer usage, late plantings and managerial limitations contribute to crop failure.

Cotton production by smallholders in South Africa is not intensive and cash expenses are largely limited to purchase of seed and insecticides. Most labour is either provided by the household or labour groups that are paid in food and drink. Before Bt, expenditure on seed represented 40–60 per cent of the total input cost. Adoption of Bt caused this share to increase to 70–80 per cent due to the extra technology fee and a decrease in the expenditure on insecticides (Fok *et al.* 2007). The increase in the relative share of seed in the total input cost is an important issue for farmers in marginal environments. It can be argued that the increase implies greater financial risk as more expense is incurred before planting and cannot be adjusted later in the season, when farmers can reduce the use of other inputs in response to adverse climatic conditions. Smallholders require some type of insurance, such as that offered to commercial farmers in the technology fee contract. It might be possible for smallholders to pay the technology fee at harvest time, based on the results of the season, but such a system would incur significant administrative costs.

Farm-level impact of Bt cotton

Studies on the performance of Bt cotton in South Africa

Even though large-scale farmers produce the bulk of the South African cotton crop, almost all research on the impact of Bt cotton has focused on the small-holder experience. Large-scale South African cotton farmers compete on a very different playing field than that of their subsidized American counterparts, but their production techniques and managerial skills are comparable, and the fact that they were able to benefit from Bt cotton adoption did not come as too much of a surprise. On the other hand, the South African smallholder experience was of much more interest to the technology owner, farmers and policymakers in developing countries, as well as to pro- and anti-GM advocacy groups.

Given the modest size of South Africa's small-scale cotton sector, the number of peer-reviewed publications analysing the Bt cotton experience is quite high. But despite the large number of publications, the analyses are based on only a few data sets. The first survey was carried out in November 2000 by the University of Pretoria (UP) in collaboration with the University of Reading. The sample consisted of 100 smallholder farmers who produced cotton on the Makhathini Flats. The stratified sample of 100 farmers included 40 non-Bt cotton growers and 60 Bt growers from the 1999–2000 season. The same farmers were also asked to recall information from the previous (1998–99) season, when 19 of them had grown Bt cotton. Data were collected by two Zulu-speaking enumerators, and most of the interviews were conducted when farmers visited the Vunisa depot. (At that time, Vunisa was the sole input supplier and seed cotton buyer on the Flats.) Data on household demographics, farming practices and cotton production were collected for the past two seasons. In addition to relying on farmer recall, some information was also obtained from Vunisa's records. A number of publications made use of this data, including Ismael *et al.* (2002), Thirtle *et al.* (2003), Gouse *et al.* (2005), Shankar and Thirtle (2005) and Gouse *et al.* (2008). In addition, these smallholder data were also used to compare with the performance of Bt cotton produced by large-scale cotton farmers in Limpopo Province, Northern Cape and Mpumalanga (Gouse *et al.* 2003, 2004).

In an effort to expand the information available from the original data set of 100 farmer interviews, researchers from the University of Reading approached Vunisa in order to make use of the records held for farmers who received input credit from Vunisa and delivered their seed cotton to the firm's ginnery. Vunisa supplied seed and insecticides to farmers and provided cash for hiring labour (for land preparation, planting, insecticide application, weeding and harvesting). The researchers were able to obtain 1283 records for 1998–99, 441 records for 1999–00 and 499 for 2000–01 (Bennett *et al.* 2006). They validated these records by comparing them to the data from the first survey as well as to the findings of an additional survey conducted among 32 members of one farmer organization. This second set of data was used in a number of publications, including Morse *et al.* (2004), Bennett *et al.* (2004), Morse *et al.* (2006) and Bennett *et al.* (2006).

Beginning with the 2001–02 production season, the Centre de Coopération Internationale en Recherche Agronomique pour le Développement (CIRAD), jointly with the UP, conducted more technical assessments of Bt cotton use in South Africa. The research included evaluation of expression and effectiveness of the Bt gene, gene flow and the evolution of the pest complex on Bt cotton plots. As part of the research, a smallholder sample of 10 Bt adopters and 10 non-adopters on the Makhathini Flats was followed for the 2002–03 and 2003–04 seasons and detailed data were collected for insect management and labour for pest control. Publications from this research include Hofs *et al*. 2006b, 2006c and 2006d.

CIRAD and UP conducted an additional survey among a larger number of farmers in order to study their production practices (Hofs *et al*. 2006a; Fok *et al*. 2007). The survey covered eight villages of the Ubombo and Ngwavuma districts on the Makhathini Flats during the 2002–03 season. The survey sample size was less than initially anticipated because of the low number of farmers planting cotton that season (only 353), and data were collected for 56 farmers. The questionnaires were translated into Zulu and farmers were interviewed in three phases at their homes or fields.

There are a number of factors that must be borne in mind when interpreting the analyses based on these smallholder data sets. First, the two larger data sets are based on farmer recall from previous seasons and ginnery records, and only the more recent, smaller data sets are based on information and observations collected at the farm. Second, the rapid growth in the use of Bt cotton by smallholders means that after a few seasons it was difficult to find non-users who could serve as a control group. Third, most of the studies have surveyed relatively small numbers of farmers over only one or two seasons. Rainfall and weather conditions have a considerable impact on the infestation level of the insects targeted by Bt cotton as well as on yield potential. As can be seen from Figure 9.4, the rainfall during the crucial months has historically been erratic and it is clear that an assessment based on only one or even two seasons for research could be misleading. Fourth, small samples and the variable conditions of rain-fed farming sometimes make it difficult to find statistically significant differences in results.

The use of Vunisa's records by the University of Reading researchers offered a way of overcoming some of the problems of small data sets. However, these data are not without problems. Cash loans for inputs do not necessarily result in the purchase of the agreed products or quantities. When inputs are supplied in kind, it does not necessarily mean that the total quantity will be applied; for instance, Vunisa believes that some farmers used insecticides supplied in the cotton loan for their vegetable plots. Using records of cash loaned for labour as a proxy for the amount of actual labour hired for cotton production is also problematic, and it does not account for family labour. In addition, basing yields on records of delivery at the ginnery may be misleading. It was not uncommon for farmers to deliver their seed cotton under different names or to have it delivered by another family member. It is not clear whether or how these anomalies were addressed in the studies based on this data set.

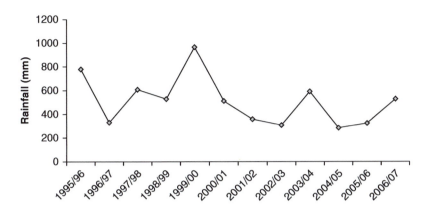

Figure 9.4 Total October to March rainfall for Makhathini according to production season

Source: Weather SA.

An additional factor that must be considered in assessing yield differences is the range of conventional cotton varieties that are compared to the Bt varieties. In studies covering the 1998–99 and 1999–2000 seasons, all the Bt cotton growers were using NuCottn 37B; 60 per cent of the farmers planting conventional cotton were using its isoline (DP 90) but the rest were using other varieties including Sicala, CA223 and the better-yielding DeltaOPAL. The more recent CIRAD/UP studies compare the Bt variety NuOPAL with its isoline DeltaOPAL. (Isolines are not necessary for making useful comparisons between the performance of transgenic and conventional varieties, but the absence of equivalent germplasm introduces an additional element of variability.)

The Bt cotton experience

This chapter does not aim to provide a comprehensive analysis of the findings from all the studies to date, but it does endeavour to put some of the findings into context. All the studies found yield increases with the use of Bt cotton compared to conventional varieties (Table 9.5). Almost all of the studies showed savings in insecticide expenditure as well; the only exception is the results from a one-year farm-level study of 20 farmers (Hofs *et al.* 2006b). Even though most of the yield differences were substantial, some were found not to be statistically significant, mainly due to small sample sizes and large variability in the data. The proportional yield gain resulting from the use of Bt cotton by South African smallholders (above 50 per cent according to the early studies based on farmer recall and company records) is higher than that found in most other countries. (Yield gains found in later studies based on farm-level interviews and observations are somewhat less.) One of the reasons for the substantial percentage increase is that the base yield (with non-Bt cotton) is very low and thus a small absolute change may be translated into a high relative increase. In addition, financial and human capital

Table 9.5 Summary of the findings of the major studies

	Non Bt yield (kg/ha)	Bt yield (kg/ha)	Diff%	Non Bt seed cost	Bt seed cost	Diff	Non Bt insecticide cost	Bt insecticide cost	Diff	Non Bt gross margin	Bt gross margin	Diff
Smallholders												
1998–99[1]	452	738	63%	138	278	−140	153	72	81	502	1033	531
1999–2000[1]	264	489	85%	190	413	−223	222	104	118	−11	376	387
2000–01[1]	501	783	56%	176	260	−84	305	113	192	348	1090	742
2002–03[2]	423	522	23%	206	392	−186	285	207	78	464	672	208
1999–2000[3]	395	576	46%	n.a	n.a	−163	129	97	32	n.a	n.a	367
Large scale												
Dryland 2000–01[3]	832	947	14%	n.a	n.a	−234	192	79	113	n.a	n.a	194
Irrigation 2000–01[3]	3413	4046	19%	n.a	n.a	−419	519	226	293	n.a	n.a	1615

Sources
1 Bennett *et al.* (2006)
2 Fok *et al.* (2007)
3 Gouse *et al.* (2003)

Note: Expenditure cost and differences indicated in Rands/ha.

constraints cause smallholders to under-invest in chemical pest control. Shankar and Thirtle (2005) showed that the average insecticide application level of small-holder farmers on the Flats is less than 50 per cent of the optimal level and it is thus not surprising that Bt cotton is able to substantially reduce the yield loss caused by bollworms.

The experience of large-scale South African farmers with Bt cotton is similar to that reported for commercial cotton farmers in other countries. Although they experience some yield increase, the major saving is in insecticide costs. These trends are consistent with findings elsewhere; in Argentina large-scale commercial farmers enjoyed a 19 per cent yield increase while smallholders reported a 41 per cent increase (Qaim and de Janvry 2003).

Gouse *et al.* (2003) compared smallholders' reasons for adoption with those of large-scale farmers. Large-scale farmers felt that the increased yield was not that important. Although more than 50 per cent of large-scale farmers indicated increased yield as a benefit of Bt cotton, it was seen more as a bonus. The big advantage for large-scale farmers is that insect-resistant cotton gives them the peace of mind and the managerial freedom to go on with other farming activities. For large-scale farmers, insecticide application requires more capital and management than labour; farmers with irrigation have difficulty fitting spraying in between the rain and irrigation schedules. In contrast, 63 per cent of the Bt adopters surveyed on the Makhathini Flats indicated insecticide saving as the most important benefit. Pesticide application implies huge difficulties for small-scale cotton farmers. Many small-scale farmers indicated that they were not even able to apply pesticides on their whole field due to a lack of time, knapsack sprayers, labour and the cost of insecticides. Water has to be fetched from communal water points and farmers may have to rely on water trucks or any other transport available. Low education levels make the mixing of pesticides and the calibration of spraying nozzles difficult, and the efficacy and efficiency of insecticide applications is questionable for many smallholder farmers (Gouse 2007).

Institutions and GM technology

The smallholder cotton sector

A number of attempts to establish sustainable smallholder cotton projects over the past 15 years have been less than successful. Limited funds, lack of skills to manage projects and funds, lack of coordination between government departments and initiatives, lack of long-term government commitment, limited knowledge of cotton farming, late approval of funds (and resulting delays in delivery of inputs), unclear farmer selection procedures, limited profitability of cotton farming and the struggle to adapt to a liberalized system have all contributed to projects collapsing within a couple of seasons. The main smallholder cotton areas remain Makhathini and Tonga, although a recent project in the Eastern Cape, partly supported by the private sector, has been reasonably successful.

Table 9.6 indicates the smallholder production areas and number of farmers, by province, for the last two production seasons and illustrates the small areas and

Table 9.6 Smallholder production according to province

	Dryland area in hectares		Irrigation area in hectares		Estimated number of farmers	
	2005–06	*2006–07*	*2005–06*	*2006–07*	*2005–06*	*2006–07*
North West	0	0	3	13	10	10
Northern Cape	0	0	11	11	16	16
KwaZulu Natal	5200	1900	1560	1030	2260	853
Limpopo	0	60	0	0	0	?
Mpumalanga	910	561	14	0	199	740
Eastern Cape	0	270	61	100	364	686
Total	6110	2791	1649	1154	2849	2305

Source: Cotton SA.

numbers of farmers involved in smallholder cotton. Makhathini Flats in KwaZulu Natal is the predominant source of smallholder cotton. (The area of irrigation farming in KwaZulu Natal in Table 9.6 is misleading as these 'smallholder' irrigation plots are rented out and planted by a commercial company.) The average yield for South African smallholders is barely more than 500 kg of seed cotton per hectare and the profitability of these small farms cannot be compared to those in China, India or Francophone Africa, where higher yields mean that a farmer can make a living on a small plot.

History of the Makhathini Flats

The early history of cotton production in the Makhathini area is uncertain, although records show that white farmers near Ndumo were planting rain-fed cotton as early as 1919. There have been attempts to establish cotton cultivation in the Ohlalwini, Mboza and Jobe areas but substantial production only became viable with the damming of the Pongola River to provide a controllable supply of water to the Flats (Witt *et al.* 2006). The Jozini dam was built in 1972 for the initial purpose of supplying irrigation water to a proposed project for small-scale white farmers planting sugar cane. However, falling international sugar prices and domestic over-production in the late 1970s, combined with rapid economic development that created employment for poor whites, meant that the scheme never materialized. The major share of land on the Flats belonged to the state and in 1979 the apartheid regime declared this a 'black area' along with the already existing KwaZulu (former Zululand) area. In the early 1980s the government decided to develop the necessary infrastructure to settle Zulu farmers on small commercial farming units to produce cotton and other crops under irrigation. The Makhathini Irrigation Scheme was expected to fill the role of a 'growth engine' for the region, but an incoherent and continually changing institutional framework imposed upon a background of changing developmental and political philosophies led to a lack of continuity and poor cooperation. The situation was exacerbated by inappropriate farmer selection and the initial removal and resettlement of about 5000 individuals in order to establish the irrigation scheme (Witt *et al.* 2006). These factors generated high levels of institutional mistrust and disillusionment and resulted in crippling levels of indebtedness (ibid.).

Once the Makhathini Irrigation Scheme was established it continued to rely on state support although there were constant changes in the management of the scheme. In 1984 the previous government manager, the Corporation for Economic Development (CED), was disbanded and the South African Development Trust Corporation (STK/SADT) and more specifically its subsidiary – Mjindi Farming – was appointed as the new managing agent. Under STK, the irrigation scheme was directed primarily towards the production of cotton. Extension services were expanded to also include dryland cotton farmers and by the late 1980s, nearly 2000 ha of irrigated and 1000 ha of rain-fed cotton were under production. Surging interest in cotton as the key cash crop offering government support triggered a decrease in food crop production in the area (Witt *et al.* 2006).

During the late 1980s two ginning companies, Clark Cotton and Tongaat Cotton, were active on the Flats, supplying credit and inputs and buying cotton from small-scale farmers. The two companies shared a weighing bridge and there was a positive attitude of cooperation. Even though some farmers borrowed production credit from one company and delivered their harvest under a different name to the other company, losses and gains generally balanced out. Around 1989 Clark and Tongaat formed a partnership called Vunisa (which means 'to harvest' in Zulu). During this period the Land Bank supplied credit, and risk of repayment default was shared between the Land Bank and Vunisa. Vunisa administrated production loans starting in the 1998–99 season and the first few years were very successful for both cotton farmers and the ginning company, with a loan recovery rate of close to 90 per cent. An important factor was the fact that Vunisa was the only buyer and, because of this monopsony power, could supply production credit to farmers who did not own their land, using the forthcoming crop as collateral. This system is not uncommon to Africa where widespread failure of credit and input markets (partly due to lack of land ownership that could serve as collateral) has led to interlocked transactions, in which a firm wishing to purchase the farm output – typically a ginner in the case of cotton – provides inputs to farmers on credit and attempts to recover the credit upon purchase of the product (Tschirley *et al.* 2006).

During the 2001–02 production season a new company, Makhathini Cotton (Pty) Ltd (MCC) erected a gin on the Flats, right next to the Vunisa depot. The MCC was founded in 2002 partly at the behest of prominent provincial politicians (Witt *et al.* 2006). With 70 per cent of the shares owned by a black South African, the MCC also fulfilled the role of an Agricultural Black Economic Empowerment company and was able to attain access to the Mjindi irrigation scheme. The MCC's vision is 'to stimulate rural development and reduce poverty on the Makhathini Flats by creating a world-class cotton agribusiness through construction of a ginnery in the heart of the area'. But by opening a competing gin they destroyed the credit system created by Vunisa and set in motion a chain of events where farmers borrowed production credit from Vunisa but delivered their harvest to the MCC. Due to substantial financial losses to Vunisa and the Land Bank, no credit was made available for 2002–03, with the effect that very few farmers were able to produce cotton that season.

The struggling smallholder sector

The drop in the number of cotton farmers in 2002–03 is clear in Table 9.7. An additional factor that contributed to farmers' low credit repayment was inadequate rainfall during the crucial months in 2001–02 and 2002–03 (Figure 9.4). A farmer who only harvests around 400 kg of seed cotton will probably not be able to repay the production loan. In 2003–04 some farmers were able to fund their own production but the low cotton price meant that many were not able or willing to continue for the next season. In 2005–06, after more than two years of negotiations, the KwaZulu Natal Department of Agriculture made available R6.4 million worth of inputs as a grant in the form of an input pack. This was supposed to be the first of three yearly grants to help farmers out of their debt trap, but in 2006–07 no funds were made available and the number of farmers dropped again. Although some suspected that funds were available for 2005–06 only because it was an election year, another grant was provided in 2007, although it was approved so late in the year that the inputs were not available for planting in the 2007–08 season.

The relatively large number of smallholders who produced cotton outside Makhathini in 2006–07 (see Table 9.7) is partly because of an increase in the number of farmers in the Eastern Cape, but mainly because the Mpumalanga Department of Agriculture provided a production grant for the farmers in Tonga that season. Again bureaucratic delay caused the inputs to arrive late and not all farmers planted. According to Cotton SA, R1.8 million of inputs were supplied but just over 300,000 Rands of seed cotton were harvested.

The correlation between smallholders' planting decision and pre-season rainfall (September to November) is weak (Figure 9.5) and planting decisions are more related to the availability of credit or grants. Similarly, few smallholders base their planting decision on predicted cotton price, due to a lack of information and a lack of options on crop choice. It is estimated that between 30 and 40 per cent of the farmers on the Flats can and do finance their own inputs (when no credit or handouts are available), but the majority of smallholders only plant when grants are provided. The farmers on the Flats who are able to produce during the seasons when credit is not available are mainly the elderly who can finance inputs with state pension income (Fok *et al.* 2007). To illustrate the precarious economics of small-scale cotton production, gross margins are frequently less than R1,000 per ha, roughly equivalent to the current monthly old-age pension.

It is also important to note that South African smallholder cotton farmers are different from their counterparts in the rest of Africa. Not only do the elderly receive a monthly pension but households also receive grants for every child

Table 9.7 Variability in smallholders' and Makhathini's contribution to the total cotton crop

	No. of smallholders	No. of smallholders on Makhathini	% of SA's smallholders on Makhathini	Dryland smallholder cotton area in hectares	Total smallholder cotton area in hectares	Share of national production	Average dryland yield: Seed cotton kg/ha
1996–97	3655	3000	82%	11,351	13,022	6.5%	403
1997–98	3062	2200	72%	12,270	14,496	13.2%	580
1998–99	3604	2200	61%	7073	9433	8.0%	545
1999–2000	3486	3000	86%	7690	8094	1.5%	777
2000–01	3312	3000	91%	4375	4404	4.9%	693
2001–02	3688	3229	88%	5031	5596	2.2%	515
2002–03	464	353	76%	1421	1476	1.2%	475
2003–04	1891	1550	82%	3395	5348	5.5%	492
2004–05	1669	548	33%	1586	3689	8.7%	521
2005–06	2543	2169	85%	6355	9086	20.9%	485
2006–07	2295	853	37%	3601	4975	18.4%	600

Source: Adapted from Fok *et al.* (2007).

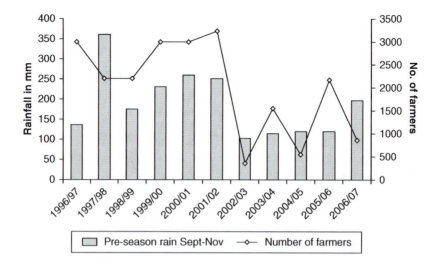

Figure 9.5 Number of smallholder cotton producers on Makhathini Flats and the correlation
with pre-season rainfall

below 16 years of age. There is an increasing labour shortage, fuelled by a growing economy that encourages labour migration and exacerbated by the impact of
HIV/AIDS. In Makhathini Flats, an estimated 42 per cent of household heads are
female and 76 per cent are over 40 years old (Gouse *et al.* 2005). Many rural
households in KwaZulu Natal receive remittances from family members working
in the cities. Makhathini farmers thus have alternative sources of income and this
influences their commitment to cotton production, especially with the marginal
profitability of recent years and the sporadic availability of government production support programs.

Inputs and information

Historically cotton gins in South Africa performed the role of a 'one-stop shop',
supplying commercial farmers with credit, advice, inputs, insect-scouting services
and transport services as well as buying the seed cotton at the end of the season.
This vertical integration allowed the cotton gins to prosper, and farmers were
dependant on the gin if they wanted to produce cotton. After liberalization of the
cotton sector in 1997 a large number of commercial farmers felt that it was more
economical to purchase inputs directly from suppliers rather than going through the
gin. In addition, some farmers tried to move into ginning, and a few farmer-owned
gins were erected. However, this period corresponded to a slump in the world cotton price; many farmers completely stopped producing cotton and a number of the
large cotton gins were closed down or sold and moved to other countries.

Vunisa performed the same service for the smallholders on the Makhathini
Flats. Vunisa supplied credit, inputs and extension services, and farmers' days
were held that provided training on subjects such as land preparation, chemical

use, and insect scouting in order to assess when spraying is necessary. The gin provided these extension services in order to ensure that they were able to source as much cotton as possible and limit their risk on the credit they supplied. (The same rationale was evident for the gins serving commercial farmers before liberalization.) With the collapse of Vunisa's system, the extension services also ceased to function, although training of farmers continued through the smallholder training program and a mentoring scheme, both supported by Cotton SA and the government Agricultural Sector Education Training Authority. MCC has also started supplying advisory services to farmers in order to increase the dryland cotton crop on the Flats.

Government extension services in the smallholder areas are inadequate and are not a reliable source of information or training for cotton growers. Some of the provincial programs supporting smallholders in the past few years have attempted to provide the most relevant inputs by soliciting advice from farmer representatives, Cotton SA and government agencies. However, the government input packages have often overlooked important differences in production practices between regions, and the government's poorly monitored procurement policy has meant that some unnecessary or inappropriate inputs found their way into the packages. There have been instances where farmers requested Bt seed and received conventional seed instead; stacked seed was supplied to farmers who do intercropping (and are thus unable to use herbicide); and foliar fertilizer was provided to farmers who had no experience using it.

D&PL opted not to sell the herbicide-tolerant variety in smallholder areas until the stacked variety was available. With almost all smallholders planting only Bt cotton for the past several years, there was concern that farmers would not spray for bollworms on the RR cotton. This indicates that D&PL and Monsanto have learned from past mistakes. When Bt cotton was first released, some smallholders (and even some commercial farmers) did not get the message that they still had to spray for sucking insects, with resulting damage to their crops. Use of herbicides is not uncommon among smallholder cotton producers and training programs and farmers' days have featured demonstrations on herbicide use. Herbicide-tolerant maize has been introduced among smallholders in other areas with great success and the minimum tillage approach has been shown to be suitable for smallholders. The performance of stacked-gene cotton among smallholders has not yet been assessed.

Because large-scale farmers use large quantities of inputs, they generally receive good service from the input suppliers, and chemical company representatives often visit farmers to deliver what is needed and to advise on new products. With the recent drop in the area of cotton planted, large farmers are also able to order their seed directly from the seed company. The situation for smallholders is different. Makhathini Flats is situated approximately 80 km from the closest large town (Pongola), and timely access to inputs is more problematic. When Vunisa was still active on the Flats, they sold inputs from a metal shipping container next to their weighing bridge. An agricultural input supplier has now taken over and sells inputs from their container close to MCC.

Some observers have suggested that the high adoption rate of Bt cotton by smallholders is misleading because farmers were given few other options (e.g.

Witt *et al.* 2006). It is certainly true that Bt cotton was the subject of considerable promotion and commercial pressure in the early years, and this influenced input availability. But it is also important to recall that Vunisa made available the inputs they felt would perform the best in order to source as much seed cotton as possible. They felt they could increase productivity and decrease the need for expensive chemicals by recommending Bt cotton. A non-Bt variety was available, but only in 25 kg bags rather than the 5 kg bags designed for smallholders. D&PL argued that it was not profitable for them to repack the conventional (DeltaOPAL) seed into small bags as the demand for the variety was minimal.

All South African farmers growing Bt cotton are required to plant a refuge to avoid the development of insect resistance. Farmers sign a contract that stipulates refuge management requirements. Large-scale farmers must purchase extra bags of conventional seed when buying Bt seed and thus D&PL at least have the assurance that the farmer bought seed for a refuge. Large-scale cotton farmers have experience of bollworms developing resistance to insecticides and it appears they have accepted the idea of stewardship for the new technology. When smallholders buy a 5 kg bag of Bt seed, an additional 500 g of conventional seed is included at no extra cost. According to Cotton SA and D&PL, the majority of large and small-scale farmers plant the required refuges. Monsanto has argued that refuge is not needed on the Flats as the small cotton plots are surrounded by wild vegetation that can serve as refuge for bollworms.

Conclusions

The Makhathini Flats experience has been hailed as proof that GM crops can benefit smallholders in Africa. Research has clearly shown that the Bt cotton technology works and that both large-scale and smallholder farmers can benefit, especially in seasons with high bollworm pressure. The fact that South Africa has a functioning regulatory framework for GMOs made it possible for cotton farmers to benefit from advances in biotechnology. Even though cotton production has decreased significantly over the past decade (due in large part to low relative prices), the market share of GM varieties has not decreased, despite the availability of conventional varieties. In fact, farmers have indicated that if it had not been for these technological advances the decline in the cotton sector would have been much more dramatic.

However, while technical solutions can help address problems such as lack of knowledge, limited access to inputs or evolution in pest pressure, it must be stressed that no technology (GM or otherwise) can resolve the fundamental institutional challenges of smallholders and agriculture in Africa. The particular case of the Makhathini Flats, and the wider story of cotton in South Africa, emphasizes that while all agricultural systems require adequate investment and appropriate technologies, their viability is determined by the policies and institutions that facilitate sustainable and profitable production. Trends in agricultural prices tend to be cyclical, and it is quite possible that the South African cotton sector will be booming again in a few years. If that happens, it will be policies and institutions, as well as technologies, that will determine the direction and equitability of cotton farming's revival.

10 Summary and conclusions

Robert Tripp

Introduction

This chapter has two purposes. It begins with a brief summary of some of the major findings of the four country case studies, in the context of what was learned from the literature reviews in Chapters 4 and 5, and it then goes on to suggest some broader implications regarding the role of transgenic crops in agricultural development.

There are obvious limitations on the possibilities of drawing general conclusions from just four cases examining a single transgenic crop. In addition, both the crop and the technology of our example have some quite distinctive characteristics, especially in the context of small-farm agriculture. Cotton is a cash crop; farmers are accustomed to using large quantities of purchased inputs to grow the crop, and they are paid for their harvest in accordance with norms and prices determined by a global industry. The technology, for insect-control, addresses a very important problem for growers, but one that is exceptionally complex and admits to no simple, one-shot solutions.

The four countries themselves are also somewhat special, and not perfectly representative of the developing world. China and India are the two largest Asian countries, and between them they include a significant proportion of the world's resource-poor farmers. But both countries have experience and capacity in agricultural technology generation and delivery that is virtually unmatched in the rest of the developing world. The other two examples, Colombia and South Africa, are middle income countries with dualistic agricultures. Although the histories of support to smallholder farming are very different in these two countries, the fact that large-scale farmers are able to exert pressure on governments and technology providers means that smallholders often benefit from the infrastructure and flow of innovations resulting from these demands.

Of course these countries were not chosen at random for our study; at this relatively early stage in the career of transgenic cotton they were virtually the only candidates. They are the 'early adopters', and just as it is useful to ask how the farmers who are early adopters of a technology differ from their neighbours, and what their characteristics indicate about the prospects for broader technology diffusion, we can ask the same question about early-adopting countries. One of the principal messages of this book has been that because these countries have the requisite institutions they have been able to take the lead in adopting transgenic cotton. Similarly, imperfections and past histories of markets, regulations, research and extension lead to inefficiencies that can help explain instances when a country has not been able to take full advantage of the new technology.

The next section reviews the performance of Bt cotton in the four case study countries. The following section summarizes the relationship between the institutions that determine the capacity to manage transgenic cotton and the farm-level results observed in the case studies. Finally, the discussion broadens to explore what the assessment of institutional performance in Bt cotton can contribute to evaluating the prospects for the wider application of transgenic crops for resource-poor farmers.

The technology and its performance

Bt cotton has spread rapidly in all four case study countries. By 2005, it was very difficult to find any farmer planting conventional varieties in the provinces of eastern China that account for two-thirds of the country's cotton-producing area. The Bt varieties spread rapidly because they provided a significant remedy for the bollworm damage that required ever-increasing investments from farmers to control. A lack of enforcement of intellectual property rights and basic seed laws meant that many breeders and seed companies in China could use the Bt gene at essentially no cost. In India, initial limited access to the transgene was broken, first by an underground seed market and then by the licensing of the transgenes to an increasing number of domestic seed companies who already had an established market for hybrid cotton seed. The government took steps to establish price limits on the seed and a significant majority of cotton farmers chose to use the transgenic varieties, which came to dominate the market.

In South Africa, the US company Delta and Pine Land (D&PL) was already a major supplier of cotton seed and was able to introduce several of its transgenic varieties to the market. One of these became very popular and spread rapidly among large farmers. At the same time it was possible to take advantage of a pre-existing credit program to introduce Bt cotton to smallholders. Initial success was followed by problems with administering the initiative, but subsequent government programs for smallholder cotton farmers also rely on transgenic cotton, which has largely replaced conventional varieties in the commercial market. In Colombia, where bollworm is not usually the major pest problem, larger, better-resourced farmers were the first to take up Bt cotton, but the technology gradually spread so that about half of the country's cotton area was planted in Bt cotton in 2007.

Chapter 4 discussed some of the difficulties in assessing the impact of a new technology. In both China and South Africa, the widespread use of Bt cotton at the time the case study research was conducted made it impossible to find a control group growing conventional varieties. In India as well, the proportion of farmers growing conventional cotton was very small. Colombia was the only one of the four case study countries where many farmers were still planting conventional cotton varieties. The study showed that those who planted Bt cotton generally achieved higher yields and higher economic returns, but usually accompanied by greater input use, including (somewhat surprisingly) more insecticide.

Our case study results on economic impact are broadly comparable to what has been reported elsewhere in the literature, although each case deserves specific attention, and there is much variability among farmers and between years. In China, yield increases due to Bt cotton are quite modest (but Chinese cotton yields were already among the world's highest). In the other countries, however, yield gains are often the primary outcome of adopting the technology. Bollworms are difficult insects to control, even in the best of circumstances. It is not surprising to find a yield gain for smallholders in South Africa or India, but it even appears to be the case for many relatively large farmers in Colombia. India's national cotton yields have increased significantly during the period when Bt cotton was becoming a dominant technology. There is surely a connection between these two phenomena, although it is difficult to say precisely how much of India's yield increase is directly due to Bt cotton.

The results for insecticide use are more surprising. The China case provides the most significant instance of insecticide reduction due to Bt cotton, although it is important to recall that this responded to a situation where farmers' excessive use of insecticides had created a treadmill of growing insect resistance and ever-increasing dependence on chemicals. Although the quantities of insecticide used on Bt cotton are now much lower, they are still among the highest in the world and include substantial insecticide use for bollworm late in the season. In India, on the other hand, the changes in insecticide practices are more modest, although farmers now use less insecticide to control bollworm. In Colombia, where boll weevil is the principal insect pest of cotton, the introduction of Bt cotton has not brought a reduction in insecticide use, and indeed most Bt users apply more insecticide than their neighbours who plant conventional varieties. The impact on South African smallholders is more difficult to gauge because they were using relatively little insecticide even before the introduction of Bt.

The gains in yield and reduction in insecticide must be balanced against the costs of the technology. We have seen that the cost is very low in China, because of the lack of intellectual property protection. But in India and Colombia Bt seed costs about twice the conventional seed, and in South Africa it is about three times as expensive. Many farmers in India were already accustomed to high-priced hybrid seed. In Colombia, farmers try to take measures to reduce their seeding rate to lower their investment in transgenic seed. For smallholders, the advantage of seed with in-built control is somewhat diminished by the fact that the additional cost must be paid at the beginning of the season, before knowing how rainfall or pest populations will affect production and crop management. No insurance schemes are available for any of the smallholders in our case studies.

The overall economic impact of the technology must be judged in relation to its accessibility for resource-poor farmers. In eastern China the technology has been universally adopted. Bt cotton is now spreading very rapidly in India. A small minority of farmers in the Maharashtra study were still not using Bt cotton, and they tended to have less land than average, but there do not appear to be any significant impediments that limit their access to the technology. In South Africa, smallholders initially obtained access to Bt cotton through an existing credit program and since then have been the beneficiaries of several local government credit packages. In Colombia, the technology is growing in popularity, but many farmers with fewer resources find that they still cannot get access to it, often because of the way that credit is organized.

But the impact of a technology on resource-poor farmers goes beyond questions of access. Even when smallholders can obtain a new technology, it is important to ask if they are able to take full advantage of it. The answer to this question is often tied to the nature of the rural institutions that serve the interests of these farmers.

Agricultural institutions and Bt cotton

Our analysis has emphasized the importance of institutions. This section reviews the relationship between several factors that have traditionally been important determinants of cotton technology choice (fibre quality, labour and credit). It then examines how the status of other institutions has shaped local response to Bt cotton, and how the introduction of the technology has affected those institutions. They include input markets, technology generation (particularly plant breeding), intellectual property (and biosafety) regulation and the provision of information.

Institutions traditionally affecting choice of cotton technology

It is useful to first review the extent to which some of the institutions that have traditionally determined cotton farmers' technology choices have been affected by the advent of Bt cotton. As outlined in Chapter 2, these include markets for fibre quality, the organization of labour and access to input credit.

There is little evidence that Bt cotton has had any significant impact on cotton fibre quality, nor has it led to any initiatives that would provide incentives to farmers for choosing technologies and management practices that would deliver fibre of different qualities. Farmers' cotton-marketing practices and options in the case study countries have remained essentially unchanged. Although the introduction of Bt cotton has often brought increased differentiation and control in seed markets, it has not led to any institutional innovation that could help farmers earn more income through more differentiated output markets.

The organization of labour has always been an important factor for determining cotton production technology. Bt cotton does not have large implications for labour, except that the potential reduction in insecticide use means less labour for spraying, and any increased yield requires more labour for harvest. The reduction in labour for spraying was especially attractive for South African smallholders, many of whose fields were a long distance from water sources. Large farmers, whose spraying regime was mechanized, instead appreciated the convenience and peace of mind of the insect-resistance technology. In China, with expanding off-farm opportunities, farmers are always looking for ways to save labour, and Bt technology (particularly combined with innovations such as hybrid use) can make some contributions. Many farmers in Colombia and India depend on hired labour for applying insecticide, but Bt cotton does not yet appear to have made any significant change to insecticide use in those countries. Larger cotton farmers in South Africa and Colombia often find herbicide tolerance at least as attractive as insect resistance in transgenic cotton, and of course the widespread use of herbicides has more profound consequences for the use of hired labour.

The third factor that is important in determining the technologies that cotton farmers are able to use is the availability of input credit. In South Africa, the introduction of Bt cotton to smallholders was through a system of tied credit that had been managed by the area's sole ginnery, but when a competing ginnery was established the scheme broke down and technology access was then determined by ad-hoc government programs. But during the time of its operation, the ginnery was eager to provide Bt cotton to its growers, believing it would improve their productivity (and the ginnery's profits). In Colombia, grower associations have always provided credit to their affiliates, taking advantage of government loan facilities in support of agriculture. But the expense of the Bt seed has meant that not all associations can offer it to their farmers and some of the associations view the technology as too risky for smallholders. In addition, some of these associations directly represent growers' interests while others are focused on commercial input sale, leading to different incentives for providing the new technology. In India and China, most cotton farmers obtain their inputs with cash, or with loans from sources not directly tied to input provision.

Input markets

Seed markets are among the most important determinants of farmers' access to Bt cotton. All of the case study countries have well-established seed industries, and the introduction of Bt cotton occasioned some changes in these systems. China was in the process of transformation from a state-run to a largely private seed system during the course of Bt cotton's introduction. Demand for the new technology was surely one of the factors that encouraged the proliferation of small seed companies and the wide array of varieties. Most of India's domestic cotton seed industry was initially locked out of the Bt market, but soon found a way in through various licensing agreements. Most of the major players in the Indian hybrid cotton seed market now have their own Bt varieties, and more new transgenic varieties come into the market each year.

Another unusual feature of the China and India cases is the importance of underground seed markets. In China this is largely a function of the lack of enforcement of intellectual property rights and seed regulations that were supposed to govern the nascent private seed sector. Without credible enforcement it is easy to access the genes informally and to produce and market unregistered varieties. India's underground Bt seed market was largely a reaction to the initially strict control of access to the technology and the very high prices for seed. In a country with considerable plant breeding and seed marketing experience such a reaction was probably inevitable. Although the problem is well recognized (and is susceptible to control through the enforcement of regulations that have been called into force in other cases), differences in local state government policy lead to very marked variation in the importance of the underground market. Although it is tempting to see such underground markets as taking advantage of farmers with low-quality products, both case studies show that it is surprisingly difficult to distinguish the authorized from the unauthorized seed. The fact that the underground seed is sold through essentially the same retail channels as legitimate seed means that providers have incentives to control the quality of their offerings as they do for their legitimate products. Although these underground markets may have a 'Robin Hood' image (in the face of corporate monopolies elsewhere), their long-term implications for the incentives to develop, deliver and control future genetically modified (GM) crops give cause for concern. In India, intense competition from the legitimate market (and the use of regulatory author- ity in some states) appears to be lessening the influence of the underground seed market. The situation in China is much more complex, in part because the private seed sector is of such recent origin.

The experience in South Africa and Colombia is quite different. The cotton seed market had always been in the hands of a very small number of players and Bt cotton further narrowed the field. One supplier (D&PL) provides all of the Bt cotton and the majority of the conventional varieties. Farmers in both countries initially had essentially one Bt variety (although there are now cotton varieties in those markets with herbicide tolerance).

The ability of Bt cotton to make the maximum contribution to improving the efficiency of farmers' insect control is also related to the organization of insecti- cide markets. Again, the contrast between the two sets of case countries is marked. The insecticide markets in Colombia and South Africa are essentially limited to the products of a few large (mostly multinational) companies, and qual- ity and product identity are strictly regulated. In contrast, the insecticide markets in China and India are comprised of a large number of small, local companies, presenting a bewildering array of commercial products from which farmers must choose. The advent of Bt cotton has made little difference to the character of these markets.

Plant breeding

A seed market is of little use without appropriate varieties. China and India both have very experienced and extensive public plant-breeding systems. Most Chinese Bt cotton varieties (except for those supplied directly by Monsanto) are the products of public breeding, although the changing roles of state agricultural research institutes in the newly privatized seed system makes the traditional public–private line more difficult to draw. The extensive use of hybrid cotton in India, beginning in the 1970s, provided the incentives for investment in private cotton breeding that has been responsible for the current range of Bt varieties, although much of the germplasm was initially from public sources. In both cases, the availability of Bt has certainly stimulated additional plant breeding and has not reduced the range of varieties available.

There has been some public cotton breeding in Colombia and South Africa, although in recent years most cotton varieties have been supplied by foreign seed companies. This means that farmers have a quite narrow range of varieties from which to choose. In the South Africa case, the initial Bt varieties offered by D&PL did not perform well, but their second-round offering proved to be popular with farmers. In Colombia, the initial Bt variety was well accepted, but one of the more recent stacked varieties has not performed well. Because cotton does not command a sufficiently large proportion of cultivated area to justify local public or private plant breeding in these countries, the restricted range of cotton varieties has always been a problem. The introduction of Bt technology in these two countries, while providing access to a productive technology, has somewhat narrowed the choices available to farmers. This is a dilemma for countries with small cotton sectors: dependence on productive foreign technology further lowers the chances for strengthening local plant-breeding capacity.

Intellectual property rights

The four case study countries present different strategies with respect to intellectual property rights for Bt cotton. They illustrate that adequate approaches for managing transgenic varieties in developing countries do not necessarily require recourse to patents, but they also illustrate that lack of enforcement capacity can threaten any IPR strategy.

The cotton seed markets in South Africa and Colombia are both quite small and the technology owner has little trouble controlling access to Bt varieties. Farmers sign grower agreements that forbid seed saving or unauthorized sale of the harvest, and the legal systems function sufficiently well that the owner is confident of being able to take any significant cases of violation to court.

In India, there are several foreign and domestic owners of Bt transgenes that have licensed them to local seed companies. Biosafety regulations prohibit the sale of unregistered transgenic varieties and basic seed laws provide for inspection of packaged seed offered for sale. Despite these regulations, officials in some states have been slow to move against the underground market for transgenic varieties, and those marketing such varieties attempt to argue that their sale is merely an extension of the law that permits farmers to save and exchange seed (of even transgenic varieties). To date the seed industry has seemed to tolerate the existence of the underground market, and it appears to be declining in the face of competition from the growing range of legitimate varieties. The existence of the underground market does not seem to have affected the introduction of new technology; for instance, Monsanto has been willing to license its second generation 'Bollgard II' gene to local companies.

In China, plant variety protection (PVP) regulations have only recently been modified to include cotton, so there has been little protection against a company producing the seed of its competitor. Variety registration and biosafety regulations could help limit the appearance of unapproved varieties on the market, but there has been almost no enforcement. The result is a market where it is very difficult to tell the approved from the unapproved varieties and the legitimate from illegitimate seed, as the China case study illustrated. Farmers have benefited from low prices for transgenic seed, but have limited capacity to learn about reliable suppliers and often resort to saving seed of varieties that perform satisfactorily, rather than have to try to identify them again in the market. In addition, the free flow of transgenic technology is a disincentive to further research and development. The inability to protect proprietary technology has almost certainly discouraged MNCs from introducing further innovations to the Chinese cotton market.

Biosafety regulation

The sustainability of the Bt technology will be determined in part by the success of the refuge strategies employed to limit the development of insect resistance. In Colombia and South Africa, the relatively small size of the cotton sector and the organization of the seed market make it easier to monitor and enforce refuge requirements, and there is less chance of unregistered transgenic varieties gaining a foothold.

In India, it is much more difficult to monitor refuge requirements, especially where many smallholders do not understand their purpose, but the industry is required to provide packets of refuge seed to purchasers of Bt varieties, together with instructions for its use. The study indicated that compliance is relatively good in Maharashtra, but in Gujarat, where farmers have until recently depended on an underground seed market, only a minority of those farmers now switching to approved varieties are following the refuge recommendations. (In China, there are no requirements for refuges because of the small farm size and mixed cropping patterns.)

Information

In order to take full advantage of Bt cotton, farmers need access to information about its performance and management. They should also be able to use Bt cotton as part of a broader insect-control strategy. There are various types of formal and informal institutions that can provide such information, including the input market, the farming community and extension services.

The extent of choice offered to farmers in our case studies falls into two extremes. On the one side, farmers in Colombia and South Africa must simply choose between the Bt variety and a few conventional varieties. On the other hand, Chinese and Indian farmers are faced with an overwhelming range of Bt cotton varieties. The same dichotomy is also evident for the pesticide market. Colombian farmers' choices are further restricted by the decisions of their associations, which elect the particular inputs to make available. In South Africa, large cotton farmers can get specific advice from input suppliers, but smallholders do not have this luxury, and their imperfect understanding of commercial inputs has, for instance, made the technology supplier wary about the introduction of herbicide-tolerant cotton to the small-farm sector.

In China, farmers must choose from among a large number of Bt cotton varieties. The Chinese case shows that farmers get relatively little useful information about inputs from the dealers and have almost no knowledge of the companies that supply the seed or insecticide. There is a high degree of turnover in the varieties and pesticides that farmers buy each year, and farmers' lack of confidence in information from the seed market is partly reflected in the high degree of seed saving.

Farmers in India are more accustomed to a commercial seed system, and many cotton farmers were buying proprietary hybrid seed long before the arrival of Bt cotton. Most farmers have no trouble identifying the seed and insecticides they are using, although the cotton farmers who have relied on the underground seed market are somewhat less informed about the legitimate market for Bt varieties. Despite the profusion of new Bt varieties, there is less rapid turnover of varieties and farmers often buy the same variety over a number of seasons.

Farmers the world over experiment with new technology and exchange experiences, which can help overcome other information deficiencies. In China there is evidence that farmers in the same village often favour a particular variety, but the favourites change so rapidly that it is difficult to see this as the outcome of an experimentation process. The Indian case provides more evidence of testing and experimentation, with farmers frequently planting a new variety on a small part of their land and gradually increasing its use if the results are favourable. Again, this takes place in the context of a well-established commercial seed system.

The extension service should be able to help farmers make choices, but there are few examples in our Bt cotton cases. The extension service available to smallholder cotton growers in South Africa is inadequate, although the ginneries attempt to provide some extension advice. In Colombia, farmers have been required to contract a private extension agent to help them make decisions. This is certainly a useful resource, but there are possible conflicts of interest and little incentive to strengthen farmers' own skills. In China as well there has been a contradiction between extension agents' mandate to help farmers follow rational pest control practices, on the one hand, and their reliance on input sales to fund the extension office, on the other. The extension service is simply not in evidence in the India case.

Without adequate extension or other information to help farmers manage the new technology, it is not surprising that the impact of Bt cotton on pest management is not as significant as it might be. In China, farmers still overuse insecticides, applying an average of 13 different products. In both China and India, farmers often mix two or more insecticides in a single application. In India, nearly half of the (infrequent) visits of outside agencies to farmers' fields have been from pesticide or seed companies, and farmers get most of their information about insecticides from dealers. In Colombia, farmers have access to contracted extension advice, but the damage caused by boll weevil and other insects, and a lack of incentives for insecticide reduction, has meant that those who grow Bt cotton often use more insecticide than other farmers. A national program to control boll weevil requires the participation of all grower associations, as well as farmer understanding, but it has been difficult to elicit the required support.

Unless there is more investment in building farmers' skills (and providing more reliable outside advice), it is unlikely that an innovation such as Bt cotton will achieve its potential impact on resource-poor farmers. We have seen that the yield advantages of the new technology have been welcomed by most farmers, and farmers' capacities to identify appropriate varieties are related to the nature of the seed systems already in place. Similarly, their abilities to use Bt cotton as part of a comprehensive insect management strategy are dependent on extension systems and other sources of information about crop management. As those are almost universally deficient, the technology's impact on insecticide reduction has often been disappointing.

Biotechnology and resource-poor farmers

Transgenic cotton varieties offer the possibility of significantly improving cotton productivity. This type of technology, if fairly priced and offered through well-organized input markets, can certainly make a contribution to improving smallholder farming. But it is important to try to place what we have learned about the successes and setbacks of transgenic cotton in the context of a wider debate about the future of agricultural biotechnology in developing countries.

Technological possibilities

One problem in making an assessment is that it is difficult to foresee what transgenic crops will be able to offer. Most current examples are based on a very few technologies. The case of Bt cotton is one where a transgenic crop provides protection against certain insects that can cause significant yield losses in a commercial crop that already requires considerable cash investment from any smallholder. Other opportunities for transgenic crop protection could achieve similar results, but there are relatively few of these at the present time. Bt maize is now available in several developing countries, and the possibility of insect resistance in a few vegetable crops in India (where pesticide use is even greater than in cotton) may be one of the most likely near-term innovations (Krishna and Qaim 2007). A number of other insect- or disease-resistant crop varieties are under development, but it is not clear when any of these will be available.

The major use of transgenic technology worldwide is for herbicide tolerance (James 2007), and advances are still being made in expanding the number of herbicides and the number of crops for which this technology is available. We have seen that herbicide tolerance in cotton has achieved growing importance among large-scale farmers, sometimes attracting more demand (and higher technology fees) than insect resistance. The issue of herbicide tolerance (and herbicide use in general) for smallholders remains controversial (Lipton 2007; Herring 2007). There are certainly dangers that such technology could displace the landless or near-landless who depend on weeding labour as an important source of income. However, there is a growing use of herbicide in small-farm agriculture, partly in response to rising rural wage rates, especially where the non-farm economy is thriving (Naylor 1994). Indeed, it is unlikely that a transgenic, herbicide-tolerant crop would be a farmer's first experience with herbicide use; it is much more probable that farmers who have already adopted herbicide would be attracted to the added convenience of transgenic varieties. Thus herbicide tolerance should not be discounted as a possible near-term innovation in some small-scale farming systems, but such a shift would likely be part of a broader evolution in technology use and input markets.

Insect resistance and herbicide tolerance continue to account for almost all of worldwide transgenic crop area, but we read almost daily of research that could provide crops the ability to withstand drought, high temperatures, salinity and other stresses, or crops with greater efficiency in extracting and utilizing soil nutrients. Although most of this research is being conducted by private firms whose market is the commercial farmers of industrialized countries, there is hope that these could also be the basis of pro-poor biotechnology (Fukuda-Parr 2007) or be applied to the orphan crops that are so important to resource-poor farmers (Naylor *et al.* 2004). A few breakthroughs of this type could provide spectacular gains, but no one has the requisite crystal ball to predict a reasonable timeframe for such advances. Although the hope and energy devoted to these possibilities is entirely appropriate for stimulating further scientific breakthroughs, more than a decade of experience with transgenic crops (and their relatively limited scope) also serves as a warning that such promises should not be used to divert attention from more immediate challenges. Even the journal *Nature Biotechnology* recently expressed concerns about the excessive emphasis on biotechnology as an imminent solution to the world's problems (Anon, 2008b).

Institutional challenges

Institutional deficiencies constitute the primary reason for being cautious about the immediate poverty-reducing potential of transgenic crops. Institutional problems for the diffusion of biotechnology are the subject of some analysis in the literature, but the range of factors discussed tends to be very narrow. In a very thorough analysis of barriers to the spread of transgenic crops in developing countries, Paarlberg (2001: 156) argues for two basic changes. Developing country policymakers should 'balance hypothetical biosafety risks from GM crops against the nation's real food production needs' (to ensure that biosafety regulation is not subverted by anti-GM pressure groups) and there should be more public sector investment in research on transgenic crops. A more recent study makes the argument more specifically for Sub-Saharan Africa (SSA) (Paarlberg 2008). Another recent study echoes these recommendations, adding that adequate patent regimes are also required (Fukuda-Parr 2007).

Effective biosafety regimes and investment in biotechnology research are of course essential if transgenic crops are to prosper, but the conclusion of this book is that there are other, broader institutional issues that need to be addressed if biotechnology is going to have an impact in most developing countries. There is a danger that a concentration on biosafety and support for investment in genetic engineering will provide too myopic a vision, one that may cause analysts and policymakers to stumble over the other impediments that stand in the way of achieving the delivery of useful transgenic technology to resource-poor farmers.

Chapter 2 attempted to show how the political and economic context in which cotton farmers around the world have operated helps determine their use of technology. Despite widely differing environments and circumstances, many of the institutional factors have been similar. Thus a pair of examples from the USA may help illustrate the challenges for developing country cotton farmers. A questionnaire sent to US cotton farmers in 2007 asked them to identify and rank the innovations that had made the greatest impact on their production in the past decade. The top responses (with more than 80 per cent of farmers ranking them as important) were transgenic varieties and the integrated pest management (IPM) program for boll weevil control. In addition, at least 65 per cent of the farmers gave similar rankings to cotton modules (machinery used in post-harvest handling), conservation tillage, disease resistance and growth regulators (Marra and Martin 2007). Thus these farmers see a wide range of innovations as contributing to increased productivity, including advances in transgenic and conventional plant breeding, crop management, IPM, chemistry and engineering. These innovations are the products of private investment, public research and extension, and industry support.

In the second example, a study investigating the controversy over US cotton subsidies points to other factors that provide advantages for cotton growers.

> In the United States, the farms work, the market works, the government works, the science works, and the universities work; and all of those elements work together in a type of virtuous circle that is decades away from the poorest countries in the world.
>
> (Rivoli 2005: 7)

This may be a somewhat rosy view of the US cotton system, and is of course not a defence for the producer subsidies that favour US cotton interests, but it is a very relevant reminder of all the other factors that stand between smallholders and the achievement of a respectable farm income. Both world trade reforms and biotechnology can make important contributions, but significant institutional development, supporting the generation and delivery of a range of technology, the provision of information and the organization of markets, is required as well.

The rest of this section outlines some of the institutional challenges for the provision of transgenic technology in developing countries. The discussion will attempt to identify some principles that could help policymakers and donors as they consider how to support the development of biotechnology for resource-poor farmers. The discussion will focus on three areas – technology generation, technology provision and farmer capacity – but these should not be seen in terms of a linear marketing sequence, where technology is developed in isolation and then delivered to grateful farmers. Instead, we need to understand that there are various interests at play and a range of incentives that govern performance. Our focus is on farmers, and in particular the smallholders that account for the majority of agricultural production in most developing countries. But final outcomes are determined by a much broader range of interests, including those of scientists in the public and private sector; agricultural input and commodity industries and the markets and labour forces that serve them; consumers; and a range of rural residents including large and small farmers and landless labourers. The efficiency and equity of outcomes is determined by the institutions that mediate the interactions among these players. Our particular concern is the role of smallholders, how their interests are represented in technology generation, their participation in input and credit markets, the efficacy of information provision and education aimed at strengthening their capacities, and the extent to which the relevant regulatory regimes are responsive to farmers' concerns.

The discussion is organized around the following themes: agricultural research, the seed industry, input markets, input regulation, intellectual property rights, information provision and agricultural policy.

Agricultural research

Everyone agrees that resource-poor farmers' access to transgenic crops will be determined to a considerable extent by the capabilities and investments of public agricultural research in developing countries. All of the examples to date feature transgenic varieties of crops (cotton, maize, soybean) bred for commercial farmers in industrialized countries that have also been relevant for some smallholders; in developing countries with a well-established private plant-breeding sector, these innovations may be carried further (as with cotton in India). But for farmers who depend on cassava, millet or pigeonpea, or whose production constraints fall outside the interests or incentives of the private sector, there is need for a significant investment in public research.

Unfortunately, the current status of public agricultural research does not provide great optimism. A recent assessment shows that developing country investment in scientific research is generally low; for instance, SSA accounts for 10 per cent of world population but only 0.5 per cent of investment in science (Pardey *et al.* 2006). The exceptions to the rule are not surprising; China and India account for 39 per cent of the developing world's investment in agricultural R&D. The 1990s saw a high rate of growth in agricultural research investment in India and China, but only a 1 per cent growth in SSA, where half of the countries invested less in 2000 than a decade earlier.

The countries with traditionally high investment in public agricultural research have a long history of developing crop varieties for their farmers. Even in India, where there has been significant growth in private plant breeding, much of the germplasm (and the training of personnel) comes from a strong public research sector. But there are many countries with very poor track records in public plant breeding, where there is little in farmers' fields to reflect an investment in public research. In those cases, simply promoting biotechnology is not going to reverse the pattern; more fundamental changes are required.

A study of the prospects for incorporating biotechnology in public agricultural research presents a classification featuring three types of countries (Byerlee and Fischer 2002). Type I includes the few large, strong national programs such as Brazil, China and India. Type II includes countries with fairly strong applied breeding programs that can incorporate biotechnology techniques developed elsewhere, and Type III covers those countries with weak plant-breeding programs and little capacity in molecular biology. The analysis suggests distinct strategies for each type of research program, with particular emphasis on priority setting. National research programs need to identify specific niches where they have advantages and not try to duplicate what the private sector is doing. They also need to ensure a coordinated research effort among various national institutions and participation in international networks. For many of the smaller countries, the immediate priorities would likely be concentrated in conventional applied research.

The lack of capacity to define priorities and carry through on a comprehensive research strategy is one of the primary weaknesses of many public agricultural research programs. This requires careful analysis as well as responsiveness to public policy and farmer interests. For instance, the so-called orphan crops may or may not present immediate priorities for investment in biotechnology. On the one hand, they are certainly ignored by commercial research, but on the other hand their orphan status reflects the chronic lack of investment in conventional research, which needs to be reversed. The greater the range of plant variety requirements and the more varied the farming systems, the higher the per-product cost. Alston (2004) points to the low investment in horticultural crop biotechnology in the USA, which can be explained by the same impediments of high regulatory and research costs relative to limited markets. Genetic engineering offers one of the most promising means of addressing some of the serious production problems of bananas in countries where they are an important food staple, but which of Uganda's 200 banana clones should be the first target for transformation (Eicher *et al.* 2006)? For rain-fed staples, a character such as drought tolerance is an obvious candidate for attention, but how many national research programs have the capacities of their private sector counterparts (who are apparently well along in developing transgenic tolerance to moisture stress) to map out and define the precise conditions and needs of their potential customers? And although any discussion of biotechnology focuses on plant breeding, many of the innovations that may be offered by transgenic crops must be complemented by good crop management technology, as we have seen for the case of IPM in cotton; how much effort should be directed to these activities?

Adequate answers to such questions can only be expected from strong public research organizations. There are many trade-offs and competing interests to be considered, so that a 'pro-poor research agenda' (Fukuda-Parr 2007: 226) is neither straightforward nor easily pursued. The skills and experience of research administrators and policymakers, and the capacities of farmers to make their voices heard, determine the effectiveness of the planning process. In most cases, public research management capacities need to be strengthened.

The seed industry

Public seed systems in developing countries have had an almost uniformly dismal history, and there is general recognition that the incentives and organization of the private sector are needed to ensure a reliable seed delivery service. The emergence of the private seed sector is usually accompanied by a shift towards private plant breeding as well, but this shift is rarely complete. There will be strong justifications for public plant breeding for many years to come, but its products will increasingly be delivered by commercial seed enterprises. In an age when seed production in industrialized countries is increasingly dominated by a few multinational giants, it is easy to lose sight of the fact that emerging (and often mature) seed industries are usually based on local enterprises. For most developing countries there is every reason to believe that small- and medium-scale enterprises will be the backbone of the national seed industry for the foreseeable future.

However, it must be acknowledged that the path to a viable commercial seed sector in many countries is not going to be an easy one, and the potential availability of a few transgenic crop varieties will not be enough to clear the way forward. Commercial seed enterprises can only thrive where farmers are relatively frequent purchasers of seed, and this is not the case in most developing countries. The majority of smallholders rely on farm-saved seed, usually for good reasons. As agricultural economies evolve there is a more consistent supply of new varieties, and the quality and convenience of commercial seed increasingly justify its purchase, but this is a slow process.

In all of the instances to date of transgenic variety use in developing countries, the farmers were already accustomed to using commercial seed markets. But for many other crops, where farmers have had little experience with the private seed sector, the introduction of a transgenic variety will be much more challenging. It is possible to imagine an initial public-sponsored distribution of seed of a transgenic crop aimed at the subsistence sector (such as insect-resistant cowpea in SSA), but this raises a number of difficult questions. Where will farmers turn once they need to replace that seed a few years hence? How do you maintain the integrity and identity of a variety that is subsequently diffused from farmer to farmer? How can farmers be sure if the seed they have acquired still has adequate expression of the transgenic character? And how does one manage biosafety regulations when the seed is being informally reproduced and distributed?

It is difficult to avoid the conclusion that a viable commercial seed industry is required if there is any hope that transgenic varieties will become widely available, and the best way to pursue that goal is by promoting the commercial seed production of the conventional crop varieties that are already available. But seed industries do not emerge overnight, and considerable policy support and financial assistance will be required in many countries before a seed delivery system is in place that could meet the demands of transgenic crops.

Input markets

The development of a commercial seed industry must be complemented by an input delivery system that reaches smallholders. Input dealers not only deliver products such as seed and fertilizer but also can help provide information that helps farmers to choose what inputs to acquire. Commercial reputation remains an essential requirement in input marketing, and its growth takes time, as the frequent reports of fraudulent seed and chemicals from many developing countries attest. Even where commercial reputations are well developed, some kind of regulatory system that provides consumer protection is also needed, and this is still the exception in developing countries.

If transgenic seed is to be delivered to smallholders, the information transmission responsibilities of the input marketing system are crucial. If the number of transgenic crops and technologies grows, the challenges will increase. The growing availability of stacked varieties that include two (or more) transgenes with distinct functions will add to the complexity and make even greater demands on the technical expertise of input dealers.

The delivery of good quality seed of conventional crop varieties and, eventually, transgenic ones will only be achieved when national policies provide an adequate environment for the growth of small businesses, the exercise of commercial reputation, the development of technical expertise for input merchants and consumer protection. And effective performance of reputation and consumer protection can only take place when farmers themselves have adequate knowledge about the products they are purchasing and the capacity to punish unacceptable behaviour in the marketplace or in the courtroom.

Regulation of inputs

Most of the discussion of the regulation of transgenic crops has focused on biosafety. The special properties of transgenic crops have called forth the development of regulatory procedures related to the health implications and environmental impact of the new technology. As noted in Chapter 1, there are a number of other issues of food and agricultural safety that are unrelated to biotechnology and that also deserve regulatory attention. The effectiveness of national biosafety regulation will be linked to the competence and adequacy of broader regulatory performance. Because so much discussion elsewhere has been devoted to biosafety the subject will not be further examined here. Instead we emphasize that the regulatory regimes used for conventional agricultural inputs deserve attention, with or without transgenic crops.

Because it is difficult for farmers to detect variations in seed quality at the time of purchase, regulatory systems often monitor variety identity and seed quality. An efficient certification system costs relatively little and provides additional confidence for farmers purchasing seed. If a certification system is not in place or is badly managed there is the danger that bad quality seed will enter the market. There are many developing countries without efficient seed certification systems.

The challenges of product approval and quality regulation are not confined to seed. Approval processes for novel products such as biopesticides (which may give farmers safer options for pest control than conventional products) are often the subject of bureaucratic inflexibility, and adulterated fertilizers and pesticides are often found in the markets of developing countries, lowering farmers' incentives to try new technologies.

External regulation is called for in these cases because the transactions do not allow the efficient interchange of information that takes place in other types of market. When those conditions change, there are alternatives to third-party regulation; when companies have well-recognized reputations to defend, or when independent bodies (such as universities or producer associations) provide testing services, then the regulatory environment is altered. It is futile to argue that a particular type of regulatory system is required; the point is rather that the institutions (government, commercial, civil society) that govern and encourage the exchange of information must be in place. The exact configuration will depend on the circumstances that are present, and as markets and economies grow the regulatory regime adjusts. This must happen with or without transgenic crops, and in many countries the process is still at an early stage.

Intellectual property rights

Intellectual property regimes have an important bearing on the future of transgenic crops in developing countries. Much has been written about the necessity of establishing national patent systems that allow private technology owners to protect their innovations, but we have seen with Bt cotton that comprehensive patent laws are not necessarily required for the transfer and protection of transgenic varieties in developing countries and, on the other hand, the mere access to patent law does not guarantee an attractive business environment unless enforcement capacity is in place.

We have also seen that there is a range of instruments (including types of plant variety protection and the application of basic seed laws) that can allow technology owners to protect their innovations from unauthorized use by competitors. The structure of the industry providing seed of transgenic varieties, and the extent to which it is reasonable or feasible to restrict the extent to which seed of such varieties is saved or exchanged informally among farmers, depends on the conditions of farming in each country and the nature of the particular crop and transgenic technology. There are thus no simple, universally applicable formulas available; instead, each country needs to develop and enforce adequate seed and intellectual property legislation that meets its own conditions and provides adequate incentives for the development of public and private innovation. Providing adequate but balanced property right protection is a prerequisite for the development of the seed industry, with or without transgenic crops.

These issues are also relevant for public sector biotechnology development in Byerlee and Fischer (2002) emphasize the need for public research velop their capacities for accessing proprietary technology and entering into partnerships and exchanges. (This of course is not limited to trans-genic technology but is important for acquiring other types of proprietary innovation as well.) Despite a considerable amount of research and accomplishment by the public sector in agricultural biotechnology worldwide there is not yet the coordination among public institutes, nor consistent strategies governing public–private interactions, that would allow publicly developed biotechnology to be applied in an effective manner (Graff *et al.* 2003). Policymakers responsible for public agricultural research need to promote the development of capacities for intellectual property management that will ensure that research innovation has the best chance of being put to good use in the field.

Information

The discussion above regarding the seed industry and input provision has emphasized the importance of transparency in these markets, so that farmers can recognize the varieties that are most suitable for their circumstances. In addition to information provided through input markets, farmers also require considerable information about crop management that the private input sector is unlikely to provide.

Some of those who have been cautious about the long-term impact of an innovation like Bt cotton point out that its immediate gains in pesticide savings must be seen against a background of inefficient and dangerous pesticide management practices (Pemsl 2006). A transgenic insect control technology is most likely to be used effectively if it is part of a broader pest management strategy, involving a range of technologies and, crucially, farmer management skills. Much of the responsibility for transmitting this kind of information and building these skills might have traditionally fallen to public agricultural extension services, but most of these are now moribund. It is not clear what modalities will replace or supplement public extension. The rapid development and accessibility of various information and communication technologies offers some hope, but this hardware must be complemented by farmers' own organization and their capacities to access and exchange information. This is not the place to debate the roles of farmer associations, public agricultural education or private extension in providing this information, but the institutions currently available are not adequate for that task and alternatives must be sought.

Policies on who benefits

This discussion has identified a number of areas in the enabling environment that need attention before contemplating the potential contribution of transgenic crops to smallholder farming systems. In addition, it is necessary to articulate clearer strategies on who benefits from the technology. In many developing countries the majority of the farming population may be classified as 'resource-poor', but this masks such significant variability that the identification of unequivocally 'pro-poor' policies becomes a real challenge.

De Janvry and Sadoulet (2000) have described four types of pathway leading from rural poverty: households may 'exit' agriculture through migration or the development of rural employment opportunities; some may follow an 'agricultural path' that connects them with agricultural markets; others can follow a 'pluriactive path' that combines off-farm income with subsistence farming; and finally some households must be provided an 'assistance path' through income or food transfers that allows immediate survival and eventual opportunities to follow other paths. This typology offers an important reminder of the complexity of devising biotechnology policies that serve 'smallholders'.

Those following the 'exit' and 'assistance' paths are likely to gain from transgenic crops if they provide additional labour opportunities or serve to lower food prices. Those on the 'agricultural' path can benefit from those crops with strong market demand. Those on the 'pluriactive' path (of whom there are many) could benefit from varieties that reduce their farm labour, help them lower pesticide use or improve their resource conservation. National policymakers need to assess the prevalence and the trajectories of these various classes of farmer in order to formulate policies on crop technology that maximize their contribution to poverty reduction.

Summary

The previous section burdened the reader with a long list of recommendations, but it is important to emphasize that a few quick changes to allow the entry of transgenic crops is not the answer for promoting poverty reduction among smallholder farmers. The new technology can certainly make a contribution, but much more attention needs to be focused on the development of local institutions. These include institutions that support public and private capacity for technology generation; technology delivery through markets, extension and regulations; and farmer capacities to demand services, participate in markets and comprehend the technology they are using.

Edgerton (2006) argues that we can be deceived into believing that certain technologies define historical periods, cause revolutionary change and then are replaced by entirely new discoveries. 'In recent years one could be forgiven for believing that there was no invention going on outside information and biotechnology' (ibid: 188). Attention to conventional techniques and infrastructure, and the human capital to support them, is not an attractive prospect for policymakers or donors who want to focus on 'cutting-edge' technology. But in many countries that kind of attention is exactly what is required if transgenic crops are eventually to make a significant contribution to small-scale farming. While we may indeed be on the threshold of the 'Biotechnology Age', the reality of smallholder farming indicates that other conventional technologies will complement, contribute to and (more often than not) be more relevant than transgenic crops for the foreseeable future.

A recent study of technology diffusion in developing countries notes that many older technologies (such as power grids and transport networks) were provided by the state, and their current use within a country is only weakly correlated with income (World Bank 2008). In contrast, many newer technologies require less infrastructure and are often provided by the private sector, but their diffusion is more highly correlated with income. There are a few outstanding examples of rapid diffusion (mobile phones being the most prominent), but the general experience is that although new technologies may achieve rapid initial penetration, they often spread slowly in developing countries. The report identifies a number of factors that influence technology diffusion, including the microeconomic and governance environment, financing for innovation and human capital. Although the study does not include agricultural technology, many of these factors are similar to those identified for transgenic crops. If we see activities such as conventional plant breeding, seed production and information provision as 'older technologies', then one of the report's recommendations is particularly relevant.

> Because of the complementarity of technologies and infrastructure, countries where older technologies have yet to penetrate deeply may also face limits to the extent to which other technologies are able to diffuse. Therefore, the authorities should focus on ensuring that publicly supported technological services are available as widely, reliably and economically as possible, whether they are provided by the state or private firms
>
> (World Bank 2008: 14).

The services required for supporting biotechnology are largely dependent on local institutions. 'Institution building' is a concept with an undistinguished career in the development industry. If institutions are seen as 'the rules of the game' (North 1990), then we must recognize that these rules cannot be imposed, but rather evolve in response to local circumstances. This calls for a change in the strategies and competencies of national governments and donors. It means that assistance cannot only be concerned with new laboratories but also with the capacity to organize research that responds to the needs and demands of various types of farmers; there is not simply talk of public–private partnerships but encouragement of sustained, hands-on interaction between public entities and local businesses; investments do not simply support extension campaigns but also identify opportunities for farmers to organize and lobby for services; there is not just increased availability of farm inputs, but attention is given to farmers' capacities and rights as consumers; and donors do not simply transplant biosafety regulations, seed laws and intellectual property regimes from elsewhere but rather develop local skills to negotiate relevant rules.

If we return to the West African village described in this book's introduction, we recognize that there is a great deal that needs to be done to provide a more secure and productive harvest for those farmers. Transgenic crops may make an important contribution, but even their most ardent supporters should agree that many other things must be in place in order for farmers to take full advantage of the technology. Many of the institutional concerns described in this book deserve more immediate attention. If these are not addressed, then there is little prospect for widespread access to transgenic crops. In addition, the strengthening of these institutions is required for equitable agricultural development, even where there is no immediate prospect for transgenic crops. This requires a re-ordering of priorities for development assistance and national policy, otherwise we are in danger of putting the cart before horse. The exceptional controversy engendered by agricultural biotechnology has pushed us into asking the wrong kinds of questions and engaging in the wrong types of debate. Transgenic crops offer enormous possibilities, but we need a more balanced, and a more comprehensive, approach.

References

Adamczyk, J.J. and Gore, J. (2004) 'Laboratory and field performance of cotton containing Cry1Ac, Cry1F, and both Cry1Ac and Cry1F (Widestrike) against beet armyworm and fall armyworm larvae (Lepidoptera: Noctuidae)', *Florida Entomologist*, 87: 427–32.

Adamczyk, J. and Meredith, W. (2004) 'Genetic basis for variability of Cry1Ac expression among commercial transgenic *Bacillus thuringiensis* (Bt) cotton cultivars in the United States', *Journal of Cotton Science*, 8: 17–23.

Adamczyk, J.J., Hardee, D.D., Adams, L.C. and Sumerford, D.V. (2001a) 'Correlating differences in larval survival and development of bollworm (Lepidoptera: Noctuidae) and fall armyworm (Lepidoptera: Noctuidae) to differential expression of Cry1A(c) delta-endotoxin in various plant parts among commercial cultivars of transgenic *Bacillus thuringiensis* cotton', *Journal of Economic Entomology*, 94: 284–90.

Adamczyk, J.J., Adams, L.C. and Hardee, D.D. (2001b) 'Field efficacy and seasonal expression profiles for terminal leaves of single and double *Bacillus thuringiensis* toxin cotton genotypes', *Journal of Economic Entomology*, 94: 1589–93.

Adams, M. and Moss, M. (2008) *Food Microbiology,* 3rd edn, Cambridge: Royal Society of Chemistry.

AgBios GM Database (2005a) MON-ØØ531-6, MON-ØØ757-7 (MON531/757/1076). Available at: <http://www.agbios.com/dbase.php?action=ShowProd&data=MON531%2F757%2F1076&frmat=LONG>

――― (2005b) MON-15985-7 (15985). Available at: <http://www.agbios.com/dbase.php?action=ShowProd&data=15985&frmat=LONG>

――― (2005c) DAS-21Ø23-5 x DAS-24236-5. Available at: <http://www.agbios.com/dbase.php?action=ShowProd&data=DAS-21%D823-5+x+DAS-24236-5&frmat=LONG>

――― (2005d) SYN-IR1Ø2-7 (COT102). Available at: <http://www.agbios.com/dbase.php?action=ShowProd&data=COT102&frmat=LONG>

Agee, J. and Evans, W. (1965) *Let Us Now Praise Famous Men*, London: Peter Owen.

Ahouissoussi, N., Wetzstein, M. and Duffy, P. (1993) 'Economic returns to the boll weevil eradication program', *Journal of Agricultural and Applied Economics*, 25: 46–55.

Alston, J. (2004) 'Horticultural biotechnology faces significant economic and market barriers', *California Agriculture*, 58(2): 80–1, 84–8.

American Academy of Microbiology (2002) *100 Years of Bacillus thuringiensis: A Critical Scientific Assessment*, Washington, DC: American Academy of Microbiology.

AMS (Agricultural Marketing Service) (2007) *Cotton Varieties Planted. 2007 Crop*, Memphis, TN: USDA, AMS – Cotton Program.

Anon. (2008a) 'Pesticide trade name to be banned in China', *Crop Protection China News*, 2(1): 2–3.

—— (2008b) 'Join the dots', *Nature Biotechnology*, 26(8): 837.

Antilla, L. (2006) 'Documentary support for continuation of a special local need registration in Arizona for maximized use of Bt cotton in a sanctioned pink bollworm eradication program', FIFRA Scientific Advisory Panel. Available at: <http://www.epa.gov/scipoly/sap/meetings/2006/october/documentarysupport.html>

Ayer, H. and Schuh, G.E. (1972) 'Social rates of return and other aspects of agricultural research: The case of cotton research in São Paulo, Brazil', *American Journal of Agricultural Economics*, 54: 557–69.

Baffes, J. (2005) 'The "cotton problem"', *World Bank Research Observer*, 20: 109–44.

Bagwell, R.D., Cook, D.R., Leonard, B.R., Micinski, S. and Burris, E. (2001) 'Status of insecticide resistance in tobacco budworm and budworm in Louisiana during 2000', in *Proceedings of the Beltwide Cotton Conference*, 9–13 January, Anaheim, CA, Memphis TN: National Cotton Council of America.

Baker, G. H., Tann, C.T. and Fitt, G.P. (2008) 'Production of *Helicoverpa spp.* (Lepidoptera, Noctuidae) from different refuge crops to accompany transgenic cotton plantings in eastern Australia', *Australian Journal of Agricultural Research*, 59: 723–32.

Bambawale, O., Singh, A., Sharma, O., Bhosle, B., Lavekar, R., Dhanpadani, A., Kanwar, V., Tanwar, R., Rathod, K., Patange, N. and Pawar, V. (2004) 'Performance of Bt cotton (MECH-162) under Integrated Pest Management in farmers' participatory field trial in Nanded district, Central India', *Current Science*, 86(2): 1628–33.

Barton, J. (2000) 'Reforming the patent system', *Science*, 287: 1933–4.

Bassett, T. (2001) *The Peasant Cotton Revolution in West Africa. Côte d'Ivoire, 1880–1995*, Cambridge: Cambridge University Press.

Basu, A., Mannikar, N. and Narayanan, S. (1990) *Cotton Scenario in India*, New Delhi: ICAR.

Bennett, R., Ismael, Y., Morse, S. and Shankar, B. (2004) 'Reductions in insecticide use from adoption of Bt cotton in South Africa: Impacts on economic performance and toxic load to the environment', *Journal of Agricultural Science*, 142: 665–74.

Bennett, R., Morse, S. and Ismael, Y. (2006) 'The economic impact of genetically modified cotton on South African smallholders: Yield, profit and health effects', *Journal of Development Studies*, 42: 662–77.

Berdan, F. (1987) 'Cotton in Aztec Mexico: Production, distribution and uses', *Mexican Studies*, 3(2): 235–62.

Bingen, R.J. (1998) 'Cotton, democracy and development in Mali', *Journal of Modern African Studies*, 36(2): 265–85.

—— (2006) 'Cotton in West Africa' in J. Bingen and L. Busch (eds) *Agricultural Standards. The Shape of the Global Food and Fiber System*, Dordrecht: Springer, pp. 219–42.

Bird, L.J. and Akhurst, R.J. (2004) 'Relative fitness of Cry1A-resistant and -susceptible *Helicoverpa armigera* (Lepidoptera, Noctuidae) on conventional and transgenic cotton', *Journal of Economic Entomology*, 97: 1699–1709.

—— (2005) 'Fitness of Cry1A-resistant and -susceptible *Helicoverpa armigera* (Lepidoptera: Noctuidae) on transgenic cotton with reduced levels of Cry1Ac', *Journal of Economic Entomology*, 98: 1311–9.

—— (2007) 'Effects of host plant species on fitness costs of Bt resistance in *Helicoverpa armigera* (Lepidoptera: Noctuidae)', *Biological Control*, 40: 196–203.

Birner, R. and Linacre, N. (2008) *Regional Biotechnology Regulations. Design Options and Implications for Good Governance*, IFPRI Discussion Paper 753, Washington, DC: IFPRI.

Boquet, D. (2005) 'Cotton in ultra-narrow row spacing: Plant density and nitrogen fertilizer rates', *Agronomy Journal*, 97: 279–85.

Bowman, D., May, O. and Creech, J. (2003) 'Genetic uniformity of the U.S. upland cotton crop since the introduction of transgenic cottons', *Crop Science*, 43: 515–8.

Brennig, J. (1998) 'Textile producers and production in late seventeenth-century Coromandel' in M. Mazzaoui (ed.) *Textiles: Production, Trade and Demand*, Aldershot, UK: Ashgate, pp. 333–54.

Briggs, F. and Knowles, P. (1967) *Introduction to Plant Breeding*, New York: Reinhold Publishing.

Brooks, N. (2001) *Characteristics and Production Costs of U.S. Cotton Farms*, Economic Research Service Statistical Bulletin No. 974-2, Washington, DC: USDA.

Brush, S. (1992) 'Reconsidering the green revolution: Diversity and stability in cradle areas of crop domestication', *Human Ecology*, 20: 145–67.

Burd, A.D., Gould, F., Bradley, J.R., Van Duyn, J.W. and Moar, W.J. (2003) 'Estimated frequency of nonrecessive Bt resistance genes in bollworm, *Helicoverpa zea* (Boddie) (Lepidoptera: Noctuidae) in eastern North Carolina', *Journal of Economic Entomology*, 96: 127–42.

Byerlee, D. and Echeverría, R. (eds) (2002) *Agricultural Research Policy in an Era of Privatization*, Wallingford, UK: CABI.

Byerlee, D. and Fischer, K. (2002) 'Accessing modern science: Policy and institutional options for agricultural biotechnology in developing countries', *World Development*, 30: 931–48.

Byerlee, D. and Hesse de Polanco, E. (1986) 'Farmers' stepwise adoption of technological packages: Evidence from the Mexican Altiplano', *American Journal of Agricultural Economics*, 68: 519–27.

Byerlee, D., Akhtar, M. and Hobbs, P. (1987) 'Reconciling conflicts in sequential cropping patterns through plant breeding: The example of cotton and wheat in Pakistan's Punjab', *Agricultural Systems*, 24: 291–304.

Carley, P. (1989) 'The price of the plan. Perceptions of cotton and health in Uzbekistan and Turkmenistan', *Central Asian Survey*, 8(4): 1–38.

Carrière, Y. and Tabashnik, B.E. (2001) 'Reversing insect adaptation to transgenic insecticidal plants', *Proceedings of the Royal Society London B*, 268: 1475–80.

Carrière, Y., Dennehy, T.J., Pedersen, B., Haller, S., Ellers-Kirk, C., Antilla, L., Haller, S., Liu, Y.B., Willott, E. and Tabashnik, B.E. (2001) 'Large-scale management of insect resistance to transgenic cotton in Arizona: Can transgenic insecticidal crops be sustained?', *Journal of Economic Entomology*, 94: 315–25.

Carrière, Y., Ellers-Kirk, C., Sisterson, M., Antilla, L., Whitlow, M., Dennehy, T.J. and Tabashnik, B.E. (2003) 'Long-term regional suppression of pink bollworm by *Bacillus thuringiensis* cotton', *Proceedings of the National Academy of Sciences*, 100: 1519–23.

Carrière, Y., Sisterson, M.S. and Tabashnik, B.E. (2004a) 'Resistance management for sustainable use of *Bacillus thuringiensis* crops', in A.R. Horowitz and I. Ishaaya (eds) *Insect Pest Management, Field and Protected Crops*, New York: Springer, pp. 65–95.

Carrière, Y., Dutilleul, P., Ellers-Kirk, C., Pedersen, B., Haller, S., Antilla, L., Dennehy, T. and Tabashnik, B.E. (2004b) 'Sources, sinks, and the zone of influence of refuges for managing insect resistance to Bt crops', *Ecological Applications*, 14: 1615–23.

Carrière, Y., Ellers-Kirk, C., Kumar, K., Heuberger, S., Whitlow, M., Antilla, L., Dennehy, T.J. and Tabashnik, B.E. (2005a) 'Long-term evaluation of compliance with refuge requirements for Bt cotton', *Pest Management Science*, 61: 327–30.

Carrière, Y., Ellers-Kirk, C., Biggs, R., Degain, B., Holley, D., Yafuso, C., Evans, P., Dennehy, T.J. and Tabashnik, B.E. (2005b) 'Effects of cotton cultivar on fitness costs associated with resistance of pink bollworm (Lepidoptera: Gelechiidae) to Bt cotton', *Journal of Economic Entomology,* 98: 947–54.

Carrière, Y., Ellers-Kirk, C., Biggs, R.W., Nyboer, M.E., Unnithan, G.C., Dennehy, T.J. and Tabashnik, B.E. (2006) 'Cadherin-based resistance to Bt cotton in hybrid strains of pink bollworm: Fitness costs and incomplete resistance', *Journal of Economic Entomology,* 99: 1925–35.

Cattaneo, M.G., Yafuso, C., Schmidt, C., Huang, C.Y., Rahman, C.M., Olson, C., Ellers-Kirk, C., Orr, B.J., Marsh, S.E., Antilla, L., Dutilleul, P. and Carrière, Y. (2006) 'Farm-scale evaluation of transgenic cotton impacts on biodiversity, pesticide use, and yield', *Proceedings of the National Academy of Sciences,* 103: 7571–6.

Chao, K. (1977) *The Development of Cotton Textile Production in China,* Cambridge, MA: Harvard University Press.

Chari, S. (2004) 'Provincializing capital: The work of an agrarian past in South Indian industry', *Comparative Studies in Society and History,* 46(4): 760–85.

Charles, D. (2001) *Lords of the Harvest,* Cambridge, MA: Perseus.

Chen, D., Ye, G., Yang, C., Chen, Y. and Wu, Y. (2005a) 'Effect of introducing *Bacillus thuringiensis* gene on nitrogen metabolism in cotton', *Field Crops Research,* 92: 1–9.

——— (2005b) 'The effect of high temperature on the insecticidal properties of Bt cotton', *Environmental and Experimental Botany,* 53: 333–42.

Chitkowski, R.L., Turnipseed, S.G., Sullivan, M.J. and Bridges, W.C. (2003) 'Field and laboratory evaluations of transgenic cottons expressing one or two *Bacillus thuringiensis* var. *kurstaki* Berliner proteins for management of noctuid (Lepidoptera) pests', *Journal of Economic Entomology,* 96: 755–62.

Christian Aid (1999) *Selling Suicide. Farming, False Promises and Genetic Engineering in Developing Countries,* London: Christian Aid.

Collings, G. (1926) *The Production of Cotton,* New York: John Wiley.

Constantine, J., Alston, J. and Smith, V. (1994) 'Economic impacts of the California one-variety cotton law', *Journal of Political Economy,* 102: 951–74.

Conway, G. (1997) *The Doubly Green Revolution,* London: Penguin.

Cook, G. (2004) *Genetically Modified Language,* London: Routledge.

Coviella, C.E., Stipanovic, R.D. and Trumble, J.T. (2002) 'Plant allocation to defensive compounds: Interactions between elevated CO_2 and nitrogen in transgenic cotton plants', *Journal of Experimental Botany,* 53: 323–31.

Cowan, R. and Gunby, P. (1996) 'Sprayed to death: Path dependence, lock-in and pest control strategies', *The Economic Journal,* 106: 521–42.

Dalrymple, D. (1988) 'Changes in wheat varieties and yields in the United States, 1919–1984', *Agricultural History,* 62: 20–36.

Day, R. (1967) 'The economics of technological change and the demise of the sharecropper', *American Economic Review,* 57(3): 427–49.

De Janvry, A. and Sadoulet, E. (2000) 'Rural poverty in Latin America. Determinants and exit paths', *Food Policy,* 25: 389–409.

Denevan, W. (1992) 'The pristine myth: The landscape of the Americas in 1492', *Annals of the Association of American Geographers,* 82: 369–85.

Dent, D. (2000) *Insect Pest Management,* 2nd edn, Wallingford, UK: CABI.

Dev, S.M. and Rao, N.C. (2006) *Socio-Economic Assessment of Bollgard Cotton in Andhra Pradesh,* Hyderabad, India: Centre for Social and Economic Studies.

Dietrich, C. (1972) 'Cotton culture and manufacture in early Ch'ing China' in W. Willmott (ed.) *Economic Organization in Chinese Society,* Stanford, CA: Stanford University Press, pp. 109–35.

Djurfeldt, G., Holmén, H., Jirström, M. and Larsson, R. (eds) (2005) *The African Food Crisis. Lessons from the Asian Green Revolution,* Wallingford, UK: CABI.

DoA (2001) *The Strategic Plan for South African Agriculture,* Pretoria: Department of Agriculture, Government of South Africa.

Dong, H.Z. and Li, W.J. (2007) 'Variability of endotoxin expression in Bt transgenic cotton', *Journal of Agronomy and Crop Science,* 193: 21–9.

Dong, H.Z., Li, W.J., Tang, W. and Zhang, D.M. (2004) 'Development of hybrid Bt cotton in China: A successful integration of transgenic technology and conventional techniques', *Current Science,* 86: 778–82.

Dong, H., Li, W., Li, Z., Tang, W. and Zhang, D. (2005) 'Evaluation of a production system in China that uses reduced plant densities and retention of vegetative branches', *Journal of Cotton Science,* 9: 1–9.

Douglas, M. and Wildavsky, A. (1983) *Risk and Culture. An Essay on the Selection of Technical and Environmental Dangers,* Berkeley, CA: University of California Press.

Downes, S., Mahon, R. and Olsen, K. (2007) 'Monitoring and adaptive resistance management in Australia for Bt-cotton: Current status and future challenges', *Journal of Invertebrate Pathology,* 95: 208–13.

Duck, N. and Evola, S. (1997) 'Use of transgenes to increase host plant resistance to insects: Opportunities and challenges', in N. Carozzi and M. Koziel (eds) *Advances in Insect Control: The Role of Transgenic Plants,* Bristol, PA: Taylor & Francis Ltd, pp. 1–20.

Duvick, D. (1992) 'Genetic contributions to advances in yield of U.S. maize', *Maydica,* 37: 69–79.

———— (1998) 'The United States' in M. Morris (ed.) *Maize Seed Industries in Developing Countries,* Boulder, CO: Lynne Rienner, pp. 193–212.

Dyson, F. (1999) *The Sun, the Genome, and the Internet,* Oxford: Oxford University Press.

Earle, C. (1992) 'The price of precocity: Technical choice and ecological constraint in the Cotton South, 1840–1890', *Agricultural History,* 66(3): 25–60.

Edgerton, D. (2006) *The Shock of the Old. Technology and Global History Since 1900,* London: Profile Books.

Eicher, C., Maredia, K. and Sithole-Niang, I. (2006) 'Crop biotechnology and the African farmer', *Food Policy,* 31: 504–27.

Ellis, F. (1998) 'Household strategies and rural livelihood diversification', *Journal of Development Studies,* 35: 1–38.

Ellstrand, N. (2003) *Dangerous Liaisons? When Cultivated Plants Mate with Their Wild Relatives,* Baltimore, MD: Johns Hopkins University Press.

Escobal, J., Agreda, V. and Reardon, T. (2000) 'Endogenous institutional innovation and agroindustrialization on the Peruvian coast', *Agricultural Economics,* 23: 267–77.

Evans, L.T. (1993) *Crop Evolution, Adaptation and Yield,* Cambridge: Cambridge University Press.

Falck-Zepeda, J., Traxler, G. and Nelson, R. (1999) *Rent Creation and Distribution from the First Three Years of Planting Bt Cotton,* ISAAA Brief 14-1999, Ithaca, NY: ISAAA.

Farnie, D. (2004) 'The role of cotton textiles in the economic development of India, 1600–1990' in D. Farnie and D. Jeremy (eds) *The Fibre that Changed the World,* Oxford: Oxford University Press, pp. 395–430.

Fernandez-Cornejo, J. (2004) *The Seed Industry in U.S. Agriculture,* Washington, DC: USDA.

Fernandez-Cornejo, J. and McBride, W. (2002) *Adoption of Bioengineered Crops,* ERS Agricultural Economics Report No. AER810, Washington, DC: USDA.

Ferré, J. and Van Rie, J. (2002) 'Biochemistry and genetics of insect resistance to *Bacillus thuringiensis*', *Annual Review of Entomology*, 47: 501–33.

Fitt, G.P. (1989) 'The ecology of *Heliothis* species in relation to agro-ecosystems', *Annual Review of Entomology*, 34: 17–52.

—— (2003) 'Implementation and impact of transgenic Bt cottons in Australia' in *Cotton Production for the New Millennium. Proceedings of the Third World Cotton Research Conference*, Cape Town, South Africa, March 2003, Pretoria: Agricultural Research Council.

Fitt, G. P. and Daly, J.C. (1990) 'Abundance of overwintering pupae and the spring generation of *Helicoverpa* spp. (Lepidoptera: Noctuidae) in northern New South Wales, Australia: Implications for pest management', *Journal of Economic Entomology*, 83: 1827–36.

Fitt, G.P., Andow, D.A., Carrière, Y., Moar, W.J., Schuler, T., Omoto, C., Kanya, J., Okech, M., Arama, P. and Maniania, N.K. (2004) 'Resistance risks and management associated with Bt maize in Kenya', in A. Hilbeck and D. Andow (eds) *Environmental Risk Assessment of Genetically Modified Organisms, Volume 1: A Case Study of Bt Maize in Kenya*, Wallingford, UK: CABI International, pp. 209–50.

Fok, M. (2003) 'Progress and challenges in making productivity gains in cotton production by smallholders in Sub-Saharan Africa (SSA)'. in *Proceedings of the Third World Cotton Research Conference*, Cape Town, South Africa, March 2003, Pretoria: Agricultural Research Council.

Fok, M., Hofs, J.L., Gouse, M. and Kirsten J.F. (2007). 'Contextual appraisal of GM cotton diffusion in South Africa', *Life Sciences International Journal*, 1: 468–82.

Francks, P. (1984) *Technology and Agricultural Development in Pre-War Japan*, New Haven, CT: Yale University Press.

Frankel, F. (1971) *India's Green Revolution*, Princeton, NJ: Princeton University Press.

Fransen, L., La Vina, A., Dayrit, F., Gatlabayan, L., Santosa, D.A. and Adiwibowo, S. (2005) *Integrating Socio-Economic Considerations into Biosafety Decisions*, Washington, DC: World Resources Institute.

Freidberg, S. (2004) *French Beans and Food Scares. Culture and Commerce in an Anxious Age*, Oxford: Oxford University Press.

Frisvold, G. (2004) 'Diffusion of Bt cotton and insecticide use', Paper prepared for Annual Meeting of Western Agricultural Economics Association, Honolulu, July 2004.

Frisvold, G., Reeves, J. and Tronstad, R. (2006) 'Bt cotton adoption in the United States and China: International trade and welfare effects', *AgBioForum*, 9(2): 69–78.

Fryxell, P. (1979) *The Natural History of the Cotton Tribe*, College Station, TX: Texas A&M University Press.

Fukuda-Parr, S. (ed.) (2007) *The Gene Revolution*, London: Earthscan.

Gassmann, A.J., Stock, S.P., Carrière, Y. and Tabashnik, B.E. (2006) 'Effects of entomopathogenic nematodes on the fitness cost of resistance to Bt toxin Cry1Ac in pink bollworm (Lepidoptera, Gelechiidae)', *Journal of Economic Entomology*, 99: 920–6.

Gassmann, A.J., Carrière, Y. and Tabashnik, B.E. (2009) 'Fitness costs of insect resistance to *Bacillus thuringiensis*', *Annual Review of Entomology*, 54: 147–63.

Gibbon, P. (1998) *Peasant Cotton Cultivation and Marketing Behaviour in Tanzania Since Liberalisation*, CDR Working Paper Subseries i.98.16, Copenhagen: CDR.

Goldberg, E. (2004) *Trade, Reputation, and Child Labor in Twentieth-Century Egypt*, New York: Palgrave.

Goodman, R., Vieths, S., Sampson, H., Hill, D., Ebisawa, M., Taylor, S. and van Ree, R. (2008) 'Allergenicity assessment of genetically modified crops – what makes sense?', *Nature Biotechnology*, 26(1): 73–81.

Gore J., Leonard, B.R., Church, G.E. and Cook, D.R. (2002) 'Behavior of bollworm (Lepidoptera: Noctuidae) larvae on genetically engineered cotton', *Journal of Economic Entomology,* 95: 763–9.

Gould, F. (1998) 'Sustainability of transgenic insecticidal cultivars: Integrating pest genetics and ecology', *Annual Review of Entomology,* 43: 701–26.

Gould, F., Martinez-Ramirez, A. Anderson, A., Ferré, J., Silva, F.J. and Moar W.J. (1992) 'Broad-spectrum resistance to *Bacillus thuringiensis* toxins in *Heliothis virescens*', *Proceedings of the National Academy of Sciences,* 89: 7986–8.

Gould, F., Cohen, M.B., Bentur, J.S., Kennedy, G.G. and Van Duyn, J. (2006) 'Impact of small fitness costs on pest adaptation to crop varieties with multiple toxins: A heuristic model', *Journal of Economic Entomology*, 99: 2091–9.

Gouse, M. (2007) 'South Africa: Revealing the potential and obstacles, the private sector model and reaching the traditional sector' in S. Fukuda-Parr (ed.) *The Gene Revolution*, London: Earthscan, pp. 175–98.

Gouse, M., Kirsten, J. and Jenkins, L. (2003) 'Bt cotton in South Africa: Adoption and the impact on farm incomes amongst small-scale and large-scale farmers', *Agrekon*, 42: 15–28.

Gouse, M., Pray, C. and Schimmelpfennig, D. (2004) 'The distribution of benefits from Bt cotton adoption in South Africa', *AgBioForum*, 7: 187–94.

Gouse, M., Kirsten, J., Shankar, B. and Thirtle, C. (2005) 'Bt cotton in KwaZulu Natal: Technological triumph but institutional failure', *AgBiotechNet,* 7: 1–7.

Gouse, M., Shankar, B. and Thirtle, C. (2008) 'The decline of cotton in KwaZulu Natal: Technology and institutions', in W. Moseley and L. Gray (eds) *Hanging by a Thread*, Athens, OH: Ohio University Press, pp. 103–21.

Govereh, J. and Jayne, T. (1999) *Effects of Cash Crop Production on Food Crop Productivity in Zimbabwe: Synergies or Trade-Offs?,* MSU International Development Working Paper No.74, East Lansing, MI: Michigan State University.

Graff, G., Cullen, S., Bradford, K., Zilberman, D. and Bennett, A. (2003) 'The public-private structure of intellectual property ownership in agricultural biotechnology', *Nature Biotechnology*, 21(9): 989–95.

Gray, L. (1933) *History of Agriculture in the Southern United States to 1860*, Washington, DC: Carnegie Institution.

Green, C. (1956) *Eli Whitney and the Birth of American Technology*, Boston, MA: Little, Brown and Company.

Greene, J.K., Turnipseed, S.G., Sullivan, M.J. and May, O.L. (2001) 'Treatment thresholds for stink bugs (Hemiptera: Pentatomidae) in cotton', *Journal of Economic Entomology,* 94: 403–9.

Greene J.K., Bundy, C.S., Roberts, P.M. and Leonard, B.R. (2006) 'Identification and management of common boll-feeding bugs in cotton'. Available at: <http://www.clemson.edu/psapublishing/Pages/Entom/EB158.pdf>

Greenplate, J.T., Mullins, J.W., Penn, S.R., Dahm, A., Reich, B.J., Osborn, J.A., Rahn, P.R., Ruschke, L. and Shappley Z.W. (2003) 'Partial characterization of cotton plants expressing two toxin proteins from *Bacillus thuringiensis*: Relative toxin contribution, toxin interaction, and resistance management', *Journal of Applied Entomology*, 127: 340–7.

Griffin, K. (1975) *The Political Economy of Agrarian Change*, London: Macmillan.

Grigg, D. (1982) *The Dynamics of Agricultural Change*, London: Hutchinson.

Griliches, Z. (1957) 'Hybrid corn: An exploration in the economics of technical change', *Econometrica,* 25: 501–22.

Guha, S. (2007) 'Genetic change and colonial cotton improvement in 19th and 20th century India' in R. Chakrabarti (ed.) *Situating Environmental History*, Delhi: Manohar, pp. 307–22.

Gujar, G.T., Kalia, V., Kumari, A., Singh, B.P., Mittal, A., Nair, R. and Mohan, M. (2007) '*Helicoverpa armigera* baseline susceptibility to *Bacillus thuringiensis* Cry toxins and resistance management for Bt cotton in India', *Journal of Invertebrate Pathology*, 95: 214–9.

Guo, H.-N., Wu, J.-H., Chen, X.-Y., Lu, R., Shi, Y.-J., Qin, H.-M., Xiao, J.L. and Tian, Y.-C. (2003) 'Cotton plants transformed with the activated chimeric *Cry1Ac* and *API-B* genes', *Acta Botanica Sinica*, 45(1): 108–13.

Gupta, P. (1998) 'Mutation breeding in cereals and legumes' in S. Jain, D. Brar and B. Ahloowalia (eds) *Somaclonal Variation and Induced Mutations in Crop Improvement*, Dordrecht: Kluwer, pp. 311–32.

Habib, I. (1999) *The Agrarian System of Mughal India 1556–1707*, New Delhi: Oxford University Press.

Hahn, S. (1983) *The Roots of Southern Populism*, Oxford: Oxford University Press.

Han, L. (2004) 'Genetically modified microorganisms' in S. Parekh (ed.) *The GMO Handbook*, Totawa, NJ: Humana Press, pp. 29–51.

Haney, P., Lewis, W. and Lambert, W. (1996) *Cotton Production and the Boll Weevil in Georgia: History, cost of control and benefits of eradication*, Georgia Agricultural Experiment Stations Bulletin No. 428, Athens, GA: University of Georgia.

Harriss-White, B. (1996) 'Free market romanticism in an era of deregulation', *Oxford Development Studies*, 24: 27–45.

Hazell, P. and Ramasamy, C. (1991) *The Green Revolution Reconsidered: The Impact of High Yielding Rice Varieties in South India*, Baltimore, MD: Johns Hopkins University Press.

Head, G., Moar, W., Eubanks, M., Freeman, B., Ruberson, J., Hagerty, A. and Turnipseed, S. (2005) 'A multi-year, large-scale comparison of arthropod populations on commercially managed Bt and non-Bt cotton fields', *Environmental Entomology*, 34: 1257–66.

Hearn, A.B. and Fitt, G.P. (1992) 'Cotton cropping systems', in C. J. Pearson (ed.) *Ecosystems of the World: Field Crop Ecosystems, Vol. 18*, New York: Elsevier, pp. 85–142.

Hebbar, K.B., Perumal, N.K. and Khadi. B.M. (2007a) 'Photosynthesis and plant growth response of transgenic Bt cotton (*Gossypium hirsutum* L.) hybrids under field condition', *Photosynthetica*, 45: 254–8.

Hebbar K.B., Rao M.R.K. and Khadi B.M. (2007b) 'Synchronized boll development of Bt cotton hybrids and their physiological consequences', *Current Science*, 93: 693–5.

Heinicke, C. and Grove, W. (2005) 'Labor markets, regional diversity, and cotton harvest mechanization in the post-World War II US', *Social Science History*, 29(2): 269–97.

Heisey, P., Smale, M., Byerlee, D. and Souza, E. (1997) 'Wheat rusts and the costs of genetic diversity in the Punjab of Pakistan', *American Journal of Agricultural Economics*, 79: 726–37.

Helferich, G. (2007) *High Cotton. Four Seasons in the Mississippi Delta*, New York: Counterpoint.

Henneberry, T.J., Jech, L.F. and de la Torre, T. (2001) 'Mortality and development effects of transgenic cotton on pink bollworm larvae', University of Arizona, Arizona Cotton Report. Available at: < http://cals.arizona.edu/pubs/crops/az1224/az12247d.pdf >

Herring, R. (2007) 'Stealth seeds: Bioproperty, biosafety, biopolitics', *Journal of Development Studies*, 43: 130–57.

Heuberger, S., Ellers-Kirk, C., Yafuso, C., Gassmann, A.J., Tabashnik, B.E., Dennehy, T.J. and Carrière, Y. (2008a) 'Effects of refuge contamination by transgenes on Bt resistance in pink bollworm (Lepidoptera: Gelechiidae)', *Journal of Economic Entomology*, 101: 504–14.

Heuberger, S., Yafuso, C., Tabashnik, B.E., Carrière, Y. and Dennehy, T.J. (2008b) 'Outcrossed cotton seed and adventitious Bt plants in Arizona refuges', *Environmental Biosafety Research*, 7: 87–96.

Higginson, D.M., Morin, S., Nyboer, M., Biggs, R., Tabashnik, B.E. and Carrière, Y. (2005) 'Evolutionary trade-offs of insect resistance to Bt crops: Fitness costs affecting paternity', *Evolution,* 59: 915–20.

Hilder, V.A., Gatehouse, A.M.R. and Boulter, D. (1989) 'Potential for exploiting plant genes to genetically engineer insect resistance, exemplified by the cowpea trypsin inhibitor gene', *Pesticide Science,* 27: 165–71.

Hillocks, R. (2005) 'Is there a role for Bt cotton in IPM for smallholders in Africa?', *International Journal of Pest Management,* 51(2): 131–41.

Hobson, S. and Le Roux, H. (2005) *Proposals to Increase Black Economic Participation in the South African Cotton Industry. New Farmers Development Company*, Pretoria: Cotton SA.

Hofs, J.-L., Fok, M., Gouse, M. and Kirsten, J. F. (2006a) 'Diffusion du coton génétiquement modifié en Afrique du Sud : Des leçons pour l'Afrique Zone Franc', *Revue Tiers Monde,* 188: 799–823.

Hofs, J.-L., Fok, M. and Vaissayre, M. (2006b) 'Impact of Bt cotton adoption on pesticide use by smallholders: A 2-year survey in Makhatini Flats (South Africa)', *Crop Protection,* 25(9): 984–8.

Hofs, J.-L., Hau, B. and Marais, D. (2006c) 'Boll distribution patterns in Bt and non-Bt cotton cultivars I. Study on commercial irrigated farming systems in South Africa', *Field Crops Research,* 98: 203–9.

Hofs, J.-L., Hau, B. Marais, D. and Fok, M. (2006d) 'Boll distribution patterns in Bt and non-Bt cotton cultivars II. Study on small-scale farming systems in South Africa', *Field Crops Research,* 98: 210–5.

Hossain, F., Pray, C.E., Lu, Y., Huang, J., Fan, C. and Hu, R. (2004) 'GM cotton and farmers' health in China: An econometric analysis of the relationship between pesticide poisoning and GM cotton use in China', *International Journal of Occupational and Environmental Health,*10: 307–14.

House of Lords Select Committee on Economic Affairs (2005) *The Economics of Climate Change,* London: The Stationery Office.

Hu, R., Pray, C., Huang, J., Rozelle, S., Fan, C. and Zhang, C. (2006) 'Reforming intellectual property rights, bio-safety management and the seed industry in China: Who benefits from policy reform?', Unpublished paper. Beijing: CCAP.

Huang, F.N., Leonard, B.R. and Andow, D.A. (2007) 'Sugarcane borer (Lepidoptera: Crambidae) resistance to transgenic *Bacillus thuringiensis* maize', *Journal of Economic Entomology,* 100: 164–71.

Huang, J., Hu, R. and Rozelle, S. (1999) 'China's seed industry toward 21st century', *Journal of Agrotechnical Economics,* 1999(2): 14–21 [In Chinese].

Huang, J., Hu, R., Fan, C., Pray, C. and Rozelle, S. (2002a) 'Bt cotton benefits, costs and impacts in China', *AgBioForum,* 5(4): 153–66.

Huang, J., Hu, R., Rozelle, S., Qiao, F. and Pray, C. (2002b) 'Transgenic varieties and productivity of smallholder cotton farmers in China', *Australian Journal of Agricultural and Resource Economics,* 46(3): 367–87.

Huang, J., Rozelle, S., Pray, C. and Wang, Q. (2002c).'Plant biotechnology in China', *Science,* 295: 674–7.

Huang, J., Hu, R., Pray, C., Qiao, F. and Rozelle, S. (2003) 'Biotechnology as an alternative to chemical pesticides: A case study of Bt cotton in China', *Agricultural Economics,* 29: 55–67.

Huang, J., Hu, R., van Meijl, H. and van Tongeren, F. (2004) 'Biotechnology boosts to crop productivity in China: Trade and welfare implications', *Journal of Development Economics,* 75: 27–54.

Huang, J., Lin, H., Hu, R., Rozelle, S. and Pray, C. (2007) 'Impact of Bt cotton adoption on pesticide use on secondary pests', *Journal of Agrotechnical Economics*, 2007 (1): 1–12 [In Chinese].

Huang, J., Qi, L. and Chen, R. (2008) 'Information, knowledge, risk preference and farmers' pesticide use', *Management World*, 2008(5): 71–6 [In Chinese].

Hutchinson, J., Silow, R. and Stephens, S. (1947) *The Evolution of Gossypium and the Differentiation of the Cultivated Cottons,* London: Oxford University Press.

ICAC (International Cotton Advisory Committee) (2004) 'Zero insecticide pest control system in Syria', *ICAC Recorder*, 22(2): 9–12.

Isaacman, A. and Roberts, R. (eds) (1995) *Cotton, Colonialism, and Social History in Sub-Saharan Africa,* London: James Currey.

Ismael, Y., Bennett, R. and Morse, S. (2002) 'Benefits from Bt cotton use by smallholder farmers in South Africa', *AgBioForum,* 5: 1–6.

Jackson, R.E., Bradley, J.R. and Van Duyn, J.W. (2003) 'Field performance of transgenic cotton expressing one or two *Bacillus thuringiensis* endotoxins against bollworm, *Helicoverpa zea* (Boddie)', *Journal of Cotton Science*, 7: 57–64.

Jackson, R.E., Bradley, Jr., J.R. and Van Duyn, J.W. (2004) 'Performance of feral and Cry1Ac-selected *Helicoverpa zea* (Lepidoptera: Noctuidae) strains on transgenic cottons expressing either one or two *Bacillus thuringiensis* ssp. *kurstaki* proteins under greenhouse conditions', *Journal of Entomological Science,* 39: 46–55.

Jacobson, T. and Smith, G. (2001) *Cotton's Renaissance. A Study in Market Innovation*, Cambridge: Cambridge University Press.

James, C. (2006) *Global Status of Commercialized Biotech/GM Crops: 2006*, ISAAA Brief No. 35, Ithaca, NY: ISAAA.

———— (2007) *Global Status of Commercialized Biotech/GM Crops: 2007*, ISAAA Brief 37. Ithaca, NY: ISAAA.

Janmaat, A.F. and Myers, J.H. (2005) 'The cost of resistance to *Bacillus thuringiensis* varies with the host plant of *Trichoplusia ni*', *Proceedings of the Royal Society London B*, 272: 1031–8.

Jayaraman, K.S. (2002) 'Poor crop management plagues Bt cotton experiment in India', *Nature Biotechnology*, 20: 1069.

———— (2004a) 'India produces homegrown GM cotton', *Nature Biotechnology*, 22: 255–6.

———— (2004b) 'Illegal seeds overtake India's cotton fields', *Nature Biotechnology* 22: 1333–4.

Jech, L.F. and Henneberry, T. (2005) 'Lepidopterous larval mortalities and Cry1Ac toxic protein in Bollgard, non-Bollgard and Roundup Ready cottons', in *Proceedings of the Beltwide Cotton Conference*, 4–7 January, New Orleans, LA, Memphis, TN: National Cotton Council of America.

Jost, P., Shurley, D., Culpepper, S., Roberts, P., Nichols, R., Reeves, J. and Anthony, S. (2008) 'Economic comparison of transgenic and nontransgenic cotton production systems in Georgia', *Agronomy Journal*, 100(1): 42–51.

Jurat-Fuentes, J.L., Gould, F.L. and Adang, M.J. (2003) 'Dual resistance to *Bacillus thuringiensis* Cry1Ac and Cry2Aa toxins in *Heliothis virescens* suggests multiple mechanisms of resistance', *Applied and Environmental Microbiology*, 69: 5898–906.

Keeley, J. (2003) *Regulating Biotechnology in China: The Politics of Biosafety.* IDS Working Paper 208, Brighton, UK: Institute of Development Studies.

Khouri, F. (1997) 'Syrian Arab Republic' in *Cotton Pests and their Control in the Near East.* FAO Plant Production and Protection Paper 141, Rome: FAO.

King, J. and Schimmelpfennig, D. (2005) 'Mergers, acquisitions and stocks of agricultural biotechnology intellectual property', *AgBioForum*, 8:83–8.

Kirsten, J. and Gouse, M. (2003) 'The adoption and impact of agricultural biotechnology in South Africa', in N. Kalaitzandonakes (ed.) *The Economic and Environmental Impacts of Agbiotech*, New York: Kluwer Academic / Plenum Publishers, pp. 243–59.

Kooistra, K., Pyburn, R. and Termorshuizen, A. (2006) *The Sustainability of Cotton. Consequences for Man and the Environment*, Science Shop Wageningen University and Research Center Report No. 223.

Kranthi, K., Kranthi, S., Naidu, S., Dhawad, C., Mate, K., Wadasakar, R., Chaudhary, A., Bharose, A., Siddhabhatti, P. and Patil, E. (2004) 'IRM and Bt cotton', paper presented at the International Symposium *Strategies for Sustainable Cotton Production – A Global Vision*, Dharwad, India, November 2004.

Kranthi, K., Naidu, S. Dhawad, C., Tatwawadi, A., Mate, K., Patil, E., Bharose, A., Behere, G., Wadaskar, R. and Kranthi, S. (2005) 'Temporal and intra-plant variability of Cry1Ac expression in Bt-cotton and its influence on the survival of the cotton bollworm, *Helicoverpa armigera* (Hübner) (Noctuidae: Lepidoptera)', *Current Science*, 89(2): 291–8.

Krishna, V. and Qaim, M. (2007) 'Estimating the adoption of Bt eggplant in India: Who benefits from public-private partnership?', *Food Policy*, 32: 523–43.

Kryder, R., Kowalski, S. and Krattiger, A. (2000) *The Intellectual and Technical Property Components of pro-Vitamin A Rice (Golden Rice)*, Ithaca, NY: ISAAA.

Kurtz, R.W., McCaffery, A. and O'Reilly, D. (2007) 'Insect resistance management for Syngenta's VipCotTM transgenic cotton', *Journal of Invertebrate Pathology*, 95: 227–30.

Lanjouw, P. and Stern, N. (1993) 'Agricultural change and inequality in Palanpur 1957–1984' in K. Hoff, A. Braverman and J. Stiglitz (eds) *The Economics of Rural Organization: Theory, Practice and Policy,* New York: Oxford University Press, pp. 543–68.

Larson, J., Roberts, R. and Gwathmey, C. (2007) 'Herbicide-resistant technology price effects on the plant density decision for ultra-narrow-row cotton', *Journal of Agricultural and Resource Economics*, 32(2): 383–401.

Lee, M.K., Walters, F.S., Hart, H., Palekar, N. and Chen, J.S. (2003) 'The mode of action of the *Bacillus thuringiensis* vegetative insecticidal protein Vip3A differs from that of Cry1Ab delta-endotoxin', *Applied and Environmental Microbiology*, 69: 4648–57.

Leigh, G. (2004) *The World's Greatest Fix. A History of Nitrogen and Agriculture*, Oxford: Oxford University Press.

Li, E. and Yan X. (2005) 'The development of seed company and industry in China', *China Seed Industry*, 1: 5–6 [In Chinese].

Li, G.-P., Wu, K.-M., Gould, F., Wang, J.-K., Miao, J., Gao, X.-W. and Guo Y.-Y. (2007) 'Increasing tolerance to Cry1Ac cotton from cotton bollworm, *Helicoverpa armigera*, was confirmed in Bt cotton farming area of China', *Ecological Entomology*, 32: 366–75.

Li, H., Oppert, B., Higgins, R.A., Huang, F., Buschman, L.L., Gao, J.R. and Zhu, K.Y.(2005) 'Characterization of cDNAs encoding three trypsin-like proteinases and mRNA quantitative analysis in Bt-resistant and susceptible strains of *Ostrinia nubilalis*', *Insect Biochemistry and Molecular Biology*, 35: 847–60.

Lipton, M. (2007) 'Plant breeding and poverty: Can transgenic seeds replicate the "Green Revolution" as a source of gains for the poor?', *Journal of Development Studies*, 43: 31–62.

Lipton, M. and Longhurst, R. (1989) *New Seeds and Poor People*, London: Unwin Hyman.

Liu, E. (2008) 'Time to change what to sow: Risk preferences and technology adoption decisions of cotton farmers in China'. Unpublished paper, Department of Economics, Princeton University, Princeton, NJ. Available at: http://www.princeton.edu/~eliu/jmpaper.pdf

Llewellyn, D.J., Mares, C.L. and Fitt, G.P. (2007) 'Field performance and seasonal changes in the efficacy against *Helicoverpa armigera* (Hübner) of transgenic cotton expressing the insecticidal protein Vip3A', *Agricultural and Forest Entomology*, 9: 93–101.

Lovejoy, P. (1978) 'Plantations in the economy of the Sokoto Caliphate', *Journal of African History*, 19: 341–68.

Lukefahr, M., Houghtaling, J. and Cruhm, D. (1975) 'Suppression of *Heliothis* spp. with cotton containing combinations of resistant characters', *Journal of Economic Entomology*, 68(6): 743–6.

Luttrell, R. (1994) 'Cotton pest management: Part 2. A US perspective', *Annual Review of Entomology*, 39: 527–42.

Luttrell, R., Fitt, G., Ramalho, F. and Sugonyaev, E. (1994) 'Cotton pest management: Part 1. A worldwide perspective', *Annual Review of Entomology*, 39: 517–26.

MacIntosh, S.C., Stone, T.B., Sims, S.R., Hunst, P.L., Greenplate, J.T., Marrone, P.G., Perlak, F.J., Fischhoff, D.A. and Fuchs, R.L. (1990) 'Specificity and efficacy of purified *Bacillus thuringiensis* proteins against agronomically important insects', *Journal of Invertebrate Patholology*, 56: 258–66.

McKenzie, J.A. (1996) *Ecological and Evolutionary Aspects of Insecticide Resistance*, Austin, TX: R. G. Landes Co. and Academic Press.

McNeill, J. (2000) *Something New Under the Sun. An Environmental History of the Twentieth Century,* London: Allen Lane.

Mahon, R.J., Olsen, K.M., Garsia, K.A. and Young, S.R. (2007) 'Resistance to *Bacillus thuringiensis* toxin Cry2aB in a strain of *Helicoverpa armigera* (Lepidoptera: Noctuidae) in Australia', *Journal of Economic Entomology,* 100: 894–902.

Malkarnekar, A., Waible, H. and Pemsl, D. (2005) 'Why some Indian cotton farmers do not adopt Bt cotton', poster presented at Tropentag 2005, University of Hohenheim, Stuttgart, 11–13 October 2005. Available at: http://www.tropentag.de/2005/abstracts/posters/298.pdf (accessed 16 July 2008)

Marchosky, R., Ellersworth, P.C., Moser, H. and Henneberry, T.J. (2001) 'Bollgard® and Bollgard II® efficacy in near isogenic lines of "DP50" upland cotton in Arizona', University of Arizona, Arizona Cotton Report. Available at: <http://ag.arizona.edu/pubs/crops/az1224>

Marra, M. and Martin, S. (2007) 'An assessment by U.S. cotton growers and other cotton experts of important innovations in cotton production in the last decade (1996–2006)', *Journal of Cotton Science*, 11: 259–65.

Marvier, M., McCreedy, C., Regetz, J. and Karieva, P. (2007) 'A meta-analysis of effects of Bt cotton and maize on non-target invertebrates', *Science*, 316: 1475–7.

Matthews, G.A. (1993) 'Pesticide registration, formulation and application in India', *Chemistry and Industry* February 1993: 115–8.

Matthews, G.A. and Tunstall, J.P. (1994) *Insect Pests of Cotton,* Cambridge: CAB International.

May, O. and Lege, K. (1999) 'Development of the world cotton industry' in C. W. Smith and J.T. Cothren (eds) *Cotton: Origin, History, Technology and Production*, New York: John Wiley, pp. 65–97.

Men, X.Y., Ge, F., Edwards, C.A. and Yardim, E.N. (2005) 'The influence of pesticide applications on *Helicoverpa armigera* Hübner and sucking pests in transgenic Bt cotton and non-transgenic cotton in China', *Crop Protection*, 24: 319–24.

Mendelsohn, M., Kough, J., Vaituzis, Z. and Matthews, K. (2003) 'Are Bt crops safe?' *Nature Biotechnology*, 21: 1003–9.

Minot, N. and Daniels, L. (2005) 'Impact of global cotton markets on rural poverty in Benin', *Agricultural Economics*, 33: 453–66.

Moar, W.J., Pusztai-carey, M. and Van Faassen, H. (1995) 'Development of *Bacillus thuringiensis* Cry1C resistance by *Spodoptera exigua* (Hübner) (Lepidoptera: Noctuidae)', *Applied Environmental Microbiology*, 61: 2086–92.

Mohanty, B. (2005) '"We are like the living dead": Farmer suicides in Maharashtra, Western India', *Journal of Peasant Studies*, 32(2): 243–76.

Mokyr, J. (1990) *The Lever of Riches. Technological Creativity and Economic Progress*, Oxford: Oxford University Press.

Moore, J. (1956) 'Cotton breeding in the old South', *Agricultural History*, 30(3): 95–104.

Morin, S., Biggs, R.W., Sisterson, M.S., Shriver, L., Ellers-Kirk, C., Higginson, D., Holley, D., Gahan, L.J., Heckel, D.G., Carrière, Y., Dennehy, T.J., Brown, J.K. and Tabashnik, B.E. (2003) 'Three cadherin alleles associated with resistance to *Bacillus thuringiensis* in pink bollworm', *Proceedings of the National Academy of Sciences*, 100: 5004–9.

Morse, S., Bennett, R. and Ismael, Y. (2004) 'Why Bt cotton pays for small-scale producers in South Africa', *Nature Biotechnology*, 22(4): 379–80.

—— (2005) 'Comparing the performance of official and unofficial genetically modified cotton in India', *AgBioForum*, 8(1): 1–6.

—— (2006) 'Environmental impact of genetically modified cotton in South Africa', *Agriculture, Ecosystems and Environment*, 117(4): 277–89.

Mullins, W., Pitts, D. and Coots, B. (2005) 'Sister-line comparisons of Bollgard II versus Bollgard and non-Bt cottons', paper presented at the Beltwide Cotton Conference, New Orleans, LA, January 2005.

Murugkar, M., Ramaswami, B. and Shelar, M. (2007) 'Competition and monopoly in Indian cotton seed market', *Economic and Political Weekly*, 42(37): 3781–9.

Napompeth, B. (2007) 'Current status of biotech cotton in Thailand', *ICAC Recorder*, 25(2): 15–6.

Naranjo, S.E. (2005) 'Long-term assessment of the effects of transgenic Bt cotton on the abundance of non-target arthropod natural enemies', *Environmental Entomology*, 34: 1193–210.

Narayanamoorthy, A. and Kalamkar, S.S. (2006) 'Is Bt cotton cultivation economically viable for Indian farmers?', *Economic and Political Weekly*, 41(26): 2716–24.

NASS (National Agricultural Statistics Service) (2007) *Acreage*. Washington, DC: USDA. Available at: <http://www.usda.gov/nass/PUBS/TODAYRPT/acrg0607.pdf> (accessed 13 May 2008).

Navon, A., Hare, J.D. and Federici, B.A. (1993) 'Interactions among *Heliothis virescens* larvae, cotton condensed tannin and the Cry1A(c) delta-endotoxin of *Bacillus thuringiensis*', *Journal of Chemical Ecology*, 19: 2485–99.

Naylor, R. (1994) 'Herbicide use in Asian rice production', *World Development*, 22: 55–70.

Naylor, R., Falcon, W. Goodman, R., Jahn, M., Sengooba, T., Tefera, H. and Nelson, R. (2004) 'Biotechnology in the developing world: A case for increased investments in orphan crops', *Food Policy*, 29: 15–44.

Nibouche, S., Martin, P. and Vaissayre, M. (2003) 'A modeling approach of sustainability of Bt cotton by small farmers in West Africa', *Resistant Pest Management Newsletter*, 13: 55–8.

Nibouche, S., Guérard, N., Martin, P. and Vaissayre, M. (2007) 'Modelling the role of refuges for sustainable management of dual-gene cotton in West African smallholder farming systems', *Crop Protection*, 26: 828–36.

North, D.C. (1990) *Institutions, Institutional Change and Economic Performance*, Cambridge: Cambridge University Press.

NRC (National Research Council) (2002) *Environmental Effects of Transgenic Plants. The Scope and Adequacy of Regulation*, Washington, DC: NRC.

Nuffield Council on Bioethics (1999) *Genetically Modified Crops: The Ethical and Social Issues*, London: Nuffield Council on Bioethics.

OECD (2006) *Cotton in West Africa. The Economic and Social Stakes*, Paris: OECD.

Olmstead, A. and Rhode, P. (2002) 'The red queen and the hard reds: Productivity growth in American wheat 1800–1940', *Journal of Economic History*, 62: 929–66.

Olsen, K.M. and Daly, J.C. (2000) 'Plant-toxin interactions in transgenic Bt cotton and their effect on mortality of *Helicoverpa armigera* (Lepidoptera: Noctuidae)', *Journal of Economic Entomology*, 93: 1293–9.

Olsen, K.M., Daly, J.C. and Tanner G.J. (1998) 'The effect of cotton condensed tannin on the efficacy of the Cry1Ac δ-endotoxin of *Bacillus thuringiensis*', in *Proceedings of the 9th Australian Cotton Conference*, 12–14 August, Broadbeach, Queensland, Wee Waa, NSW: Australian Cotton Growers' Research Association.

Olsen, K.M., Daly, J.C., Holt, H.E. and Finnegan, E.J. (2005) 'Season-long variation in expression of *cry1Ac* gene and efficacy of *Bacillus thuringiensis* toxin in transgenic cotton against *Helicoverpa armigera* (Lepidoptera: Noctuidae)', *Journal of Economic Entomology*, 98: 1007–17.

O'Reilly, D.R., Walters, F., Palekar, N., Boyer, A. and Kurtz, R.W. (2007) 'Laboratory studies to determine the high dose status of VipCot cotton', in *Proceedings of the Beltwide Cotton Conference*, 9–12 January, New Orleans, LA, Memphis, TN: National Cotton Council of America.

Overton, M. (1996) *Agricultural Revolution in England. The Transformation of the Agrarian Economy 1500–1850*, Cambridge: Cambridge University Press.

Oxfam (1999) *Genetically Modified Crops, World Trade and Food Security*, Oxford: Oxfam.

——— (2002) *Cultivating Poverty. The Impact of US Cotton Subsidies on Africa*, Oxfam Briefing Paper 30. Oxford: Oxfam.

Paarlberg, R. (2001) *The Politics of Precaution*, Baltimore, MD: The Johns Hopkins University Press.

——— (2008) *Starved for Science. How Biotechnology is Being Kept Out of Africa*, Cambridge, MA: Harvard University Press.

Panos (2005) *The GM Debate – Who Decides?*, London: The Panos Institute.

Pardey, P., Beintema, N., Dehmer, S. and Wood, S. (2006) *Agricultural Research. A Growing Global Divide?*, Washington, DC: IFPRI.

Pearson, M. (2006) '"Science", representation and resistance: The Bt cotton debate in Andhra Pradesh, India', *The Geographical Journal*, 172: 306–17.

Pemsl, D. (2006) *Economics of Agricultural Biotechnology in Crop Protection in Developing Countries – The Case of Bt-Cotton in Shandong Province, China*. Pesticide Policy Project Publication Series No. 11, Hannover, Germany: University of Hannover.

Pemsl, D., Waibel, H. and Orphal, J. (2004) 'A methodology to assess the profitability of Bt cotton: Case study results from the state of Karnataka, India', *Crop Protection*, 23: 1249–57.

Pemsl, D., Waibel, H. and Gutierrez, A. (2005) 'Why do some Bt cotton farmers in China continue to use high levels of pesticides?', *International Journal of Agricultural Sustainability*, 3(1): 44– 56.

Perlak, F.J., Deaton, R.W., Armstrong, T.A., Fuchs, R.L., Sims, S.R., Greenplate, J.T. and Fischhoff, D.A. (1990) 'Insect resistant cotton plants', *Nature Biotechnology*, 8: 939–43.

Persley, G., Giddings, L. and Juma, C. (1993) *Biosafety. The Safe Application of Biotechnology in Agriculture and the Environment*, ISNAR Research Report 5. The Hague: ISNAR.

Peterson, P. (2001) 'Stem rust of wheat: Exploring the concepts' in P. Peterson (ed.) *Stem Rust of Wheat. From Ancient Enemy to Modern Foe*, St Paul, MN: APS Press, pp. 1–15.

Pettigrew, W.T. and Adamczyk, J.J. (2006) 'Nitrogen fertility and planting date effects on lint yield and Cry1Ac (Bt) endotoxin production', *Agronomy Journal*, 98: 691–7.

Pietrantonio P.V., Junek T.A., Parker R., Mott D., Siders K., Troxclair N., Vargas-Camplis J., Westbrook J.K. and Vassiliou V.A. (2007) 'Detection and evolution of resistance to the pyrethroid cypermethrin in *Helicoverpa zea* (Lepidoptera: Noctuidae) populations in Texas', *Environmental Entomology*, 36: 1174–88.

Poehlman, J. and Sleper, D. (1995) *Breeding Field Crops*, Ames, IA: Iowa State University Press.

Pope, H. (2005) *Sons of the Conquerors*, New York: Overlook Duckworth.

Potrykus, I., Bilang, R., Futterer, J., Sautter, C. and Schrott, M. (1998) 'Genetic engineering of crop plants', in A. Altman (ed.) *Agricultural Biotechnology*, New York: Marcel Dekker, Inc, pp. 119–59.

Poulton, C., Gibbon, P., Hanyani-Mlambo, B., Kydd, J., Maro, W., Larsen, M., Osorio, A., Tschirley, D. and Zulu, B. (2004) 'Competition and coordination in liberalized African cotton market systems', *World Development*, 32: 519–36.

Pray, C., Ma, D., Huang, J. and Qiao, F. (2001) 'Impact of Bt cotton in China', *World Development*, 29: 813–25.

Pray, C., Huang, J., Hu, R. and Rozelle, S. (2002) 'Five years of Bt cotton in China: The benefits continue', *The Plant Journal*, 31(4): 423–30.

Pretty, J, (ed.) (2005) *The Pesticide Detox*, London: Earthscan.

Qaim, M. (2003) 'Bt cotton in India: Field trial results and economic projections', *World Development,* 31: 2115–27.

Qaim, M. and de Janvry, A. (2003) 'Genetically modified crops, corporate pricing strategies, and farmers' adoption: The case of Bt cotton in Argentina', *American Journal of Agricultural Economics,* 85: 814–28.

Qaim, M. and Zilberman, D. (2003) 'Yield effects of genetically modified crops in developing countries', *Science*, 299: 900–2.

Qaim, M. and de Janvry, A. (2005) 'Bt cotton and pesticide use in Argentina: Economic and environmental effects', *Environment and Development Economics*, 10: 179–200.

Qaim, M., Subramanian, S., Naik, G. and Zilberman, D. (2006) 'Adoption of Bt cotton and impact variability: Insights from India', *Review of Agricultural Economics*, 28: 48–58.

Qayum, A. and Sakkhari, K. (2005) *Bt Cotton in Andhra Pradesh. A Three-Year Assessment*, Hyderabad, India: Deccan Development Society.

Radosevich, S., Holt, J. and Ghersa, C. (1997) *Weed Ecology. Implications for Management,* New York: John Wiley.

Ramaswami, B., Pray, C. and Lalitha, N., (forthcoming) *The Limits of Intellectual Property Rights: Lessons from the Spread of Illegal Transgenic Seeds in India*, GIDR Working Paper, Ahmedabad: Gujarat Institute of Development Research.

Raymond, B., Sayyed, A.H. and Wright, D.J. (2005) 'Genes and environment interact to determine the fitness costs of resistance to *Bacillus thuringiensis*', *Proceedings of the Royal Society London B*, 272: 1519–24.

Raymond, B., Sayyed, A.L. and Wright, D.J. (2006) 'Host plant and population determine the fitness costs of resistance to *Bacillus thuringiensis*', *Biological Letters*, 3: 82–5.

Rifkin, J. (1998) *The Biotech Century*, New York: Jeremy P. Tarcher/Putnam.

Rigg, J. (1989) 'The new rice technology and agrarian change: Guilt by association?', *Progress in Human Geography*, 13: 374–99.

Rivoli, P. (2005) *The Travels of a T-Shirt in the Global Economy*, Hoboken, NJ: John Wiley.

Roberts, R. (1996) *Two Worlds of Cotton. Colonialism and the Regional Economy in the French Soudan, 1800–1946,* Stanford, CA: Stanford University Press.

Rogers, E. (1995) *Diffusion of Innovations*, 4th edn, New York: Free Press.

Rola, A. and Pingali, P. (1993) *Pesticides, Rice Productivity, and Farmers' Health*, Manila: IRRI.

Romeis, J., Shelton, A. and Kennedy, A. (eds) (2008) *Integration of Insect-Resistant Genetically Modified Crops within IPM Programs*, Berlin: Springer.

Roush, R.T. (1998) 'Two-toxin strategies for management of insecticidal crops: Can pyramiding succeed where pesticide mixtures have not?', *Philosophical Transactions of the Royal Society London B*, 353: 1777–86.

Roy, D., Herring, R. and Geisler, C. (2007) 'Naturalising transgenics: Official seeds, loose seeds and risk in the decision matrix of Gujarati cotton farmers', *Journal of Development Studies*, 43: 158–76.

Royal Society (2000) *Transgenic Plants and World Agriculture*, London: The Royal Society.

Royle, J.F. (1851) *On the Culture and Commerce of Cotton in India and Elsewhere*, London: Smith, Elder and Co.

Ruddiman, W. (2005) *Plows, Plagues and Petroleum*, Princeton, NJ: Princeton University Press.

Ryan, B. and N. Gross (1943) 'The diffusion of hybrid seed corn in two Iowa communities', *Rural Sociology*, 8: 15–24.

Sachs, E.S., Benedict, J.H., Stelly, D.M., Taylor, J.F., Altman, D.W., Berberich, S.A. and Davis, S.K. (1998) 'Expression and segregation of genes encoding Cry1A insecticidal proteins in cotton', *Crop Science*, 38: 1–11.

Sadao, N. (1984) 'The formation of the early Chinese cotton industry' in L. Grove and C. Daniels (eds) *State and Society in China*, Tokyo: University of Tokyo Press, pp. 17–77.

Sahn, D. (1990) 'The impact of export crop production on nutritional status in Côte d'Ivoire', *World Development*, 18: 1635–53.

Satya, L. (1997) *Cotton and Famine in Berar 1850–1900*, New Delhi: Manohar.

Schnepf, E., Crickmore, N., Van Rie, J., Lereclus, D., Baum. J., Feitelson, J., Zeigler, D.R. and Dean, D.H. (1998) '*Bacillus thuringiensis* and its pesticidal crystal proteins', *Microbiology and Molecular Biology Reviews*, 62: 775–806.

Scoones, I. (2005) *Science, Agriculture and the Politics of Policy*, New Delhi: Orient Longman.

Sequeira, R.V. and Playford, C.L. (2001) 'Abundance of *Helicoverpa* (Lepidoptera: Noctuidae) pupae under cotton and other crops in central Queensland: Implications for resistance management', *Australian Journal of Entomology*, 40: 264–9.

Shankar, B. and Thirtle, C. (2005) 'Pesticide productivity and transgenic cotton technology: The South African smallholder case', *Journal of Agricultural Economics*, 56: 97–116.

Sharma, H.C. (1993) 'How wide can a wide cross be?', *Euphytica*, 82: 43–64.

Sharma, H.C. and Pampapathy, G. (2006) 'Influence of transgenic cotton on the relative abundance and damage by target and non-target insect pests under different protection regimes in India', *Crop Protection*, 25: 800–13.

Shephard, G. (2003) 'Aflatoxin and food safety: Recent African perspectives', *Toxin Reviews*, 22(2&3): 267–86.

Showalter, A.M., Heuberger, S., Tabashnik, B.E. and Carrière, Y. (forthcoming) 'A primer for the use of insecticidal transgenic cotton in developing countries', *Journal of Insect Science*.

Shukla, S., Arora, R. and Sharma, H.C. (2005) 'Biological activity of soybean trypsin inhibitor and plant lectins against cotton bollworm/legume pod borer, *Helicoverpa armigera*', *Plant Biotechnology Journal*, 22: 1–6.

Sidhu, M.S. (1999) 'Impact of intellectual property rights on the Indian seed industry', *Indian Journal of Agricultural Economics*, 54: 370–9.

Singh, P.K., Kumar, M., Chaturvedi, C.P., Yadav, D. and Tuli, R. (2004) 'Development of a hybrid delta-endotoxin and its expression in tobacco and cotton for control of a polyphagous pest *Spodoptera litura*', *Transgenic Research*, 13: 397–410.

Singh, S. (2006) 'Organic cotton supply chains and small producers', *Economic and Political Weekly*, 41(52):5359–66.

Sisterson, M.S., Antilla, L., Carrière, Y., Ellers-Kirk, C. and Tabashnik, B.E. (2004) 'Effect of insect population size on evolution of resistance to transgenic crops', *Journal of Economic Entomology*, 97: 1413–24.

Sisterson, M.S., Carrière, Y., Dennehy, T.J. and Tabashnik, B.E. (2005) 'Evolution of resistance to transgenic crops: Interactions between insect movement and field distribution', *Journal of Economic Entomology*, 98: 1751–62.

Sisterson, M.S., Biggs, R.W., Manhardt, N.M., Carrière, Y., Dennehy, T.J. and Tabashnik, B.E. (2007) 'Effects of transgenic Bt cotton on insecticide use and abundance of two generalist predators', *Entomologia Experimentalis et Applicata*, 124: 305–11.

Skinner, D.Z., Muthukrishnan, S. and Liang, G.H. (2004) 'Transformation: A powerful tool for crop improvement', in G. H. Liang and D. Z. Skinner (eds), *Genetically Modified Crops: Their Development, Uses, and Risks,* New York: Food Products Press, pp. 1–16.

Slusarenko, A., Fraser, R. and van Loon, L. (eds) (2000) *Mechanisms of Resistance to Plant Diseases,* Dordrecht: Kluwer.

Smale, M. (1997) 'The green revolution and wheat genetic diversity: Some unfounded assumptions', *World Development*, 25: 1257–69.

——— (ed.) (2006) *Valuing Crop Biodiversity. On-Farm Genetic Resources and Economic Change,* Wallingford, UK: CABI.

Smale, M., Zambrano, P., Falck-Zepeda, J. and Gruère, G. (2006a) *Parables: Applied Economics Literature About the Impact of Genetically Engineered Crop Varieties in Developing Economies.* EPT Discussion Paper 158, Washington, DC: IFPRI

Smale, M., Zambrano, P. and Cartel, M. (2006b) 'Bales and balances: A review of the methods used to assess the economic impact of Bt cotton on farmers in developing economies', *AgBioForum*, 9(3): 195–212.

Smith, C., Cantrell, R., Moser, H. and Oakley, S. (1999) 'History of cultivar development in the United States' in C.W. Smith and J.T. Cothren (eds) *Cotton: Origin, History, Technology and Production*, New York: John Wiley, pp. 99–171.

Smith, R.H., Smith, J.W. and Park, S.H. (2004) 'Cotton transformation: Successes and challenges', in G. H. Liang and D. Z. Skinner (eds) *Genetically Modified Crops: Their Development, Uses, and Risks*, New York: Food Products Press, pp. 247–57.

Sneller, C. (2003) 'Impact of transgenic genotypes and subdivision on diversity within elite North American soybean germplasm', *Crop Science*, 43: 409–14.

Srinivasan, C. (2003) 'Concentration in ownership of plant variety rights: Some implications for developing countries', *Food Policy*, 28: 519–46.

Stephens, S. (1975) 'Some observations on photoperiodism and the development of annual forms of domesticated cotton', *Economic Botany*, 30: 409–18.

Stewart, S.D., Adamczyk, J.J., Knighten, K.S. and Davis, F.M. (2001) 'Impact of Bt cottons expressing one or two insecticidal proteins of *Bacillus thuringiensis* Berliner on growth and survival of noctuid (Lepidoptera) larvae', *Journal of Economic Entomology*, 94: 752–60.

Stockbridge, M., Smith, L. and Lohano, H. (1998) 'Cotton and wheat marketing and the provision of pre-harvest services in Sindh Province, Pakistan' in A. Dorward, J. Kydd and C. Poulton (eds) *Smallholder Cash Crop Production under Market Liberalisation*, Wallingford, UK: CABI, pp. 177–239.

Stoll, S. (2002) *Larding the Lean Earth. Soil and Society in Nineteenth Century America*, New York: Hill and Wang.

Stone, G. (2004) 'Biotechnology and the political ecology of information in India', *Human Organization*, 63: 127–40.

—— (2007) 'Agricultural deskilling and the spread of genetically modified cotton in Warangal', *Current Anthropology*, 48: 67–103.

Tabashnik, B.E. (1994a) 'Evolution of resistance to *Bacillus thuringiensis*', *Annual Review of Entomology*, 39: 47–79.

—— (1994b) 'Delaying insect adaptation to transgenic plants: Seed mixtures and refugia reconsidered', *Proceedings of the Royal Society London B*, 255: 7–12.

Tabashnik, B.E. and Carrière, Y. (2008) 'Evolution of insect resistance to transgenic plants', in K. Tilmon (ed.) *Specialization, Speciation and Radiation. Evolutionary Biology of Plant and Insect Relationships*, Berkeley, CA: University of California Press, pp. 267–79.

Tabashnik, B.E., Patin, A.L., Dennehy, T.J., Liu, Y.B., Carrière, Y., Sims, M.A. and Antilla, L. (2000) 'Frequency of resistance to *Bacillus thuringiensis* in field populations of pink bollworm', *Proceedings of the National Academy of Sciences*, 97: 12980–4.

Tabashnik, B.E., Dennehy, T.J., Sims, M.A., Larkin, K., Head, G.P., Moar, W.J. and Carrière, Y. (2002) 'Control of resistant pink bollworm by transgenic cotton with *Bacillus thuringiensis* toxin Cry2Ab', *Applied and Environmental Microbiology*, 68: 3790–4.

Tabashnik, B.E., Carrière, Y., Dennehy, T.J., Morin, S., Sisterson, M.S., Roush, R.T., Shelton, A.M. and Zhao, J.Z. (2003) 'Insect resistance to transgenic Bt crops: Lessons from the laboratory and field', *Journal of Economic Entomology*, 96: 1031–8.

Tabashnik, B.E., Gould, F. and Carrière, Y. (2004) 'Delaying evolution of insect resistance to transgenic crops by decreasing dominance and heritability', *Journal of Evolutionary Biology*, 17: 904–12.

Tabashnik, B.E., Dennehy, T.J. and Carrière, Y. (2005) 'Delayed resistance to transgenic cotton in pink bollworm', *Proceedings of the National Academy of Sciences*, 43: 15389–93.

Tabashnik, B.E., Fabrick, J.A., Henderson, S., Biggs, R.W., Yafuso, C.M., Nyboer, M.E., Manhardt, N.M., Coughlin, L.A., Sollome, J., Carrière, Y., Dennehy, T.J. and Morin, S. (2006) 'DNA screening reveals pest resistance to Bt cotton remains rare after a decade of exposure', *Journal of Economic Entomology*, 99: 1525–30.

Tabashnik, B.E., Gassmann, A.J., Crowder, D.W. and Carrière, Y. (2008) 'Insect resistance to Bt crops: Evidence versus theory', *Nature Biotechnology*, 26: 199–202.

Tanksley, S. and McCouch, S. (1997) 'Seed banks and molecular maps: Unlocking genetic potential from the wild', *Science*, 277:1063–6.

Tansey, G. and Rajotte, T. (eds) (2008) *The Future Control of Food*, London: Earthscan.

Taylor, M. and Cayford, J. (2003) *American Patent Policy, Biotechnology, and African Agriculture: The Case for Policy Change*, Washington, DC: Resources for the Future.

Terán-Vargas, A.P., Rodrígues, J.C., Martínez-Carrillo J.L., Cibrián-Tovar, J., Sanchez-Arroyo, H., Rodríguez-Del-Bosque, L.A. and Stanley, D. (2005) 'Bollgard cotton and resistance of tobacco bollworm (Lepidoptera: Noctuidae) to conventional insecticides in southern Tamaulipas, Mexico', *Journal of Economic Entomology*, 98: 2203–9.

Thirtle, C., Beyers, L., Ismael, Y. and Piesse, J. (2003) 'Can GM-technologies help the poor? The impact of Bt cotton in Makhatini Flats, KwaZulu-Natal', *World Development*, 31: 717–32.

Thompson, W.M., Anderson, J., Ibendahl, G. and Hudson, D. (2007) 'The impacts of GM seed technology on cotton: Cost of production in Mississippi, 1996–2005', paper presented at the Southern Agricultural Economics Association Annual Meeting, Mobile, Alabama, February 2007.

Tiberghien, Y. (2007) 'Europe: Turning against agricultural biotechnology in the late 1990s' in S. Fukuda-Parr (ed.) *The Gene Revolution*, London: Earthscan, pp. 51–68.

Tinjuangjun, P. (2002) 'Snowdrop lectin gene in transgenic plants: Its potential for Asian agriculture', *AgBiotechNet*, 4 July: ABN 091.

Traxler, G. (2007) 'US: Leading science, technology and commercialization' in S. Fukuda-Parr (ed.) *The Gene Revolution*, London: Earthscan, pp. 36–50.

Traxler, G. and Godoy-Avila, S. (2004) 'Transgenic cotton in Mexico', *AgBioForum*, 7: 57–62.

Traxler, G., Godoy-Avila, S., Falck-Zepeda, J. and Espinoza-Arellano, J. (2003) 'Transgenic cotton in Mexico: Economic and environmental impacts' in N. Kalaitzandonakes (ed.) *Economic and Environmental Impacts of First Generation Biotechnologies,* New York: Kluwer Academic, pp. 183–202.

Tripp, R. (ed.) (1997) *New Seed and Old Laws. Regulatory Reform and the Diversification of National Seed Systems*, London: Intermediate Technology Press.

—— (2001a) *Seed Provision and Agricultural Development*, Oxford: James Currey.

—— (2001b) 'Can biotechnology reach the poor? The adequacy of information and seed delivery', *Food Policy*, 26: 249–64.

—— (2006) *Self-Sufficient Agriculture. Labour and Knowledge in Small-Scale Farming*, London: Earthscan.

Tschirley, D., Poulton, C. and Boughton, D. (2006) *The Many Paths of Cotton Sector Reform in Eastern and Southern Africa: Lessons from a Decade of Experience*, Michigan State University International Development Working Paper No. 88, East Lansing, MI: MSU.

Twyman, R.M., Christou, P. and Stoger, E. (2002) 'Genetic transformation of plants and their cells', in K.M. Oksman-Caldentey and W.H. Barz (eds) *Plant Biotechnology and Transgenic Plants,* New York: Marcel Dekker Inc, pp. 111–41.

Udikeri, S.S., Patil, B.V., Khadi, B.M., Vamadevaiah, H.M., Basavangoud, K. and Kulkarni, K. (2007) 'Performance of new generation Bt cotton hybrids in Indian rainfed eco-system', in *Proceedings of the World Cotton Research Conference*, 10–14 September, Lubbock, Texas.

United States Department of Justice (2005) 'Monsanto Company charged with bribing Indonesian government official: Prosecution deferred for three years', Available at: <http://www.usdoj.gov/opa/pr/2005/January/05_crm_008.htm>

United States Environmental Protection Agency (2001) *Biopesticides Registration Action Document – Bacillus thuringiensis Plant-Incorporated Protectants*, Available at: <http,//www.epa.gov/pesticides/biopesticides/pips/bt_brad.htm>

—— (2005a) *Bt Cry1F/Cry1Ac Widestrike Cotton Registration Action Document*, Available at: <http://www.epa.gov/pesticides/biopesticides/ingredients/tech_docs/brad_006512-006513.pdf >

——— (2005b) Bt *Cry1F/Cry1Ac Widestrike Cotton Registration Action Document*, Available at: <http://www.epa.gov/oppbppd1/biopesticides/ingredients/tech_docs/brad_006512.pdf >

Van Esbroeck, G., Bowman, D., Calhoun, D. and May, O. (1998) 'Changes in the genetic diversity of cotton in the USA from 1970 to 1995', *Crop Science*, 38: 33–7.

Venette, R.C., Hutchison, W.D. and Andow, D.A. (2000) 'An in-field screen for early detection and monitoring of insect resistance to *Bacillus thuringiensis* in transgenic crops', *Journal of Economic Entomology*, 93: 1055–64.

Venkateshwarlu, D. and Da Corta, L. (2001) 'Transformations in the age and gender of unfree workers on hybrid cotton seed farms in Andhra Pradesh', *Journal of Peasant Studies,* 28(3): 1–36.

Wallace, H. and Brown, W. (1988) *Corn and Its Early Fathers,* Ames, IA: Iowa State University Press.

Wan, P., Huang, M.S. and Wu, K.M. (2004) 'Seasonal pattern of infestation by pink bollworm *Pectinophora gossypiella* (Saunders) in field plots of Bt transgenic cotton in the Yangtze River Valley of China', *Crop Protection*, 23: 463–7.

Wan, P., Zhang, Y.J., Wu, K.M. and Huang, M.S. (2005) 'Seasonal expression profiles of insecticidal protein and control efficacy against *Helicoverpa armigera* for Bt cotton in the Yangtze River Valley of China', *Journal of Economic Entomology*, 98: 195–201.

Wang, S., Just, D. and Pinstrup-Andersen, P. (2006) 'Tarnishing silver bullets: Bt technology adoption, bounded rationality and the outbreak of secondary pest infestations in China', paper presented at the American Agricultural Economics Association Annual Meeting, Long Beach, CA, July 2006.

Wang, Z., Lin, H., Huang, J., Hu, R., Rozelle, S. and Pray, C. (2009) 'Bt cotton in China: Are secondary insect infestations offsetting the benefits in farmer fields?', *Agricultural Sciences in China,* 8(1): 83–90.

Ware, J. (1936) 'Plant breeding and the cotton industry', in *Yearbook of Agriculture*. Washington, DC: US Department of Agriculture pp. 657–744.

Watt, G. (1907) *The Wild and Cultivated Cotton Plants of the World*, New York: Longmans, Green and Co.

Wendel, J. (1989) 'New World tetraploid cottons contain Old World cytoplasm', *Proceedings of the National Academy of Sciences*, 86: 4132–6.

Whitehouse, M.E.A., Wilson, L.J. and Fitt, G.P. (2005) 'A comparison of arthropod communities in transgenic Bt and conventional cotton in Australia', *Environmental Entomology*, 34: 1224–41.

Whitehouse, M.E.A., Wilson, L.J. and Constable, G.A. (2007) 'Target and non-target effects on the invertebrate community of Vip cotton, a new insecticidal transgene', *Australian Journal of Agricultural Research*, 58: 273–85.

Wilkes, G. (1994) 'Germplasm conservation and agriculture' in K. Kim and R. Weaver (eds) *Biodiversity and Landscapes*, Cambridge: Cambridge University Press, pp. 151–70.

Williamson, S. (2003) *The Dependency Syndrome: Pesticide Use by African Smallholders,* London: Pesticide Action Network, UK.

Willrich, M.M., Braxton, L.B., Richburg, J.S., Lassiter, R.B., Langston, V.B., Haygood, R.A., Richardson, J.M., Haile, F.J., Huckaba, R.M., Pellow, J.W., Thompson, G.D. and Mueller, J.P. (2005) 'Field and laboratory performance of Widestrike insect protection against secondary lepidopteran pests', in *Proceedings of the Beltwide Cotton Conference*, 4–7 January, New Orleans, LA, Memphis, TN: National Cotton Council of America.

Wilson, F.D., Flint, H.M., Deaton, W.R., Fischhoff, D.A., Perlak, F.J., Armstrong, T.A., Fuchs, R.L., Berberich, S.A., Parks, N.J. and Stapp, B.R. (1992) 'Resistance of cotton lines containing *Bacillus thuringiensis* toxin to pink bollworm (Lepidoptera: Gelechiidae) and other insects', *Journal of Economic Entomology*, 85: 1516–21.

Witt, H., Patel, R. and Schnurr, M. (2006) 'Can the poor help GM crops? Technology, representation and cotton in the Makhatini Flats, South Africa', *Review of African Political Economy,* 109:497–513.

Wolfenbarger, L.L., Naranjo, S.E., Lundgren, J.G., Bitzer, R.J. and Watrud, L.S. (2008) 'Bt crops effects on functional guilds of non-target arthropods: A meta-analysis', *Plos One* 3: 1–11. Available at: <http://www.plosone.org/article/info:doi%2F10.1371%2Fjournal. pone.0002118>

Wolson, R.A. and Gouse, M. (2005) 'Towards a regional approach to biotechnology policy in Southern Africa: Phase I, situation and stakeholder analysis—South Africa', Pretoria: Food, Agriculture and Natural Resources Policy Analysis Network (FANRPAN). Available at: <http://www.fanrpan.org/documents/d00073>

World Bank (2006) *Intellectual Property Rights. Designing Regimes to Support Plant Breeding in Developing Countries*, Washington, DC: World Bank.

——— (2008) *Global Economic Prospects. Technology Diffusion in the Developing World,* Washington, DC: World Bank.

——— (forthcoming) *Comparative Analysis of Organization and Performance of African Cotton Sectors: Learning from Experience of Cotton Sector Reform in Africa.* Washington, DC: World Bank.

Wu, F. and Butz, F. (2004) *The Future of Genetically Modified Crops. Lessons from the Green Revolution*, Santa Monica, CA: Rand Corporation.

Wu, K. (2007) 'Monitoring and management strategy for *Helicoverpa armigera* to Bt cotton in China', *Journal of Invertebrate Pathology*, 95: 220–3.

Wu, K. and Guo, Y. (2003) 'Influences of *Bacillus thuringiensis* Berliner Cotton planting on population dynamics of the cotton aphid, *Aphis gossypii* Glover, in Northern China', *Environmental Entomology*, 32: 312–8.

——— (2005) 'The evolution of cotton pest management practices in China', *Annual Review of Entomology*, 50: 31–52.

Wu, K., Li, W., Feng, H. and Guo, Y. (2002) 'Seasonal abundance of the mirids, *Lygus lucorum* and *Adelphocoris* spp. (Hemiptera: Miridae) on Bt cotton in northern China', *Crop Protection,* 21: 997–1002.

Wu, K.M., Guo, Y.Y., Lv, N., Greenplate, J.T. and Deaton, R. (2003) 'Efficacy of transgenic cotton combining a *cry1Ac* gene from *Bacillus thuringiensis* against *Helicoverpa armigera* (Lepidoptera: Noctuidae) in northern China', *Journal of Economic Entomology*, 96: 1322–8.

Wu, K., Mu, W., Liang, G. and Guo, Y. (2005) 'Regional reversion of insecticide resistance in *Helicoverpa armigera* (Lepidoptera: Noctuidae) is associated with the use of Bt cotton in China', *Pest Management Science*, 61(5): 491–8.

Xu, N. and Fok, M. (2007) 'Multiple-factor adoption of GM cotton in China: Influence of conventional technology development and rural change in Jiangsu Province', paper presented at World Cotton Research Conference, Lubbock, TX, September 2007.

Xue, Q.Z., Zhang, X.Y. and Zhang, Y. (2006) 'Development of biotech crops in China', in N. Halford (ed.) *Plant Biotechnology: Current and Future Applications of Genetically Modified Crops*, San Francisco: John Wiley.

Yafa, S. (2005) *Big Cotton,* New York: Viking.

Yang, P., Li, K., Shi, S., Xia, J., Guo, R., Li, S. and Wang, L. (2005a) 'Impacts of transgenic Bt cotton and integrated pest management education on smallholder cotton farmers', *International Journal of Pest Management*, 51(4): 231–24.

Yang, P., Iles, M., Yan, S. and Jolliffe, F. (2005b) 'Farmers' knowledge, perceptions and practices in transgenic Bt cotton in small producer systems in Northern China', *Crop Protection,* 25: 229–39.

Zechendorf, B. (1998) 'Agricultural biotechnology: Why do Europeans have difficulty accepting it?', *AgBioForum,* 1: 8–13.

Zhang, B.H., Liu, F., Yao, C.B. and Wang, K.B. (2000) 'Recent progress in cotton biotechnology and genetic engineering in China', *Current Science,* 79: 37–44.

Zhao, J.Z., Li, Y.X., Collins, H.L., Cao, J., Earle, E.D. and Shelton, A.M. (2001) 'Different cross-resistance patterns in diamondback moth (Lepidoptera: Plutellidae) resistant to *Bacillus thuringiensis* toxin Cry1C', *Journal of Economic Entomology,* 94: 1547–52.

Zhao, J.Z., Cao, J., Collins, H.L., Bates, S.L., Roush, R.T., Earle, E.D. and Shelton, A.M. (2005) 'Concurrent use of transgenic plants expressing a single and two *Bacillus thuringiensis* genes speeds insect adaptation to pyramided plants', *Proceedings of the National Academy of Sciences,* 102: 8426–30.

Zhou, G.Y., Weng, J., Zeng, Y., Huang, J., Qian, S. and Liu, G. (1983) 'Introduction of exogenous DNA into cotton embryos', in R. Wu, L. Grossman and K. Moldave (eds) *Methods in Enzymology: Recombinant DNA, Part C, vol. 101,* New York: Academic Press, pp. 433–81.

Zitnak, A. and Johnston, G. (1970) 'Glycoalkaloid content of B5141-6 potatoes', *American Potato Journal,* 47: 256–60.

Zummo, G.R., Segers, J.C. and Benedict, J.H. (1984) 'Seasonal phenology of allelochemicals in cotton and resistance to bollworm (Lepidoptera: Noctuidae)', *Environmental Entomology,* 13: 1287–90.

Index

aflatoxin 13
Africa: and cotton subsidies 27; colonial cotton production 24, 25; fibre quality 29; input credit 32
agricultural change 5–7; *see also* Green Revolution
agricultural research 20–1, 237–9
Agricultural Research Council (South Africa) 207
Agricultural Sector Education Training Authority (South Africa) 223
agriculture: and environment 9–10
Agrobacterium-mediated transformation 50
Agrobacterium tumefaciens 50
Alabama argillacea 195
Aleyrodidea 210
American bollworm *see Helicoverpa armigera*
Andai 89, 110
Andhra Pradesh: Bt cotton performance 63, 75; experimentation 100–1; hybrid cotton use 139; net benefits of Bt cotton 80–1; pesticides 99; seed choice 150, 151; seed price 78
Anhui Province 105, 116, 118, 120, 129–30, 132
Anthonomus grandis (boll weevil) 35, 38, 40; control 41, 176–7, 195–6, 198, 233–4, 236
aphids *see Aphis gossypii*
Aphis gossypii (aphids) 40, 56, 57, 58
Aral Sea 26
Argentina: areas of cotton planted 46, 47; Bt cotton impact variability 82; insecticide use changes 76; intellectual property rights 94–5, 97; net benefits of Bt cotton 80; pest control 101; refuge policies 85–6; seed and input industry

88–90, 99; seed laws 98; seed price 78–9; yield 76
Arizona: pink bollworm 68–9
armyworms *see Spodoptera* spp. and *Spodoptera frugiperda*
Australia: areas of cotton planted 46, 47; *Helicoverpa armigera* 69–70; insecticide use changes 73–4, 103; intellectual property rights 95; refuge policies 84–5; seed and input industry 88–90, 99; seed laws 98; seed price 78–9; yield changes 73–4

Bacillus thuringiensis (Bt) 10, 42
Bacillus thuringiensis cotton *see* transgenic cotton
bananas 238
Banco Agrario (Agrarian Bank) 173, 175
Bayer Crop Science 88, 90
Bemisia tabaci (whitefly) 40, 57, 58
Benin: cotton income 28; farmer unions 27
Biocentury 89, 90
biodiversity: Bt cotton effect on 86; and environment 11–13
biopesticides 241
biosafety regulation 115, 232, 240–1
biotechnology future 234–43; policies on who benefits 242–3; technological possibilities 234–5
boll weevil *see Anthonomus grandis*
Bollgard cotton 44, 88; Cry1Ac concentration 59–60
Bollgard II: in Burkina Faso 89; characteristics 54; in Colombia 178, 196; in India 147, 150, 157, 164, 165; licensing 88, 90; toxins in 53, 66
bollworms *see Helicoverpa* spp.
Brazil: Bt cotton 46; plant breeding 36

Bt cotton *see* transgenic cotton
Bt maize 206, 234
Burkina Faso: Bt cotton 46, 89

Campo Unido (Colombia) 184
Cartagena Protocol on Biosafety 17
Center for Chinese Agricultural Policy
  (CCAP) 105; GM crops database 107
child labour 30
China: agricultural research 237, 238;
  areas of cotton planted 46, 47;
  biodiversity 86; Bt cotton impact
  variability 82; Bt cotton net benefits 81;
  Bt cotton performance 115–17; Bt toxin
  expression 116–17; cotton subsidies 27;
  crop management 37; data sources
  107–8; farmers' pest control practices
  123–33; farmers' seed practices 117–23;
  future policy 134; GM crop regulation
  114–17; *Helicoverpa armigera* 69–70;
  hybrid technology 96; insecticide
  purchase 126–8; insecticide use 73–6,
  116–17, 128–33, 227, 233; intellectual
  property rights 94–8, 231–2; IPM 41,
  102; pesticide market 124–5; pink
  bollworm 69; plant breeding 36, 230–1;
  refuge policies 84–5, 232; seed and
  input industry 88–90, 99–100, 229–30;
  seed laws 97–8, 110; seed market
  distribution 110–14; seed market
  evolution 109–10; seed price 78–80,
  118, 227; seed purchase 118–21; seed
  saving 121–3; seed sector 109–17; yield
  performance 73–6, 116, 227
China's Biosafety Committee (CBC)
  115–17, 120–2
Chinese Academy of Agricultural Sciences
  (CAAS) 89, 95, 105; Cotton Research
  Institute (CRI) 110; Institute of
  Biotechnology Research (IBR) 110;
  Institute of Plant Protection (IPP) 108;
  transgene 106, 108, 115–16
CIRAD 214–15
Clark Cotton 207, 219
Coker (cotton variety) 51
Coleoptera 40
Colombia: areas of cotton planted 46, 47;
  biodiversity 86; biosafety framework
  169; boll weevil control 176–7, 195–6,
  198, 233–4, 236; Bt cotton adoption
  179–86; Bt cotton production
  economics 186–96; cotton grower
  associations 173–7, 179, 180–1;
  cotton-growing regions 168, 169; cotton

land distribution 171; cotton production
  organization 170–9; cotton sector
  support 170–1; farmers 171–3;
  genetically modified products 169;
  insecticide access 177; insecticide use
  195–6, 227, 233–4; intellectual property
  rights 94, 231; land access 171–3; pink
  bollworm 195; plant breeding 231;
  refuge policies 85, 178, 232; seed
  access 177–9; seed and input industry
  88–90, 99–100, 230; seed laws 98; seed
  price 78–9, 194, 227; survey description
  169–70, 179, 182; weather effects 194;
  yield performance 186–94, 227
Colombian Agricultural Institute (ICA)
  169, 177
Colombian Cotton Confederation *see*
  CONALGODÓN
commercial transgenic cultivars:
  development 51–2; seed production 52
Commonwealth Scientific and Industrial
  Research Organization (CSIRO) 89
Compañia Agricola Colombiana 178
CONALGODÓN 168, 169, 171, 176, 197
cooperatives 32
Córdoba: armyworm control 196; Bt
  cotton adoption 182–5, 191–3; cotton
  farmer characteristics 184–5; cotton
  grower associations 173, 179, 180–1;
  cotton production 169; cotton
  production costs 186–9; cotton variety
  use 172, 183; cotton yields 186–9,
  191–4; farm sizes 172; survey sample
  characteristics 182; weather effects 194
CORPOICA 178
corporate concentration 15, 16
corporate control of technology 15–17
Corporation for Economic Development
  (CED) 219
Côte d'Ivoire: colonial cotton 29;
  cotton cash crop 26; farmer unions
  27; labour 30
cotton: cultivation history 23–8;
  distribution 24–5; how grown 28–33;
  and intellectual property 34, 231–2; *see
  also Gossypium* and transgenic cotton
cotton aphids *see Aphis gossypii*
Cotton Board (South Africa) 202
cotton bollworm *see Helicoverpa zea*
cotton bugs *see Dysdercus* spp.
cotton grower associations 173–7,
  179, 180–1
Cotton Incorporated 36
cotton insects 39–40

cotton leafworm *see Spodoptera litura*
Cotton Marketing Committee (South
    Africa) 202
cotton production technology 33–42; and
    institutions 42, 228–9; variety
    development 33–4; *see also* technology
    fees; technology performance
Cotton Research Institute (CRI) 110
Cotton SA 202, 207, 220, 223, 224
Cotton Seed Distributors (CSD) 89, 90
cotton stainers *see Dysdercus* spp.
cowpea trypsin inhibitor (CpTI) 53
credit *see* input credit
crop management 37–8
cross-pollination 35
cross-resistance 66–7
crystalline (Cry) toxins 53

D&PL *see* Delta and Pine Land
DDT 38, 41
Delta Opal 178, 194, 196, 215, 224
Delta and Pine Land (D&PL) 44, 76,
    88–90; in Colombia 178; in South
    Africa 22, 205–7, 210–12, 223, 224
DeltaOPAL RR 207
desi cotton 140, 141, 144
diamondback moth 10
Diparopsis spp. (red bollworm) 39, 57–8
DNA insertion 49–51
Dow AgroSciences 88
DP 90 variety 178, 194, 207, 215
DP Lebombo 210
Dysdercus spp. (cotton stainers) 39

Earias spp. (spotted bollworm) 39, 56–8
early adopters 18, 225–6
East India Company 25
Egypt: child labour 30; cotton production
    25; plant breeding 36
Empoasca spp. (jassids) 40, 57, 58
endogeneity 190
environment: and agriculture 9–10; and
    biodiversity 11–13
environmental learning 150–2
European Union (EU): cotton
    subsidies 27
eutrophication 10
extension agents 177, 198, 233
extension services 222–3, 233

fall armyworm *see Spodoptera
    frugiperda*
farmer seed saving *see* seed saving
farmer unions 27

farmers: control of technology 19–20;
    information access 100–3, 153–4,
    232–4, 242
fibre quality 29–30, 228
fitness costs 67
food industry: GMO applications 2–3
food safety 13–14
France: African green beans 13

gene gun 50
gene patents 92, 93–5
genetic engineering: conflicting visions 2
genetic interchange 12–13
genetic transformation: methods 11, 49–51
genetically modified organisms (GMOs):
    applications 2–3
ginning 176
glycoalkaloids 13
GM food: consumer acceptance 13
GMO Act (South Africa) 205
GMOs *see* genetically modified organisms
Gossypium spp. 24
Gossypium arboreum 24, 35, 140
Gossypium barbadense 24–5
Gossypium herbaceum 24, 35
Gossypium hirsutum 24, 33, 35, 36
gossypol 43
green beans (African export) 13
Green Revolution 7–9
Gujarat: Bt cotton adoption 141–4; cotton
    yields 144–6; crops 137–8;
    experimentation 101; farmers' opinions
    about Bt cotton 164, 165; hybrid cotton
    use 139–40; insecticide information
    sources 155, 157; insecticide practices
    155–7; insecticide use on different
    varieties 159–64; location 136; refuge
    management 164, 166, 232; seed choice
    criteria 150–3; seed information sources
    154; seed price 78; survey districts
    136–7; unapproved Bt cotton use 95–6,
    101, 139–40, 143–4; underground
    market 167; varieties sown 147–50
Gujarat Agricultural University 139
Gujarat State Seed Corporation (GSSC)
    139, 140

H4 hybrid 139
Haber–Bosch process 6
Haryana: hybrid cotton use 96
Hebei Province 105, 116–23, 126–7,
    129–30, 132
Helicoverpa spp. (bollworms) 56–60;
    insecticide use for 128–32, 157–65, 224

Helicoverpa armigera (American bollworm) 39, 58, 59, 61; control 69–70; infestation levels 61–2; resistance 64–5, 69–70
Helicoverpa zea (cotton bollworm) 39, 44, 63; resistance 65, 67
Heliothis spp. 43
Heliothis virescens (tobacco budworm) 39, 44, 56–7, 63, 195; resistance 64–5, 67
Hemiptera 39–40
Henan Province 105, 116–23, 126–7, 129–30, 132
herbicide-tolerance 234–5; in transgenic cotton 44, 206–8, 223, 235; in weeds 10, 12
hybrid technology 93, 96–7
hybrid transgenic cotton: development 52; seed production 52
hybrid vigour 15

imitation effect 152–3
India: agricultural research 237, 238; areas of cotton planted 46, 47; biodiversity 86; Bt cotton adoption 141–4; Bt cotton impact variability 82, 83; Bt cotton performance 63; Bt cotton utilization 137–46; child labour 30; cotton farmers 137–8; cotton production history 25, 26; cotton seed market 147–50, 167; hybrid cotton use 96, 139; input credit 31; insect control 154–65; insecticide market 154–5; insecticide practices 155–7, 233; insecticide use changes 73–5, 162, 164, 227; insecticide use on different varieties 157–65; intellectual property rights 94–7, 231; IPM 102; net benefits of Bt cotton 80–2; plant breeding 36, 230–1; refuge policies 85–6, 164, 232; seed choice 147–54; seed choice criteria 150–3; seed information sources 153–4; seed and input industry 88–90, 99–100, 138–41, 229–30; seed laws 98; seed price 78–9, 147, 227; survey description 135–7; textile industry history 25, 27; yield performance 73–5, 144–6, 227
Indian Central Cotton Committee 36
Indian Institute of Technology 90
information access 100–3, 153–4, 232–4, 242
input credit 31–2, 173–6, 219–20, 229
input delivery 99–100, 240
input markets 88–90, 229–30, 240; *see also* seed industry

insect control 38–40; *see also* pest management
insecticide resistance management (IRM) 102, 157
insecticides: effects of reduced use 62–3; use changes with Bt cotton 73–6
Institute of Biotechnology Research (IBR) 110
Institute for Industrial Crops 201
Institute of Plant Protection (IPP) 108
institutional capacity 20–1
institutions: building 244; challenges 235–6; role in cotton production 32–3; and technology 42, 228–9
integrated pest management (IPM) 40–2, 102, 236
intellectual property rights (IPRs) 15–16; and cotton 34, 231–2; future 241–2; and transgenic crop varieties 92–3
IPM *see* integrated pest management
IPRs *see* intellectual property rights
IRM *see* insecticide resistance management

jassids *see Empoasca* spp.
Jiangsu Province 105
Jidai 89, 110
Jozini dam 218

Karnataka: Bt cotton performance 82
Kwazulu Natal 201, 203, 218, 220, 222; *see also* Makhathini Flats

labour 30–1, 228–9; *see also* child labour
Land Bank 219, 220
leafhoppers 58
lectins 53
Lepidoptera 39
Limpopo Province 213
linters 37
Lonhro 207
Lowell, Francis Cabot 34
Lygus spp. (mirids) 40, 56, 57, 58; insecticide use for 128, 130–1

Maharashtra: Bt cotton adoption 141–4; Bt cotton performance 75; cotton yields 144–6; crops 138; farmers' opinions about Bt cotton 164, 165; hybrid cotton use 140–1; insecticide information sources 155, 157; insecticide practices 155–7; insecticide use on different varieties 157–9, 162, 164; location 136; refuge management 164, 166, 232; seed

choice criteria 150–3; seed information sources 154; seed price 78; survey districts 136–7; unapproved Bt cotton varieties 140–1; varieties sown 147–50
Maharashtra State Seed Corporation 140
Mahyco 78, 83, 89–90, 140
Mahyco Monsanto Biotech (MMB) 89–90, 95, 139
maize: hybrid 7
Makhathini Cotton (MCC) 219–20, 223
Makhathini Flats: history 218–20; inputs and information 222–4; insecticide use 217; rainfall 214, 215, 220, 222; smallholder income sources 220, 222; smallholder numbers 220–2; surveys 213–17; technology fees 212
Makhathini Irrigation Scheme 218–19
Mali: cotton quality 29; crop management 38; farmer organizations 30
marginal conditions: Bt cotton performance under 63–4
marker genes 49–50
Marketing Act (South Africa) 201
Marketing of Agricultural Products Act (South Africa) 202
medicine 2
Mexico: areas of cotton planted 46, 47; insecticide use changes 74–5; intellectual property rights 94, 97; refuge policies 85; seed and input industry 88–90, 99–100; seed laws 98; seed price 77–9; yield changes 74
'Million Dollar' variety 36
minimum guaranteed price (MGP) 170–1
Ministry of Agriculture (MOA) 114–15
Ministry of Science and Technology (MOST) 114
mirids *see Lygus* spp.
mites 56, 57, 58
Mjindi Farming 219
Monsanto 88–9; Bt cotton development 43–4; in China 108, 110, 115–17; in Colombia 169, 176, 178, 184; fine 14; in India 139, 141, 147; patents 95; seed price 76–80; slogan 3; in South Africa 210–12, 223, 224
Mpumalanga 201, 203–4, 213, 220
mutation breeding 11

Nanking, University of 36
National Seed Corporation (NSC) 109
Navbharat Seeds 95–6, 139–40
NB151 hybrid 139–40
nitrates: as health hazard 10

nitrogen: and Bt concentrations 60
novice plantings 151
NuCotn 35B 207
NuCotn 37B 207, 215
NuOpal: in Colombia 86, 178, 182, 194, 196; in South Africa 86, 207, 215
NuOPAL RR 207

Ola Invernal (Colombia) 175
'one-cultivar community plan' 29
OPAL variety 207

Pakistan: Bt cotton 46; input credit 32
particle bombardment 50
patenting life 15
patents 92, 241; *see also* gene patents
Pectinophora gossypiella (pink bollworm) 39, 56–7, 195; control 68–9; resistance 65, 69
Pentatomidae spp. (stink bugs) 39, 58
Peru: cotton production 25; input credit 31–2
pest management: integrated (IPM) 40–2, 102, 236
pesticides: effects 10
Philippines: National Biosafety Framework 17
PhytoGen Seed Company 88
pink bollworm *see Pectinophora gossypiella*
plant breeding 6–7, 10–11, 230–1; for insect resistance 43
Plant Genetic Systems 43
plant pathogens 10
Plant Varieties and Farmers' Rights Act (India) 96
plant variety protection (PVP) 15, 92, 93–5, 96–9
plantation slavery 25
pollen-tube pathway 50–1
poverty reduction: pathways from rural poverty 243; technology assessment in relation to 17–21
precautionary principle 14
Pretoria, University of (UP) 213–15
promoters 49–50
protease inhibitors 53
provincial academies of agricultural sciences (PAAS) 110
Punjab: hybrid cotton use 96, 139
purchase agreements 93
PVP *see* plant variety protection
pyramid strategy 66–7
pyrethroids 63

rainfall 82–3, 214, 215, 220, 222
Reading, University of 213–14
red bollworm *see Diparopsis* spp.
redundant killing 66
refuge deployment decisions 68
refuge policies 65–6, 84–5
regulation 14, 21, 114–17, 232, 240–1
regulatory mechanisms 21
resistance management 84
rice: fertilizer-responsive 8
risk preference 131, 133
'Roundup' 44, 178
'Roundup Flex' 178
'Roundup-Ready' (RR) cotton 44, 206–8, 223
'Roundup-Ready' (RR) crops 44, 206

science-based regulation 14
Sea Island cotton 24
seed contamination 67–8
seed industry 88–90, 229–30, 239;
  see also input markets
seed laws 93, 97–8
seed price 76–80, 118
seed provision 36–7
seed purchase 118–21
seed quality and certification standards 93
seed saving 121–3; laws 93–5
Semillas Valle 178
SEMSA 178
Shandong Province 105, 116, 121–3, 126–7, 129–30, 132; pesticides 99
sharecropping 25–6
'skip-row' 38
smallholders (South Africa): cotton sector 217–18; income sources 220, 222; inputs 222–4; production by province 217–18; as struggling sector 220–2; surveys 214–15; technology fees 212; training courses 203
snowdrop lectin gene 53
social learning 150, 152–3
South Africa: biodiversity 86; Bt cotton experience 215–17; Bt cotton farm-level impact 213–17; Bt cotton impact variability 82, 83; Bt cotton net benefits 81; Bt cotton performance 213–15; cotton gins 222;cotton production areas 46, 47, 201, 203–5; cotton production history 200–1; cotton sector status 200–3; cotton seed sector 207–10; crop management 37–8; cultivars received at cotton gins 207–9; extension services 222–3, 233; and GM crops 205–7;

government smallholder cotton aspirations 202–3; insecticide use 73–6, 217, 227; institutions and GM technology 217–24; intellectual property rights 94, 231; pest control 101–2; plant breeding 231; production credit 219–20; refuge policies 85, 224, 232; seed and input industry 88–90, 99–100, 230; seed laws 98; seed price 77, 79–80, 210–12, 227; textile industry 201; yield performance 73–6, 215–17, 227;
  see also smallholders
South African Committee for Genetic Experimentation (SAGENE) 205
South African Development Trust Corporation (STK/SADT) 219
spiny bollworm *see Earias* spp.
Spodoptera spp. (armyworms) 56, 57, 58, 195; insecticide use for 157–64
Spodoptera frugiperda (fall armyworm) 39, 195
Spodoptera litura (cotton leafworm or tobacco leafworm) 39, 58
spotted bollworm *see Earias* spp.
stink bugs *see Pentatomidae* spp.
Stoneville 88, 90
Sub-Saharan Africa (SSA) 235, 237, 239
sucking pests: insecticide use for 157–65
Sucre: Bt cotton adoption 182–5, 193; cotton farmer characteristics 184–5; cotton grower associations 173; cotton production 170; cotton production costs 186–9; cotton variety use 172, 183, 194; cotton yields 186–9, 193–4; farm sizes 172; survey sample characteristics 182; weather effects 194
sustainability 64–70, 84–6
Syria: IPM 41

talukas 136
tannins 59–60
Technical Committee for Biosafety (Colombia) 169
technology diffusion 243–4
technology fees 77–8, 211–12
technology performance 18–19, 72–87, 226–8
temperature: and Bt concentrations 60
textile industry: specialization 28
Thailand: Bt cotton 46
thrips 57, 58
tobacco budworm *see Heliothis virescens*
tobacco leafworm *see Spodoptera litura*

Tolima: armyworm control 196; Bt cotton adoption 182–5, 190–3; cotton farmer characteristics 184–5; cotton grower associations 175, 179; cotton production 170; cotton production costs 186–93; cotton variety use 172, 183; cotton yields 186–94; farm sizes 172, 189–90; insecticide use 195–6; seeding rate 195; survey sample characteristics 182; weather effects 194

Tonga 203, 217, 220

Tongaat Cotton 219

transgenic cotton 42–6; areas planted (by country) 46, 47; commercially available (by country) 45; economic performance in field 72–87, 226–8; herbicide-tolerant 44, 206–8, 223, 235; impact variability 82–4; insect-resistant 42–4; management 61–4; net benefits 80–2; resistance management 64–70; 'stacked' 44

transgenic cotton cultivars: characteristics 54–5, 58–60; development 49–52

transgenic crops: creation 10–11; differences about 9–17; *see also* 'Roundup-Ready' (RR) crops

transgenic toxins in cotton: efficacy against insect pests 53, 56–8; factors affecting expression 58–61; types 53

Uganda 238

UK: African green beans 13

'ultra narrow row' 38, 77

UPOV 92

USA: areas of cotton planted 46, 47; biodiversity 86; Bt cotton impact variability 83–4; cotton production history 25–6; cotton subsidies 27, 236; crop management 38; Green Revolution 8; harvesting technology 30–1; insecticide use changes 73–4, 76, 103; intellectual property rights 95; IPM 40–1, 236; maize yields 7; net benefits of Bt cotton 81; plant breeding 35–6; refuge policies 85; seed and input industry 88, 99; seed laws 98; seed price 77, 78–80; yield changes 73–4

Uzbekistan 26; child labour 30

variety mandates 29–30

variety release procedures 93

vegetative insecticidal proteins (Vip) 53

Vick, Henry W. 36

Vikram Seeds 140

Vunisa 212, 213, 214, 219–20, 222–4

Washington University (St Louis) 43

weeds: herbicide-tolerance 10, 12

West Africa: *Helicoverpa armigera* 69–70

wheat dwarfing 8

whitefly *see Bemisia tabaci*

Whitney, Eli 34

wilt disease 36

World Trade Organization (WTO) 56

yield: changes with Bt cotton 73–6, 227

Zimbabwe: cotton cash cropping 26

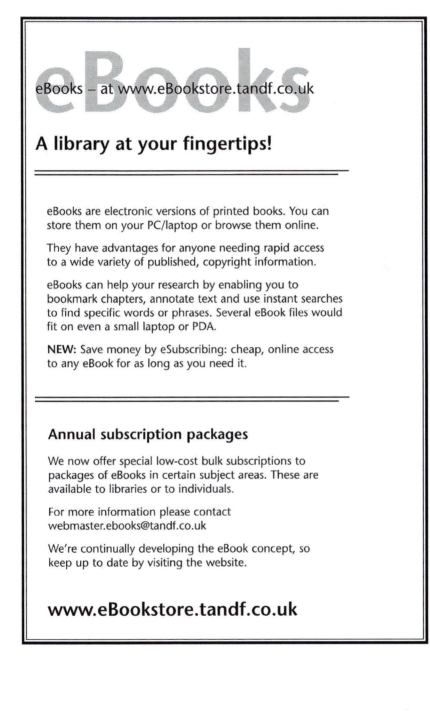